Toeing the Line

SUNY series in American Constitutionalism

Robert J. Spitzer, editor

Toeing the Line

The US Supreme Court and Affirmative Action Politics

NINA M. MOORE

SUNY
PRESS

EU GPSR Authorised Representative:
Logos Europe, 9 rue Nicolas Poussin, 17000, La Rochelle, France
contact@logoseurope.eu

For information, contact State University of New York Press, Albany, NY
www.sunypress.edu

Library of Congress Cataloging-in-Publication Data

Name: Moore, Nina M., author.
Title: Toeing the line : the US Supreme Court and affirmative action politics / Nina M. Moore.
Description: Albany : State University of New York Press, [2025]. | Series: SUNY series in American Constitutionalism | Includes bibliographical references and index.
Identifiers: ISBN 9798855805550 (hardcover : alk. paper) | ISBN 9798855805574 (epub) | ISBN 9798855806984 (PDF) | ISBN 9798855805567 (pbk. : alk. paper)
Further information is available at the Library of Congress.

In memory of my sisters,
Sunshine and Etta Jane,
until we meet again.

Contents

Illustrations

Figures

Tables

Introduction

The policy views dominant on the Court are never for long out of line with the policy views dominant among the lawmaking majorities of the United States. Consequently it would be most unrealistic to suppose that the Court would, for more than a few years at most, stand against any major alternatives sought by a lawmaking majority.

—Robert Alan Dahl, "Decision-Making in a Democracy: The Supreme Court as a National Policy Maker"

The 2023 US Supreme Court ruling that effectively outlawed race-conscious college admissions met stinging criticism, above all the charge that it was yet another sign of a conservative supermajority out of touch with the rest of America.[1] President Joe Biden said the ruling was proof that "this is not a normal court." Critics lumped[2] *Students for Fair Admissions v. Harvard* (*SFFA*, 2023)[3] together with the 2022 abortion ruling[4] that overturned *Roe v. Wade*, pointing out that a clear majority of Americans identify as "pro-choice."[5] *SFFA* was folded in also with 2018 and 2023 rulings[6] that shielded businesses that refused service to LGBTQ+ couples, at a time when national polls show 71 percent support for same-sex marriage.[7] According to one news report more Americans are warming to the idea of court reform "in the face of a six-three conservative supermajority issuing decisions largely out of step with the country's principles and priorities."[8] This book's multi-decade analysis of affirmative action jurisprudence and politics challenges the notion that *SFFA* fits in the same box as these other judicial outcomes.

Students for Fair Admissions v. Harvard is not a case of the Supreme Court at odds with the body politic. The exact opposite is true. The main holding that the equal protection clause of the US Constitution bars race-specific admissions policies actually moved the Court closer to where

1

the general public and politicians have stood for quite some time. In the decades leading up to *SFFA* the Court repeatedly rejected colorblind constitutionalism, despite the fact that Americans continually endorsed it. Chief Justice Roberts and his five counterparts did not act unilaterally in disposing of racial preference in college admissions. Indeed the fallout from the decision reveals that critics and defenders of *SFFA* credit the 6–3 conservative majority with greater independence than is warranted. It assumes a degree of inner fortitude on the part of Supreme Court justices that does not and never has existed, most especially where race is concerned.

To fully grasp that *SFFA* is but the latest extension of 45 years of preferential policy rulings that mirror the political impulses of the day, we must analyze more than the final vote and, instead, unpack the logic and reasoning behind the vote. Upon doing so, we gain a clearer view of the breadth and depth of policy and political agreement between the justices and the rest of America. Our tendency to reduce affirmative action decisions to up or down votes obscures this substantive agreement. The final votes are important to the extent that they dispose of the litigant claims that are formally before the Court. But the rationalizations offered by the justices to explain and justify the judgments are the stuff of real-life policy change beyond judicial process. Significant for our purposes is that they are a window into the Court's disposition toward the larger policy issues and problems that are implicated in the cases they take up.

This book's deep dive into the constitutional-legal arguments behind the final outcome in *SFFA* and prior affirmative action rulings reveals that the justices of the Supreme Court wrestle with the same concerns and questions about race that preoccupy politicians and citizens at large. And, critically, they also reason through politically charged racial matters the same as the rest of America. The written opinions in affirmative action cases supply the proof, as they are the justices' platform for chiming in on issues at the heart of America's racial politics. Alongside the final judgments is revealing commentary on a range of pivotal racial matters. By comparing key elements of the racial discourse that takes place inside the courthouse to the conversation about race outside of the courthouse this book demonstrates that the Court and the body politic have been saying the same thing about race.

The ideational symmetry between the Court and the polity exists on 13 recurring themes or "flashpoints" in national racial politics, which can be grouped into four categories. The first category bears on Supreme Court positioning around racial history and, specifically, whether the past has any bearing on the current state of race in America. It links, more specifically, to the ongoing debate whether racial preferences are justified by the history of slavery and government-sanctioned exclusion, whether existing racial dispar-ities can be blamed on systemic racism, or if Black Americans simply need to pull themselves up by their own bootstraps the same as once-maltreated Italian, Irish, and Jewish Americans. Affirmative action rulings also channel the justices' perspective on the fundamental nature of race and racism in contemporary America. They chime in on whether motives and context are important for adjudging race-awareness as good or bad, whether racial disproportionality constitutes racism, if affirmative action conflicts with core American ideals like individualism and equal rights, and finally, the extent to which race-specific policies are harmful to Whites as well as Blacks.

In a third category are the justices' beliefs about the limits of racial reform initiatives, as reflected in the guiding principles and policy constraints delineated over the years in preferential rulings. Affirmative action rulemaking conveys the Supreme Court's regard for colorblind constitutionalism, which types of race-specific policy goals are allowable in the name of racial equality, and the specific mechanisms employed to achieve those policy goals. Last is the Court's expansive conception of "diversity," one that departs from the conception behind the original affirmative action policy. The Court overhauled the traditional take on whether "diversity" encompasses Whites as well as Blacks, men as well as women, the haves and the have-nots alike. Also mapped out in its opinions is guidance on precisely who and what affirmative action is for. Is it primarily intended to level the playing field for racial-ethnic minorities or to bolster the fortunes of the nation as a whole?

Toeing the Line offers a detailed descriptive analysis of the correspondence across multiple decades between the US Supreme Court and the American polity on these defining issues in national racial politics. The main question that guides the analysis is: To what extent and how do the explanations and pronouncements set forth in racial preference decisions emulate those of the larger body politic? Does the way in which the Court reasons through, high-profile contests over racial matters differ from how lay citizens and politicians negotiate these issues? Or, do the Harvard- and Yale-trained Supreme Court justices engage in modes of intellection similar to everyday citizens and lawmakers when it comes to controversial racial matters?

The book's main conclusion that racial preference judgments closely parallel national racial politics is grounded in a two-part examination. First is the most comprehensive probe of race-based affirmative action case law to date in a single volume. The analysis of opinions takes in the entire series of Supreme Court racial preference rulings, it dissects the 13 core concerns addressed across the rulings, and it traces these jurisprudential developments over a 45-year period from the first ruling in 1978 in *Bakke* to its 2023 ruling in *Students for Fair Admissions*. The second half of the analysis details how the 13 themes are negotiated by national public opinion, the two major political parties, presidential politics from Roosevelt through Biden, and grassroots developments on a range of hot button issues from critical race theory to Confederate symbols to immigration trends and diversity, equity, and inclusion (DEI) politics, and more. This portion of the study draws extensively from original national databases. The Supreme Court's posture on racial history, racism, policy mechanisms, and diversity conceptions is placed side by side with the rest of the country's posture. The comparative analysis establishes that the populist character of affirmative action rulings is reflected not only in the ideological thrust of final case outcomes; it is evident also in the explanations put forth in Court opinions as justification of final outcomes.

While this book's analysis is descriptive and not causal, it nonetheless contains some insight into the most common explanations proffered in the scholarship on race and the US Supreme Court. Theories that construe racial preference rulings as the making of a status quo–oriented legal process, or conservative political movements, or individual justices' preferences and ideology are certainly helpful in broadening our understanding of why the Court rules as it does in affirmative action cases. However, the data and analysis compiled here imply that such theories are only partial explanations. It is true that constitutionalism and judicial process inexorably limit what reformists can accomplish by way of judicial policy. But, it is also true that, one, judges have options and, two, given the right conditions courts can bring about major social reform.[9] Moreover, if conservative justices are to blame for the constricting nature of preferential rulings, then it is arguable that liberal justices share part of the blame too, because they embrace many of the same controlling principles and precepts as those embraced by conservative justices. A bottom-line takeaway from this work is that any scholarly explanation that reduces 45 years of affirmative action case law to just one or another legal or political influence necessarily overlooks the broader, more complex set of forces in play.

This investigation proves that every major political front in national American politics shares Supreme Court justices' views on race and is, therefore, a viable suspect in assessing culpability for affirmative action decisions. Whether the focus is on *Students for Fair Admissions* (SFFA, 2023) or its predecessors, the fact is mass public opinion, the national Democratic and

Republican Parties, presidents from Roosevelt through Biden, and a growing number of states, academicians, and others are on the same page as Supreme Court justices in regard to the enduring challenges in American racial politics. Whatever the root driver, the Supreme Court consistently ends up toeing the line of national racial politics, right alongside the other major entities within the body politic.

Aside from illuminating the empirical relationship between affirmative action rulings and politics *Toeing the Line* has broader theoretical and practical implications also for the study of courts, race, and democratic politics. Given the evidence of toeing the political line, we have reason to question the conventional understanding of the US Supreme Court's past and present impact on the civil rights policy front. The Warren Court is considered to have laid the moral foundation for the 1960s civil rights revolution, the Burger-Rehnquist Court a civil rights retreat thereafter, the Roberts Court a champion of colorblindness in a time of hardening racial tensions. The common thread across these viewpoints is the sense that, on sensitive racial matters, the Court has and is acting of its own accord. The analytical findings in this book suggest that we should rethink whether the Warren Court is properly regarded as heroic, given that the justices were, in effect, leading the country where it was already headed; whether the Burger-Rehnquist Court is any more disappointing than the rest of the body politic in its turnabout on the civil rights front; and whether the Roberts Court's post-racialism is as much of an outlier in a political order where distinctively *racial* interests are frequently drowned out by the sheer multiplicity of competing equal treatment demands.

Perhaps it is time to abandon too the sense that the federal judiciary is structurally suited to be a protector of minority rights. Alexander Hamilton's *Federalist No. 78* expressed the constitutional framers' plan for the federal judiciary to operate above the fray of majority politics. Over the course of judicial history, marginalized causes have often advanced more readily through litigation than through other governmental processes. Spann explains that the Civil War amendments are partly why "we have now come to vest the Supreme Court, rather than the political process, with the primary responsibility for protecting the interests of racial minorities from disregard by the majoritarian branches of government."[10] To Spann's analysis we might add the common belief that *Brown v. Board of Education* (1954)[11] broke ground for the Black civil rights movement and the historic legislative reforms that followed. The same can be said of the LGBTQ+ movement in regard to state courts and particularly the Hawaii Supreme

Court's first-ever pro-marriage equality decision of 1993. Nonetheless, as evidenced by Spann's study, the evidence in this book urges a second look at the idea that the federal judiciary or any judiciary will lead the way in advancing and protecting minority interests.[12]

Enough political change preceded *Brown* for us to reasonably hypothesize that Chief Justice Warren and his colleagues blazed a trail on a pathway already laid by major political players outside of the Court. LGBTQ+ state and federal court successes in various policy areas were likewise preceded by a marked shift in mass public opinion. We can throw into the mix also *Dred Scott* (1857), *Plessy* (1896), the Japanese Internment cases, and others, which show that, at times when it mattered most, the Court did not stand in the gap for racial-ethnic minorities in the face of majority excess.[13] Inasmuch as this probe of affirmative action judgments shows that they mirror the ebb and flow of racial politics, then perhaps too the most monumental of civil rights cases are best understood as signs of the times, instead of instances of Supreme Court justices shielding minorities from or sacrificing them to overbearing majorities.

The fact that there is a kinship between affirmative action jurisprudence and racial politics furthermore suggests that there are certain circumstances where we can anticipate that the Court will rule one way or another on the civil rights front. What are the most likely political conditions under which we should expect judicial process to work to the benefit of Blacks and other racial minorities? What is the writing on the wall in the larger political arena that helps us to game out the most likely winners and losers within the courthouse? Do certain constitutional-legal questions in affirmative action cases evoke more or less countermajoritarian behavior on the part of the justices?

Last are inferences to be drawn regarding the received wisdom on the influence of judicial partisanship on judicial decision-making. Republican appointees Justices Sandra Day O'Connor and Lewis Powell played pivotal roles in the most important rulings that permitted racial preferential policy to continue. Meanwhile, liberal Justices William Brennan and Thurgood Marshall were appointed by a Republican and Democratic president, respectively, yet ascribed to constitutional principles and doctrines that served to restrict the scope and impact of race-based affirmative action. Preeminent among these is the foundational precept that race is an inherently suspect construct that demands strict scrutiny. The Republican-versus-Democrat-appointed paradigm comes up short too in accounting for the mostly Republican Rehnquist and Roberts Courts' defense of LGBTQ+ rights in several areas, including validation of same-sex marriage and equal treatment in the workplace.[14] Recent 2023 rulings that expand and protect racial minority voting rights also do not fit the ideology-centered narrative.[15] It seems shortsighted to expect that more favorable civil rights judgments will be secured only by adding Democratic appointments. If jurisprudential developments coincide with political tides, then civil rights rulings are not solely a function of whether a judge is Democrat or Republican appointed or a conservative or liberal. The tide itself figures into the equation.

What can we say about the political tide that the June 29, 2023, *Students for Fair Admissions* (*SFFA*) ruling rode in on, specifically the part that outlawed race-based college admissions? That tide consisted of a wave of anti–affirmative action national public opinion. In the weeks leading up to the ruling in *SFFA* an *Economist*/YouGov poll[16] found that 65 percent opposed race-aware admissions and a YouGov/CBS poll[17] found that 70 percent opposed. Just over two months before the June 2023 ruling a Pew Research Center poll showed that 50 percent of respondents disapproved of "colleges and universities taking race and ethnicity into account in admissions decisions in order to increase the racial and ethnic diversity of the school." Only 33 percent approved.[18] A February 2023 Reuters/Ipsos poll showed that 62 percent of Americans expressed that race should not be a factor in college and university admissions.[19] Additionally, parties have straddled the fence on affirmative action more often than not, with Republicans quick to condemn quotas yet support Minority Business Enterprises. Meanwhile, Democrats spurn quotas at the same time that they endorse results-oriented programming. In presidential politics, President Bill Clinton's 1995 "Mend It, Don't End It" policy was a sign that Presidents Ronald Reagan and George W. Bush were not the only modern presidents to back away from affirmative action. Only one out of five public universities consider race in admissions, thanks to ballot measures that officially ban affirmative action.

Prior affirmative action rulings rode the same political wave as *SFFA*. Albeit without outlawing race-based admissions policies, the Supreme Court displayed unease with race awareness as long ago as 1978, in *Bakke*, its first affirmative action ruling. Writing 25 years later in 2003 for the majority in *Grutter*, Justice Sandra Day O'Connor projected race-based affirmative action would meet its end 25 years hence. During the interim the policy barely survived scrutiny by a bench that was always sharply divided over whether the Constitution demanded colorblindness. From 1978 to 2016, roughly half of the race-based affirmative action rulings were settled by a sharply split vote in favor of the policy, and the other half by a closely divided court opposed to it.

Despite the political uproar it spurred, *SFFA* shifted the Court's position on just one of the 13 questions taken up in this book. It held that diversity learning does not constitute a compelling interest that justifies race-aware college admissions because courts cannot assess when the interest has been met. Beyond this, *SFFA* stuck to the script for race and public policy that prior affirmative action rulings had already written. The severely restrictive nature of the constitutional-legal standards used in previous cases were applied also in *SFFA*. Chief Justice Roberts gave a ringing endorsement to colorblind constitutionalism as a matter of principle but stopped short of insisting on it as a matter of blanket policy practice. The extremely broad conception of diversity that prevailed in earlier cases continued in *SFFA* too, such that well-to-do White applicants may count as "diversity." In short, the June 2023 ruling echoed much of what the rest of America and the justices of the Supreme Court had been saying about racial history, racism, policy implementation, and DEI for more than 40 years.

Toeing the Line uses a variety of original qualitative and quantitative data to illustrate the substantive agreement between the Supreme Court and the flow of national racial politics from 1978 through 2023. The discussion is divided into six chapters. Chapter 1 lays out the institutional, empirical, and historical reasons why it should be unsurprising that the US Supreme Court toes the line with respect to affirmative action. This opening chapter contains a discussion of the applicable literature on the Supreme Court and judicial politics. It also lays out the study's analytical focus, data, sources, and methodology. Finally, it offers a brief primer on affirmative action policy and history.

Chapter 2 unpacks judicial and political appraisal of the present-day relevance of Black history. It shows that the Supreme Court, policymakers, and the masses concede that the past is not entirely in the past and that it is important to be mindful of the legacy of slavery. But the consensus on the Court and in the country at large is that America's racial past is not enough to justify race-conscious policymaking. Another key facet of racial preference opinions is the justices' and much of America's belief that racism is not the root cause of racial inequality. Both are persuaded that everything cannot be explained by race, and that the explanatory power of socioeconomic class surpassed that of race, from the early 1960s onward. Last in the Black history category of themes is evidence that the Supreme Court treats the difference between past state-enforced bigotry against Blacks and the barriers once faced by White ethnics as a difference without a distinction. This same parallelism between Black and White ethnic histories in affirmative action rulings is advanced in the political process, on both sides of the party aisle and by presidents across the political spectrum, including Democratic presidents.

Chapter 3 shows that across the series of affirmative action rulings the justices redefined race and racism to mean something quite different from how they are construed within traditional civil rights perspectives. The Supreme Court insists on heightened scrutiny for all things racial yet simultaneously treats race as a malleable construct. The justices' denomination of race as inherently problematic channels the sentiments of a sizeable segment of the average citizenry. On this point, the symmetry between the Court's rationalizations and that of national political parties and presidents is not quite as seamless as that between the public and Court doctrine. Alongside treatment of race as irredeemably troublesome is repeated rejection of the notion that racial disparity of itself constitutes evidence of racism. More and more for the Court and the country racism is a matter of the mind, in that racial matters are increasingly negotiated through a lens predominately trained on something other than concretes (e.g., measurable racial inequality and minority disadvantage). Public opinion polling and the "happy talk" in which both major political parties frequently engage reflect this phenomenon. With the exception of President Barack Obama, we observe limited regard for material inequality on the part of recent presidents too. A third point of focus in chapter 3 is the justices' views about treating individuals as members of racial groups, instead of as individuals. This, they believe, contravenes core American ideals. Across the United States we find a shared sense on the part of lay citizens and politicians that affirmative action runs afoul of American individualism and equal treatment principles. Republicans and Democrats are not that far from the Court on this issue. Neither is a growing number of states whose fierce and quick reactions to critical race theory (CRT) curricula jive with the framing of race and race-specific policies within Supreme Court rulings.

The final concern of chapter 3 is how Supreme Court opinions construe racial preferences as discriminatory against Whites by way of excluding them and harmful to Blacks by virtue of reinforcing negative racial stereotypes. The same is true of the political world beyond judicial process where it is believed that the discriminatory dynamics of preferential policy operate along two continuums, one that caricatures Blacks as unqualified and the other that effectively envisages Whites as the new Blacks. While the Republican

Party and the Supreme Court are at one with respect to the reverse discrimination claim, the Democratic Party is arguably complicit too, in that
it is silent on whether preferential policies discriminate against Whites and
stereotype Blacks. The same cannot be said of President Bill Clinton, who
joined a chorus line of presidents that amplified White anger about preferential policies, or President Donald Trump who used White working-class
angst to secure his electoral victory in 2016. On the ground too, not only
are Americans as equally disinclined as the Court to summarily characterize
the Black population in any particular fashion, but the idea that Whites are
increasingly shortchanged has gained traction. In much the same way that
the Court has been expressly attentive to *White* rights and *White* burdens,
so too the arbitration of White interests as *White* interests is now normalized
in mainstream politics.

In chapter 4 we examine the Supreme Court's disposition toward
colorblindness. Even though the justices cautiously approved race-aware
policies (by slim vote margins) from *Bakke* (1978) through *Fisher* (2016),
most Americans were never on the same page—put off by the "racial" and
"preferential" aspects of affirmative action. They prefer preferential policies
that are race neutral and tied to other forms of marginalization. Decades-long
state-level politics trends likewise suggest that Supreme Court endorsement
of race consciousness is an instance of judicial policy misalignment with
the thrust of grassroots racial politics. *Students for Fair Admissions* (2023)
brought greater harmony, but not perfect harmony between the Court and
ordinary people. On the other hand, given that *SFFA* left the door open
for remedial affirmative action and for race consciousness in military school
admissions, prison assignments, and college applicant essays, it maintained
a longstanding alignment between the Court, parties, and presidents.

Notwithstanding rejection of the idea that the Constitution and civil
rights laws always demand race-blind policymaking, from 1978 through
2023 affirmative action rulings have imposed ever-restrictive stipulations.
These policy restrictions are consistent with widely shared beliefs in the
political arena, especially the prohibition on tackling systemic racism and on
correcting racial imbalances. And just as the rulings gloss over the unique
barriers that racial minorities face, a large segment of the US population is
about as likely to believe that widespread racism against Whites is a serious
problem as widespread racism against Blacks. Equivalents to the Supreme
Court's stance on racial balancing are observed in national party politics as
well, couched there in terms of equal opportunity versus equal results. When
the Court first began to flesh out its equal opportunity guidance in *Bakke*

in 1978, it did so against the backdrop of a matching bipartisan consensus that lasted until 2020. The consensus around opportunity as opposed to outcomes has been bolstered by every modern US president, including its first Black president, President Barack Obama.

Until the ruling in *Students for Fair Admissions* in 2023 only two race-based affirmative action policy goals were deemed permissible under the Constitution and civil rights laws, namely policies designed to foster diversity and policies to recompense specified instances of individual discrimination. The latter mandate that race-based remedial action target only particularized instances of identified discrimination is supported by public opinion. The same picture emerges in regard to political parties and remedial action, as their decades of pledges to fight discrimination is the natural outgrowth of a political history filled with overtures to the idea that the American dream consists of equal opportunity, of the removal of exclusionary barriers, and a fair shot for all. There is no shortage of presidential speeches that wax on about the valiant struggle to outlaw barriers to racial equality. The second policy goal initially approved by Supreme Court rulings—increasing diversity—is likewise anchored in values and traditions embraced across the board by the general public, major parties, and presidents over the years. None more than the notion that America is a melting pot and a nation of immigrants. However, *SFFA* muted the Court's ringing praise of diversity, by questioning whether courts can reliably measure how racial diversity impacts learning in the college classroom. At least in degree though not in kind, *SFFA* thusly creates a difference between the Court and the rest of America in regard to the generalized diversity principle.

Finally, chapter 4 details the multi-pronged constitutional test that was crafted across several rulings. The test all but guarantees that affirmative action policy is not and cannot be a viable means of achieving meaningful, large-scale racial reform in the US. The way in which Supreme Court decisions hamstring implementation of racial preferences is in accord with public discontent over how racial classifications are employed in the college admissions process, the workplace, and elsewhere. A majority of America wants the policy changed, in the same way that the justices insist on continual reassessment and adjustment of race-conscious programs. Three-quarters of Americans are disinclined to sanction permanency for affirmative action programs, in the same way that the justices insist on temporariness. As well, the distaste for rigidity manifest throughout affirmative action rulings mirrors the disdain for quotas on the part of not only the general public, but the Republican Party and Democratic Party as well. President Clinton's

"Mend It, Don't End It" policy announced in 1995 marked a turning point in presidential politics on racial matters, as Democratic presidents also began to hold the line against rigidity.

Chapter 5, titled "All Lives Matter: DEI and the Death of Affirmative Action," lays out how the Court-approved diversity standard diminished the political weight of distinctively *racial* minority concerns and interests. The Court's conception of diversity takes in almost every conceivable iteration of human differentiation. A critical first step to its catchall diversity standard was to upend the Black-White paradigm and, in doing so, decenter Blacks in diversity, equity, and inclusion (DEI) politics and policymaking. To underscore the "other aspects of diversity" that he believed should not be sacrificed, Justice Kennedy instanced "the star athlete or musician whose grades suffered because of daily practices and training . . . a talented young biologist who struggled to maintain above-average grades in humanities classes . . . a student whose freshman-year grades were poor because of a family crisis but who got herself back on track in her last three years of school."[20] Judicial process is not the only place where Blacks and racial-ethnic minorities have been decentered. We see the same dynamic in public opinion data. The vast majority prefers a "catchall" approach. So do both major political parties, as evident in the bipartisan universalist approach that took shape over several decades. No president has embraced a more wide-reaching definition of diversity than President Joseph Biden, who included under his administration's rubric rural residency, veteran status, pregnancy and pregnancy-related conditions, among a host of other things. An interesting twist is that progressive DEI politics on the college campus supplied the nail in the coffin of traditional race-centered affirmative action.

The second finding of chapter 5 is that in sharp contrast with the original stated goals of affirmative action—to increase opportunities for marginalized racial minority groups—the race-based diversity programs initially approved by the Supreme Court had to be designed to benefit nonminorities and the nation as a whole. *Bakke* (1978) insisted that a diverse student body cannot be an end in itself. Rather, it was the "transcendent value of academic freedom" that shields race-conscious diversity policies from constitutional attack, Justice Powell wrote. Coinciding with the Supreme Court's initial approval of race consciousness being conditioned on student learning benefits, the rest of America is not fully convinced that it improves the quality of higher education or is a net good for the country. On the other hand, Supreme Court framing of diversity as a benefit to the nation is a view that the general public, Democrats and Republicans, and American presidents agree with.

The upshot of *Toeing the Line* is that there is little daylight between the racial beliefs and arguments of the justices, on the one hand, and, on the other, that of ordinary American citizens and politicians in regard to the 13 key affirmative action issues that preoccupy both sides of the equation. A great deal of synchronicity is observed between the complex constitutional-legal proclamations pronounced within the courtroom and the nitty gritty of national racial politics outside the courtroom. The body of proof consists of mass public opinion data, party platforms, presidential positioning, and grassroots developments. Placed side by side with written court opinions, these data show that justices of the US Supreme Court toe the same line as lawmaking majorities when it comes to racial preferences in the policy process.

Although this is not a book about affirmative action, and is instead a look at the nature and extent of symmetry between Supreme Court case law and national racial politics, a word is in order about the usual challenges tied to discussions that touch on affirmative action. Despite its clearly stated theoretical and analytical aim, I suspect that this book will not be spared the intense feelings, partisanship, and gut reaction analysis that goes with the territory in some spaces. This is all the more so against the backdrop of recent political developments, such as historic polarization within the party system and the electorate, competing coalitions on the Political Right spurred by Trumpism and Make America Great Again (MAGA) politics, and analogous divisions on the Left that are recently exacerbated by the border crisis and Israel-Hamas War, among other things.

Personally, I consider it extremely unfortunate that even in some scholarly quarters the study of race and affirmative action does not escape the intense emotionalism that often drowns out sober analysis and reasoning beyond the Ivory Tower. Too often within academe there are "sides" of the affirmative action debate that are dug in in ways that render objective analysis not only difficult but, in some corners, spurned. One is expected to take a side, for or against. Failure to do so prompts some to read between the lines and draw their own conclusions about the analyst's politics, on the assumption that the writer's own politics somehow overtake the data, analysis, and conclusions. The fact that one's politics is frequently assumed (or imputed) on the basis of skin color, gender, sexual orientation, and the like adds yet another unhelpful dimension. The result is that, as compared to other academic subjects, the study of affirmative action is uniquely dogged by emotionalism, unresearched assertions, and politicization. This point is borne out by rigorous research that shows race is more prone to emotionalism than other political subjects and among the "easy" issues in American politics that typically do not involve as much cognitive effort, but frequently knee-jerk emotional responses.[21]

Some readers may be disappointed by this study's attempt to focus squarely on the empirical evidence that depicts where things have and continue to stand between the Court and body politic, instead of where things should or should not stand. Some may take issue with the fact that the discussion and analysis do not explicitly take a side. The Court probe here does not set out to take down or condemn court opinions or rationalizations, including those with which I personally disagree. The politics side of the analysis does not advocate but simply explicates what has been done and said by major players outside the courthouse in regard to race-conscious policies. The core research chapters do not advocate one way or another on the complex question whether affirmative action policy and programs are effective or not, whether just or not, whether supporters and detractors are good or bad people, whether it should remain as is, be mended, or ended. These very worthy normative and analytical assessments I leave to the many scholars whose research already ably tackles them.[22] In the main, I present this research project as a decidedly academic enterprise, with the overarching goal of making plain what the Court has been "saying" about racial matters for decades, and to offer evidence-based conclusions about the extent to which the body politic has been "saying" the same thing for decades.

All this is not to say that I do not have a dog in the fight, so to speak. I do. Race jurisprudence and America's racial politics are obviously a matter of great concern to not only those of us who devote time and energy to digging out oftentimes sobering truths and empirical realities about the intra- and extra-institutional dynamics of race. Affirmative action policy and its politics are a matter of great interest also to those who sincerely care whether things out there in the real world get better for Blacks, Latinos, First Peoples, Asians, Jews, and every other racial-ethnic minority group. Accordingly, the epilogue is where I offer summary remarks on a potential strategy forward. I affirm here at the outset that my wish is for a Supreme Court that lives up to its calling in *Federalist No. 78* to be a protector of minority rights and interests, an institution that racial-ethnic minorities can turn to in *times* of democratic excess and indifference, and an institution *composed* of justices that do more than simply toe the line when it comes to the promise of racial equality. The research in this book establishes that we are not there yet. By "we" I mean not only the justices but also voters, the political parties that purportedly act on our behalf, and the presidents we elect. Hopefully, this book is counted among those that offer helpful clues on how we can get there and where to start or, more aptly, with whom to start.[23]

Chapter One

Affirmative Action Jurisprudence in Institutional, Political, and Historical Context

US Supreme Court rulings on race are often viewed as the making of a court acting contrarily or unilaterally. The proffer of proof is usually watershed decisions like *Dred Scott* (1857), the Japanese internment cases, or *Brown* (1954) and *Loving* (1967), along with the so-called civil rights retreat of the Burger and Rehnquist Courts. The rulings on racial preference are similarly branded as somehow divergent from the liberal politics of the 1960s and the decades to follow. A common thread running through this line of thinking is that, whether in a conservative or liberal direction, whether in ways that are helpful or harmful to minority interests, the Court is acting in ways that are strikingly distinguishable from the body politic as a whole when it comes to emotionally charged racial issues. In contrast with these perspectives, the discussion to follow highlights many institutional, political, and historical considerations that challenge the notion of a trailblazing judiciary in the American policy process, especially on the racial policy front. These considerations supply ample reasons to expect US Supreme Court affirmative action rulings to closely mirror the racial political and policy preferences of the day.

Institutional Context of the Supreme Court

In the classic 1957 work that laid the foundation for much of the scholarship on the politics of the US Supreme Court, Dahl insisted that the president and Congress's authority over the appointment process is an important constraint on the countermajoritarian impulse of the Court. According to O'Brien's *Storm Center: The Supreme Court in American Politics*, "judges and scholars perpetuate the myth of merit," but the reality is that "every appointment is political."[1]

In doing their part to fill vacancies on the bench presidents seek to advance their own political agendas.[2] They choose nominees who share their beliefs and values, what O'Brien refers to as their "ideological kin."[3] It is a tradition that began with America's first president, George Washington.[4] Presidents seek out not only their ideological kin but those who share their position on specific policy matters, mainly those that are central to the president's legislative agenda. The fact that some appointees may drift[5] away from their original ideological leanings and vote against the policies of the president that nominated them does not negate the fact that such nominations are strategic and that appointees fulfill presidential policy expectations more often than not.[6] "Ideological drift" has more to do with the interplay between justices and changing mass political preferences[7] than with maverick tendencies on the justices' part. Presidents, and by extension the majorities that put them in office, typically carry the day, both in terms of the 93 percent confirmation rate[8] and in terms of the impact of presidential preferences on judicial policymaking.[9]

The US Senate confirmation process is another part of the Supreme Court's constitutional design where national politics seep in. Senators, whose elections necessarily reflect majority voter preferences, bring their own politics to the table. They too support nominees who share their ideology. Besides ideology, party politics and other factors amp up the degree of political contestation[10] within the confirmation process, impacting every stage of that process—from questioning during Judiciary Committee hearings to parliamentary procedures on the floor. Overby and colleagues detail how the contentious Senate confirmation vote on Justice Clarence Thomas was a way of courting constituents.[11] The ideological and partisan inputs that are channeled through the coordinate branches are themselves a function of electoral considerations. Kastellec and colleagues highlight a strong link between constituency opinion and voting on Supreme Court nominees.[12] Explaining the nexus, Cameron, Cover, and Segal say that a "senator can generally expect to gain electorally (or at least not to lose electorally) from voting as constituents wish and can expect to incur losses from flouting constituents' desires, regardless of the actual outcome of a vote."[13]

Opportunities for lawmakers to try to engineer Supreme Court rulings do not stop at shaping the makeup of the bench; they extend also to the structural and policymaking capacity of the federal judiciary. Which cases are taken up, when, and how are matters that Article III of the US Constitution leaves primarily to lawmakers to decide. All aspects of the judiciary's business are in some way subject to Congress's Article III powers—from the judiciary's budget,[14] to the rules[15] that govern case handling, to management of buildings and grounds,[16] the Court's calendar, its and caseload, and more.[17] By extension, all operate under the amalgam of electoral, policy, and special interests in play within the legislature. There are well-known episodes in which legislators played politics with the size of the Court as during the Roosevelt years,[18] along with the less well-known congressional enactments before and afterward.[19] There are historical examples too where Congress used its control over other aspects of court infrastructure and resources to further a policy agenda, such as the creation of circuit courts, new judgeships, judicial salaries,[20] removals,[21] and more.[22, 23] The Court's ability to set a policy agenda exists thanks to a congressional enactment, the Judiciary Act of 1925. This legislative authorization enables Supreme Court justices to choose cases from among the 8,000–10,000 petitions submitted each year, which petitions touch on major public policy concerns ranging from gun control, First Amendment rights, LGBTQ+ equality, and virtually everything else.[24] That adjustments to this discretionary authority are not confined to the far gone past is evident from the fact that Congress eliminated much of what remained of the mandatory docket in 1988.[25] Agenda-setting is subject to legislative control also through the Article III power to construe appellate jurisdiction.[26]

Article III powers are rarely used because their mere presence incentivizes restraint, mainly through political calculus. Scholars show that if and when justices fear a legislative reversal, there is a ripple effect that prompts them to feel constrained in constitutional cases as well.[27] More broadly, Casillas, Enns, and Wohlfarth point out that "decisions ignoring the prevailing tides of public mood risk alienating the mass public, inciting negative reactions from the elected branches, and perhaps compromising the Court's legitimacy."[28] A number of studies shed additional empirical light on this point. Segal, Westerland, and Lindquist found that concerns about institutional maintenance impart a measure of sensitivity in the Court toward the elected branches and a tendency to "modify its decisions accordingly."[29] Variation across time, population segments, and issues[30] in public confidence in the Court[31] suggests there are times when the Court is particularly vulnerable to encroachments and will tread more carefully. Recent efforts drive home the point that Supreme Court justices know what the president and Congress *could* do if ever sufficiently motivated by pressure from the electorate. They have good reason to worry. In April 2021, President Joseph Biden charged a newly established Presidential Commission on the Supreme Court of the United States[32] to appraise the merits of various reform proposals, ranging from the length of service and size of the Court to case selection, rules, and practices. *The Washington Post* reports that term limit proposals are popular also with the general public.[33] And, a contemporary version of court-packing has gained steam in a more concerted fashion than at any time since 1937, according to a report of the Center for American Progress.[34]

Although the dangers of structural dependency were front and center in Alexander Hamilton's *Federalist No. 78*, the federal judiciary was nonetheless left without means of independently enforcing its own court orders, another factor that forces justices to be more politically minded. Casillas, Enns, and Wohlfarth's work shows that nonimplementation is a special concern that the justices actively weigh,[35] as does Hall's study of Supreme Court decisions from 1951 to 2007.[36] Other scholars reach the same conclusion, that implementation of Court edicts is never guaranteed, that the Court is constrained by the fact that the Executive Branch can refuse implementation, and that Congress can thwart the intent of the judiciary.[37] McGuire and Stimson explain that "since the justices do not have the institutional capacities to give their rulings full effect, they must calculate the extent to which popular decision makers will support their policy initiatives."[38] Consequently, "strategic justices must gauge the prevailing winds that drive reelection-minded politicians and make decisions accordingly."[39]

The history of national racial politics figures largely in regard to each of the previously discussed pathways where politics can seep into the work of the Supreme Court. As to the nominations process, knowing beforehand where President H. W. Bush nominee Samuel Alito stood on affirmative action and abortion was very important to 46 percent of Americans and somewhat important to 31 percent.[40] The same was true during President Obama's tenure, when 48 percent of US adults reported that it was very important to know Justice Sonia Sotomayor's stance on issues such as affirmative action and abortion with 28 percent citing it as somewhat important.[41] Further, since race is a defining feature of America's party politics,[42] racial controversy also influences senators' behavior in the confirmation process. Affirmative action is prominent among the "litmus test" policy issues that bear on constituency pressures and ultimately Senate votes. Nearly 80 percent of Republican and Democrat voters said that a senator's vote on confirmation of Chief Justice John Roberts should be based in part on Roberts's position on issues such as affirmative action and abortion.[43] A year prior to Roberts's confirmation, when asked whether "the Senate should only consider a judge's background, experience and qualifications, or should the Senate also consider a judge's views on such issues as abortion, gun control and affirmative action," fully 60 percent of respondents chose the latter.[44]

Race has shaped Congress's use of its greatest power over the Supreme Court. There have been five constitutional reversals,[45] two of which involved racial matters—the Thirteenth and Fourteenth Amendments' reversal of *Dred Scott* (1857) is of particular note to this study. Congress's tool to overturn rulings that interpret federal law, legislative reversals, are more frequent[46] and consequential.[47] The Civil Rights Restoration Act of 1991 was expressly enacted by Congress "to respond to recent decisions of the Supreme Court by expanding the scope of relevant civil rights statutes in order to provide adequate protection to victims of discrimination."[48] Alone, it reversed or modified up to six separate conservative rulings handed down between 1989 and 1991.[49] Among these was *Richmond v. Croson* (1989), a major affirmative action case.

An historic race-related case proves the uncertainty of implementation too. More than 500 anti-*Brown* measures were enacted in the South to defy the desegregation ruling, prompting President Dwight Eisenhower to dispatch the National Guard in order to secure compliance. Gerald N. Rosenberg's seminal analysis of judicial impact in *The Hollow Hope: Can Courts Bring About Social Change?*[50] shows that, unless and until political conditions are in alignment with its judgments, the Court can do little on its own. Here too we can turn to the *Brown* decision for support. It did not measurably change the racial makeup of southern schools until after Congress, the president, and local officials aided implementation.

Empirical Research on Political Influences and the Supreme Court

The ideological, personal, and professional experiences of the justices that sit on the US Supreme Court provide additional opportunities where politics can enter the judicial process.[51] In two major works Segal and Spaeth argue that justices decide cases based partly on their own attitudes and personal views on the Constitution and policy issues, as well as interpretation of the law.[52] Supported by a probe of 2,418 votes and cases, their "attitudinal model" illustrates that judges' own preferences consistently trump legal precedents.

As Ulmer put it, judges are normal human beings that are no more or less immune to political thinking than the rest. They are "Black-robed homo sapiens."[53] They are no less so when tackling the highly emotional subject that is race-conscious decision-making.

Macropolitical phenomena too converge on judicial process in ways that yield special lessons for civil rights jurisprudence. In deciding what to decide and how, the Court targets the same matters that concern most of America and in the same way, according to the late Chief Justice William Rehnquist. He offered that "judges, so long as they are relatively normal human beings, can no more escape being influenced by public opinion in the long run than can people working at other jobs. . . . Judges need not 'tremble before public opinion' in the same way that elected officials may, but it would be remarkable indeed if they were not influenced by . . . currents of public opinion."[54] The shift in the Court's docket from mostly economic cases during 1900–1940 to mostly civil liberties cases during 1950–1990[55] coincided with a shift in national attention away from the Great Depression and toward the social justice politics of the 1950s and 1960s. And as the country embraced a more liberal stance on racial equality, women's rights, prisoner rights, voting rights, and more, we observe the same evolution in the rulings handed down by the Vinson and Warren Courts across the same policy areas. The post-1968 turnabout that revealed increased racial conservativism beyond the South was comparably embodied in Supreme Court rulings that gradually chipped away at the liberal decisions of the Warren Court.

Political science studies document an empirical link between court rulings and public opinion.[56] Gibson cautions that "in the final analysis it is simply not clear whether the Court responds to public opinion, or shapes public opinion, or whether it responds to the same sort of factors that themselves shape public opinion."[57] Casillas, Enns, and Wohlfarth tried to resolve the "chicken-or-egg" dilemma by controlling for societal forces and found that public mood has both significant short- and long-run influence on the Supreme Court's decisions.[58] Baum and Devins similarly conclude that when the general public and elites are on the same page, then the Court is more likely to align itself with that consensus.[59] Coming from a different angle, Giles, Blackstone, and Vining argue that "justices' preferences shift in response to the same social forces that shape the opinions of the general public."[60] Elaborating, McGuire and Stimson posit "that the Supreme Court's outcomes may comport with popular opinion is scarcely a wonder; it is merely a manifestation of selecting ideologically driven justices whose preferences roughly match those of the electorate more generally."[61] As Exhibit A, they offer the following from the late Justice Antonin Scalia: "The justices of the Court are taken from society . . . and however impartial they may try to be, they are going to bring with them those societal[al] attitudes."[62]

There are dozens of occasions on which the Supreme Court thwarts policy majorities by exercising judicial review (i.e., the power to declare acts of Congress and the president null and void).[63] But, striking down federal policies is more an exception than the rule. In his classic study of judicial review in the 150+ years to follow the foundational *Marbury v. Madison* ruling of 1803, Bickel avers that the Court typically takes the bold step of invalidating congressional and presidential power only when it is politically safe to do so.[64] There is disagreement among judicial politics scholars about the precise pathways and direction of the relationship between the Court and the body politic. Nonetheless, the bottom line is that there is ample qualitative and quantitative proof that political considerations seep into judicial decision-making, somehow, someway, and to some extent. For these reasons, coupled with the weight of the evidence from the judicial politics literature, we should anticipate that affirmative action case law is in accord with the national politics of affirmative action.

The History of Race Jurisprudence

The body of literature that is dedicated to US Supreme Court race and affirmative action jurisprudence highlights a number of pathways through which national politics filter into court decision-making specifically on this policy front. These works may be classified into four models for explaining affirmative action rulings. One focuses on the justices, another on legalism, a third on the colorblind doctrine and its politics, and the last on macro racial politics.

The first model homes in on the racial ideology, philosophy, and politics of individual judges. Constitutional scholar and political scientist Chemerinsky deems the Court derelict in fulfilling one of its preeminent purposes, which is to protect the rights of minorities.[65] Chemerinsky's expansive look at legal history up through the Roberts Court unpacks several areas of law, with special attention to the Supreme Court's record of protecting racial minorities. The antebellum cases are featured as instances of failure wherein the justices protected the rights of slave owners and denied all rights to those who were enslaved. Significant for our purposes is that Chemerinsky argues that, due to the "open-ended language in the Constitution," the decisions in these important civil rights cases "are products of who is on the Court and their personal views."[66] Likewise, in a major work where Spann takes on affirmative action decisions on race and remedies over a 25-year period heavy emphasis is placed on the explanatory significance of voting blocs on the high court.[67] Without articulating a causal claim, Perry traces the story of the Michigan affirmative action cases—from the district to the appellate to the high court. Her field research unpacks the national civil rights politics that led to *Bakke* (1978), in addition to Michigan state politics, the legal briefs submitted to the Supreme Court in *Grutter* (2003) and *Gratz* (2003), interviews of the personalities and interest groups behind the lawsuits, and oral arguments in these companion cases. The result is a compelling account that underscores the crucial role of Justice Sandra Day O'Connor as a swing voter and Court opinion author. It is a role that, according to Perry, loops back to O'Connor's "personal, professional, and judicial backgrounds."[68]

A second model exhibited in *Race Against the Court: The Supreme Court and Minorities in Contemporary America*[69] by Girardeau Spann draws our attention to the ways in which legal principles interact with majority and minority preferences. According to Spann, "The Supreme Court has often interpreted legal principles to mean whatever the majority says that they mean." The study details just how far the Court's actual performance diverges from the ideal of a countermajoritarian institution. Based on an extended look at *Brown v. Board of Education* (1954) and the law of affirmative action, Spann postulates "the discrepancy between actual and model Supreme Court performance is sufficient to preclude the existence of any meaningful difference between Supreme Court adjudication and ordinary politics."[70] The reason? The constraints of legalism and constitutional principle within which the Court must operate make it vulnerable to the same political forces that drive majoritarian responses. The only difference of note between political and judicial dispositions of minority interests, he maintains, is that judicial majoritarianism functions with undetected effectiveness precisely because it transpires behind the veil of legalism, namely judicial review. The Court is "inherently conservative" because two phenomena—lifetime tenure and judicial independence—cause it to function as a political force for the status quo. Because racial minorities are disadvantaged by the existing status quo, it follows that efforts to achieve racial equality are inevitably impaired by the Court's inherent conservatism. As we seek to better understand affirmative action outcomes, then, this line of reasoning supplies additional cause to investigate not only who sits on the bench, but the way in which constitutional-legal standards drive how those who are on the bench navigate the real-world racial status quo.

The connection between colorblind constitutionalism and the racial power hierarchy is front and center in a third model of Supreme Court race jurisprudence. Golub construes colorblind constitutionalism as more than mere doctrine and instead as part of a longstanding historical dialectic in which Supreme Court rulings render the pursuit of racial equality in the US a violation of White rights. Carefully dissecting the history and reasoning in *Plessy v. Ferguson* (1896), Golub concludes that "Harlan's dissent is motivated less by a rejection of racial difference as such than by concern over the majority opinion's posture of legal formalism, by which it disavows the evident meaning of the law it defends."[71] Likewise, Golub insists that "today's color-blind conservatives more closely resemble the *Plessy* majority than the dissent that they champion."[72] Since *Brown* (1954) the notion of a colorblind Constitution serves as a foundation for aggressive rights-based activism by conservative critics of civil rights. It is worth pointing out Golub's claim that misapplication of the colorblind principle in contemporary constitutional discourse is inevitable because constitutionalism functions in the broader sense of constituting the nation or people in whose name its authority is exercised.

Goldstone's detailed account of the failure to protect minority voting rights in the decades after the Civil War likewise points to the Court's indifference to racialized power structures. Placing the final judgments in voting rights cases side by side with the political battles outside the Court, Goldstone argues the justices of the Supreme Court "contented themselves with taking refuge in parsing language, debating the meaning of this clause or that, or deciding whether or not a definition of a term meant what it said or something else."[73] All of this was to purposely turn a blind eye to the brutality inflicted on Blacks by white supremacists bent on disenfranchisement. For Goldstone too, to fully understand the nature of Supreme Court behavior we must examine the justices' conscious alliance with political forces that are hostile or agnostic to racial reform.

A fourth model for explaining affirmative action that emerges from scholarly works is concerned with the overall political context in which racial matters are negotiated. Dahl's classic treatise on the Supreme Court stresses the critical significance of lawmaking majorities. The article, "Decision-Making in a Democracy: The Supreme Court as a National Policy Maker," analyzes "the fifteen or so cases in which the Court used the protections of the Fifth,

Thirteenth, Fourteenth and Fifteenth Amendments to preserve the rights and liberties of a relatively privileged group at the expense of the rights and liberties of a submerged group." Specifically, the Court privileged slaveholders "at the expense of the enslaved, White people at the expense of colored people, and property holders at the expense of wage earners and other groups."[74] Dahl's analysis notes the seismic shift in the political and economic order that would have occurred had the Court decided otherwise. A different set of rulings would have meant "thoroughly basic shifts in the distribution of rights, liberties, and opportunities in the United States where, moreover, the policies sustained by the Court's action have since been repudiated in every civilized nation of the Western world, including our own."[75] Yet, precisely because such monumental changeover in the basic distribution of privilege was at stake, Dahl deemed it "futile" for us "to suppose that the Court could have possibly acted much differently in these areas of policy from the way in which it did in fact act."[76] He concludes that it is "most unrealistic to suppose that the Court would, for more than a few years at most, stand against any major alternatives sought by a lawmaking majority."[77]

Kennedy also bottoms the relationship between politics and affirmative action case law on the larger political context. Kennedy offers an incisive look at affirmative action within the history of racial politics, the Left and Right assertions within the national affirmative action policy debate, and Supreme Court case law through 2013. He finds that "the Supreme Court's handling of the controversy over affirmative action in higher education mirrors the thinking and sentiments of the nation's governing elite."[78] Kennedy contends as well that "the Court has made a series of ambiguous, ad hoc rulings that reflect the country's racial anxieties."[79]

Using an historical lens that takes in civil rights rulings and politics from 1895 to 1965, Klarman too posits the former as inextricably tied to the latter. For him, the Supreme Court's role in the fight for racial equality is a prime example of the fact that "judicial decision making involves a combination of legal and political factors."[80] These factors constitute a "legal axis" (which consists of sources such as text, originalism, and precedent) and a "political axis" (composed of factors such as judicial values, the social and political context of the times, and external political pressures). Instead of conceptualizing the two axes as fixed, Klarman urges the need to adjudge them on a continuum of determinacy to indeterminacy, in one instance, and strong political preferences to weak ones, in the other. Different judges will accord different weights to these two axes, at different times, and with different case facts in mind. To fully grasp the dynamics of the stretch of cases from *Plessy* (1896) to *Brown* (1954), therefore, one must examine how most justices during the respective time periods understood their jobs in light of the broader social and political context of the times. As the broader social and political context of the times change, so will justices' rulings . . . or not.

We are led to the same conclusion by Davis and Graham's *Supreme Court, Race, and Civil Rights*.[81] Their 194-year review of the role of the Supreme Court in civil rights policymaking shows that the Court has at times furthered equality and, at others, frustrated equality goals. This pattern and the politically disadvantaged group's quest for equality are best understood, the authors explain, by appreciating the interaction between politics and law in the area of civil rights. Supreme Court policymaking is not independent from the influences of its external environment. For Davis and Graham a critical mechanism is membership change on the Court, which is itself the result of the policy preferences of the appointing president, which preferences are, in turn, those of lawmaking majorities.

Sunstein illuminates the broader political and policy backdrop of Supreme Court affirmative action decisions in "Casuistry," urging that "the issue of affirmative action should be settled democratically, not judicially."[82] Until then, affirmative action is best evaluated by the Court on a case-by-case basis and with close attention to policy consequences, because some race-conscious programs likely serve important goals, others possibly disserve their intended beneficiaries, and still others fall somewhere in between. Sunstein's primary "defense of casuistry" is based on the notion that the Supreme Court can stimulate the kind of public debate that is more inclusive, more deliberative, and substantive. Although less authoritative and decisive, the Court's casuistical approach to affirmative action is the kind of judicial particularism that can promote the kind of democratic virtues of participation and responsiveness that could forestall the kind of public backlash that presumedly precipitated California's enactment of Proposition 209. A casuistical approach may confront the problems of legitimacy associated with a policy proliferated by government bodies in the absence of fulsome public debate. To Sunstein's list of potential outcomes of a more deliberative racial politics and at the risk of oversimplification, I would add enough public buy-in to amass a lawmaking majority.

To conclude the foregoing review of scholarly clues that affirmative action case law toes the line, it is my interest in the latter—namely, building and mobilizing a lawmaking majority consensus around racial reform—that is the motivation behind this book. My interest is not guided by a belief that it is preferable to resolve America's race problem democratically, but rather the sense that it is unavoidably necessary to do so as long as America is a democratically governed polity in which the majority rules and in which Supreme Court justices and their actions are borne out of the polity. Hopefully without displaying too much hutzpah (considering that the just-discussed studies are authored by the nation's leading scholars on race jurisprudence), my aim in this study is to build on the important theoretical foundation that they have laid. I will do so by methodizing analysis of doctrinal developments, systematically tracing those developments over time, and using a structured themes-centered framework to assess correspondence over time between Supreme Court affirmative action policy and racial politics. The end result is a merger of the study of racial politics and jurisprudential developments.

In what follows I explain the focus, data, and analytical goal of this study.

Methods: Study Focus, Data, and Analytical Goal

To assess whether the Supreme Court and the lay public engage in similar modes of intellection when it comes to emotionally charged racial matters the study's research analysis examines, first, the way in which Supreme Court justices reason through affirmative action rulings and, second, the way in which the larger body politic reasons through racial matters.

COURT OPINION ANALYSIS

This study's focus on the substance of Supreme Court opinions takes in a different set of analytics than those employed in most empirical examinations of judicial politics. Scholars typically rely on either output (e.g., votes on certiorari and on the merits); the ideological tilt of final judgments; or automated content analysis tools that use coding algorithms, such as word scoring[83] (i.e., treating words as statistical data points). By training our lens on the logic and substantive components of the rulings, we can grasp not only whether final outputs comport with the politics of the day, but whether the stated justifications and controlling legal principles do as well. Taking a cue from Hansford and Spriggs, the analysis launches also from the premise that "the importance of the U.S. Supreme Court for American politics resides in its ability to set legal and public policy. The rules and procedures set forth in Court opinions serve important informational functions."[84] In short, the focus exclusively on formal written opinions as a way to construct a portrait of Supreme Court affirmative action logic is based on an understanding of official court opinions as pivotal.

Majority opinions are where the Supreme Court's policymaking power resides.[85] Opinions are the official platform on which the Supreme Court codifies, explicates, and disseminates its policy positions on the issues of the day. The majority or plurality opinions capture the prevailing institutional logic of the Court in the most cohesive fashion possible, in that they set forth the collective or controlling consensus that officially decides. As justices craft opinions, they are actively and conscientiously engaged in a political and policy discourse with the public.[86] Thus, a series of opinions supply a window into the ongoing dialectic that is imbedded in court judgments on a single policy subject. According to Black and colleagues and also Wedeking and Zillis, Supreme Court justices endeavor to write clear opinions and choose less disagreeable rhetoric in an attempt to bolster public support and dull public opposition.[87] Specifically in regard to affirmative action rulings Cass R. Sunstein frames the Court's casuistical approach as the justices' way to emphasize the "content of particular programs, their stated goals, and the link between those goals and the affirmative action measures undertaken," in order to "trigger public debate."[88]

Following the lead of Chief Justice John Roberts and Justice O'Connor, this analysis employs the majority or "Court" opinion to pinpoint the institutional consensus. When warning against reliance on dissents for the Court's position, Roberts quipped in *Students for Fair Admissions v. Harvard* (2023), "A dissenting opinion is generally not the best source of legal advice on how to comply with the majority opinion."[89] In the absence of a majority opinion, the plurality or principal opinion serves as the point of focus. Precedent corroborates reliance on principal opinions as a way of gauging the prevailing consensus, as O'Connor clarifies in *Grutter* (2003):

> In the wake of our fractured decision in *Bakke*, courts have struggled to discern whether Justice Powell's diversity rationale, set forth in part of the opinion joined by no other Justice, is nonetheless binding precedent under *Marks*. In that case, we explained that "when a fragmented Court decides a case and no single rationale explaining the result enjoys the assent of five Justices, the holding of the Court may be viewed as that position taken by those Members who concurred in the judgments on the narrowest grounds."[90]

A key feature of the study's design is its all-inclusive approach to probing written opinions. Well beyond statements and conclusions and dicta, every component of each case is considered—from the author's selection of supporting facts, to specification of questions to be decided, to the choice of supporting precedents, political implications of noncontrolling dicta, evidence cited, focus of historical reviews, critique of concurring and dissenting opinions, footnotes, and more. The Court's multi-stage, behind-the-scenes vetting process serves to confirm that every part of an opinion is intended for a particular purpose.[91]

A total of 31 race-based affirmative action case opinions anchor the court analysis. Many legal and political science scholars classify as "affirmative action" cases a much larger subset than is selected here. This study's threshold interest is in race ethnicity. Accordingly, the cases were selected based, first, on whether they are explicitly denoted by court opinions as pertaining to "affirmative action," "racial classification," "racial preference," "racial quotas," "racial set-asides," and the like.[92] Spann's account numbers racial affirmative action rulings from 1974 to 2000 at 32.[93] The second consideration is whether the plaintiff expressly petitioned the Court for a ruling on the validity of a racial preference program or policy. A third criterion was whether the litigation stemmed from allegations of "benign" or "reverse" racial discrimination, as opposed to "traditional" civil rights discrimination claims. Finally, while public school busing and redistricting cases often involve challenges to benign racial classifications, time and space do not permit a comprehensive review of these cases too. The 31 race-based affirmative action cases are listed in table 1.1.

An issue-focused framework is used to probe opinion content. The framework centers on 13 recurring constitutional-legal questions and topics in affirmative action case law. This approach is informed partly by Girardeau A. Spann's layout of affirmative action case "issues" in *The Law of Affirmative Action: Twenty-Five Years of Supreme Court Decisions on Race and Remedies.*[94] By deconstructing written affirmative action opinions we can undertake a systematic multi-decade correspondence analysis that compares the specific ways that race is operationalized in judicial process to the specifics of how race is negotiated within the larger political process. The 13 themes or flashpoints that are examined here were identified through an exhaustive distillation of each of the main opinions in race-based affirmative action cases.

The 13 themes are grouped into four camps based on their relatedness to one another, and each group is analyzed in one of the book's four research chapters. In the first camp are questions that concern the significance of

Table 1.1. Race-Based Affirmative Action Cases, 1974–2023

Year	Case		Citation
1974	*DeFunis v. Odegaard*		416 U.S. 312
1974	*Morton v. Mancari*		417 U.S. 353
1978	*Regents California v. Bakke*		438 U.S. 265
1979	*U.S. Steel Workers v. Weber*		443 U.S. 193
1980	*Fullilove v. Klutznick*		448 U.S. 448
1981	*Minnick v. California Dept. of Corrections*		452 U.S. 105
1982	*Weinberger v. Rossi*		456 U.S. 25
1984	*Firefighters Local 1784 v. Stotts*		467 U.S. 561
1986	*Wygant v. Jackson*		476 U.S. 267
1986	*Local 28 of Sheet Metal Workers' v. EEOC*		478 U.S. 421
1986	*Firefighters v. City of Cleveland*		478 U.S. 501
1987	*U.S. v. Paradise*		480 U.S. 149
1987	*Johnson v. Transportation Agency*		480 U.S. 616
1989	*Richmond v. Croson*		488 U.S. 469
1989	*Martin v. Wilks*		490 U.S. 755
1990	*Metro v. FCC*		497 U.S. 547
1993	*Northeastern v. Florida*		508 U.S. 656
1995	*Adarand Constructors v. Pena*		515 U.S. 200
2000	*Adarand Constructors v. Slater*		528 U.S. 216
2001	*Adarand Constructors v. Mineta*		534 U.S. 103
1999	*Texas v. Lesage and U.S.*		528 U.S. 18
2003	*Gratz v. Bollinger*		539 U.S. 244
2003	*Grutter v. Bollinger*		539 U.S. 306
2007	*Parents Involved v. Seattle, Meredith v. Jefferson*		551 U.S. 701, 551 U.S. 701
2009	*Ricci v. DeStefano*		557 U.S. 557
2013	*Fisher v. University of Texas*		570 U.S. 297
2014	*Schuette v. Coalition to Defend AA*		572 U.S. 291
2016	*Fisher v. University of Texas II*		Docket 14-981
2023	*Students for Fair Admissions v. Harvard*		Docket 20-1100, Docket 21-707

Source: Created by the author.

America's racial past in today's politics. Does it still matter that Blacks were once enslaved or is the past simply that, the past? The second camp concerns the issue of what constitutes racism, whether race awareness itself is racism, and whether racial disparity constitutes racism. The formal policy proscriptions and prescriptions stipulated in race-based rulings comprise the third category. Do the rules set down by the Court accord with what the public and politicians want? The final group of themes centers on diversity, equity, and inclusion (DEI) policy and politics. To what extent and how has the Court's new conception of "diversity" decentered Blacks and racial minorities generally? And, is its "All Lives Matter" conception of diversity concordant with that embraced by everyday citizens? Finally, to what end must DEI policies be chiefly directed, the betterment of minorities or America as a whole?

Although we will see why Justice Sandra Day O'Connor described the Court's first affirmative action ruling in *Bakke* (1978) as the "touchstone for constitutional analysis of race-conscious admissions policies,"[95] this study does not suggest that there is a seamless trajectory of rulings from 1978 onward, meaning they steadily move in one direction or another. Nor does it suggest that the many parts fit together in a sensible fashion. In the words of Cass R. Sunstein: "From the standpoint of the rule of law, the cases are truly a mess," an instance of "case-by-case particularism."[96] The point of emphasis here is on how the Court wrestles with issues, not how neatly it does so.

Racial Politics Analysis

The second part of the analysis is a systematic description of national racial politics on several fronts, including: mass public opinion, national party politics, presidential policy positioning, state level trends, and grassroots developments. It draws from primary sources of political data to build the multi-decade probe of symmetry between Supreme Court affirmative action rulings and racial politics.

The public opinion analysis is designed to gauge how national majorities are aligned. While public opinion can be disaggregated by racial-ethnic, gender, sexual orientation, class, and other important demographic differences, the aim of this study is to map out the stance of the collective, that is to say the sum of the whole body politic, not its parts. (Tables 1.3 and 1.4 highlight racial and partisan differences, respectively.) The public opinion analysis in this study has a view toward Robert A. Dahl's treatise on "lawmaking majorities." It is the majority of the adult population in the US that ultimately chooses who is elected and empowered to make the laws by which we are governed. Partisan and regional differences in attitudes matter too. So does context, such that enactment of California Proposition 209 in 1995 ratcheted up the political saliency of affirmative action. There is also what Sunstein laments as the "laundering effect" of political correctness.[97] Additionally important is the impact of question wording as indicated in table 1.2. It shows that binary questions tend to yield lower support for affirmative action. A Cato Institute analysis shows differences between questions with an explanation versus those without explanation.[98] Instrumentation

Table 1.2. Framing of Affirmative Action Survey Questions, US, 2009 and 2013

Year	Survey Question	Select Responses (%)
2013	Are you in favor of affirmative action? (*Economist*/YouGov, June 24, 2013)	Favor: 32 Oppose: 41 Not sure: 27
2013	Are you in favor of affirmative action programs for racial and ethnic minorities? (*Economist*/YouGov, June 24, 2013)	Favor: 36 Oppose: 41 Not sure: 23
2009	Are you in favor of affirmative action? (*Economist*/YouGov, July 15, 2009)	Favor: 25 Oppose: 39 Not sure: 36
2009	Are you in favor of affirmative action programs for racial and ethnic minorities? (*Economist*/YouGov, July 15, 2009)	Favor: 23 Oppose: 44 Not sure: 33
2009	Do you generally favor or oppose affirmative action programs for women? (Associated Press/GFK, June 2, 2009)	Strongly favor: 33 Somewhat favor: 30 Somewhat oppose: 15 Strongly oppose: 14 Don't know/no response: 9
2009	Do you generally favor or oppose affirmative action programs for racial and ethnic minorities? (Associated Press/GFK, June 2, 2009)	Strongly favor: 24 Somewhat favor: 32 Somewhat oppose: 17 Strongly oppose: 19 Don't know/no response: 9

Source: Survey data obtained from *Polling the nations*. (n.d.). Topic: Affirmative action. Last accessed 4/25/2022 from https://ptn-infobase-com.exlibris.colgate.edu/topics/VG9waWM6 NTI=?aid=14265.

Table 1.3. Perceptions of Civil Rights Progress, US, by Race, 2018

	Black Respondents (percent who say little or no progress has been made)	White Respondents (percent who say little or no progress has been made)
Fair treatment by police	73	39
The criminal justice system	66	40
Fair coverage by the media	57	21
Political representation	56	18
Equal economic opportunities	51	21
Access to loans and mortgages	49	18
Access to good jobs	44	18
Access to affordable housing	41	22
Access to good education	40	14
Reducing segregation in public life	39	15
Voting rights	33	9
Access to good health care	31	16

Source: Associated Press-NORC Center for Public Affairs Research. (2018, March). *50 years after Martin Luther King's assassination: Assessing progress of the civil rights movement.* https://apnorc.org/projects/50-years-after-martin-luther-kings-assassination-assessing-progress-of-the-civil-rights-movement/.

Table 1.4. Partisan Differences in Perception of Discrimination, US, by Party, 2021

	Republican Respondents	Democrat Respondents
Black people	63	93
Hispanic people	60	89
Asian people	56	82
White people	63	20

Note: The table shows the percent of Republican and Democrat respondents who say there is "A lot" or "Some" discrimination against each of the groups listed.

Source: Daniller, A. (2021, March 18). Majorities of Americans see at least some discrimination against Black, Hispanic and Asian people in the U.S. Pew Research Center. https://www.pewresearch.org/fact-tank/2021/03/18/majorities-of-americans-see-at-least-some-discrimination-against-Black-hispanic-and-asian-people-in-the-u-s/.

and methodology pose their own conundrums that bear on interpretation. Research by Bobo much more fully fleshes out the range of methodological challenges in measuring racial attitudes.[99] Thankfully, his and many other studies devote careful treatment to the attitudes of various subpopulations.

To help ameliorate some of the usual challenges of public opinion survey data and methodology, multiple polling sources are relied upon. A wide range of affirmative action–related questions are used that stretch from 1990 through 2023. The more than 200 survey questions reported on here consist of single standalone polls as well as time-series data. To help home in on the particular concerns of this study and to fill in gaps as needed, several nationally representative 1,000–1,500 sample size surveys were commissioned and fielded for this study by YouGov.

National political party positioning around race and affirmative action is ascertained from the official platform adopted quadrennially by the two major parties. All platforms were obtained from the American Presidency Project database (which I describe in the next paragraph). They are the most reliable means of pinpointing the Democratic and Republican Party positions on various policy and political subjects over multiple decades because they represent the intraparty consensus that is built through back-and-forth negotiations at the national convention in committee sessions. Kidd succinctly characterizes their significance as follows, "Even in an era of candidate-centric politics, political party platforms spell out the general programs offered by the parties, and the platforms are heavily influenced by the policy positions of the candidates themselves. In addition, the political platform is the one document that spells out the entire program of the party. Individual candidate speeches capture only snippets (at best) of the policy choices offered to voters."[100] Fagan provides strong time-series evidence that legislative agendas are influenced by the platform of the president's party in the short term, with variations across agenda types and issues.[101] Platforms also give voters a sense of what a party will do if it wins the election, according to Ginsberg and Monroe.[102] Studies additionally establish that voters use party platforms to draw conclusions. For instance, Simas and Evans show that citizens are able to use party platforms in their assessments of presidential candidates.[103]

The most reliable indicators for mapping the extent of agreement between presidents and the Supreme Court on affirmative action policy are executive orders, official proclamations, administrative regulations and guidance, speeches, interviews briefings, legislative endorsements and vetoes, and the like. To systemize sourcing of these documents, I rely exclusively on the publicly available American Presidency Project (APP) online database.[104]

The website is maintained by Gerhard Peters and John Wooley through the University of California at Santa Barbara. Materials on presidents include almost all documents from two canonical collections of presidential papers: *Messages and Papers of the Presidents of the United States* and *The Public Papers of the Presidents*. The site is regularly updated with materials from the White House media office, the Government Printing Office, and the National Archives and Records Administration (NARA). Unlike other sources of presidential documents (e.g., presidential libraries, depositories, and the *Federal Register*), APP compares its documents against other documentary sources to resolve any discrepancies. APP is the most complete compilation. APP's online search tool was used to select documents. Filters included a president's years in office, along with a list of pertinent search terms (e.g., "affirmative action," "quotas," "preferences," "set-asides," "diversity," etc.). Almost all of these terms were used for every president from Roosevelt through Trump. I then reviewed the documents yielded by this search to determine which offered the most robust statement versus a passing reference.

The analysis and discussion contextualize the preceding data with supplementary information pertaining to "on the ground" trends and developments. State legislative trends, headline news, election politics, culture war discourses, and academic and political commentary shed light on how race and affirmative action controversies play out in real time. As an example, to appreciate the political significance of critical race theory (CRT) in the divide over race awareness, it is important to know not only what presidents like Donald J. Trump said and did relative to CRT, but also how state legislatures across the country and, perhaps most of all, how proponents and opponents of CRT framed it. The same for slave reparations and several other critical issues in the ongoing racial discourse across the US.

Correspondence Analysis

The end goal of this study's correspondence analysis is to compare the Supreme Court's position to that of the polity, on each of the selected 13 affirmative action issues, in order to establish the degree to which both are in sync with one another. Each chapter proceeds along two tracks. The first track is a detailed description of Supreme Court pronouncements and reasoning on the themes or "flashpoints" at the center of race-based affirmative action cases decided between 1978 and 2016. The second track describes how the same flashpoints are mediated in the political arena by lay citizens, national political parties, presidential administrations, and grassroots politics, highlighting how these are aligned with Court reasoning and pronouncements.

It does not advance a claim about causation. Taking a page from a wide swath of the judicial politics literature, the discussion uses terms like "correspondence," "synchronicity," "symmetry," and the like, instead of "responsiveness" because the overriding aim is to assess agreement, not control.[105] Indeed, one of the takeaways from the analysis is that neither necessarily leads or follows the other. There are instances where we will see the Court moving ahead of the public, although there are more where the public and politicians arrive at a conclusion about race and preferential treatment well before the Court does. It bears mentioning too that this book does not posit a perfect one-to-one match but emphasizes instead the basic thrust of rationalizations of the Supreme Court and the body politic.

To reiterate, this is a study of the empirical relationship between the Supreme Court and the larger body politic on affirmative action issues, politics, and policy. It is a study of kinship and relationship or, more aptly, relatedness. This is *not* a book about affirmative action policy. There are countless studies that afford impressive descriptions and explanations of the ins and outs of racial preferences. Furthermore, the analytical lens here is largely trained on the African American experience and does not take in the experience of every racial and ethnic demographic in the US. The experience of Latinos, Native Americans, Asians, LGBTQ+s, immigrants, women, among others, are critical to studies of marginalization and policy behavior, particularly as they relate to immutable characteristics. The choice to focus on the Black American experience stems partly from the fact that, as the discussion will show, national affirmative action originated out of a particularized (though not exclusive) concern for African Americans and the long-term effects of enslavement. There is also an abundance of governmental and nongovernmental data and sources that allow us to readily assess changes across several decades in the Black American experience, writ large. Finally, there are the usual constraints of time and space. My hope is that this book helps to lay groundwork for further research on the substantive components of Supreme Court pronouncements and the politics of these other groups' experience. I am confident that the book will speak to their journey as well.

Brief Primer on Affirmative Action

The following brief primer on affirmative action should help readers more easily follow the probe of Court pronouncements and political developments.

There are a great many books that provide rich and detailed overviews of what it is, who it benefits, how it originated, how it is debated, and more. Here, I sketch out only the basics of the origins and definition of affirmative action.

The most important of these to note is that affirmative action policy originated as a remedial policy designed to help undo the socioeconomic, political, and cultural damage brought on by centuries of systematic racial and ethnic exclusion. It was founded on the promise of equality in the Fourteenth Amendment's equal protection clause. Harvard Law Professor Randall Kennedy elaborates how the remedial justification for affirmative action remains central to the actual practice.[106] The concept of compensatory action was first advanced during the Civil War era in connection with the Forty Acres and a Mule promise, tethered to the belief that special amends were needed to fully secure the freedom and well-being of newly freed enslaved Blacks. Later, Lyndon B. Johnson, who in 1965 issued the executive order that for decades remained the legal basis for federal affirmative action (EO 11426), set forth the underlying rationale. In a speech at Howard University on June 4, 1965, Johnson presented the "shackled runner thesis." Using the metaphor of a track race, it compares a shackled runner to an unshackled runner to stress the importance of either starting on equal footing or the need to make up for the uneven start.[107] This point is further elaborated by Melvin I. Urofsky in *The Affirmative Action Puzzle: A Living History from Reconstruction to Today*.[108] The original policy intent behind affirmative action was to incentivize employers and others to move beyond mere passive nondiscrimination to actively extend opportunities to marginalized minority groups.

The seeds of race-based national affirmative action policy as we know it were planted during the Roosevelt years, according to Terry H. Anderson's *The Pursuit of Fairness: A History of Affirmative Action*.[109] On the other hand, Urofsky's as well as Leiter and Leiter's research dates remnants of the policy back to Reconstruction.[110] So does Kennedy's *For Discrimination: Race, Affirmative Action, and the Law*, which highlights the 1866 Civil Rights Act as the race-sensitive precursor to what we now know as affirmative action.[111] The Congressional Research Service (CRS) report on the history of the largest affirmative action program in the country, the Small Business Administration's 8(a) program, pinpoints the formal starting point with President Kennedy's Executive Order 10925.[112] Additional features were incrementally built out, first by the Lyndon B. Johnson administration, which created the President's Test Cities Program (PTCP). According to the CRS report,

PTCP involved a small-scale use of the SBA's authority under Section 8(a) to award contracts to firms willing to locate in urban areas and hire unemployed individuals, largely African Americans, or sponsor minority-owned businesses by providing capital or management assistance. Under Johnson's PTCP small businesses did not have to be minority-owned to receive subcontracts under Section 8(a). It was the Richard Nixon administration that later restructured PTCP so that it was "larger and focused more specifically on minority-owned small businesses."[113]

The task of defining what "affirmative action" refers to today is quite complex. Professor Kennedy provides a list of eight different definitions used by scholars.[114] The complexity stems from the fact that in the decades to follow Kennedy, Johnson, and Nixon's efforts, the term "affirmative action" evolved to mean myriad things that are only peripherally related to reparative justice for the formerly enslaved and their descendants. It means different things to different segments of the population and to decision-makers. It varies also depending on the context, whether employment, education, housing, or voting rights.[115] All, in turn, embrace a varied mix of aims, justifications, and beneficiaries that often change with time. The survey data on the public's understanding, shown in table 1.5, make clear that average Americans' understanding runs the gamut. The 2021 Moore/YouGov survey data show that a larger share views affirmative action as "quotas," while the smaller share believes it is "increased outreach." In 1995, at the height of the controversy over California Proposition 209 and announcement of Bill Clinton's "Mend It, Don't End It" policy, respondents were as likely to identify disabled persons as beneficiaries, as Hispanic and Asian Americans.

Now lumped under the banner of "affirmative action" is a broad spectrum of policies. At one end are strict, legalistic policies, such as federal, state, and local government-imposed mandates. For the federal government alone, there are dozens of different types of preferential policies across dozens of agencies. At the other end of the spectrum are looser versions. Court-ordered hiring goals prompted by discrimination lawsuits, for instance, are denoted "affirmative action" in equal measure as voluntary efforts by employers and labor unions to raise awareness about discriminatory workplace practices. There are also "soft" versions[116] that intently weigh racial minority status as a "plus" or that simply encourage minorities to apply. "Hard" versions of federal preferential policy were not formulated until issuance of Order No. 4 by the Office of Federal Contract Compliance (OFCC) under the Nixon administration in 1971. The order required a written plan that established goals based on an underutilization analysis and

Table 1.5. Public Understanding of Affirmative Action Policies, US,
1995–2021, Select Years

Year	Survey Question	Select Responses (%)
2021	When you hear about affirmative action for Blacks and Hispanics in hiring and college admissions, do you think of it more as setting quotas or fixed numbers of positions, or increasing outreach efforts to find qualified Black and Hispanic job and college applicants?[a]	Quotas or fixed numbers: 59 Increased outreach: 41
2009	Which do you think is the best term to describe these programs—affirmative action or preferences? (Quinnipiac University, June 3, 2009)*	Affirmative action: 36 Preferences: 51
2003	When I mention affirmative action for Blacks and Hispanics in college and university admissions, do you think of it more as setting quotas or fixed numbers of positions for Blacks and Hispanics in college admissions, or increasing outreach efforts to find qualified Black and Hispanic college applicants? (*Newsweek*, January 18, 2003)	Setting quotas: 38 Increasing outreach: 44
1997	When you hear the term "affirmative action," what one word or phrase comes to mind? (*New York Times*, December 13, 1997)	Don't know/no answer: 35 Equal rights: 14 Discrimination: 11 Doesn't work: 3 General negative: 8 General positive: 6 Other: 9
1995	How well do you understand what affirmative action is: very well, fairly well, not very well, or not at all? (Kaiser Family Foundation, September 1995)	Very well: 21 Fairly well: 48 Not very well: 23 Not at all: 8
1995	Do you think African Americans, White men, women, Hispanic Americans, Asians, gay men and lesbian women, the disabled, poor people are generally covered or not under federal affirmative action laws? (Kaiser Family Foundation, September 1995)	African Americans: 78 White men: 44 Women: 69 Hispanic Americans: 69 Asians: 65 Gay men and lesbian women: 35 The disabled: 64 Poor people: 42

Year	Survey Question	Select Responses (%)
1995	When you hear the term "affirmative action," what one word or phrase comes to mind? (*New York Times*/CBS News Poll, April 4, 1995)	Don't know: 37 Generally negative: 10 General equal rights: 9 Generally positive: 7 General discrimination: 6 Blacks only: 4 Quotas: 3 Contracts, college: 2 Outdated: 2 Equal rights for Blacks only: 1 Equal rights for women: 1 Giving preference for jobs, Racism: 1 Nothing: 1 Other: 15
1995	How often do you think affirmative action programs designed to help women and minorities get better jobs or education end up using quotas: almost always, quite a lot, only occasionally, or almost never? (*Los Angeles Times*, March 22, 1995)	Almost always: 22 Quite a lot: 32 Only occasionally: 32 Almost never: 4 Don't know: 11

Sources: Except where indicated, survey data in the table were obtained from *Polling the nations*. (n.d.). Topic: Affirmative action. Last accessed 4/25/2022 from https://ptn-infobase-com.exlibris.colgate.edu/topics/VG9waWM6NTI=?aid=14265.

[a]Moore, N./YouGov. (2021, May 18–20). *Affirmative Action Omnibus*.

*The preceding question was "Now let me read you two brief statements on affirmative action programs and ask which one comes closer to your own point of view. Affirmative action programs are still needed to counteract the effects of discrimination against minorities, and are a good idea as long as there are no rigid quotas; or affirmative action programs have gone too far in favoring minorities, and should be ended because they unfairly discriminate against Whites. Do you feel strongly about that, or not?"

a timetable for reaching those goals. "Hard" versions of affirmative action may entail the use of concrete numerical goals that simply guide hiring or admissions decisions. Or, they can entail firm quotas and set-asides that are allocated strictly to racial-ethnic minorities. Meanwhile, colleges and universities employ "diversity" and "inclusive" policies that encompass a host of things, many of them nonracial. For many financial institutions it entails simply signaling to prospective customers that the institution is committed to nondiscriminatory practices.

The multiplicity of aims and contexts further problematizes the definitional challenge.[117] At best, we can summarily describe the hodgepodge of different initiatives as benign race-conscious policies. For purposes of this study, the term "affirmative action" will be used as a referent to all policies and programs that use race-conscious mechanisms for ostensibly beneficial purposes. This includes those designed as such either explicitly or implicitly, "hard" and "soft" versions, temporary or permanent programs, and those geared toward remediation or diversification. "Affirmative action" will be used interchangeably with racial preference, preferential policies, race consciousness, racial classifications, race awareness, race-specific, set-asides, and so forth.

Notwithstanding the wide and varied conceptions of just what affirmative action is, the national debate rages on all the more so in the wake of the 2023 Supreme Court ruling that ended race awareness except in select situations. Two works—Kennedy's *For Discrimination: Race, Affirmative Action, and the Law* and Leiter and Leiter's *Affirmative Action in Antidiscrimination Law and Policy*—offer the most thorough and thought-provoking account of the national debate over affirmative action.[118] Hopefully without oversimplifying, we can boil down the main arguments in the debate as centered around the present-day effects of the racial past; the policy significance of race versus that of class; conceptions of fairness, justice, and racism; and the intended beneficiaries, aims, and impact. Despite the formal end of race-based affirmative action policy as we've known it, the issues that gave rise to affirmative action and that informed use and implementation of it, support and opposition to it, and its potential all remain critical issues in racial discourse.

In the chapters to follow, we learn where the US Court and the majority of Americans stand on many of these debate topics and whether they stand on the same side, both before and after the June 2023 ruling in *Students for Fair Admissions v. Harvard*.

Chapter Two

Burying the Past

That Was Then; This Is Now

Neither US Supreme Court justices nor the general public and politicians believe that the extended history of slavery or systemic racism matters much when it comes to policymaking now. Many are convinced that the country's difficult racial past is real and it is regrettable, but that it has no policy-relevant bearing on the present. Contemporary racial inequality, they believe, is most immediately caused by income inequality or other race-neutral causes. As a result, the Court and the polity believe that universal policies are the answer, not racial ones. It is widely believed too that Blacks are not the only racial-ethnic group in America to have been severely victimized by past bigotry and exclusion. European White ethnics once were too. Yet, maltreated Irish, Italian, and Jewish immigrants managed to pull themselves up by their own bootstraps and without special help, as far as the Court and the body politic are concerned. As presumedly evidenced by the success story of disfavored European immigrants of the late 19th century, so too with Black victims of historical mistreatment: that was then; this is now.

Black History Is Passé

Court Opinion on Slavery and the Past

Students for Fair Admissions v. Harvard (2023) reiterated something long ago established in regard to the constitutional significance of societywide discrimination. Roberts stressed for the 6–3 majority that, in the wake of *Bakke*, "the Court repeatedly held that ameliorating societal discrimination does not constitute a compelling interest that justifies race-based state action." Supreme Court justices began the burial process for America's racial past in 1978 in *Bakke*. The position that they reinforced in the years to follow is that past injustices and broad societal discrimination are real, but they do not justify preferential treatment for Blacks and other racial-ethnic minorities. We observe this in two precepts articulated by the Court. First is that the racial past has no constitutional-legal value in individual affirmative action cases. Second is that, even in accepting that the past and its tangible repercussions are worrisome still today, race-conscious remediation should proceed only when there is concrete evidence of racial exclusion and on a case-by-case basis.

In the run-up to *SFFA* from *Regents of the University of California v. Bakke* (1978) through *Fisher v. Texas* (2016) the Court repeatedly declared the legal insignificance of American Black history writ large. In its first affirmative action case, *Bakke*, the goals of the set-aside admissions program were linked to past racial discrimination in the US. Its architects asserted the plan was aimed partly at "countering the effects of societal discrimination." As the swing vote in the two-part ruling, we can look to Justice Powell's opinion for the prevailing consensus. Powell elaborated the program's goal as follows, "It is said that preferences for Negro applicants may compensate for harm done them personally, or serve to place them at economic levels they might have attained but for discrimination against their forbears."

Powell ultimately sided with Respondent's Equal Protection challenge partly because of his take on anti-Black history. Citing the *Slaughter-House Cases* (1873), he acknowledged that the "initial view of the Fourteenth Amendment was that its 'one pervading purpose' was the freedom of the slave race, the security and firm establishment of that freedom, and the protection of the newly-made freeman and citizen from the oppressions of those who had formerly exercised dominion over him." He believed, however, that by 1978 the equal protection clause of the Fourteenth Amendment was no longer restricted to the plight of "the slave race."[1] Indeed, as of the early 1930s, he wrote, "it was no longer possible to peg the guarantees of the Fourteenth Amendment to the struggle for equality of one racial minority."

The Court's minimalist treatment of racial history has maintained even in cases where there are on-the-record admissions of past systemic bias.[2] *Minnick v. California Department of Corrections* (1981) involved a state prison system affirmative action plan. The department and state officials were sued by two White male correctional officers and their union for implementing a plan that required "that an Agency's percentage of minority personnel should be at least 70% of that minority in its service (inmate population)." Department officials admitted that "the impact of their past practices had resulted in a disproportionate hiring and promotion of White males." Still the US Supreme Court dismissed the writ of certiorari due to "uncertainty concerning the precise issue to be decided." Writing for an 8–1 majority, Justice John Paul Stevens dove into the weeds of the evidentiary findings of the lower courts. The state trial court had denied a motion to reopen the case in order to provide "detailed evidence of past discriminatory practices." Most significant to Stevens were "ambiguities in the record." He was concerned that the trial court declared the affirmative action plan discriminatory but "did not indicate the extent to which such discrimination had occurred." Hence, the Supreme Court should not address the constitutional issues until the state court proceedings were completed. Absent from his extended discussion of evidence gaps is any reference to the state's admissions concerning the racial impact of past practices, the trial court's dismissal of the Corrections Department motion to submit "detailed evidence of past discriminatory practices," and the broader legacy of racial exclusion.

In a 1986 lawsuit against race-based teacher layoffs the justices acknowledged the country's difficult racial past while at the same time dismissing its constitutional-legal relevance. Justice Powell's plurality opinion in *Wygant v. Jackson Board of Education* asserted, "No one doubts that there has been serious racial discrimination in this country. But as the basis for imposing discriminatory *legal* [*sic*] remedies that work against innocent people, societal discrimination is insufficient and over-expansive." Also, whereas *Sheet Metal Workers* (1986) affirmed that race consciousness can be employed to "dissipate the lingering effects of pervasive discrimination" and to eliminate "the last vestiges of an unfortunate and ignominious page" in history, it was measured. The kind of "lingering effects" to which liberal Justice William Brennan's majority opinion was referring were not systemwide, but individualized. He framed the race-aware union membership goals and procedures in the case as responsive to identified instances "where an employer or a labor union [had] engaged in persistent or egregious discrimination."

The most forceful commentary on the legal inconsequence of past exclusion came in *Richmond v. Croson* (1989), where the capitol of the Confederacy was rebuffed for enacting "legislation designed to address the effects of past discrimination." Adopted in 1983, the set-aside in *Croson* required prime city contractors in Richmond, Virginia, to subcontract at least 30 percent of the dollar amount of the contract to one or more designated minority business enterprises (MBEs). The plan defined an MBE as a business anywhere in the US that was at least 51 percent owned and controlled by minority group members, which included citizens who were Black, Spanish-speaking, Orientals, Indians, Eskimos, or Aleuts. The plan was adopted by the Richmond city council as a remedial measure to promote wider participation by MBEs in the construction of city public projects. It was informed by an analysis that revealed the residential population of Richmond was 50 percent Black, but only 0.67 percent of the city's prime construction contracts were awarded to MBEs. The plan was challenged by J. A. Croson Company manager Eugene Bon, who had submitted a bid for installation of plumbing in the city jail, reached out to several MBEs to no avail, was twice denied a waiver of the MBE requirement, then later notified that his bid was rejected and that the city rebid the project. The Croson Company argued that the city's affirmative action plan was unconstitutional on its face and as applied in his case.

Justice Sandra Day O'Connor's opinion for the Court in *Croson* picked up in 1989 where *Bakke* left off in 1978 regarding racial history. She too stressed that "the history of discrimination in society at large" could not justify the city's set-aside, just as societal discrimination could not ground the medical school set-aside in *Bakke*. O'Connor underlined that "there was no direct evidence of race discrimination on the part of the city in letting contracts or any evidence that the city's prime contractors had discriminated against minority-owned subcontractors." Also, "the history of school deseg-regation in Richmond and numerous congressional reports, [did] little to define the scope of any injury to minority contractors in Richmond." Among the other analyses rejected in *Croson* as grounds for Richmond's set-aside were: proponents' representations about past discrimination in Richmond's construction industry, underrepresentation of MBEs in city contracting, and the small number of minorities in contractors' associations. For the 6–3 majority in *Croson*, "none of these 'findings,' singly or together, provide the city of Richmond with a 'strong basis in evidence for its conclusion that remedial action was necessary.'"

It bears highlighting that these statements about the limited value of racial history were intertwined with acknowledgments of the long-term effects of past race discrimination. Justice O'Connor wrote, "While there is no doubt that the sorry history of both private and public discrimination in this country has contributed to a lack of opportunities for Black entre-preneurs, this observation, standing alone, cannot justify a rigid racial quota in the awarding of public contracts in Richmond, Virginia." She pushed back against the suggestion in Justice Marshall's dissent that the Court was blind to continued racial bias. Citing *Wygant* (1986) she replied that the justices did not "view racial discrimination as largely a phenomenon of the past" or that "government bodies need no longer preoccupy themselves with rectifying racial injustice."

Companion rulings in 2007 further solidified the Supreme Court's burial of racial history. *Parents Involved v. Seattle School District* and *Meredith v. Jefferson County* involved two school districts that employed race-based school assignment plans. In *Parents Involved* the objective was to mitigate the consequences of de facto residential segregation and, in *Meredith*, to eliminate the "vestiges of its prior policy of segregation." Both the Jefferson County and Seattle School District plans were struck down by the Court. A majority of justices was unmoved by the fact that a federal district court had earlier imposed a court-ordered desegregation decree from 1975–2000, based on a finding that the Jefferson County Public School system in Louisville, Kentucky, maintained a segregated school system. Writing for a 5–4 panel Chief Justice Roberts countered that "once Jefferson County achieved unitary status, it had remedied the constitutional wrong that allowed race-based assignments" and that "any continued use of race must be justified on some other basis" than past racial segregation. Roberts further asserted that not only was the past wrong remedied, but that the once-legally segregated Jefferson County School District had actually come to rest "on the same footing as any other school district." Meaning, the county's past segregation was no longer implicated in the ongoing racial segregation.

The same diminishment of past discrimination in cases involving state and local government action in *Parents Involved, Croson, Wygant, Sheet Metal, Minnick,* and *Bakke* was eventually applied in a case concerning congressional power. Initially Congress was given greater latitude. *Bakke*'s principal opinion remarked in 1978, "We have previously recognized the special competence of Congress to make findings with respect to the effects of identified past discrimination and its discretionary authority to take appropriate remedial measures." The same is true of *United Steelworkers of America v. Weber* (1979). There, the United Steelworkers of America (USWA) and Kaiser Aluminum & Chemical Corporation entered into a voluntary collective bargaining agreement for 15 plants in order to increase work opportunities for Blacks. In the Gramercy, Louisiana, plant only 1.83 percent of the skilled craft workers were Black, whereas the local work force was 39 percent Black. To help to meet the race-based hiring goals that were set, an on-the-job training program reserved 50 percent of its openings for Black employees until the percentage of Black workers reflected the percentage of Blacks in the local labor force. Seven Black and six White craft trainees from the plant's production workforce were admitted to the training program.

One of the rejected White production workers, Brian Weber, filed a class action lawsuit in federal court alleging discrimination against White employees because the most senior Black trainee had less seniority than some of the rejected White production workers. The training program was invalidated by the district court and the Fifth Circuit Court of Appeals as a violation of Title VII of the Civil Rights Act of 1964, but later upheld by the Supreme Court, which assumed a deferential posture toward congressional intent. Justice William Brennan concluded for the five-person majority[3] in *Weber* that Title VII of the Civil Rights Act of 1964 did not prohibit employers and unions from taking race-conscious remedial steps. Instead the language in the act was intended to "eliminate, so far as possible, the last vestiges of an unfortunate and ignominious page in this country's history." The purposes of the Kaiser-USWA plan mirrored the statute's aims.

An even broader reading of Congress's power to remediate past discrimination can be found in *Fullilove v. Klutznick* (1980), a 6–3 decision upheld the minority business enterprise (MBE) provision of the federal Public Works Employment Act of 1977. The lead opinion by Chief Justice Burger and joined by Justices White and Powell articulated a broad interpretation of Congress's Spending Power under Article I of the Constitution. Burger expressed that Congress was constitutionally empowered to tackle macro-level discrimination. He explained the "legislative objectives of the MBE provision must be considered against the background of ongoing efforts directed toward deliverance of the century-old promise of equality of economic opportunity." The House Committee report on the Small Business Association (SBA) concluded "that, over the years, there has developed a business system which has traditionally excluded measurable minority participation. In the past more than the present, this system of conducting business transactions overly precluded minority input." Burger deferred to congressional findings that MBEs' "competitive position is impaired by the effects of disadvantage and discrimination."

The deferential posture in *Fullilove* and *Weber* was abandoned in *Adarand* (1995). With four other justices, Justice O'Connor insisted that Congress cannot act on broad assertions of racial exclusion but must make individualized findings, like every other entity. She highlighted the Court's failure in the internment of Japanese Americans during World War II, saying that it led to "most unfortunate results" and that "a grave injustice was done to both citizens and permanent resident aliens of Japanese ancestry." The takeaway for O'Connor and her colleagues from that chapter in American history was that "all racial classifications, imposed by whatever federal, state, or local governmental actor, must be analyzed by a reviewing court under strict scrutiny." O'Connor essentially used a review of racial history to discount its constitutional-legal significance.

POLITICS OF SLAVERY AND PAST DISCRIMINATION

In concert with the Supreme Court, the general public too acknowledges that the past is not entirely in the past and that it is important to recognize that the impacts of slavery continue to reverberate. But also like the Court, there is little public support for the idea that race-conscious remediation is justified by things that happened long ago. The public opinion data in table 2.1 show support for the idea that the past matters. A 2019 Associated Press/ NORC survey reveals that fully 60 percent believe the history of slavery affects Blacks still today. Further, a nationally representative poll designed and fielded for this study asked respondents whether the "country is better off if we all try to forget about the history of racial discrimination against Blacks in the U.S." This YouGov/Moore 2016 survey reveals that almost half (49%) believe that we should be mindful of the past. Most share the sense also that *something* should be done about the effects of slavery. The same YouGov/Moore survey asked whether policymakers should "at least try to eliminate any long-term negative impact that slavery may have upon the economic and educational progress of Blacks in the U.S." A 56 percent majority either strongly or somewhat agreed.

Nonetheless, as with the justices of the Supreme Court Americans do not believe that race-aware policies are the solution to the long-term effects of slavery and past discrimination. Most don't believe that even an apology is in order, let alone reparations. The multi-sourced data in table 2.2 are drawn from questions that specifically mention "past discrimination" or allude in some way to its broad effects. The 2019 Harris Poll that asked whether "America today should be a society in which minorities receive special treatment to make up for racism and past discrimination or should people of all races receive equal treatment" shows that over 80 percent opted for the latter. Notwithstanding the 2009 NBC News/*Wall Street Journal* survey and the 2007 NPR/Pew surveys that show a large majority supportive of remediating the past, up against the lengthier list that portrays a deeper divide, there is a clear takeaway from table 2.2. There is no public consensus

Table 2.1. Public Opinion on Slavery and Its Effects, US, 2016 and 2019

Year	Survey Question	Select Responses (%)
2019	How much do you think the history of slavery in this country affects Black people in American society today?[a]	A great deal/quite a lot: 60 Not much/not at all: 39
2019	Do you think the US federal government should or should not officially apologize for the history of slavery in this country?[a]	Should apologize: 46 Should not apologize: 52
2019	Do you think the US federal government should or should not pay reparations for slavery and racial discrimination in this country by making cash payments to the descendants of enslaved people?[a]	Should pay reparations: 29 Should not pay reparations: 68
2019	How much, if at all, do you think the legacy of slavery affects the position of Black people in American society today?[b]	A great deal/fair amount: 63 Not much/not at all: 35
2016	Please indicate how strongly you agree or disagree with the following statement: This country is better off if we all try to forget about the history of racial discrimination against Blacks in the US.[c]	Strongly/somewhat agree: 36 Neither agree nor disagree: 15 Strongly/somewhat disagree: 49
2016	Please indicate how strongly you agree or disagree with the following statement: Policymakers should at least try to eliminate any long-term negative impact that slavery may have upon the economic and educational progress of Blacks in the US.[c]	Strongly/somewhat agree: 56 Neither agree nor disagree: 23 Strongly/somewhat disagree: 421

Sources:

[a]Associated Press/NORC. (2019, September 20–23). *The legacy of slavery.* Last accessed 4/25/2022 from https://apnorc.org/projects/the-legacy-of-slavery/.

[b]Pew Research Center. (2019, January 22–February 5). *American Trends Panel Wave 43.* Final topline. file:///C:/Users/nmoore/Downloads/W43-topline_final_diversity_report%20(1).pdf.

[c]Moore, N./YouGov. (2016, September 3–6). *Racial Profiling Omnibus.*

Table 2.2. Causality and Present Effects of Past Discrimination, US, 1995–2019, Select Years

Year	Survey Question	Select Responses (%)
2019	Do you think America today should be a society in which minorities receive special treatment to make up for racism and past discrimination or should people of all races receive equal treatment? (Harris Poll, August 2019)	Minorities receive special treatment: 19 All races receive equal treatment: 81
2013	Which comes closer to your own point of view: Affirmative action programs are still needed to counteract the effects of discrimination against minorities, and are a good idea as long as there are no rigid quotas; or affirmative action programs have gone too far in favoring minorities, and should be ended because they unfairly discriminate against Whites? (NBC News/*Wall Street Journal*, June 10, 2013)	Still needed: 45 Should be ended: 45
2009	Which comes closer to your own point of view: Affirmative action programs are still needed to counteract the effects of discrimination against minorities, and are a good idea as long as there are no rigid quotas; or affirmative action programs have gone too far in favoring minorities, and should be ended because they unfairly discriminate against Whites? (NBC News/*Wall Street Journal*, June 17, 2009)	Still needed, feel strongly/do not feel strongly: 63 Should be ended, feel strongly/do not feel strongly: 28
2009	Which comes closer to your view regarding affirmative action programs in the workplace: We should have affirmative action programs to overcome past discrimination; We should have affirmative action programs to increase diversity; We should not have affirmative action programs? (Quinnipiac University, June 3, 2009)	To overcome past discrimination: 20 To increase diversity: 27 Should not have: 47

continued on next page

Table 2.2. Continued.

Year	Survey Question	Select Responses (%)
2008	In your view, should government programs that are designed to address economic inequality give special consideration to Blacks because of past racial discrimination, or should these programs only take into account a person's economic situation?[a]	Give special consideration: 9 Only consider economic situation: 87
2007	In order to overcome past discrimination, do you favor or oppose affirmative action programs, which give special *preferences* to qualified Blacks in hiring and education? (NPR/Pew Research Center, November 13, 2007)	Favor: 46 Oppose: 40
2007	In order to overcome past discrimination, do you favor or oppose affirmative action programs designed *to help* Blacks get better jobs and education? (NPR/Pew Research Center, November 13, 2007)	Favor: 60 Oppose: 30
2003	Do you think affirmative action programs are needed today to help minorities such as Blacks and Hispanics overcome discrimination, or are they not needed today? (Associated Press, March 12, 2003)	Needed: 51 Not needed: 43
2000	Which comes closer to your own view: Affirmative action programs are still needed to counteract the effects of discrimination against minorities, as long as there are no rigid quotas; affirmative action programs have gone too far in favoring minorities, and should be phased out because they unfairly discriminate against non-minority groups? (Kaiser Family Foundation/MTV, September 2000)	Still needed: 50 Should be phased out: 44 Neither/both: 3

Year	Survey Question	Select Responses (%)
2000	Which comes closer to your own point of view: Affirmative action programs are still needed to counteract the effects of discrimination against minorities, and are a good idea as long as there are no rigid quotas; Affirmative action programs have gone too far in favoring minorities, and should be phased out because they unfairly discriminate against Whites? (Wall Street Journal/NBC News Poll, March 2000)	Still needed: 54 Should be phased out: 37
1995	Affirmative action is deserved compensation for past injustice. (KAET-TV, September 20, 1995)	
1995	Which of these three statements comes closer to your view? "We need to continue affirmative action because discrimination is still common," or "Discrimination is still common, but affirmative action has simply gone on too long," or "Affirmative action is no longer needed because discrimination has been largely eliminated." (*Los Angeles Times*, March 22, 1995)	Continue: 46 Has gone on too long: 35 No longer needed: 13

Sources: Except where indicated, survey data in the table were obtained from *Polling the nations.* (n.d.). Topic: Affirmative action. Last accessed 4/25/2022 from https://ptn-infobase-com.exlibris.colgate.edu/topics/VG9waWM6NTI=?aid=14265.

[a]Gallup, Inc. (n.d.). *Race relations.* Last accessed 4/25/2022 from https://news.gallup.com/poll/1687/race-relations.aspx.

behind the idea that societal discrimination, notably past discrimination, demands race-conscious policy attention, preferential treatment, or set-asides.

Equally correspondent to affirmative action rulings is bipartisan recognition of the troubling history of discrimination in the US and its lasting impacts. And like the justices both major parties reject the notion that "racial discrimination is largely a phenomenon of the past." The sense of both national parties is that something should be done about it. However and importantly, there is no cross-party agreement on what to do about it. National parties' acknowledgment of widespread racism and the need to redress it actually precedes the Court's. The 1940s Democratic Party platforms folded a long list of promises into the party's first-ever acknowledgment of pervasive discrimination, including a pledge to adopt "legislative safeguards against discrimination in government service and benefits" and to eliminate "unfair and illegal discrimination based on race, creed or color."[4] Around the same time Republicans demanded that "discrimination in the civil service, the army, navy, and all other branches of the Government" be eradicated; advocated effective universal suffrage "for the Negro citizen"; and called for legislation to combat "discrimination against Negroes who are in our armed forces."[5] In the 1950s Republican calls for other anti-discrimination measures amped up and took the form of advocacy for the abolition of poll taxes, anti-lynching legislation, anti-discrimination clauses in federal employment and federal contracts, and more.

Both parties maintain, as the Court does, that the country continues to struggle with race discrimination. Democrats are more explicit about the myriad ways that societal bias is operationalized, asserting during the 1960s that "racial discrimination was present in every section of the country."[6] In the 1980s they again stressed that "the age-old scourge of discrimination and prejudice against many groups in American society is still rampant." As of the 2000s liberals' messaging is louder in decrying the pervasiveness of racial bias. During the 2020 election cycle they declared that "the intolerable racial injustice that still stains the fabric of our nation" works "profound and lasting inequities" in a host of areas.[7] Over the years liberals homed in on racial problems in housing and redlining, education and segregation, employment and wage disparity, policing and profiling, criminal justice and the school-to-prison pipeline, church burning, insurance rates, discriminatory lending practices and home appraisals, voting, and more. Republicans frame the race problem as a national problem too, but in a more circumscribed fashion. In the heat of the 1960s civil rights movement conservatives admitted that "discrimination is not a problem localized in one area of the country, but rather a problem that must be faced by North and South alike."[8] They put meat on the bones later in the 1980s and 1990s when highlighting, for instance, the disproportionately harmful outcomes of the foster care system on Blacks, the spate of Black church burnings, racial disparities in health, and so on.[9]

On top of alignment with the Supreme Court around the belief that systemic racial bias persists, partisans also embrace *Sheet Metal*'s bottom-line conclusion about the need to eliminate "the last vestiges of an unfortunate and ignominious page" in history. Democrats' sense in 1960 was that "victims of past discrimination must be encouraged and assisted."[10] Decades later they pressed the federal government and private employers to make special efforts to "aid minority Americans in overcoming both the historic patterns and the historic burdens of discrimination."[11] On the other side of the aisle is a decades-long track record of Republicans calling attention to the need to "provide alternative means of assisting the victims of past discrimination to realize their full worth as American citizens,"[12] based on the belief that, as late as 1980, "this nation has not yet eliminated all vestiges of racism over the years."[13] In elections to follow, Republican platform attention to slavery would be connected chiefly to the party's abolition history.[14]

As in Supreme Court rulings, also in national party politics there is no clear policy plan from either party on the pivotal question of what to do today about the effects of slavery. Democrats' answer is to study it. In 2000 they advocated creation of a commission "to examine the history of slavery, discrimination, and exclusion suffered by all minorities to report on the continuing effects of those tragic chapters in our history; and to make appropriate recommendations on behalf of the American people."[15] Again in 2020 they asserted "there can be no realization of the American dream without grappling with the lasting effects of slavery, and facing up to the centuries-long campaign of violence, fear, and trauma wrought upon Black Americans,"[16] and they proposed a commission to study reparations and the effects of slavery and Jim Crow segregation.

It is important to interject here that racial preferences are not Democrats' fix for the effects of slavery and societal racism insofar. Instead, they envisage a wide spectrum of marginalized groups as beneficiaries of affirmative action, not just Black descendants of the enslaved or victims of systemic racism.[17] Meanwhile, 1976 was the only year the Republican Party platform made a case for tackling historical bias straight on. It contended, "Wiping out past discrimination requires continued emphasis on providing educational opportunities for minority citizens, increasing direct and guaranteed loans to minority business enterprises, and affording qualified minority persons equal opportunities for government positions at all levels."[18] That is the sum and substance of Republicans' policy proposals over the years for dealing with slavery and societal discrimination.

There is even greater harmony with the Supreme Court on the presidency front of affirmative action politics, both in regard to the persistence of systemic racism and the question of what to do about it. It bears underlining that presidents also staked out their position on these issues before *Bakke* (1978) and *Brown* (1954). Anderson carefully unpacks the pivotal role of civil rights leader A. Philip Randolph in pressuring President Franklin D. Roosevelt to do more.[19] Roosevelt's 1941 Executive Order 8802 asserted there was "evidence that available and needed workers have been barred from employment in industries engaged in defense production solely because of consideration of race, creed, color, or national origin."[20] EO 8802 was followed by Executive Order 9346 (1943), which purposed to "eliminate discriminatory practices" and stipulated that, in addition to federal government contracting, "there shall be no discrimination in the employment of any person in war industries or in Government by reason of race, creed, color, or national origin."[21]

More orders in this vein were signed by Presidents Truman and Dwight D. Eisenhower, namely Executive Orders 10308 in 1951, 10479 in 1953, and 10557 in 1954. Then, in 1955 Executive Order 10590 extended the nondiscrimination requirement to federal employment and established a committee to "advise the President periodically as to whether the civilian employment practices in the Federal Government are in conformity with the non-discriminatory employment policy."[22] Then–Vice President Richard M. Nixon and chair of the President's Committee on Government Contracts decried the fact that the "U.S. Employment Service, which provided funds for state-operated employment bureaus, encouraged skilled Blacks to register for unskilled jobs, accepted requests from White employers and made no efforts to get employers to accept African American workers."[23] As vice president, Nixon believed "that such indifference was more prevalent than overt discrimination, and called for remedial steps."[24]

From the 1940s through 2020, the only president to break from this shared institutional perspective on persistent and widespread racism is President Donald J. Trump. A September 15, 2017, Proclamation 9642 that recognized HBCU week as a reminder of "the historic and ongoing struggle for equal access that led to the establishment of HBCUs in our Nation" is one of few instances in which his administration directly addressed slavery and systemic racism. Later, the administration's tune changed. During a September 15, 2020, televised town hall meeting moderated by ABC News analyst George Stephanopoulos, when pressed to say whether he believed there were systemic racial problems in the US, Trump repeatedly deflected. Asked about statistics that suggest that criminal justice racial disparities are "a real systemic problem," whether he believed it, and whether he would address it, Trump pivoted to polls that purportedly showed Blacks want more policing.[25] Much of Trump administration officials' talk about systemic racism was in connection with violent crime, abortion, and HIV-AIDs.[26] As an example, HUD Secretary Ben Carson asserted, "What is racist is the fact that African Americans have the highest abortion rate."[27]

Instead of agreeing with his predecessors' sense of pervasive bias Trump devoted considerable energy to denouncing critical race theory (CRT). He derided CRT as one of several "one-sided and divisive accounts" of "America's history related to race." His October 30, 2020, Proclamation 10110 complained that "adherents to Critical Race Theory and other associated ideologies believe that America is an inherently racist and sexist country, defined by oppression and hierarchies of victimhood, rather than freedom and equality." Race-centered theories were the focal point of Trump's November 2, 2020, Executive Order 13958 too.[28] The order established the President's Advisory 1776 Commission to push back against the view of "America as an irredeemably and systematically racist country." A previously issued September 22, 2020, Executive Order 13950 bashed teachings about systemic racism and sexism as "pernicious." Trump made clear during the September 29, 2020, presidential debate in Cleveland that he eliminated racial sensitivity training in federal agencies in order to prevent teaching that America is a racist country.

It was Trump's Republican predecessors that were more closely hewed to the Court's recognition of continued pervasive racism. President Ronald Reagan echoed those aspects of affirmative action judgments that conceded pervasive bigotry. He matter-of-factly proclaimed in a radio address on civil rights, "Discrimination is still not yet a thing of the past."[29] On another occasion Reagan disputed the notion of racial utopia, saying of the country's history of slavery and bigotry against Jews, "The way has never been easy, and even our best efforts have left us far short of utopia."[30] Admitting that "we've had our share of bigotry" and that "we've outgrown a lot of that nonsense," Reagan declared, "It's time we erased the last vestiges of intolerance, bigotry, and unkindness from our hearts. Decency demands this and so does our history."[31] He did the same on numerous occasions up until a 1987 address on the Dr. Martin Luther King Jr. holiday where he stated, "Today the job that Martin Luther King, Jr., started is ours to finish."[32]

Also for the George H. W. Bush administration we observe symmetry between SCOTUS and POTUS on the issue of pervasive race discrimination. The effects of structural racial bias were stipulated, explained, and studied at length by the US Commission on Minority Business Development. It documented in 1992 how "stereotypical images of minority owned firms limit their access to the factors of production" and that "our nation's history has created a 'cycle of negativity' that reinforces prejudice through its very practice; restraints on capital availability lead to failures, in turn, reinforce a prejudicial perception of minority firms as inherently high-risks, thereby reducing access to even more capital and further increasing the risk of failure."[33] Bush himself remarked at a meeting of the National Urban League, "Discrimination—of course it still exists. Race hate, born of ignorance and inhumanity, still exists. The day of the poll tax is over. The day of Jim Crow is gone. Today bigotry and bias may take more subtle forms; but they persist, and as long as they do, my work is not over; your work is not over; our work is not over."[34]

As to the question of what to do about the legacy of slavery and discrimination and particularly the value of race-aware policies, we again observe the Court and presidents in sync with one another. But, two presidents stand out as outliers on this issue. President Lyndon B. Johnson drew a straight line from racial history to public policy. In a speech at Howard University on June 4, 1965, he unveiled his "shackled runner thesis." Under it, "you do not take a person who, for years, has been hobbled by chains and liberate him, bring him up to the starting line of a race and then say, 'you are free to compete with all the others,' and still justly believe that you have been completely fair."[35] Years later President Bill Clinton likewise expressed that affirmative action is an appropriate policy response to systemic racism. In his July 19, 1995, affirmative action speech Clinton explained that the "purpose of affirmative action is to give our Nation a way to finally address the systemic exclusion of individuals of talent on the basis of their gender or race, from opportunities to develop, perform, achieve, and contribute."[36]

However, at the same time that he framed affirmative action as a way to confront the disadvantages faced by minorities, in the end Clinton declined to offer a mere apology for slavery, after a call to do so from Ohio Democrat Representative Tony Hall in 1997. Hall's reasoning was that an apology would not fix "the lingering injustice resulting from slavery but reconciliation begins with an apology."[37] Instead, on a 12-day visit to Africa in March of 1998 Clinton simply expressed regret for America's role in the slave trade.

President Barack Obama voiced the same sentiments of *Bakke* (1978) and *Parents Involved* (2007) concerning the infeasibility of crafting public policy based on racial history. Where *Bakke* made much of the practical difficulty of identifying long ago victims of discrimination, President Obama similarly deemed race-specific programs such as reparations politically "impractical" and "unachievable." He characterized their advocacy as stemming from "the desire, the legitimate desire, for that history to be recognized." By comparison, expansion of universal programs "doesn't speak to the hurt, and the sense of injustice, and the self-doubt that arises out of the fact that we're behind now, and it makes us sometimes feel as if there must be something wrong with us."[38] Responding to questions about slavery reparations from author Ta-Nehisi Coates, Obama drilled down on the political challenge. He said:

> Theoretically, you can make, obviously, a powerful argument that centuries of slavery, Jim Crow, discrimination are the primary cause for all those gaps. That those were wrongs done to the Black community as a whole, and Black families specifically, and that in order to close that gap, a society has a moral obligation to make a large, aggressive investment, even if it's not in the form of individual reparations checks, but in the form of a Marshall Plan, in order to close those gaps. It is easy to make that theoretical argument. But as a practical matter, it is hard to think of any society in human history in which a majority population has said that as a consequence of historic wrongs, we are now going to take a big chunk of the nation's resources over a long period of time to make that right.[39]

President Joseph R. Biden's positioning around slavery and public policy was also not remarkably distinctive from the Supreme Court's. Biden bemoaned the damage wrought by slavery, but only went so far as to support H.R. 40,[40] a congressional bill proposal to establish a commission whose charge was "to study and consider a national apology and proposal for reparations for the institution of slavery, its subsequent de jure and de facto racial and economic discrimination against African Americans, and the impact of these forces on living African Americans," among other things.[41]

We see alignment with Supreme Court views on the racial past in other social, cultural, and political discourses. The present-day relevance of Black history is frequently contested in high-profile legislative and academic debates over reparations, the Confederate flag, and the role of race in American history. Federal legislation to create a commission to study reparations for Black Americans was first introduced by House Democrat John Conyers Jr. in 1989, but stalled for three decades. According to *The Washington Post* Conyers introduced the bill 20 times from 1989 to 2017, after which Representative Sheila Jackson Lee took on the cause.[42] H.R. 40

was finally reported out of committee in 2021. The bill, named after the Civil War–era Forty Acres and a Mule concept, launches from the premise that "slavery is America's original sin, and this country has yet to atone for the atrocities visited upon generations of enslaved Africans and their descendants," as Jackson Lee wrote.[43]

How to "atone" for America's original sin is much disputed in intellectual debates. In reply to a 2014 pro-reparations article by Ta-Nehisi Coates in *The Atlantic*, Hoover Institution's Peter and Kirsten Bedford Senior Fellow Richard A. Epstein authored a rebuttal titled "The Case Against Reparations for Slavery."[44] In it Epstein asserts, "One does not have to believe in reparations to recall with horror the sins of the past," after which he pivots to argue the impossibility of identifying the victims of slavery or of pinpointing its generational effects upon Blacks as well as Whites.[45] In a separate piece staff writer at *The Atlantic* David Frum conjectured, "Within the target population, will all receive the same? Same per person, or same per family? Or will there be adjustment for need? How will need be measured? Will convicted criminals be eligible? If not, the program will exclude perhaps one million African Americans. If yes, the program would potentially tax victims of rape and families of the murdered for the benefit of their assailants."[46]

Key elements of the history of slavery are themselves a subject of debate. Disputes over the Confederate flag reignited after the Charleston Church Massacre in South Carolina when a White supremacist and Confederate flag admirer killed nine Black churchgoers on June 17, 2015. Calls to remove the flag from the grounds of the state capitol followed.[47] South Carolina state lawmakers countered with arguments that pertained as much to slavery and the Civil War as to the Confederate flag. State House Representative Eric M. Bedingfield declared, "This particular war was fought over many different things. When it comes to fighting an oppressive federal government, I still do it in this chamber today."[48] Representative Michael A. Pitts offered a string of amendments and speeches during the legislative debate, during which he asserted, "The misrepresentation and the abduction—not the co-opting, the abduction—by despicable hate groups that took that flag as a symbol, was not what I grew up with."[49] Significantly, removal of Confederate flags and other Confederate symbols narrowly musters a national majority, with 51 percent of Americans supporting the removal of statues and only 10 percent believing they should be completely destroyed, according to an NBC News/*Wall Street Journal* poll.[50] To date, 100 Confederate monuments were removed in 2020, but 700 remain, plus another 2,100 public Confederate symbols.[51]

Sharp disagreements over the breadth and depth of America's past racism headlined political news in 2020. The coverage featured two initiatives that offered competing narratives about the extent to which the history of Black slavery and exclusion are interwoven in American history. *The New York Times Magazine*'s 1619 Project, led by Pulitzer Prize winner and author Nikole Hannah-Jones reframed American history by placing slavery and its continuing legacy at the center of the nation's story, starting with the 1619 arrival of the first enslaved Blacks in Jamestown. Hannah-Jones points out that "as the reach of the 1619 Project grew, so did the backlash."[52] Meanwhile, the 1776 Commission established by Executive Order 13958 condemned the 1619 Project in the following:

> The recent attacks on our founding have highlighted America's history related to race. These one-sided and divisive accounts too often ignore or fail to properly honor and recollect the great legacy of the American national experience—our country's valiant and successful effort to shake off the curse of slavery and to use the lessons of that struggle to guide our work toward equal rights for all citizens in the present. Viewing America as an irredeemably and systemically racist country cannot account for the extraordinary role of the great heroes of the American movement against slavery and for civil rights.[53]

SECTION SUMMARY

To sum up, the Supreme Court's burial of America's racial past resembles a similar dynamic in national racial politics and on every major political front. Most Americans believe that slavery impacts Black lives still today and that we should not forget the stain of slavery. Yet, they also reject the sense that race-specific policies are the best way to amend the effects of slavery. When asked whether minorities should receive "special treatment to make up for racism and past discrimination," Americans overwhelmingly prefer the alternative, that "all races receive equal treatment." Since the 1940s Democrats and Republicans too have acknowledged the need to somehow confront the legacy of slavery and past racial exclusion. However, Democrats' policy answer is to study slavery, while Republicans are ever-more detached from the policy relevance of slavery. Echoes of the justices' logic regarding slavery and systemic racism are also in presidential politics. With the exception of Donald J. Trump, every president from Roosevelt to Biden concedes the harms wrought by slavery and that "discrimination is still not yet a thing of the past," in the words of Ronald Reagan. Whereas Lyndon B. Johnson advanced the "shackled runner" thesis in an unqualified fashion, others, including Barack Obama cautiously pointed to the practical challenges of moving the "majority population" to channel resources toward "historic wrongs." Across America's frontlines we see deep divisions over the impacts of slavery—whether around slave reparations, removal of Confederate flags and symbols, or simply the 1619 Project versus 1776 Commission narratives about the historical reach of slavery. All in all, the Court has not acted alone in burying racial history.

What's Slavery Got to Do with It?

Pushback against the central claim of critical race theory (CRT) is embedded within Supreme Court reasoning about the history of slavery and discrimination in the US. Affirmative action jurisprudence deems it a "speculative leap" and "unprecedented" to assume that racial disparities are principally the result of discrimination. Alternatively, the view advanced over the years by conventional civil rights discourse as well as CRT is that the generational effects of slavery, pervasive racial violence, state-sanctioned exclusion, Black generational disadvantage, White privilege, and the like are the main engines that perpetuate the racial status quo.[54] Political scientist Ronald J. Fiscus offers that "accepting the nonracist premise of true equality at birth requires the conclusion that racism directly or indirectly accounts for all behavioral and attitudinal differences between Whites and Blacks as groups, including all that are relevant to the attainment of the society's generally recognized goods."[55] However, the justices insist that persistent racial disparities are not traceable to the history of racial exclusion and state-sanctioned discrimination. Not only a majority of justices but the lay public, national political parties, and a long line of presidents are also convinced that something other than slavery and past discrimination lies at the root of today's racial inequality.

COURT OPINION ON CAUSES OF RACIAL INEQUALITY

Hailed the "touchstone of constitutional analysis for race-conscious admissions policies," *Regents v. Bakke*'s rejoinder to critical race theory and other structural explanations is that the causal connection between the legacy of slavery and present-day disparities is extremely attenuated.[56] Writing for the

5–4 majority that invalidated the University of California at Davis Medical School set-aside program in *Bakke*, Justice Powell picked apart the dissents' claims about history. For Powell and his counterparts—Justices Stevens, Stewart, Rehnquist, and Chief Justice Burger—assertions about the cause of disparities in medical schools and the medical field were not evidently due to discrimination. He took exception to Justices Brennan, White, Marshall, and Blackmun's conclusion that "there is reason to believe" that the disparate impact sought to be rectified by the program was the "product" of some form of discrimination against the preferred minority groups by "society at large." Powell wrote in *Bakke* that it was a "speculative leap" to claim "that the failure of minorities to qualify for admission at Davis under regular procedures was due principally to the effects of past discrimination." "Not one word in the record supports this conclusion, and the authors of the opinion offer no standard for courts to use in applying such a presumption of causation." Powell also instanced a *New England Journal of Medicine* study that concluded the cause of Black underrepresentation in the medical profession was "traceable to the poor premedical experiences of Black undergraduates, and can be remedied effectively only by developing remedial programs for Black students before they enter."

An occasion on which the Court upheld racial preference based on alleged links between macro discrimination and disparate outcomes was out of deference to Congress, which deference proved to be short-lived. For the plurality in *Fullilove v. Klutznick* (1980) Chief Justice Burger wrote that Congress "had before it, among other data, evidence of a long history of marked disparity in the percentage of public contracts awarded to minority business enterprises." Further, "this disparity was considered to result not from any lack of capable and qualified minority businesses, but from the existence of maintenance of barriers to competitive access which had their roots in racial and ethnic discrimination, and which continue today, even absent intentional discrimination or other unlawful conduct." *Fullilove* and its deferential stance were overturned in *Adarand* (1995).

Otherwise, the same line of reasoning in *Bakke* was decisive in later cases, such as *Wygant* (1986). It rejected a lower court ruling that endorsed the school board's claim that "statistical disparities were the result of general societal discrimination, not of prior discrimination by the Board." In *Wygant* Powell again contended, "There are numerous explanations for a disparity between the percentage of minority students and the percentage of minority faculty, many of them completely unrelated to discrimination of any kind." *Richmond v. Croson* (1989) followed suit, concluding that a 30 percent racial set-aside designed to "ameliorate the effects of past discrimination" was based on "statistical generalizations" and "sheer speculation." O'Connor elaborated that the policy speculated about "how many minority firms there would be in Richmond absent past societal discrimination, just as it was sheer speculation how many minority medical students would have been admitted to the medical school at Davis absent past discrimination in educational opportunities." Regarding the evidence of past discrimination proffered by the city, O'Connor countered with a list of nonracial factors that she said "would seem to face a member of any racial group attempting to establish a new business enterprise, such as deficiencies in working capital, inability to meet bonding requirements, unfamiliarity with bidding procedures, and disability caused by an inadequate track record." *Croson* concluded that, to accept the claim "that past societal discrimination alone can serve as the basis for rigid racial preferences would be to open the door to competing claims for 'remedial relief' for every disadvantaged group."

The Politics of Causality

Justice Powell's contention in *Wygant* (1986) that "there are numerous explanations" for racial imbalance is a belief that corresponds with the prevailing consensus in American politics. A majority of citizens and politicians do not believe that existing racial inequality can be blamed on the legacy of slavery and bias. Many in this camp don't dispute that past bigotry played a role in the creation of Black disadvantage. Rather, they believe that the explanatory power of class surpassed that of race decades ago.

That everyday citizens believe something other than slavery and past discrimination lies at the root of today's racial inequality is borne out by survey data. While we learned earlier that many believe that Blacks are still affected by the past, most also believe that living near the bottom of the class strata is more consequential than being Black. Figure 2.1 reveals that fewer and fewer people believe that societal discrimination is why Blacks experience lower levels of prosperity than their White (and Chinese) counterparts, and that this belief stretches over decades. The number that rejects discrimination as determinative actually grew during the 1990s and 2000s, reaching as high as 65 percent in 2014. There was a time when the country believed that racial differences were due to "lack of will," 65 percent as of 1977, then declining to 37 percent by 2018. Half of Americans are convinced that inequality stems specifically from differences in education that themselves stem from poverty. In 2018, 50 percent of respondents pointed to education-related causes, as in 1977 when 51 percent believed the same.

Figure 2.1. Public Opinion on Causes of Racial Inequality. *Source*: Davern, M., Bautista, R., Freese, J., Morgan, S. L., & Smith, T. W. (n.d.). *General social surveys, 1972–2021*. NORC, 2021: NORC at the University of Chicago [producer and distributor]. Last accessed 2/16/2021 from the GSS Data Explorer website at gssdataexplorer.norc.org.

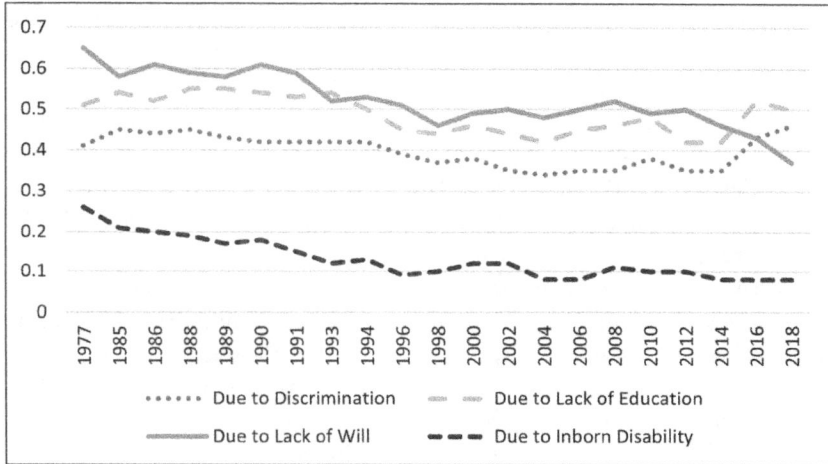

For quite some time national political parties too were at one with the Supreme Court in regard to the overriding significance of race-neutral forces. For decades both channeled *Bakke* (1978), *Croson* (1989), and *Wygant's* (1986) sense that "there are numerous explanations for a disparity between the percentage of minority students and the percentage of minority faculty, many of them completely unrelated to discrimination of any kind." Politicians on the left only recently centered their messaging in the view that race always matters. For today's Democrat racism is a centrifugal force deeply embedded in America's socioeconomic and political structures. Claims of systemic racism were widely promulgated in 2016, as liberals maintained that "race still plays a significant role in determining who gets ahead in America and who gets left behind," but they stopped short of denoting its role as determinative.[57] In the 2020 election cycle, Democrats turned a corner and developed a sharper focus on systemic racism that situated the party farther away from the Court's position. Democrats proclaimed that "historic wrongs and abuses perpetrated against Native Americans, two and a half centuries of slavery, a hundred years of Jim Crow segregation, and a history of exclusionary immigration policies have created profound and lasting inequities in income, wealth, education, employment, housing, environmental quality, and health care for communities of color."[58]

Prior to the 2020 election cycle, however, the Democratic Party parroted the same race-neutral mantra as that advanced by the Court and Republicans. At the same time that the Supreme Court fine-tuned its claims about nonracial forces from the 1970s through 2016, Democrats leaned into a message that highlighted economic disadvantage as much as racial disadvantage. Even at the height of the 1960s Black civil rights movement Democrats urged that economic and educational policies were critical to breaking down structural barriers to minority employment.[59] By the late 1960s they joined Republicans' call to expand minority business opportunities. Liberals added more culprits to the list of nonracial influences in the decades to follow. Along with failed federal housing policies,[60] also folded into Democrats' universal explanations were economics-centered policy proposals, such as job training for minorities, federal funding for historically Black colleges and universities, and economic development.[61]

Democrats amped up their claim that class inequality mattered as much as past racism during the 1980s, asserting that their "commitment to civil rights embraces not only a commitment to legal equality, but a commitment to economic justice as well."[62] By the 1990s universal policies became a key part of their calling card in the form of pledges to end "savage inequalities" and to eliminate the achievement gap.[63] Into the 2000s they stressed the importance of expanding economic opportunity for the disadvantaged and eliminating healthcare disparities among "minorities, American Indians, women, low-income people through better research and better funded community-based health centers."[64]

Republicans had embraced economic solutions to racial problems long before the Supreme Court countered the civil rights race-centered explanations. In the 1940s they pledged that "American citizens of Negro descent shall be given a square deal in the economic and political life of this nation."[65] Zeroing in on the economics of racial inequality a decade later Republicans called for legislation to expand employment opportunities specifically for minorities. From 1968 on, conservatives were convinced that, at the core of the race problem was a poverty problem. That "the inability of the poor to cope meaningfully with their environment is compounded by problems which blunt opportunity—inadequate income, inferior education, inadequate healthcare, slum housing, limited job opportunities, discrimination and crime."[66]

Conservatives folded their plan for Black America into a larger agenda for poverty and economic development during the 1970s, with minority business enterprise (MBE) programs as the centerpiece. By the 1980s Republicans banked almost exclusively on economic development as the cure to racial ills, declaring, "Our fundamental answer to the economic problems of Black Americans is the same answer we make to all Americans—full employment without inflation through economic growth."[67] Recent decades manifest the same thinking in a series of pledges to allocate more federal funding to historically Black colleges and universities and the mantra "No child in America should be segregated by low expectations."[68] Conservatives attribute racial disparities also in housing to money problems, to wit: "The most significant barrier to homeownership is the down payment."[69]

No less than in Supreme Court affirmative action rulings, mass opinion, and party messaging, there is a long history of pointing to multiple causes of racial disparities also in presidential politics. Every modern American president has embraced the view that slavery and past discrimination are not the sole reason that Blacks lag behind Whites, and that other nonracial factors figure into the equation. When the US Equal Employment Opportunity Commission issued regulations in 2012 that situated the economic and social conditions of minorities within "a larger pattern of restriction, exclusion, discrimination, segregation, and inferior treatment of minorities and women in many areas of life," the nation's first Black president helped to supply the rationale.[70] President Barack Obama frequently merged the role of race together with socioeconomic disadvantage and values. In an interview with author Ta-Nehisi Coates Obama explained:

> If you want to get at African American poverty, the income gap, wealth gap, achievement gap, that the most important thing is to make sure that the society as a whole does right by people who are poor, are working class. . . . Higher minimum wages, full-employment programs, early-childhood education: Those kinds of programs are, by design, universal, but by definition, because they are helping folks who are in the worst economic situations, are most likely to disproportionately impact and benefit African Americans. They also have the benefit of being sellable to a majority of the body politic.[71]

Drilling down on the significance of class-related factors in a separate interview, Obama said that progress over the last half century was progress "that middle-class African Americans enjoy in ways that really impoverished African-Americans do not yet feel."[72] As to the role of personal values, during a panel discussion on poverty at Georgetown University, the president asserted that "broad economic trends" are "turbocharged by technology and globalization, a winner-take-all economy that allows those with even slightly better skills to massively expand their reach and their markets. . . . But there are values and decisions that have aided and abetted that process."[73]

Within the text of the same speech that originally unveiled the intellectual framework for affirmative action, universal factors, especially family breakdown, were underscored as much as racism. President Lyndon B. Johnson began his 1965 Howard University speech by highlighting the pivotal role of racism and discrimination in the form of the "shackled runner thesis" as explained earlier. But just a few sentences down he shifted to class factors, explaining: "Ability is stretched or stunted by the family that you live with, and the neighborhood you live in—by the school you go to and the poverty or the richness of your surroundings. It is the product of a hundred unseen forces playing upon the little infant, the child, and finally the man." Among all, he claimed, the "most important—its influence radiating to every part of life—is the breakdown of the Negro family structure," something that the controversial Moynihan report would serve to reinforce once it became public later.[74] Hence, Johnson's answer to the race problem was tied largely to jobs, partly to decent homes, welfare and social programs, care for the sick, and to fixing "the crumbling of the Negro family."

The comprehensive affirmative action review that President Clinton ordered in 1995 concluded that, while "current discrimination, past discrimination, and the lingering effects of that past discrimination" were important factors that explained minority underrepresentation in key professions and in higher education, "increasingly, educational institutions are the engines of opportunity."[75] Expressing agreement with conservative thought leaders like Ward Connerly, Abigail Thernstrom, and Stephan Thernstrom, Clinton shared his own frustration that affirmative action benefits only about 10 percent of the people, and not the educationally disadvantaged who "didn't get the preparation and continuing support that they needed" and whom he thought should be the focus.[76] In the longest-ever affirmative action speech by a US president, Bill Clinton was emphatic about the importance of class over and above race, saying that "we must also admit that affirmative action alone won't solve the problems of minorities and women who seek to be a part of the American dream."[77] To do that, "we have to have an economic strategy that reverses the decline in wages and the growth of poverty among working people. Without that, women, minorities, and White males will all be in trouble in the future."[78] Accordingly, Clinton revamped the Minority Small Business and Capital Ownership Development Program in 1998 and changed the program's name in order "to emphasize that individuals need not be members of minority groups and to stress the importance of assisting participating firms in their overall business development."[79] The newly assigned race-neutral name was "8(a) Business Development Program."

The Supreme Court's emphasis on nonracial, socioeconomic influences is most closely mirrored in the policies of Presidents Donald J. Trump and Richard M. Nixon. During the interim President George H. W. Bush committed his administration to a version of affirmative action that would "inspire people of *all* [emphasis added] races to nurture affirmative values, affirmative views of themselves, affirmative lives."[80] That entailed reform of public housing to increase ownership through the "HOPE" initiative (Homeownership and Opportunity for People Everywhere), through enterprise zones, anti-crime legislation, community power, and family-oriented policies. Of all of these, Bush believed that, over and above "opportunity, education, advancement, equality," the "number-one threat" to inner cities where minorities are concentrated was illegal drugs.[81]

President Trump rarely discussed the problems of Black America as distinctively *racial* in nature.[82] He boasted on several occasions about how he helped Blacks, such as in his January 31, 2020, Proclamation on National African American History that detailed policies he believed helped Blacks. The policies included everything from employment growth to tax cuts, opportunity zones, criminal justice reform, support for HBCUs, and more. Trump touted much the same at several gatherings, including a September 2020 "Black Voices for Trump" rally in Atlanta, Georgia. Asked in the first year of his administration how he planned to tackle the growing racial divide in the country, he offered, "I really think jobs can have a big impact. I think if we continue to create jobs—over a million, substantially more than a million . . . I think that's going to have a tremendous impact—positive impact on race relations."[83] In a televised election town hall meeting, pressed by moderator George Stephanopoulos to say whether there is a "race problem in America," President Trump replied by pointing to improvements in the "income levels," "job situation," and "unemployment numbers" of the Black community.[84]

Despite the boldness of Order No. 4[85] issued by his Office of Federal Contract Compliance, President Nixon deracialized federal race policy years before the Supreme Court expressed its views on nonracial determinants. Nixon declared that the kind of "civil rights policy" to which his administration was committed focused on "earning power."[86] He also spoke on multiple occasions about the need to aim federal programs at "correcting the effects of past discrimination"[87] and to "eliminate racial discrimination in housing—some of which he conceded was intentional."[88] As well, Nixon pushed back against the idea that "economic segregation" is the equivalent of "racial segregation," insisting that "the terms 'poor' and 'Black' were not interchangeable," that "the issues involved are separate, and those who would treat effectively with race and poverty must take care to maintain the distinction."[89]

In concert with affirmative action case law Nixon nonetheless maintained that the factors driving housing patterns were "immensely complex and intricately balanced."[90] Regarding schools too he said, "The key factor is not race but the kind of home the child comes from . . . the distinction between educational difficulty as a result of race, and educational difficulty as a result of social or economic levels, of family background, of cultural patterns, or simply of bad schools." For Nixon, providing better education for the disadvantaged required a more sophisticated approach than mere racial mathematics.[91] He went on to outline his belief that "to foster the economic status and the pride of members of our minority groups we must seek to involve them more fully in our private enterprise system . . . we need to remove commercial obstacles which have too often stood in the way of minority group members—obstacles such as the unavailability of credit, insurance, and technical assistance."[92] This rationale undergirded the agenda to tackle what his administration termed "enormous economic inequities."[93] Hence, Nixon's executive orders squarely concentrated on socioeconomic factors more than racial factors. His 1969 Executive Order 11458 established the Office of Minority Business Enterprise (OMBE).[94] A later order (EO 11625) expanded the scope of the OMBE's minority business programs to encompass grants for technical and management assistance to minority business enterprises (MBEs).

Alongside presidents, parties, and the public, also parroting Justice Sandra Day O'Connor's assertion in *Richmond v. Croson* (1989) that the dearth of minority businesses could be attributed to "deficiencies in working capital" is a diverse chorus of civil rights advocates, academics, and candidates for elected office. Indeed, national discourse outside the courthouse long beforehand tilted away from policies to address systemic racism and toward those designed to redress class inequality. The post-1960s turnabout was not entirely the making of the Political Right. The civil rights movement had already shifted its focus toward poverty, though not with the intent of minimizing the importance of race. The last major march that Dr. Martin Luther King planned was the Poor People's March, as detailed in David

J. Garrow's *Protest at Selma: Martin Luther King, Jr., and the Voting Rights Act of 1965*.[95] A civil rights organization devoted to expanding economic opportunity for Blacks, Operation Breadbasket was established in 1966, with Dr. King appointing civil rights leader Jesse Jackson as its national director. Conservatives originated the class inequality narrative to counter the race discrimination thesis during the 1970s.[96] The latter fine-tuned it, none more than Charles Murray whose widely read 1984 book *Losing Ground* blamed government welfare programs for the rise in female-headed households within the Black population and increased Black poverty rates.[97]

Scholarly research by noted Harvard University sociologist William Julius Wilson enormously impacted the national conversation about race in his award-winning book *The Declining Significance of Race: Blacks and Changing American Institutions*. In it, Wilson argues that the explanatory power of race began to decline in the early 1960s.[98] Racism and exclusion accounted for much of lagging Black progress up until the 1960s. From the 1960s on, however, socioeconomic class mattered more, he contends. The shift in the labor market from mostly goods-producing to mostly service-producing jobs hit the inner city hardest, where Blacks are disproportionately concentrated and reliant on disappearing factory jobs. Affirmative action, Wilson argues, primarily benefits the Black middle class. Whereas, for disadvantaged Blacks, universal policies hold more promise than race-centered policies. Precisely this point is documented in a compelling analysis in Richard D. Kahlenberg's *The Remedy: Class, Race, and Affirmative Action*.[99] Like Wilson, Kahlenberg insists that because it benefits middle-class Blacks, affirmative action should be refashioned as a class-based policy, so that it benefits the truly disadvantaged, regardless of race.

The race versus class academic debate regularly spills over into national political discourse, including in 2016 and 2020. Presidential candidates Bernie Sanders and Elizabeth Warren as well as other Progressives centered their platforms around declining wages and the concentration of wealth in the hands of the top 1 percent earners. Black and Brown minorities are disproportionately disadvantaged, they maintained, not because they are Black and Brown, but because they are disproportionately poor. Hence, the best approach to tackling racial inequality is universal policies that tackle poverty. For many progressives and conservatives, race policy talk was largely off the table in 2016, eclipsed by preoccupation with class inequality. The protests that followed the murder of an unarmed Black man, George Floyd, by a White police officer in 2020 momentarily refocused national attention squarely on race. Floyd's death was widely viewed as clear evidence of systemic racism in law enforcement.[100] But, little time passed before nonracial factors were thrown into the mix. Differences in rates of criminality, modes of law enforcement, and socioeconomic class differences moved to center stage alongside race-centered arguments. The policy reform proposals aimed at the racial dynamics of law enforcement stalled in Congress, such as the George Floyd Justice in Policing Act.[101] Within just a few months the Black Lives Matter mantra was countered with "Blue Lives Matter," "All Lives Matter," "Gay Lives Matter," and myriad other race-neutral expressions.

SECTION SUMMARY

In all, on the critical question whether the legacy of slavery and race discrimination is to blame for persistent racial inequality, Supreme Court affirmative action jurisprudence settles on the same conclusion as the rest of America: It is not. Most Americans blame racial disparities on poverty and deficits in educational opportunity. Right up until 2020, the Democratic Party embraced race-neutral theories of inequality just as much as the Republican Party. In presidential politics too Presidents Nixon and Trump negotiated race as a chiefly economic matter. President Obama likewise called attention to the fact that middle-class African Americans and impoverished African Americans did not share the same plight. So did President Clinton, who point-blank stated that "affirmative action alone won't solve the problems" of minorities and that a sound economic strategy was needed. So did President Lyndon B. Johnson, whose commentary on the legacy of slavery in his "shackled runner" speech immediately pivoted to significant impacts of family, neighborhood, and schools. Leading academics chimed in on the race versus class debate in ways that carried weight and that continued to find voice in the 2016 and 2020 national elections and later. To close, Justice Powell's claim that it is "speculative" to argue that slavery and racism are the root cause of continuing racial inequality is a claim that captures the dominant view across the political field.

White History Equivalency:
We Were All Victims at Some Point or Another

The Supreme Court and America at large scarcely see a distinction between the centuries-long, legally mandated racism that expressly targeted forcibly removed Blacks, on the one hand, versus the shorter-lived societal bias that faced Italian, Irish, Polish, and German immigrants upon their voluntary arrival to the US, on the other. In national racial politics, talk of "bootstraps," "opportunity for all," and the value of a "strong work ethic" undercut claims about Black versus White ethnic histories. American citizens, politicians, and academics are just as apt as Supreme Court justices to impute a legal, moral, and historical equivalency between Black and White histories.

Court Opinion on White History Equivalency

Racial preference rulings by the Supreme Court treat the difference between past, state-enforced exclusion of Blacks and the societal barriers that White ethnics once encountered as a difference without a distinction. Against this backdrop *Students for Fair Admissions*' (2023) rejection of the idea that Blacks and Whites are differently situated under the Fourteenth Amendment is consistent with the long line of rulings that preceded it. Chief Justice Roberts's majority opinion in *SFFA* insisted that the Court's first reading of the equal protection clause in *Strauder v. West Virginia* (1880) was that "the law in the States shall be the same for the Black as for the White: that all persons, whether colored or White, shall stand equal before the laws of the States." And while the Court failed to live up to the clause's core commitments for over half a century after *Plessy v. Ferguson*, by 1950 the "inevitable truth of the Fourteenth Amendment" reemerged, which was that separate treatment of races was inherently unequal.

It was *Bakke* (1978) that first blurred the line of demarcation between the lived experience of Blacks and non-Blacks. Justice Powell's principal opinion quashed the idea that one could ascribe exceptionalism to Black history beyond the 1930s. Powell rejected what he termed the artificial line of a "two-class theory" of the Fourteenth Amendment, whereby maltreated racial minorities could be differentiated from a privileged White majority. He insisted, "The guarantee of equal protection cannot mean one thing when applied to one individual and something else when applied to a person of another color. If both are not accorded the same protection, then it is not equal." The amendment was framed in universal terms in order to state a principle that is responsive to the racial, ethnic, and cultural diversity of the country. It was "strangled in infancy by post-civil-war judicial reactionism" up until the mid- to late 1930s. But, "by that time it was no longer possible to peg the guarantees of the Fourteenth Amendment to the struggle for equality of one racial minority." This, because "the White majority" itself is composed of various minority groups, most of which can lay claim to a history of prior discrimination. It is true, he reasoned, that landmark decisions in equal protection law such as *Brown v. Board of Education* (1954), *Shelley v. Kraemer* (1948), and *Yick Wo v. Hopkins* (1886) "arose in response to the continued exclusion of Negroes from the mainstream of American society" and could "be characterized as involving discrimination by the 'majority' White race against the Negro minority." Nonetheless, "they need not be read as depending upon that characterization for their results."

Powell's commentary stressed the difficulty of sorting the stigmatized from the nonstigmatized. Such that, during the period intervening between the Civil War and the era of substantive due process in the 1930s "the United States had become a Nation of minorities. Each had to struggle—and to some extent struggles still—to overcome" prejudices. Under his *Bakke* reasoning "members of various religious and ethnic groups, primarily but not exclusively of Eastern, Middle, and Southern European ancestry, such as Jews, Catholics, Italians, Greeks, and Slavic groups, continue to be excluded" from various jobs "because of discrimination based upon their religion and/ or national origin." Powell continued, "Not all of these groups can receive preferential treatment . . . for then the only 'majority' left would be a new minority of White Anglo-Saxon Protestants."

The notion that differences between Black and White history lack constitutional-legal significance was advanced with added force in the years to follow *Bakke*. By 1986, *Wygant* stipulated that the Supreme Court had fully settled on the view "that the level of scrutiny does not change merely because the challenged classification operates against a group that historically has not been subject to governmental discrimination." *Croson* (1989) reiterated the same, quoting *Bakke*'s assertion that "the guarantee of equal protection cannot mean one thing when applied to one individual and something else when applied to a person of another color." *Croson* too challenged the traditional "majority" versus "minority" paradigm. Justice O'Connor pointed out that the set-aside plan in *Croson* was the making of a majority-Black city council in order to dispute the notion that racial preferences consistently represent instances in which "the 'White majority' places burdens upon itself."

Chief Justice Roberts doubled down in 2007 on his sense that it is impossible to determine which races deserve preferential treatment and what representativeness entails. In *Parents Involved* Roberts picked apart the "tipping point" concept that guides diversity planning, which is the point at which a sufficient level of diversification is achieved. He seized upon testimony from a Seattle school district expert concerning the importance of attaining a critical mass of minority students in district schools in order to "avoid students feeling any kind of specter of exceptionality." The chief justice questioned whether avoidance of racial isolation was "more likely to be achieved at a school that is 50 percent White and 50 percent Asian-American . . . than at a school that is 30 percent Asian-American, 25 percent African-American, 25 percent Latino, and 20 percent White." In short, Roberts rebuffed the idea of a universal ideal level of representativeness, especially when a multitude of minority groups in the US lay claim to a history racial exclusion.

POLITICS OF WHITE HISTORY EQUIVALENCY

The equivalency between Black and White ethnic histories that is imputed in affirmative action jurisprudence parallels a related thread in discourses across the country. The centuries-long, legally enforced subordination of Blacks no longer plays the lead role in the American story of racial victimization. Harvard University Law Professor Cass R. Sunstein makes the case that it should, that the equal protection clause is best understood as anti-caste, rather than simply anti-discrimination. Such that, "in the area of race, the principal target of the Civil War amendments was the system of racial caste, a system that turned the highly visible and morally irrelevant characteristics of race into a basis for second-class citizenship."[102] Under this conception of the Fourteenth Amendment, Sunstein concludes, "there is nothing fundamentally illegitimate about affirmative action programs."[103]

But, anti-caste thinking does not resonate with the overall American public any more than it does with Supreme Court justices. Mass public opinion data illustrate that everyday citizens believe the recipe for Black success is no different than the one that forged White ethnic groups' success. When asked, "Do you agree strongly, agree somewhat, neither agree nor disagree, disagree somewhat, or disagree strongly with the following statement: Irish, Italians, Jewish and many other minorities overcame prejudice and worked their way up. Blacks should do the same without special favors," as of 1994, fully three out of four Americans agreed. Of those, 45 percent "strongly agreed," as shown in figure 2.2. By 2018, the number that lumped together the kinds of obstacles that face Blacks with those that once faced Irish, Italian, and Jewish Americans dipped to a 58 percent majority, and with just 25 percent of Americans still convinced that Black and White histories are different.

In the handful of instances in which national political parties directly address the issue in the years leading up to *Bakke* (1978), their positioning

Figure 2.2. Perceptions of White Ethnic Success: Hard Work. *Source*: Davern, M., Bautista, R., Freese, J., Morgan, S. L., & Smith, T. W. (n.d.). *General social surveys, 1972–2021*. NORC, 2021: NORC at the University of Chicago [producer and distributor]. Last accessed 2/16/2021 from the GSS Data Explorer website at gssdataexplorer.norc.org.

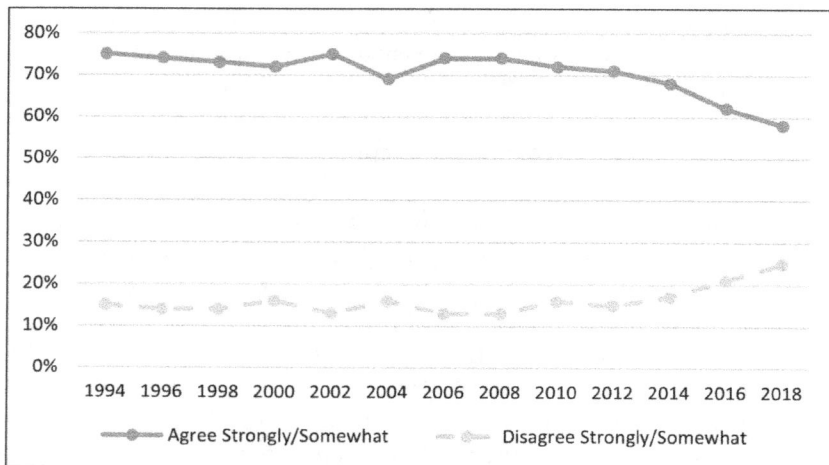

around White ethnic history was not remarkably different from the Supreme Court's. This means, by the time the Court chimed in on the subject in 1978, it was toeing a line already plotted by the general public and the party system. In line with *Bakke* (1978), both parties harp on about the melting pot forged by the large and wide variety of racial and ethnic groups, each with their own unique history of struggles and success. And, much like Powell's pronouncement that America is no longer a nation with a White majority, Democrats and Republicans likewise trumpet the notion that there is more than Black versus White history when it comes to race relations in the US.[104] The point where parties break with the Court is in connection with express equivalency claims, in that neither Republican nor Democratic leaders go so far as to publicly cosign the justices' conflation of the history of anti-Black versus anti-White exclusion.

Otherwise, liberals have long touted the political importance of the cultural heritage of White ethnics. Amid the White backlash that followed the 1960s civil rights reforms Democrats bracketed the cultural experience of White ethnics together with Blacks and other racial minorities. Their 1972 platform proclaimed that "recognition and support of the cultural identity and pride of Black people are generations overdue. The American Indians, the Spanish-speaking, the Asian Americans—the cultural and linguistic heritage of these groups is too-often ignored in schools and communities."[105] It continued, "So, too, are the backgrounds, traditions and contributions of White national, ethnic, religious and regional communities ignored." Conservatives have been more explicit about the continuing struggles of White ethnics. Their 1976 "Ethnic Americans" plank maintained that "Ethnic Americans have enriched this nation with their hard work, self-reliance and respect for the rights and needs of others."[106] They went further during the 1980s to lament, "Millions of Americans who trace their heritage to the nations of Eastern, Central, and Southern Europe have for too long seen their values neglected," because, to Republicans it was still important that these Europeans "have the opportunity to share the power."[107]

Agreement with Court pronouncements on White ethnic history is observed also in those of American presidents. Nostalgic remembrances of anti-European bias and triumph are a staple feature of presidential speech-making well into the 2000s. President Bill Clinton suggested Black and Irish histories were "the same," when he commented favorably on a book that, he said, "basically talks about how, when the Irish immigrants first came here, they really identified with the African-American slaves because they were treated the same way, and they had much the same experience."[108] When Black hip hop artist Sister Souljah reacted to the 1992 Los Angeles riots by asking, "If Black people kill Black people every day, why not have a week and kill White people,"[109] President Clinton responded by saying, "If you took the words 'White' and 'Black,' and you reversed them, you might think David Duke was giving that speech."[110] *Centrist Rhetoric: The Production of Political Transcendence in the Clinton Presidency* points out that, "to make the words of Duke and Souljah interchangeable, to posit that a reasonable person would find the vast differences between these two individuals less significant than the resemblances of their rhetoric, is a serious charge, in part because it implies that the Klan (Duke) and the Coalition (Souljah) are also potentially comparable in the same way."[111]

Clinton's Sister Souljah moment was in step with positions taken by his predecessors. President Lyndon B. Johnson compared the newly passed 1965 Immigration and Control Act that opened the door for non-European immigrants with anti-Italian policies that existed before. He noted, "Under the old system, even Christopher Columbus would have found it difficult to come to this country—simply because Christopher Columbus was born in Italy. Under the old system, a person born in England was 12 times more welcome to America than a person born in Italy."[112] President Jimmy Carter likewise remarked that "there's also been much discrimination in our society against Italian Americans," recounting the signs that read, "No Italians need apply," "No Irish need apply." For Carter, "the signs may be gone, but many of the memories remain, along with too much of the quiet, unspoken discrimination."[113] He went so far as to add bias against southerners into the mix, saying, "All of us have known the pain associated with discrimination," given the prejudice and suffering in the South and the fact that "we haven't had a President elected from the deep South since 1848."[114]

Presidents Johnson and Obama were careful to highlight fundamental differences between the history of anti-White ethnic discrimination and anti-Black history. Comparing the two, Johnson stressed that White ethnics "did not have the heritage of centuries to overcome, and they did not have a cultural tradition which had been twisted and battered by endless years of hatred and hopelessness, nor were they excluded—these others—because of race or color—a feeling whose dark intensity is matched by no other prejudice in our society."[115] President Obama recounted, "A century ago, New York City shops displayed those signs, 'No Irish Need Apply' . . . Chinese immigrants faced persecution and vicious stereotypes and were, for a time, even banned from entering America. During World War II, German and Italian residents were detained, and in one of the darkest chapters in our history, Japanese immigrants and even Japanese American citizens were forced from their homes and imprisoned in camps."[116] Significantly, however, Obama opened the same speech by declaring, "From the start, Africans were brought here in chains against their will and then toiled under the whip. They also built America."

The Supreme Court's sense of likeness between Black and White ethnic experiences was wholeheartedly embraced by Presidents Nixon and Trump. Nixon suggested that minorities and Whites are equally justified in choosing to live among their own and that "it is natural that people with a common heritage retain special ties; it is natural and right that we have Italian or Irish or Negro or Norwegian neighborhoods; it is natural and right that members of those communities feel a sense of group identity and group pride."[117] Secretary of Housing and Urban Development in the Trump administration Dr. Ben Carson suggested that the forced importation of Black enslaved peoples was a form of Black immigration. Carson explained that his definition of "immigrant" included "involuntary immigration."[118] President Trump himself advanced a "racial equivalency" argument on the heels of a 2017 Charlottesville, Virginia, White supremacist march that resulted in one dead and 35 injured. Trump's recall of the incident was to say, "You had people—and I'm not talking about the neo-Nazis and the White nationalists, because they should be condemned totally—but you had many people in that group other than neo-Nazis and White nationalists. Okay? And the press has treated them absolutely unfairly."[119]

Complementing political narratives are academic histories of Irish and Italian immigrants often used to validate the kind of reasoning offered by Justice Powell in *Bakke* (1978) and by Justice Roberts in *SFFA* (2024). Hundreds of history books and articles chronicle how Irish Americans were once caricatured as apelike, dangerous, drunken, and idle in much the same way as Blacks.[120] They highlight violent attacks on Irish Americans by Anglo-Protestant groups. Restriction to less-desirable jobs in the farming, railroad, mining, and textile industries is frequently featured in early Irish American histories.[121] Historians document as well how Italian Americans were targets of hostility and negative stereotypes, both in the past and today.[122] Often labeled during the late 19th century as a mongrel race, intellectually inferior, and disproportionally engaged in Mafia-like organized crime, Italian Americans are said to have suffered grave consequences because of these stereotypes.[123] A widely read account of 19th-century American nativism reports that the first generation of Italian immigrants were "abused in public and isolated in private, cuffed in the wards and pelted on the streets, fined and imprisoned on the smallest pretext, cheated of their wages, and crowded by the score into converted barns and tumble-down shanties that served as boarding houses."[124]

The upshot of many of these types of historical analyses is that White ethnic out-groups of the past made it to mainstream America by pulling themselves up by their own bootstraps, working hard, and embracing the right values. The logical extension is that Blacks are not faring as well as other victimized groups because Blacks do not work as hard. Rhetorical devices like "model minority" and "land of opportunity" downplay the impact of centuries-long, government-enforced racism on Blacks' socioeconomic status and at the same time play up the idea that hard work is the main driver behind the success of Asian Americans.[125] Studies show that such narratives are frequently embraced by recent Mexican and Asian immigrants, including a study of immigrant attitudes by the liberal-leaning Migration Policy Institute. It reports that a large majority (73 percent) think it is "extremely important" for immigrants "to work and stay off welfare."[126] The study adds, "In focus groups, many talked about the stark reality that greeted them when they first came to the United States—and the understanding that, without hard work, their dream of America as the land of plenty would not come true."[127]

SECTION SUMMARY

In all, the racial equivalency claims in affirmative action opinions are regularly voiced in national racial politics, more so by everyday citizens and presidents than by the major political parties. Decades of survey data show that, when asked whether Blacks should work their way up to overcome prejudice the same as Irish, Italians, Jewish, and other minorities, the overwhelming percent of respondents agree. Neither national political party goes as far as the Supreme Court does in claiming that White ethnics' historical experience with exclusion is equal to that of Blacks. However, both Democrats and Republicans regularly wax on about the cultural heritage of White ethnics and the importance of recognizing their travails. Presidents Johnson and Obama were careful to acknowledge that Irish, Italian, German, and Japanese Americans experienced racism of their own. Both were just as keen to highlight also the distinction that "Africans were brought here in chains against their will and then toiled under the whip." On the other hand, the views expressed by Presidents Carter, Nixon, and Trump and especially President Clinton's breakout "Sister Soulja" moment all match up with the Supreme Court's sense that stigmatized groups cannot be differentiated along racial lines. Academic studies serve as proof. In a nutshell, the Supreme Court's fusion of Black and White experiences with discrimination is on par with what we observe in mass survey data, national party positioning, presidential politics, and historical analyses.

Chapter Three

The Reconstruction of Race and Racism

US Supreme Court affirmative action rulings from *Bakke* (1978) through *Students for Fair Admissions* (2023) deconstructed the original meaning of race and racism in the US and constructed new conceptions in their stead. First among the four pillars of the new judicial constructions of race and racism is the foundational principle that race is always, inherently and unavoidably, problematic, and hence, colorblindness is the ultimate goal of American society. Second is that racial disparity does not—of itself—constitute evidence of racism because the equal protection clause (EPC) of the US Constitution does not require actual equality. A third pillar posits a conflict between race-conscious policies and core American ideals, namely individualist and traditional civil rights ideals. The final pillar construes Whites as victims of racial discrimination just as much as Blacks, thus negating the twin notions of universal White privilege and systematic Black disadvantage. The fundaments of Supreme Court intellection of race and racism closely resemble those of everyday voters and elected officials. Scarce daylight exists between the judicial and political perspectives, specifically in regard to the basic aversion to race consciousness, the policy significance of racial disparities, the relation between American values and race-specific policies, and beliefs about racial stereotypes and reverse discrimination.

All Race Is Suspect

COURT OPINION ON RACIAL CLASSIFICATIONS

Students for Fair Admissions' (*SFFA*) commentary on the dangers of race awareness punctuate the fact that the meaning of race underwent a seismic reconstruction by the Supreme Court over the past 40+ years. Ian Haney López's *White by Law: The Legal Construction of Race* details how, not only the Supreme Court, but other courts, justices, and lawyers redefined race in the early 20th century.[1] The contention here is that the same dynamic continued to unfold afterward, up until now. The new conception articulated in Supreme Court preferential rulings calls for a uniform approach to all things racial, yet simultaneously conceives of race as a variable concept. The only understanding that a majority of the justices consistently attach to race is that it is a thorny sociopolitical construct, always and in every situation—no matter the motives or policy aims. *SFFA* dismissed the notion that there is a consequential difference between benign and invidious race-conscious policies and, instead, cast all as deeply troubling. Chief Justice Roberts's majority opinion insisted "that all racial classifications, however compelling their goals," were "dangerous,"[2] that "racial discrimination [is] invidious in all contexts,"[3] and he remarked about "the perilous remedy of racial preferences." According to Roberts, "The entire point of the Equal Protection Clause is that treating someone differently because of their skin color is *not* like treating them differently because they are from a city or from a suburb, or because they play the violin poorly or well."

Much of what Roberts wrote in *SFFA* (2023) was lifted from earlier rulings, especially the 2003 *Grutter* majority opinion that noted "serious problems of justice connected with the idea of [racial] preference itself." *Grutter* had lifted this language from *Bakke* (1978). The underlying reasoning was that, in order to distinguish permissible from impermissible uses of race, courts must always apply the strictest form of judicial scrutiny when they encounter a racial classification. This guidance was first established in 1978 in *Regents of California v. Bakke*, a case self-described as the Court's first brush with racial preference. *Bakke* "involve[d] the use of an explicit racial classification never before countenanced" by the Court, a point reiterated by Chief Justice Roberts in 2007.[4] The race-based admissions program at the University of California at Davis Medical School reserved 16 of the 100 seats in the incoming class for minority students. Dual admissions tracks were set up; one was open to all applicants and administrated by a general admissions committee, the other operated by a special committee. The special admissions committee was composed of mostly minority members and screened applicants who checked the box to indicate their wish to be considered as members of a "minority group."[5] "Black," "Chicano," "Asian," and "American Indian"[6] applicants could elect to be considered through either the general or special admissions process. Whites could not apply through the special admissions process.

The litigant, Allan Bakke, was a White male who applied to the Davis Medical School in 1973 and 1974, was considered under the general admissions program, and rejected both years—despite having a higher grade point average, MCAT score, and committee rating than the average applicant admitted under the special program. The Supreme Court of California held that the equal protection clause provides that "no applicant may be rejected because of his race, in favor of another who is less qualified, as measured by standards applied without regard to race."[7] On appeal, the US Supreme Court sided partly with Bakke and invalidated the special admissions program based on a 5–4 majority finding that, in employing a racial classification, the university failed to satisfy the requirements of strict scrutiny.

Among the flaws in the special admissions process that Justice Powell's lead opinion highlighted were "serious problems of justice connected with the idea of preference itself." Most of all was the difficulty of ascertaining what is and is not "in fact benign." Powell worried about the unique problems posed by racial preferences. He believed "gender-based classifications are less likely to create the analytical and practical problems present in preferential programs premised on racial or ethnic criteria." And, on the other hand, that "the perception of racial classifications as inherently odious stems from a lengthy and tragic history that gender-based classifications do not share." Starting with Powell's lead opinion in *Bakke* (1978) any program or policy expressly based in part or in whole on racial considerations must satisfy the most exacting judicial review of the who's, why's, where's, when's, and how's. With this stipulation, *Bakke* dismantled the traditional civil rights view of racial set-asides for marginalized racial minorities as a net positive and beneficial use of race. Justice Powell also took down the original infrastructure of race, by effectively establishing that race could no longer be treated as a principally social and political construct with constitutional-legal roots in slavery and Jim Crow laws. Race was recast instead as a principally constitutional-legal construct with *potentially* identifiable sociopolitical roots. Reform policies would henceforth have to launch from legal principle, rather than socioeconomic realities. The central legal question taken up in *Bakke* was whether racial classifications, even when employed for the benefit of racial minorities, are constitutionally suspect and thus subject to heightened judicial scrutiny. The *Bakke* ruling's answer was "yes." Justice Powell's opinion declared that all racial classifications are inherently suspect, even pernicious, and they call for "the most exacting judicial examination," always and no matter the circumstances.[8]

It bears highlighting that the four justices who sought to uphold the set-aside program agreed with the majority on the foundational principle that race was a suspect classification that required heightened scrutiny. The point of departure for Justices Brennan, White, Marshall, and Blackmun hinged on how the standard was applied in this particular case. In an opinion that concurred in part and dissented in part, they wrote, "Our review under the Fourteenth Amendment should be strict—not '"strict" in theory and fatal in fact,' because it is stigma that causes fatality—but strict and searching nonetheless."

The strict scrutiny review standard for race-sensitive programs was fleshed out further in *Adarand Constructors, Inc. v. Pena* (1995) and later rulings. Writing for the 5–4 majority O'Connor insisted that, while there was once "lingering uncertainty in the details" of Supreme Court requirements, affirmative action precedents clearly established three things. First, any preference based on racial or ethnic criteria is subject to strict scrutiny. Second, the standard of review is not dependent on the race of those burdened or benefited.[9] Third, "Equal protection analysis in the Fifth Amendment area is the same as that under the Fourteenth Amendment."[10] The latter point was determinative in *Adarand I*, which held that congressionally approved affirmative action plans are subject to the same heightened scrutiny as that applied to state, local, and private preferential policies.[11] All the way through 2016 in *Fisher v. University of Texas*[12] a majority of Supreme Court justices insisted on strict scrutiny of all types of race-based programs. *Fisher II* added that universities and other decision-makers have a "continuing obligation to satisfy the burden of strict scrutiny in light of changing circumstances." Consequently, an affirmative action program permissible at one point in time may not survive judicial scrutiny at a later point in time.

The individualized harm brought on by race-conscious policies was also delineated in *Adarand* (1995), as well as *Wygant* (1986) and *Parents Involved* (2007), all cases where the Court invalidated affirmative action policies. *Wygant* (1986) found them "simply too pernicious to permit any but the most exact connection between justification and classification." In *Adarand* (1995) Justice O'Connor wrote that "whenever the government treats any person unequally because of his or her race, that person has suffered an injury that falls squarely within the language and spirit of the Constitution's guarantee of equal protection." Also, from Chief Justice Roberts's vantage point in *Parents Involved* (2007) race was an "irrelevant factor" in governmental decision-making and American life generally.[13] His bottom line in *Parents Involved* is that "the way to stop discrimination on the basis of race is to stop discriminating on the basis of race."

That racial classifications are inherently harmful is a position that the Court has taken in favorable as well as unfavorable affirmative action rulings. In a college admissions case where a preferential policy was upheld, *Fisher v. Texas* (2016) reasoned that "formalistic racial classifications may sometimes fail to capture diversity in all of its dimensions and, when used in a divisive manner, could undermine the educational benefits the University values." In another case that upheld affirmative action, *Fullilove v. Klutznick, Secretary of Commerce, et al.* (1980), Chief Justice Burger's lead opinion, joined by Justices White and Powell, underscored how the history of governmental tolerance of practices using racial criteria for invidious discrimination proved the need for intensive judicial examination. The justices expressed concern too about the "deleterious effects of even benign racial or ethnic classifications when they stray from narrow remedial justifications." As such, "any preference based on racial or ethnic criteria must necessarily receive a most searching examination to make sure that it does not conflict with constitutional guarantees."

Part of the calculation in these rulings is that heightened scrutiny minimizes the damage wrought by race awareness. *Grutter* (2003) explained that it is "designed to provide a framework for carefully examining the importance and the sincerity of the reasons advanced by the governmental decision-maker for the use of race in that particular context." *Wygant* (1986) likewise asserted that the point "is precisely to distinguish legitimate from illegitimate uses of race in governmental decision-making." Justice O'Connor's summation in *Croson* (1989) offered a more colorful description, concluding that "the purpose of strict scrutiny is to 'smoke out' illegitimate uses of race."

As to precisely what strict scrutiny entails in application, *Grutter* declared it "means that such classifications are constitutional only if they are narrowly tailored to further compelling governmental interests." This two-prong test that probes, first, the program or policy goal and, second, the means of achieving the goal was crafted in preliminary form in *Bakke*. A third requirement came in *Fisher I* (2013), where Justice Kennedy added that "strict scrutiny imposes on the university the ultimate burden of demonstrating, before turning to racial classifications, that available, workable race-neutral alternatives do not suffice." Writing for a seven-person majority, Kennedy cited the principal concurring opinion in *Bakke* and summarized that "strict scrutiny must not be strict in theory but feeble in fact."

The motives behind affirmative action do not matter. Chief Justice Roberts wrote for the five-person majority in *Parents Involved* and *Meredith*

(2007) that the danger of a motives test is that it would "do no more than move us from 'separate but equal' to 'unequal but benign.' " The two cases in *Parents Involved* concerned race-based school assignment plans voluntarily adopted by the Seattle School District and Jefferson County Public Schools in Louisville, Kentucky. The goal, as described by Seattle's expert witness, was to help minority students avoid feeling "any kind of specter of exceptionality." Roberts's response was to say, "Simply because the school districts may seek a worthy goal does not mean they are free to discriminate on the basis of race to achieve it, or that their racial classifications should be subject to less exacting scrutiny." He rejected the dissent's assertion that there was "no case that . . . repudiated [a] constitutional asymmetry between that which seeks to exclude [*sic*] and that which seeks to include [*sic*] members of minority races." On the contrary, Roberts contended, "we have found many. Our cases clearly rejected the argument that motives affect the strict scrutiny analysis." The same was expressed by Justice Kennedy in *Fisher v. Texas* (2013), who wrote it is "irrelevant that a system of racial preferences in admissions may seem benign." As a result, the 7–1–1 majority in *Fisher v. Texas* (2013) remanded the case because the Fifth Circuit failed to hold the university "to the demanding burden of strict scrutiny."[14]

For years, specifically from 1978 to 1995, congressionally approved preferential programs were held to a less exacting standard. *Fullilove* (1980) detailed at length how the US Constitution accorded Congress greater latitude to employ racial and ethnic criteria, whether as an exercise of its spending powers or as part of its commerce powers under Article I or as part of its power to enforce the equal protection clause of the Fourteenth Amendment. Burger wrote that "Congress has latitude to try new techniques such as the limited use of racial and ethnic criteria to accomplish remedial objectives." *Metro Broadcasting v. FCC* (1990) evinced even greater judicial deference to Congress. In that case two preferential policies adopted by the Federal Communications Commission (FCC) were challenged by separate petitioners as violative of the equal protection component of the Fifth Amendment. The first policy awarded an "enhancement" for minority ownership in the application process for licenses for new radio or television broadcast stations. The second program was the FCC's "distress sale" policy. It provided that a radio or television broadcaster under FCC investigation was permitted to transfer their license if the transferee was a minority enterprise that met certain requirements. The purpose of the policies—both adopted pursuant to the Communications Act of 1934—was to promote diversification of programming and to encourage minority participation in the broadcast industry.

Justice Brennan wrote for the 5–4 majority in *Metro* that included Justices White, Marshall, Blackmun, and Stevens. Upholding both FCC policies, he stated, "A majority of the Court in *Fullilove* did not apply strict scrutiny to the race-based classification at issue," but rather the lesser-stringent substantially related standard. He added that *Croson* concerned a municipality and, hence, "does not prescribe the level of scrutiny to be applied to a benign racial classification employed by Congress." In the instant case, "benign race-conscious measures mandated by Congress—even if those measures are not 'remedial' . . . are constitutionally permissible to the extent that they serve important governmental objectives within the power of Congress." Brennan read *Croson* as reaffirming the takeaway in *Fullilove*, that "race-conscious classifications adopted by Congress to address racial and ethnic discrimination are subject to a different standard than such classifications prescribed by state and local governments." *Metro*'s (1990) more relaxed "substantially related" standard proved to be short-lived and was overturned in *Adarand* (1995). There, it was held that Congress's motives must be scrutinized no less than that of other policymaking bodies under the strict scrutiny standard.

By 2003 Supreme Court jurisprudence that treated all race-based classifications are always suspect was declared "well-settled law." O'Connor's opinion in *Grutter* (2003) echoed the 1978 *Bakke* precept that governmental decisions that touch on an individual's race or ethnic background call for an exacting standard of judicial review. *Grutter* also echoed *Croson*'s (1989) sense that strict scrutiny helps courts to determine what is in fact "benign" or "remedial." In *Gratz* (2003) Chief Justice Rehnquist regarded the principle as reaffirmed over the years enough to proclaim, "It is by now well established that 'all racial classifications reviewable under the Equal Protection Clause must be strictly scrutinized.' "[15] With comparable certitude Rehnquist's successor Chief Justice John Roberts reiterated the same again in *Parents Involved* (2007).

Students for Fair Admissions (2023) held to the same view even as it teased out an additional component of strict scrutiny, namely that race-based policies be crafted so that the courts can independently measure the connection between the means and the ends. Chief Justice Roberts wrote, "Courts may not license separating students on the basis of race without an exceedingly persuasive justification that is measurable and concrete enough to permit judicial review." Under the precept of measurability the race-aware admissions programs at Harvard and the University of North Carolina could not "satisfy the burden of strict scrutiny," he argued, because they "cannot be subjected to meaningful review." The universities' interest in using race to achieve a diverse student body to promote various learning goals was "inescapably imponderable." He asked, "How is a court to know whether leaders have been adequately 'train[ed]'; whether the exchange of ideas is 'robust'; or whether 'new knowledge' is being developed?"

In addition to declaring all race awareness universally suspect, more-over, affirmative action jurisprudence overhauled also the conventional understanding of how race operates in the US. The Supreme Court opted for one that is more chameleonlike, in that it abandoned the perspective that imputes disadvantage to racial minorities and accords universal privilege to Whites. *Bakke* (1978) set the Court on a course whereby the meaning and ramifications of race would be construed on a case-by-case basis—by, first, examining the context in which a racial classification is employed and, then, deciding what "race" means in a more precise fashion.

The evolution of racial fluidity in Supreme Court opinions can be traced to a dissenting opinion in a 1974 case that the Court declined to decide on the merits. The White plaintiff in *DeFunis et al. v. Odegaard et al.* (416 U.S. 312), Marco DeFunis Jr., was denied admission to the University of Washington Law School and sued on grounds that he was discriminated against on account of his race in violation of the Fourteenth Amendment. The law school admissions process consisted of two tracks. One was for applicants who indicated they were "Black, Chicano, American Indian, or Filipino." The other relied on an index called the "Predicted First Year Average," which combined the Law School Admission Test (LSAT) score and grades in the last two years in college. The process yielded 147 applicants with averages above 77 who were admitted. Due to his 76.23 average, DeFunis was waitlisted and eventually declined, whereas 36 minority applicants with averages below 74.5 were accepted through the special admissions process. At oral argument the law school explained that if minority applicants had been considered under the same procedure as DeFunis, none would have been admitted. A *per curiam* opinion announced that, because DeFunis was already in his final year of law school and set to receive his degree regardless of how the Court ruled, the "case or controversy" requirement of Article III rendered the case moot.

At the same time that Justice Douglas's dissent pushed to remand the case to consider whether the LSATs should be eliminated due to built-in bias against minorities, he also put the concept of racial fluidity into play. He wrote, "The reservation of a proportion of the law school class for mem-bers of selected minority groups is fraught with . . . dangers, for one must immediately determine which groups are to receive such favored treatment and which are to be excluded, the proportions of the class that are to be allocated to each, and even the criteria by which to determine whether an individual is a member of a favored group." Douglas continued, musing how "the University of Washington included Filipinos, but excluded Chinese and Japanese; another school may limit its program to Blacks, or to Blacks and Chicanos."

In a similar vein *Bakke* (1978) remarked that "the concepts of 'majority' and 'minority' necessarily reflect temporary arrangements and judgments." Powell quoted extensively from Douglas's commentary in *DeFunis*. He reiterated that "the Court could attempt to assess how grievously each group has suffered from discrimination, and allocate proportions accordingly," but that "if that were the standard the current University of Washington policy would almost surely fall, for there is no Western State which can claim that it has always treated Japanese and Chinese in a fair and evenhanded manner." "Nor obviously will the problem be solved if next year the Law School included only Japanese and Chinese, for then Norwegians and Swedes, Poles and Italians, Puerto Ricans and Hungarians, and all other groups which form this diverse Nation would have just complaints."

Croson (1989) likewise negotiated race as a mutable construct. Announcing the judgment of a 6–3 majority, O'Connor hypothesized that it is "possible" that the Black majority in the Richmond, Virginia, city council may have actually disadvantaged a White minority when it adopted a minority set-aside in 1983. Fundamentally at issue was the traditional civil rights presumption that "such measures essentially involve a choice made by dominant racial groups to disadvantage themselves." In the instant case "Blacks constitute approximately 50% of the population of the city of Richmond," and "five of the nine seats on the city council are held by Blacks." This, she reasoned, raised the "concern that a *political* [emphasis added] majority will more easily act to the disadvantage of a minority," in this case Whites.

All in all, under Supreme Court reasoning from *Bakke* (1978) up to and including *Students for Fair Admissions* (2023) is that one's "race" no longer conveys anything on its own. Traditional civil rights views of what constitutes a racial minority, what constitutes a White majority, and even whether there is such a thing as a White majority and a racial minority are rendered contestable. Layered atop this is the notion that racial considerations are "seldom relevant" by Justice O'Connor's account and altogether "irrelevant," according to Chief Justice Roberts's *Parents Involved* opinion. To sort out when race matters, where, and how, judges must strictly scrutinize all race awareness, no matter the underlying motives. So must policymakers.

THE COLORBLIND PRINCIPLE

Students for Fair Admissions' (2023) extended remarks about the virtues of colorblindness is in accord not only with earlier affirmative action rulings, but also the beliefs of a sizeable segment of the American population. Chief Justice Roberts's blunt assertion in *Parents Involved* (2007) that "the way to stop discrimination on the basis of race is to stop discriminating on the basis of race" encapsulates the belief of many citizens and politicians in the US. Hoang Vu Tran may accurately characterize colorblind jurisprudence as an "act of Whiteness," one that refuses to recognize the salience of race.[16] But, the fact is, everyday Americans share the Court's beliefs about the colorblind principle, and the justices' unease with race awareness. They are uncomfortable with merely discussing racial issues. The 2016 Moore/YouGov survey asked a nationally representative sample of 1,000 "whether we talk about racial issues too much in this country." The results show that roughly three out of five believe that we do. The aversion is more apparent when race and merit are juxtaposed to one another.

That the public is sold on the notion of meritocracy is also reflected in the table 3.1 data. The 2016 YouGov/Moore survey also asked whether respondents agree with the statement "It is never okay to take into account a person's race when dealing with that person, such as in hiring, college admissions, renting apartments, and so on." As shown, a decisive 81 percent stated that they strongly or somewhat agreed, with 66 percent "strongly" agreeing and 15 percent "somewhat" agreeing. As well, the 2019 Pew Research Center American Trends Panel surveys (Wave 43) show a supermajority (74%) of the country believes in meritocracy. They believe that, when it comes to college admissions and decisions about hiring and promotions, companies and organizations should only take a person's qualifications into account, even if it results in less diversity. This includes a majority of Whites (78%), Hispanics (69%), as well as Blacks (54%). Specifically in regard to colleges and universities there is a supermajority consensus of 73 percent that believe race should not be a factor. The consensus breaks down by race so that 62 percent of Blacks, 78 percent of Whites, and 65 percent of Hispanics lean toward meritocratic ideals. Gallup trend data in Figure 3.1 show the same, that more than three-quarters of Americans reject race consciousness.

Table 3.1. Attitudes Toward the Colorblind Principle, US, 2016, 2019, 2023

Year	Survey Question	Select Responses (%)
2023	As you may know, some colleges and universities around the country are selective, which means they have many more applicants than they can admit. One of the factors some of these colleges take into account in admissions decisions is race and ethnicity, in order to increase the racial and ethnic diversity of the school. Do you approve of this practice?[a]	Strongly/somewhat disapprove: 50 Strongly/somewhat approve: 33
2023	Please tell us if you believe the following should be major considerations, minor considerations, or not considered at all for college/university admissions: Race or ethnicity.[b]	Should not be considered at all: 62 Major/minor consideration: 38
2022	Should a student's race ever be considered when evaluating their admission to college?[c]	No: 68 Yes: 19
2019	When it comes to decisions about hiring and promotions, do you think companies and organizations should only take a person's qualifications into account, even if it results in less diversity in the workplace?[d]	Only take qualifications into account: 74
2019	Here are some factors colleges and universities may consider when making decisions about student admissions. Do you think each of the following should be a major factor, minor factor, or not a factor in college admissions?[e]	Race-Ethnicity should not be a factor: 73
2019	When it comes to improving race relations, do you think it is more important for people to focus on . . .[f]	What different racial and ethnic groups have in common: 55
2016	Do you believe that we talk about racial issues too much in this country?[g]	Yes: 57

continued on next page

Table 3.1. Continued.

Year	Survey Question	Select Responses (%)
2016	It is never okay to take into account a person's race when dealing with that person, such as in hiring, college admissions, renting apartments, and so on.[g]	Strongly/somewhat agree: 81

Sources:

[a]Pew Research Center. (2023, June 8). More Americans disapprove than approve of colleges considering race, ethnicity in admissions decisions. https://www.pewresearch.org/politics/2023/06/08/more-americans-disapprove-than-approve-of-colleges-considering-race-ethnicity-in-admissions-decisions.

[b]Borter, G. (2023, February 15). Most Americans think college admissions should not consider race—Reuters/Ipsos poll. Accessed 1/17/2024 from: https://www.reuters.com/world/us/most-americans-think-college-admissions-should-not-consider-race-reutersipsos-2023-02-15/.

[c]YouGov. (2022, April 12–18). Last accessed 2/12/2025 from: https://today.yougov.com/politics/articles/42233-affirmative-action-yougov-poll-april-12-18-2022.

[d]Horowitz, J. M. (2019, May 8). Americans see advantages and challenges in country's growing racial and ethnic diversity. Pew Research Center. https://www.pewresearch.org/social-trends/2019/05/08/americans-see-advantages-and-challenges-in-countrys-growing-racial-and-ethnic-diversity/.

[e]Graf, N. (2019, February 25). *Most Americans say colleges should not consider race or ethnicity in admissions.* Pew Research Center. https://www.pewresearch.org/fact-tank/2019/02/25/most-americans-say-colleges-should-not-consider-race-or-ethnicity-in-admissions/.

[f]Horowitz, J. M., Brown, A., & Cox, K. (2019, April 9). Race in America 2019. Pew Research Center. https://www.pewsocialtrends.org/wp-content/uploads/sites/3/2019/04/PewResearchCenter_RaceStudy_FINAL-1.pdf.

[g]Moore, N./YouGov. (2016, September 3–6). *Racial Profiling Omnibus.*

Crosby's *Affirmative Action Is Dead; Long Live Affirmative Action* shares that "America's infatuation with justice seems to be a major reason, perhaps the major reason, why affirmative action has not received unwavering support."[17] This, even though a number of scholars challenge the notion of an American meritocracy. For instance, Duster points out that a 4.0 grade point average is often a function of both grade inflation in high schools and "advanced placement" courses, adding that wealthy students can take these special courses and increase their grade point averages significantly. Duster thus concludes that "a 4.0 GPA may simply indicate that the student had access to these advanced placement courses. In poorer areas . . . the great

Figure 3.1. Public Support for Colorblindness. *Source*: Gallup. (n.d.). In Depth: Topics A to Z, Race Relations. Last accessed 5/10/2022 from https://news.gallup.com/poll/1687/Race-Relations.aspx.

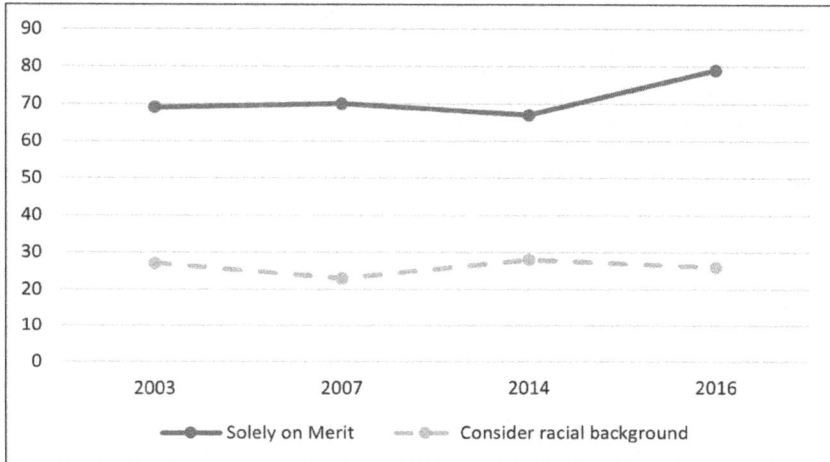

majority do not offer any advanced placement courses."[18] Meanwhile, Piven says that, aside from the class bias problem, meritocracy arguments are also morally ambiguous because "individual merit was never the main basis for success and failure in American life. . . . Harvard's admissions criteria, for example, included alumni set-asides long before they included minority set-asides—and most people knew it."[19]

The symmetry between the Supreme Court and political parties regarding race awareness is not as seamless as that between the Court and the general public. Democratic leaders do not believe that race is unavoidably challenging, whereas Republicans do, at least in principle. In the late 1960s Democrats hesitated to tackle racial problems as *racial* problems, something we glean from the fact that they balked at confronting the race riots of 1967 as principally *racial*. Their party platform reflected on the Kerner Commission report in a way that dodged its bottom line conclusion that the nation was "moving toward two societies, one Black, one White—separate and unequal."[20] The platform instead pledged a campaign against lawlessness "by attack on the root causes of crime and disorder,"[21] with no mention of the racial dimensions of the rioting or the role that systemic discrimination and police profiling played in precipitating the disorders, as detailed in the Kerner Commission report. During the same time period, Republicans were less reticent to confront racial dynamics head-on. By their estimation, "fire and looting, causing millions of dollars of property damage, have brought great suffering to home owners and small businessmen, particularly in Black communities least able to absorb catastrophic losses."[22] Aside from this 1968 outlier, however, Democrats have consistently rejected colorblindness. By 2020 they framed race awareness as not only justified but necessary, contending that "race-neutral policies are not sufficient to rectify race-based disparities."[23]

The National Republican Party has consistently locked arms with the Supreme Court in regard to colorblindness by declaring all race awareness wrongheaded, such as in their 1992 plank titled "Constitution and its guarantee of color-blind opportunity."[24] In 2008 they adopted the standout line in Chief Justice John Roberts's *Parents Involved* (2007) opinion and proclaimed, "We affirm the commonsense approach of the Chief Justice of the United States: that the way to stop discriminating on the basis of race is to stop discriminating."[25] In more recent elections Republicans continue to maintain that "merit, ability, aptitude, and results should be the factors that determine achievement in our society."[26] Later in chapter 5 we learn that while Republicans are closer to the Court's ideological positioning around colorblindness, they nonetheless advocate a range of race-aware policies, such as economic and educational policies that entail special outreach to racial minorities.

Additionally in presidential politics we observe a deracialization process that, in part, parallels the Supreme Court's rendering of race as inherently problematic. It is a process in which presidents endorse certain race-conscious policies and simultaneously praise the colorblind ideal. President Bill Clinton did much to advance deracialization on this front. He practiced colorblind and race-conscious politics at once. Clinton began by ordering a review of race-conscious federal affirmative action programs to determine whether the programs were effective. A move that clearly leaned into race neutrality was renaming of the Minority Small Business and Capital Ownership Development Program as the "8(a) Business Development Programs." The name change was expressly purposed "to emphasize that individuals need not be members of minority groups and to stress the importance of assisting participating firms in their overall business development."[27] In public statements Clinton stressed that affirmative action should not involve hiring unqualified persons.[28] Like the Court, he landed on the proposition that "all of us should embrace the vision of a colorblind society, but recognize the fact that we are not there yet."[29]

Clinton's predecessors and successors likewise advocated colorblindness and race awareness at once. President Nixon signed amendments to Title VII in the Equal Employment Opportunity Act of 1972 that the Supreme Court later relied upon as proof that Congress approved of race-conscious remedies. Presidents Reagan, Bush I, and Bush II, as well as Trump all boasted about their support for historically Black colleges and universities (HBCU). This includes Trump's Proclamation 9642 that honored HBCU week and hosted an HBCU summit.[30] All actively promoted federal funding for minority business enterprises (MBE).

On August 17, 2015, President Donald J. Trump insinuated tacit support for affirmative action in in an interview with television journalist Chuck Todd on NBC's *Meet the Press*, as follows:[31]

> CHUCK TODD: Affirmative action. Should we keep it? Yes or no.

> DONALD TRUMP: I'm fine with affirmative action. I mean, I think—

> CHUCK TODD: Should it be expanded? Or should it—

> DONALD TRUMP:—we've been having—

> CHUCK TODD:—be limited?

> DONALD TRUMP: Well, you know, you have to also go free market. You have to go capability. You have to do a lot of things. But I'm fine with affirmative action. We've lived with it for a long time. And I lived with it for a long time. And I've had great relationships with lots of people. So I'm fine with it.

These same presidents practiced their brand of colorblind politics. Richard Nixon's objections to racial busing led to calls for a national moratorium on busing and an amendment to the US Constitution. Reagan urged in a radio address on Dr. Martin Luther King, "We want a colorblind society, a society that, in the words of Dr. King, judges people 'not by the color of their skin, but by the content of their character.' "[32] The Bush I administration discouraged race-specific policies in 2008 guidance issued by the Department of Education for elementary, secondary, and postsecondary student admissions.[33] In remarks at the Journalists of Color Convention in 2004, Bush II commented on the University of Michigan affirmative action cases, expressing his belief that, "in terms of admissions policy, race-neutral admissions policies ought to be tried."[34] Importantly, however, Bush II continued saying, "If they don't work to achieve an objective, which is diversification, race ought to be a factor."[35]

Once elected to office in 2016 Trump did an about-face, indicating that he was no longer "fine" with affirmative action. He signed Executive Order 13950 that insisted, "Our Federal civil service system is based on merit principles. These principles, codified at 5 U.S.C. 2301, call for all employees to 'receive fair and equitable treatment in all aspects of person-nel management without regard to' race or sex 'and with proper regard for their . . . constitutional rights.'" Furthermore, "instructing Federal employees that treating individuals on the basis of individual merit is racist or sexist directly undermines our Merit System Principles and impairs the efficiency of the Federal service."[36]

President Joe Biden's January 20, 2021, Executive Order 13985 reflected a measure of apprehension vis-à-vis focusing solely on "racial equity" in his administration's efforts to "affirmatively advance equity, civil rights, racial justice, and equal opportunity." While the order directed each federal agency to "assess whether, and to what extent, its programs and policies perpetuate systemic barriers to opportunities and benefits for people of color and other underserved groups,"[37] immediately afterward a report of Biden's Civil Rights Division interpreted the order as designed to be as race- and gender-neutral as possible.[38] The report lauded the order for empowering federal agencies to implement a broad range of programs to expand equity and diversity "without triggering a heightened standard of review." As of this writing little has been said by Biden as to his own views directly on the utility of race consciousness, a striking contrast with his former boss Barack Obama, who strove for transparent compliance with Supreme Court rulings but at the same time called out the suspect nature of meritocracy politics.

President Barack Obama took the bold step of calling out the dou-ble standard in how the colorblind ideal is invoked. In an interview with Ta-Nehisi Coates he said:

> You know, I always talk about when I was doing civil-rights law and people would talk about the dearth of African Americans in police departments and fire departments around the country.

And they would say, "Well, this should be a meritocracy, and everybody needs to take a test, and that's objective, and anything else is affirmative action and unfair." And I'm thinking, "Well, when Officer O'Malley or Officer Krupke was walking the beat, nobody said it was a meritocracy then." What happened? We're suddenly now of the notion that somebody who's a police officer or firefighter having some affinity and familiarity with the community they are serving is completely out of bounds. What changed?[39]

Nevertheless, Obama too was mindful of the challenges posed by race consciousness. The result was that his administration walked a fine line in crafting guidelines for compliance with the Court's strict scrutiny standard, while pushing the envelope in an effort to preserve affirmative action. We see this in the 2011 guidance issued by the Departments of Justice and Education. Concerning the voluntary use of race to achieve diversity and avoid isolation in elementary, secondary, and postsecondary schools, the guidance encouraged institutions to "consider whether it can meet its compelling interest in diversity by using race-neutral approaches."[40] The guidance also set forth a workaround that employed race at the aggregate level, but not in relation to an individual's race.[41]

Beyond the world of elected politicians, Chief Justice Roberts's aspirational ideal of a colorless society is lauded by famous adherents in every field—from entertainment to sports. Academy award–winning actor Morgan Freeman and other popular figures publicly register their own distaste for race awareness. Freeman channeled the chief justice's sentiments in an interview with CBS's *60 Minutes* reporter Mike Wallace. When Wallace asked Freeman, "How are you going to get rid of racism?" Freeman replied, "Stop talking about it. I'm going to stop calling you a White man . . . And I'm going to ask you to stop calling me a Black man."[42] Star of one of the highest grossing films in 2009, *Avatar*, Zoe Saldana echoed Freeman's sentiments in an interview with *Ebony* magazine's Kelley L. Carter. Saldana stated she was not going to talk about racism, that "it's an elephant. We all see it, we all know it, but I'm not going to carry it in my heart, because I want to be a person that embodies change. Not embodies war or battles or bitterness; I want to keep moving on."[43]

The Court's reformulation of race as a function of context likewise corresponds with popular news that casts doubt on the idea that race has a fixed meaning. Among the high-profile examples are former presidential candidate Elizabeth Warren's claims of Native American ancestry (and proffer of a DNA test to prove it) and the late iconic pop star Michael Jackson and golf legend Tiger Woods's embrace of multi-racial identity. The go-to for colorblind advocates is Dr. Martin L. King's 1963 "I Have a Dream" speech. This, even though Randall Kennedy carefully details how Dr. King propounded ideas that comport with affirmative action. Reflecting on American slavery King declared that ancient common law provided for "a massive program by the government in special, compensatory measures which could be regarded as a settlement" of the appropriation of the labor of one human being by another.[44]

SECTION SUMMARY

The takeaway from the foregoing discussion is that Supreme Court justices' sense that all forms of race consciousness are suspect comes closer to mass attitudes as compared to presidential and party politics. Average Americans believe that the country is overly preoccupied with racial matters. The overwhelming majority—fully 81 percent—believe that "it is never okay to take into account a person's race when dealing with that person." The same regarding meritocracy, including a majority of Whites, Hispanics, and Blacks. Politicians, on the other hand, more often straddle the fence when it comes to colorblindness. The Court's aversion to race is at odds with Democrats embrace of race awareness. Meanwhile, Republicans endorse race neutrality in principle; yet, they tout their commitment of major federal funding to historically Black colleges and universities (HBCUs).

In presidential politics we observe a partial deracialization process. President Clinton advocated universal policies at the same time that he admitted the need for affirmative action. A similar two-step was practiced by Presidents Reagan, Bush I, and Bush II, all of whom argued for race neutrality as they bragged about supporting Republicans' minority business enterprise programs. Even Trump displayed a double mind, expressing support for affirmative action in 2015 then barring race-conscious hiring in the federal civil service toward the end of his first term. In speeches and executive actions Presidents Obama and Biden expressed skepticism as to whether meritocracy truly exists, and at the same time conceded the enormous difficulty of allocating benefits on a racial basis. Put simply, political elites have wrestled more earnestly with the colorblind ideal than have Supreme Court justices and the lay public.

Mind Over Matter

Supreme Court justices repeatedly reject the idea that racial disparity constitutes racism. They believe that material inequality along racial lines is not violative of the Constitution or federal civil rights laws, no matter how entrenched or pervasive. This precept is anchored within a larger anti-discrimination legal framework that stacks the deck against disparate claims. Hoang Vu Tran criticizes the emphasis on equal opportunity versus equal results as tied to a lack of receptivity to claims that structural racism is real and impactful. Whereas the Warren Court "emanated a racial understanding that focused on special practices and material life," the post-Warren Courts have not.[45] In what follows we see that not only inside the courthouse, but outside the courthouse too, racism is less and less about the lived experience of racial minorities and more a matter of the mind. Throughout the country racial matters are increasingly negotiated through a lens predominately trained on something other than concretes like measurable racial inequality and minority socioeconomic disadvantage.

INEQUALITY AND THE COURT

The Supreme Court's elevation of mind over matter was accomplished across several rulings. Earl E. Pollock's *Race and the Supreme Court: Defining Equality* details at least 10 types of equality—moral equality, equality of individuals, equality of groups, civil equality, political equality, social equality, gender equality, equality of access, equality of result, and equality of opportunity.[46] It is the latter that the Supreme Court validates. Under affirmative action case law, the socioeconomic gap between Blacks and Whites is permissible under the US Constitution.

The Court declared as much in 2007 when it asserted that "the Constitution is not violated by racial imbalance in the schools, without more." The occasion was companion cases in which the justices squarely confronted the question whether racial disparities are per se problematic, *Parents Involved Community v. Seattle School District* and *Meredith v. Jefferson County*. The stated intent of the set-aside plans was to correct de facto school segregation. In the Seattle, Washington, school district and the Jefferson County school district in metropolitan Louisville, Kentucky, students were assigned to a school "so that the racial balance at the school [fell] within a predetermined range based on the racial composition of the school district as a whole."

In Seattle's oversubscribed schools the district employed a tiebreaker that favored those whose race would "serve to bring the school into balance." In the Jefferson County district, if a school was racially segregated then "a student whose race would contribute to the school's racial imbalance" would not be assigned there. Both plans were invalidated on appeal. Chief Justice Roberts's Court opinion chided Justice Breyer's dissent for eliding the "distinction between *de jure* and *de facto* segregation," and for intimating that the patterns of school attendance in and of themselves reflected "illegal segregation." As far as Roberts was concerned, the district court already determined that "Jefferson County had eliminated the vestiges of prior segregation," despite the persistence of de facto segregation.

Earlier decisions had already fortified the majority's stance in *Parents*. *Croson* (1989) elaborated the constitutional-legal insignificance of racial unevenness. Justice O'Connor's majority opinion declared that "the statistics comparing the minority population of Richmond to the percentage of *prime* [*sic*] contracts awarded to minority firms had little or no probative value in establishing prior discrimination." The statistics showed that minority businesses received 0.67 percent of prime city contracts, even though minorities constituted 50 percent of the city's population. By O'Connor's estimation, an inference of discriminatory exclusion cannot arise from the mere fact of disproportionately low Black participation in an industry or trade organization. Disparity, "standing alone, cannot establish a prima facie case of discrimination."[47]

Also liberal Justice Brennan's opinion for the Court a few years later in *Sheet Metal Workers v. EEOC* (1986) stressed that during the 1964 civil rights proceedings in Congress "supporters of the bill insisted that employers would not violate Title VII simply because of racial imbalance, and emphasized that neither the Commission nor the courts could compel employers to adopt quotas solely to facilitate racial balancing." To "assuage opponents' fears," they agreed to insert language that stipulated employers, schools and labor unions could not be forced to achieve racial balance. Justice Powell's principal opinion in *Bakke* (1978) had earlier criticized Brennan's dissent in that case for misconceiving the scope of prior rulings on Title VII of the Civil Rights Act of 1964 and by suggesting that ""disparate impact" alone is sufficient to establish a violation of that statute."

Affirmative action case law is anchored within a larger constitutional-legal doctrine that stacks the deck against racial disparate claims across the board. As opposed to pervasive measurable social, political, economic, educational, and housing inequality, conclusive for the Court is whether the inequality is intentional. A sharp line of demarcation was drawn between "discriminatory intent" and "discriminatory impact" decades ago in two cases that addressed race discrimination claims, *Washington v. Davis* (1976)[48] and *Arlington Heights v. Metropolitan Housing Development Corp.* (1977).[49] Both held that discriminatory intent must be proven to establish a violation of the equal protection clause (EPC) of the Fourteenth Amendment. Absent evidence that racial imbalances are the product of intentional disparate treatment, such imbalances cannot be faulted under the EPC.

Pro-affirmative action rulings equally reinforce the Court's consensus on racial balancing. The district court in *U.S. v. Paradise* (1987) found that the Alabama Department of Public Safety intentionally excluded Blacks from employment as state troopers for almost four decades. Consequently, the court imposed a one-for-one hiring quota in 1972, so that the department was to hire one Black trooper for each White trooper until Blacks reached 25 percent of the force. Later in 1979 and again in 1981 and 1983, the National Association for the Advancement of Colored People (NAACP) sought and obtained relief for noncompliance in the form of court-ordered promotion quotas. The district court-ordered plan was upheld by Supreme Court Justices Brennan, Marshall, Blackmun, and Powell, but for reasons unrelated to persistent racial disparity in the trooper ranks. Writing for the panel, Brennan highlighted at several points in his opinion that the imbalance itself was not the problem. Instead, it was the "Department's pervasive, systematic, and obstinate discriminatory exclusion of Blacks. . . . The one-for-one mechanism was employed not to punish the Department's failure to achieve racial balance, but to remedy the Department's refusal to fulfill the commitment made in the consent decrees." Under this reasoning, Brennan wrote, "the racial imbalances in the Department are properly characterized as the effects of the Department's past discriminatory actions."

Preferential rulings go so far as to shield a practice known to exacerbate workplace disparities between White and minority employees, namely seniority systems.[50] Commenting on one such case, Ronald J. Fiscus argued against seniority and observed that "at least some of the Whites in *Stotts* would not have had seniority had it not been for past discrimination, at least some of them were not entitled to have their jobs protected at the expense of Black firefighters with less seniority."[51] In *Firefighters Local Union No. 1784 v. Stotts et al.* (1984) a federal district court invalidated a Memphis, Tennessee, Fire Department seniority system. Blacks in the department, Carl Stotts and Fred Jones, brought a class action charging that the department and city officials engaged in a pattern of hiring and promoting on the basis of race, in violation of Title VII of the Civil Rights Act of 1964. A settlement was reached and a consent decree entered by the court. When budgetary constraints necessitated layoffs, the court temporarily ordered the city to "not apply the seniority policy proposed insofar as it will decrease the percentage of Black lieutenants, drivers, inspectors and privates that are presently employed." A modified layoff plan approved by the district court avoided the racialized effects of the seniority system.

For the US Supreme Court, the central issue was whether the modified plan to minimize racial impacts was justified. Justices White, Burger, Powell, Rehnquist, O'Connor, and Stevens concluded that it was not. The fact that the fire department's seniority system disproportionately disadvantaged Black employees was not dispositive. The six-person majority rejected plaintiff's argument that the district court could bar the seniority-based layoff plan if the racial disparity allegations had been proven on the record. For the majority Justice White concluded that in order to override senior systems, lower courts must find that "the Blacks protected from layoff had been a victim of discrimination."

Supreme Court justices do not believe that racial inequality is the product of societal discrimination but rather broader forces, a point expounded in the *Ricci v. DeStefano* (2009) opinion. Justice Kennedy's opinion for the Court relied heavily on witness testimony that insisted racial differences in the New Haven, Connecticut, firefighter test results were symptoms of a pervasive problem of racial inequality that existed throughout the US, not just in New Haven or in connection with its civil service test. Kennedy spotlighted the testimony of Professor Janet Helms of Boston College, whom he described as an expert on race and culture. She asserted that "regardless of what kind of written test we give in this country . . . we can just about predict how many people will pass who are members of under-represented groups." She concluded, "No matter what test the City had administered, it would have revealed 'a disparity between Blacks and Whites, Hispanics and Whites, particularly on a written test.'" The Court upheld the test results.

POLITICS OF RACIAL DISPARITY

The same disconnect from material inequality that is observed in affirmative action case law is evident also on the main fronts of national American politics. We see this in public opinion data that, for much of the country, affirmative action is literally a matter of the mind more than measurable disadvantage. While it is thorny for a sizeable swath of the country, a large majority of Americans admit they are not directly impacted by racial preferences. Across four decades the overwhelming percentage report that they have never been passed over, discriminated against, or otherwise affected by a preferential program at work or school. Table 3.2 further details 1991 through

Table 3.2. Personal Experience with Affirmative Action, US, 1991–2023, Select Years

Year	Survey Question	Select Responses (%)
2023	Do you think that you have ever been at a disadvantage in your education, career, or job because of efforts to increase racial and ethnic diversity?[a]	No: 57
2016	How concerned are you about so-called reverse racism, or discrimination against White people, impacting your life: very concerned, somewhat concerned, not so concerned, or not concerned at all? (Quinnipiac University Poll, September 16, 2016)	Not so concerned/not at all: 57
2013	Do you believe that you have been affected by affirmative action (a policy that qualified minorities should be given special preferences in hiring and education) in higher education or the workplace? (Institute of Politics, August 30, 2013)	No: 62
2007	In your own personal career and education, have you ever been helped or hurt by an affirmative action program, or has this never affected you? (NPR/Pew Research Center, November 13, 2007)	Not personally affected: 82
2003	In your own personal career and education, have you ever been helped or hurt by an affirmative action program, or has this never affected you? Helped or hurt? (Pew Research Center, May 14, 2003)	No: 82
1999	I'm going to read to you a list of things that some people are worried about, but others are not. For each, I want you to tell me if that is something that worries you a great deal, worries you a good amount, worries you just a little, or doesn't worry you at all. Affirmative action may have gone too far to give some Blacks unfair advantages over Whites. (*Washington Post*, November 7, 1999)	Worry little/not at all: 69

continued on next page

Table 3.2. Continued.

Year	Survey Question	Select Responses (%)
1995	In your opinion, have you personally or has someone you know ever been discriminated against because of an affirmative action program for minorities or women? (*Time*/CNN/Yankelovich, March 28, 1995)	No: 71
1995	Have you personally ever thought that a racial minority where you worked got an undeserved job or promotion as a result of affirmative action programs? (*USA Today*, March 24, 1995)	No: 69
1995	Have you, yourself, ever received a job or educational opportunity as part of an affirmative action program designed to help minorities or women get ahead, or haven't you ever received such an opportunity? (*Los Angeles Times*, March 22, 1995)	No: 89
1995	Have you personally ever been helped or harmed by affirmative action? (NBC News/*Wall Street Journal* Poll, March 1995)	Not helped: 90 Not harmed: 84
1991	Have you personally or has someone you know ever been discriminated against because of an affirmative action program for Blacks? (*Time*/CNN/Yankelovich, April 29, 1991)	Yes—personally: 9 Yes—know someone: 15 No: 74

Source: Except where indicated otherwise, survey data in the table obtained from *Polling the nations*. (n.d.). Topic: Affirmative action. Last accessed 4/25/2022 from https://ptn-infobase-com.exlibris.colgate.edu/topics/VG9waWM6NTI=?aid=14265.

[a]Pew Research Center. (2023, June 8). More Americans disapprove than approve of colleges considering race, ethnicity in admissions decisions. https://www.pewresearch.org/politics/2023/06/08/more-americans-disapprove-than-approve-of-colleges-considering-race-ethnicity-in-admissions-decisions.

2023 surveys that show sizeable majorities do not believe that they will be personally affected (whether hurt or helped) by preferential policies. Such a disconnect between public perception and reality is additionally evident in public assessments of the socioeconomic condition of Black America. Most US adults concede that Blacks fare worse than Whites on the economic scale, but still feel that conditions have improved for Blacks. The General

Social Survey trend data in figure 3.2 show that respondents are much more likely to rank Black wealth toward the bottom of the seven-point scale (5, 6, and 7) than White wealth. In 2018, 7 percent ranked Whites at the bottom, compared to a sizeable 57 percent who ranked Blacks at the bottom. Despite such grim assessments, according to the Gallup data in figure 3.3, until recently most were nonetheless very satisfied or somewhat satisfied with "the position of Blacks and other racial minorities in the nation."

Major political parties' tendency toward "happy talk" is akin to Supreme Court justices' detachment from material inequality. The fact that Democrats and Republicans typically highlight progress around election time could be chalked up to grist for the mill. Except that, against the backdrop of America's perennial and pervasive race problem, bipartisan "happy talk" and Whitewashing are not without consequences. Political messaging that homes in on progress in an unqualified way necessarily counterbalances policy attention to the need for reform and improvement. Showcasing anecdotal evidence as proof of "strides" diminishes the urgency of structural reform.

Both Democrats and Republicans channeled their energies to underscore racial minority gains during the 1980s. They did so against the backdrop of a growing racially conservative public mood, White backlash in urban areas,

Figure 3.2. Assessment of Black and White Wealth. *Source*: Davern, M., Bautista, R., Freese, J., Morgan, S. L., & Smith, T. W. (n.d.). *General social surveys, 1972–2021*. NORC, 2021: NORC at the University of Chicago [producer and distributor]. Last accessed 2/16/2021, from the GSS Data Explorer website at gssdataexplorer.norc.org.

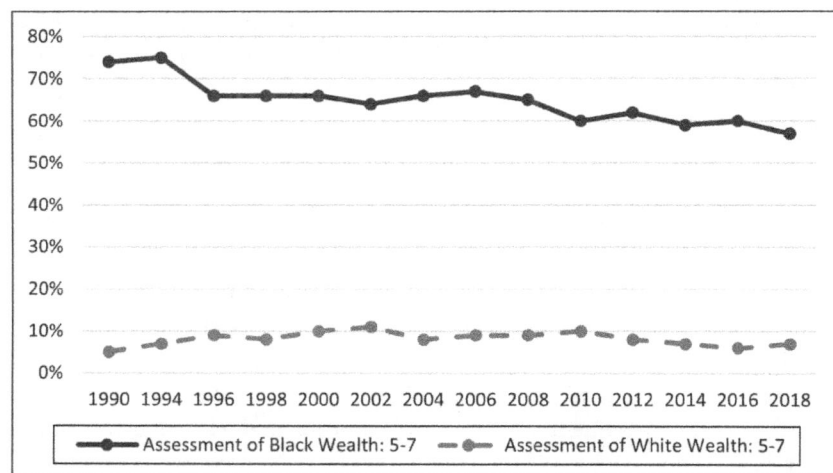

Figure 3.3. Satisfaction with Position of Blacks and Other Racial Minorities. *Source*: Gallup. (n.d.). In Depth: Topics A to Z, Race Relations. Last accessed 5/10/2022 from file:///C:/Users/nmoore/Downloads/210203SatifactionIssues.pdf.

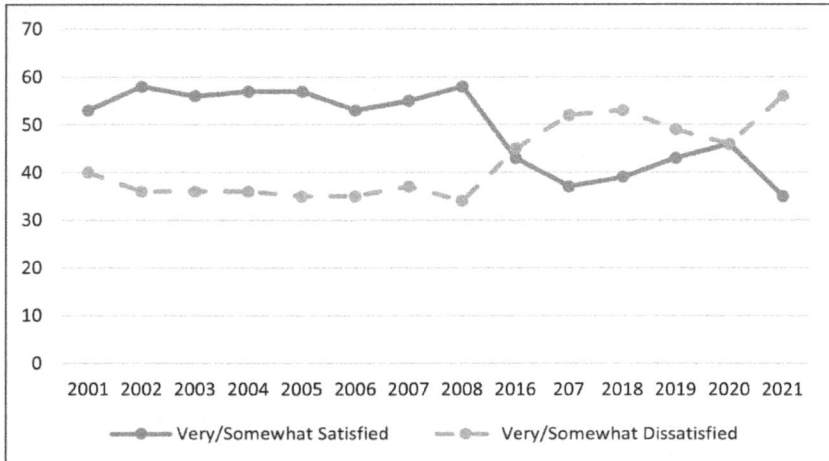

and major cuts in federal funding for social programs and services. As civil rights leaders were sounding the alarm about a rollback of civil rights gains, Republicans were gloating that for "millions of Black Americans, Hispanic Americans, Asian Americans, and members of other minority groups, the past four years [had] seen a dramatic improvement in their ability to secure for themselves and for their children a better tomorrow."[52] Near the close of the '80s they touted their strategy to "defeat discrimination by fostering opportunity for all" and highlighted a 14 percent rise in real income for Black families between 1982 and 1988.[53] This was enough for them to declare that "upward mobility for all Americans has come back strong." Similar lines about minority gains were rehearsed on the other side. Liberals more often spotlight the disproportional impact of economic recessions on "Blacks, Hispanics, other minorities, women and older workers." But when they control the White House or Congress, Democratic leaders pivot to boasting about the gains made by "all groups." During the 1970s they centered attention on the 8.5 million new jobs added to the workforce, highlighting that "about 1 million of those jobs are held by Blacks, and nearly an additional 1 million are held by Hispanics."[54] Well into the 2000s record low unemployment for African Americans and Hispanics remained a key talking point for the Left.[55]

Meanwhile, in presidential politics, shifting political winds brought the White House into closer alignment with the Supreme Court's minimal regard for material inequality. This shift is best captured by President Bill Clinton's Executive Order 13050 and its emphasis on intangibles. The order established the President's Advisory Board on Race in June 1997. Three of the four directives given to the board were to "advise the President on matters involving race and race reconciliation" concerning dialogue, understanding, tensions, and ways to specifically

> (1) Promote a constructive national dialogue to confront and work through challenging issues that surround race; (2) Increase the Nation's understanding of our recent history of race relations and the course our Nation is charting on issues of race relations and racial diversity; (3) Bridge racial divides by encouraging leaders in communities throughout the Nation to develop and implement innovative approaches to calming racial tensions; (4) Identify, develop, and implement solutions to problems in areas in which race has a substantial impact, such as education, economic opportunity, housing, health care, and the administration of justice.[56]

Civil rights leaders criticized the final report of the board for having failed to advance meaningfully concrete policy reforms.[57] The board itself terminated within one year of its start, on September 30, 1998, under a sunset clause.

After Clinton, the presidential politics of race tilted even more toward abstractions. Personal transgressions, verbal slip-ups, and long-past missteps increasingly occupy the center stage of racial discourse. President Donald Trump expended considerably more time and energy in 2020 on bashing then-candidate Joe Biden's decades-old transgressions on the race front than on Joe Biden's 2020 agenda for building back Black America. Trump called out Biden's advocacy of the 1994 crime bill and its racialized effects.[58] His administration released a statement detailing a long list of things that Biden allegedly did wrong decades ago. Trump's backward-looking attacks were matched by candidate Biden's preoccupation with the racially charged statements that Trump made over the course of his first four years in office and his decades in the public eye in New York—from his attacks on the Central Park Five to birtherism.

A similar preoccupation with insubstantial faux pas is manifest too in developments on the ground. The amount of news coverage of measurable deprivation is eclipsed by that devoted to symbols and word choices. During the run-up to the 2020 election, racial reform advocates expended a not insignificant amount of political capital on the removal of Confederate memorials and statues from public spaces. Nearly 168 Confederate symbols were removed in 2020, as noted earlier.[59] Some through government action, others by protesters. Virtually all removals were in response to the murder of an unarmed Black man, George Floyd, by a White police officer. And while their removal is a net plus for the cause of racial justice, it is not the stuff of yesterday's civil rights politics wherein legislative enactments to equalize access to housing, employment, education, and voting at the federal and state level were the measure of productive political insurgency.[60] Removal of "Color Only/White Only" signs and other front-facing signs were a by-product of transformative, macro-scaled anti-desegregation laws—not the overriding goal.

The Court's detachment from the lived experience of racial minorities is furthermore paralleled by political bouts in the national arena over academic theories, verbal slights, and soundbites. Former President Donald J. Trump was called to task by liberal advocates for telling four minority congressional representatives to "go back" to where they came from. Extended media conversations focused on whether he used the "N" word in the past. Outrage followed his "very fine people on both sides" comment in connection with the Charleston, North Carolina, White nationalist rally. Alongside these phenomena are others, such as recriminations over mispronunciation of Vice President Kamala Harris's name, failure to use the appropriate "people of color" term versus the derisive, historically rooted "colored people," whether to capitalize the term "Black" or not, whether "slaved" or "enslaved." These episodes play out alongside others in regard to microaggressions, cultural appropriation, and the like. Most are disconnected from actual social and economic policy change as the Supreme Court's disregard for racial imbalance. The fact that social media is the dominant platform for much of the day-to-day stuff of racial discourse partly evidences the trivialization of racial matters. Such trivialization is less likely on the congressional or state legislative floor where formal policy provisions are crafted, debated, enacted, and implemented with a view toward tackling the racial status quo. The superficiality fits Luskin, McIver, and Carmines's scholarly assessment of race as more prone to emotionalism than other political subjects and among the "easy" issues in American politics that typically do not involve much cognitive effort, but mostly habitual emotional response.[61]

The polity's conflation of major and minor racial matters is matched by the considerable political bandwidth allocated to critical race theory (CRF), a higher education curricular controversy that impacts fewer than

25 percent of Blacks who are able to attend as well as afford college. President Barack Obama used the term "bandwidth" to convey the idea that there is only so much of a window of opportunity for proponents of change to capture public attention and make headway on the ground.[62] The controversy over CRT upstages weightier policy discussions about the inferior quality of elementary and high school education in inner city public school districts, something that impacts nearly everyone in Black and Brown communities. CRT consumes more bandwidth than the more fundamental problem of limited access to higher education, residential resegregation and gentrification, the structural disintegration wrought by mass incarceration and overcriminalization and overpolicing, together with widespread abuse of solitary confinement, and myriad other policy problems. The uproar over another theory, replacement theory, is of a similar ilk, coupled with the implied notion that White supremacists need a theoretical framework to rationalize racial bigotry.

The overarching point here is that, on balance, in the same way that the affirmative action jurisprudence discounts the lived experience, the dominant mode of national racial politics tips the scale in the same direction.

SECTION SUMMARY

In summary, the Supreme Court's minimal regard for material racial inequality is mirrored across the polity. In the same way that the Court gazes past stark racial imbalances, a majority of Americans too acknowledge that Black wealth lags well behind White wealth while being nonetheless satisfied with "the position of Blacks." Another layer to the public's disconnect rests on the fact that large majorities deem affirmative action problematic at the same time as conceding they are not personally affected by it. Democrats as well as Republicans regularly elevate mind over matter. Both tout Black progress when it is in their best interest to do so, even though such posturing undercuts the urgency of pervasive, entrenched racial inequality. The groundwork for a shift away from concretes and toward intangibles was laid by the Clinton administration. By the time 2016 and 2020 election cycles rolled around, Donald J. Trump and Joseph R. Biden were trading blows on personal failures far and above actual policy success and failures. So did many news media outlets and reform advocates who devoted finite political bandwidth to Confederate symbols, microaggressions, allegations of Trump's use of the "N" word, and the like. The teaching of critical race theory in the college classroom centered national conversations about race, more than the inferior quality of the elementary and high schools that more than three-fourths of Blacks are forced to attend. At bottom, affirmative action rulings' detachment from measurable inequality is part of a broader historical and political dialect.

Betrayal of Individualist and Civil Rights Ideals

A majority of Supreme Court justices believe that treating individuals as members of racial groups violates a treasured American ideal, namely individual rights. They see inbuilt tension between not only individualist ideals and the basic principles of affirmative action policy, but also civil rights ideals, as articulated in the *Brown v. Board of Education* decision (1954), the civil rights movement, and the landmark Civil Rights Act of 1964. The sense that affirmative action runs afoul of American individualism and equal treatment principles is shared throughout the national political arena. Like the Court, much of American society sees serious problems of justice and equality engendered by a policy that was created to achieve greater justice and equality.

Court Opinion on Affirmative Action versus American Ideals

A core tenet of Chief Justice Roberts's majority opinion in *Students for Fair Admissions* (*SFFA*, 2023) was embraced by most other Supreme Court justices, specifically the belief that appropriating constitutional guarantees on a group basis is at odds with equal protection principles and history. *Students for Fair Admissions* (2023) drilled down on the constitutional rights of individuals as individuals. The chief justice stressed that "at the heart of the Constitution's guarantee of equal protection lies the simple command that the Government must treat citizens as individuals, not as simply components of a racial, religious, sexual or national class."[63] Accordingly, while carving out an exception where race may come into play in college admissions, Roberts insisted that any benefit to a student whose college essay details how they overcame racial discrimination or whose heritage motivated them must be tied specifically to the applicant. *SFFA* reiterated earlier rulings that also suggested the Black population in the US is not entitled to special constitutional protections or privileges as a group. Rather, the US Constitution bestows rights and privileges upon individual Black citizens, no more and no less than upon White citizens. Affirmative action jurisprudence is thusly anchored in a constitutional-legal form of American individualism.

Since 1978 preferential rulings have rebutted the contention that courts should be uniquely attuned to the plight of racial minority groups, *as groups*.

What Justice Powell saw as the "fatal flaw" in the University of California Medical School preferential program in *Bakke* (1978) was "its disregard of individual rights as guaranteed by the Fourteenth Amendment," because, he wrote, the "rights created by the first section of the Fourteenth Amendment are, by its terms, guaranteed to the individual." "The rights established are personal." To accord rights and privileges on a group basis, furthermore, would make it difficult to avoid arbitrary application of equal protection. As Powell put it, "If it is the individual who is entitled to judicial protection against classifications based upon his racial or ethnic background because such distinctions impinge upon personal rights, rather than the individual only because of his membership in a particular group, then constitutional standards may be applied consistently. Political judgments regarding the necessity for the particular classification may be weighed in the constitutional balance . . . but the standard of justification will remain consistent." Long before *SFFA* (2023) the marriage between equal protection and individualism was pronounced time and again in favorable as well as unfavorable rulings, and opinions authored by both conservative and liberal justices. Powell complained in 1986 in *Wygant* that Justice Marshall viewed the affirmative action challenge "not in terms of individual constitutional rights," but as an allocation of burdens "between racial groups." The petitioners, he insisted, were not "White teachers as a group," rather they were "Wendy Wygant and other individuals who claim that they were fired from their jobs because of their race." *Wygant* stressed that "the Constitution does not allocate constitutional rights to be distributed like block grants within discrete racial groups." Following prior precedents, a pro–affirmative action opinion penned by liberal justice William Brennan cautioned against government relief to a "class as a whole rather than to individual members." Brennan explained for the majority in *Sheet Metal Workers* (1986) that such relief was not always and, in every instance, proper, but must be judiciously "guided by sound legal principles."

As a regular swing vote on the Supreme Court, Justice O'Connor placed heavy emphasis on individual rights. Her majority opinion in *Croson* (1989) reiterated that it was critical for White contractors' "personal rights to be treated with equal dignity and respect." She bottomed her 5–4 majority opinion in *Adarand* partly on the "basic principle that the Fifth and Fourteenth Amendments to the Constitution protect *persons*, not *groups* [*sic*]." Setting forth an explanation for overturning *Metro Broadcasting v. FCC* (1990), O'Connor highlighted two of the critical flaws in that ruling. One was that it rested on an unprecedented distinction between state and federal racial classifications and the other was it "undermine[d] the fundamental principle of equal protection as a personal right."

In *Adarand* (1995) the Colorado-based contractor that Justices O'Connor, Scalia, Kennedy, Thomas, and Chief Justice Rehnquist sided with alleged that a subcontractor clause mandated by federal law violated the equal protection component of the Fifth Amendment. Although Adarand Constructors, Inc., submitted the lowest bid to complete the guardrail portion of a highway construction project, the prime contractor, Mountain Gravel & Construction Company, awarded the guardrail subcontract to Gonzales Construction Company. Mountain Gravel would have awarded the bid to Adarand "had it not been for the additional payment it received by hiring Gonzales instead." Under federal law prime contractors received additional compensation if they hired subcontractors certified as small businesses controlled by "socially and economically disadvantaged individuals." Gonzales was certified as such; Adarand was not. Under federal regulations "the contractor shall presume that socially and economically disadvantaged individuals include Black Americans, Hispanic Americans, Native Americans, Asian Pacific Americans, and other minorities, or any other individual found to be disadvantaged by the [Small Business] Administration." *Adarand* (1995) ruled that, whenever a court adjudicates a racial classification, it must ensure that the classification is "subjected to detailed judicial inquiry to ensure that the *personal* [*sic*] right to equal protection of the laws has not been infringed."

The Supreme Court has long deemed race-based classifications as more corrosive than other types of identity classifications. Chief Justice Roberts suggested in *Parents Involved* (2007) that race-based preferential policies are self-defeating insofar as they promote racial thinking. In regard to the two race-based public school assignment plans in that case Roberts wrote, "To the extent the objective is sufficient diversity so that students see fellow students as individuals rather than solely as members of a racial group, using means that treat students solely as members of a racial group is fundamentally at cross-purposes with that end." The mere act of imputing certain political and policy interests to a racial minority group serves to exacerbate racial division, according to *Schuette v. BAMN* (2014). In that case voters in the state of Michigan adopted a ballot initiative (Proposal 2) in 2006 that amended the state constitution to include Section 26, which prohibited the use of race-based preferences as part of the admissions process for state universities. A suit challenging Section 26 was brought by students, faculty, and prospective applicants to Michigan public universities, and also the Coalition to Defend Affirmative Action, Integration and Immigrant Rights and Fight for Equality by Any Means Necessary (BAMN). The District Court for the Eastern District of Michigan upheld Section 26. The Sixth Circuit Court struck it. The US Supreme Court reinstated it on appeal.

For the 6–2–1 majority[64] in *Schuette* (2014) Justice Kennedy reasoned that prior precedent rebuked judicial efforts to determine which political policies serve the "interest" of a group defined in racial terms. This was due partly to what he outlined as the difficulty of sorting individuals according to their race and interests. By Kennedy's account, this would be a venture "undertaken with no clear legal standards or accepted sources to guide judicial decision." Among other things, judges would have to determine "the policy realms in which groups defined by race had a political interest." Such a task would risk any number of policy debates being cast in terms of racial advantage or disadvantage. Under this scenario Kennedy asserted "racial division would be validated, not discouraged."

Decades before *Students for Fair Admissions* was handed down in 2023, invoking the moral force of the landmark *Brown v. Board of Education* (1954) and the 1960s Black civil rights movement was a standard refrain in affirmative action cases. The usual take is that the preeminent aim of *Brown* and the movement was to eliminate the use of skin color to deny rights and benefits to Blacks, whereas racial set-asides require that rights and benefits be accorded on the basis of skin color. *Parents Involved* and *Meredith* (2007) cited *Brown* repeatedly as it rebuked the race-based school assignment plans in those cases. Chief Justice Roberts concluded his *Parents Involved* majority opinion with a reminder that, "before Brown, schoolchildren were told where they could and could not go to school based on the color of their skin," and that the "school districts in these cases have not carried the heavy burden of demonstrating that we should allow this once again." As to the guarantee of individual rights as opposed to group rights, Roberts claimed, "This fundamental principle goes back, in this context, to *Brown* itself." Lifting from *Brown*, he added, "At stake is the *personal* [*sic*] interest of the plaintiffs in admission to public schools . . . on a nondiscriminatory basis." The chief justice declared that "the position of the plaintiffs in *Brown* was spelled out in their brief and could not have been clearer, 'The Fourteenth Amendment prevents states from according differential treatment to American children on the basis of their color or race.' "

Watershed civil rights judgments were summoned also by Justice O'Connor in her attempt to sharpen the contrast between racial classifications and civil rights ideals. Her opinion for the Court in *Adarand* (1995) walked through several such decisions, including the 1943 *Hirabayashi v. U.S.* ruling that imposed a curfew on Japanese Americans, the 1944 *Korematsu v. U.S.* decision that approved internment of Japanese Americans, a 1964 holding in *McLaughlin v. Florida* (1964)[65] that struck down a state law against interracial cohabitation, and *Loving v. Virginia* (1967),[66] which invalidated state bans on interracial marriage. O'Connor explained, "Most of the cases discussed above involved classifications burdening groups that have suffered discrimination in our society." And even though affirmative action is framed as a racial classification designed to benefit traditionally marginalized groups, "any person, of whatever race, has the right to demand that any governmental actor subject to the Constitution justify any racial classification subjecting that person to unequal treatment under the strictest judicial scrutiny.

SFFA followed the lead of these earlier rulings and likewise invoked earlier historic civil rights rulings to make the point that race-based policies ignore the lessons afforded by those cases. In addition to civil rights cases from *Strauder v. West Virginia* (1880) through *Plessy v. Ferguson* (1896), Chief Justice Roberts turned also to the *Korematsu v. United States* (1944) Japanese internment case as one that "demonstrates vividly that even the most rigid scrutiny can sometimes fail to detect an illegitimate racial classification."[67] Roberts borrowed at length from *Brown* and reiterated the plaintiffs' argument in that case that "no State has any authority under the equal-protection clause of the Fourteenth Amendment to use race as a factor in affording educational opportunities among its citizens." He noted other areas where, spurred by *Brown*, the Court "began routinely affirming lower court decisions that invalidated all manner of race-based state action."

POLITICS OF INDIVIDUAL RIGHTS

Parents Involved's (2007) rebuke of policies that treat individuals "solely as members of racial group" is on par with a way of thinking that is deeply rooted in American political thought. The idea that individual citizens should be judged solely as individuals is widely shared. Many also believe that to do otherwise pits White citizens against Black and Brown citizens, rendering affirmative action a zero-sum game in which Whites lose out. Sociologists describe the latter viewpoint as tied to "racial group threat, meaning members of one racial group perceive successes by the other as a direct threat to their own."[68] Survey data tables show that a good portion of the country ascribes to racial group threat because they, like the Supreme Court, consider affirmative action harmful to Whites. A number of surveys show a small margin of difference between those who believe Whites are losing out due to preferences for Blacks and those who believe that Blacks are losing out due to racial disadvantage. Table 3.3 reveals that there are few

Table 3.3. Racial Groups Losing Out Due to Affirmative Action, US, 1995–2017, Select Years

Year	Survey Question	Select Responses (%)
2017	Which of these do you think is the bigger problem in this country—Blacks and Hispanics losing out because of preferences for Whites, or Whites losing out because of preferences for Blacks and Hispanics? (*Washington Post*/Kaiser Family Foundation, June 17, 2017)	Blacks/Hispanics losing out: 42 Whites losing out: 28
2016	Which of these do you think is the bigger problem in this country—Blacks and Hispanics losing out because of preferences for Whites, or Whites losing out because of preferences for Blacks and Hispanics? Do you feel that way strongly or somewhat? (ABC News/*Washington Post*, March 13, 2016)	Blacks/Hispanics losing out, strongly or somewhat: 43 Whites losing out, strongly or somewhat: 23
2013	Which do you think is a bigger problem in the workplace today—minorities losing out because of racial discrimination or Whites losing out because of affirmative action? (YouGov, October 18, 2013)	Minorities losing out: 20 Whites losing out: 26
2003	Thinking about the effects of racism and affirmative action on this country, which do you think is a bigger problem today, Blacks and Hispanics losing out because of racism or Whites losing out because of affirmative action? (Associated Press, March 12, 2003)	Blacks/Hispanics losing out: 44 Whites losing out: 30
2003	Now thinking about the effects of racism and affirmative action on the society as a whole, which do you think is a bigger problem today: Blacks and Hispanics losing out because of racism, Whites losing out because of affirmative action, or neither is a big problem? (*Newsweek*, January 18, 2003)	Blacks/Hispanics losing out: 42 Whites losing out: 23

continued on next page

Table 3.3. Continued.

Year	Survey Question	Select Responses (%)
1997	Which do you think is a bigger problem in the workplace today—Blacks losing out because of racial discrimination or Whites losing out because of affirmative action? (*New York Times*/CBS News Poll, December 13, 1997)	Whites losing out: 34 Blacks losing out: 35
1996	Which do you think is a bigger problem in your local area today—qualified Blacks and other minorities being denied jobs or promotions because of racial discrimination, or qualified Whites losing out to less qualified Blacks or other minorities because of affirmative action? (*Newsweek*/Back Talk Poll, March 10, 1996)	Whites losing out: 39 Blacks/minorities denied: 18
1995	Do you think affirmative action programs giving preference to women, Blacks, and other minorities result in less opportunities for White men, or not? (*Washington Post*/ABC News Poll, March 19, 1995)	Yes: 51 No: 46
1995	If you think affirmative action programs giving preference to women, Blacks, and other minorities results in less opportunities for White men, does it bother you a lot, some, not much, or not at all? (*Washington Post*/ABC News Poll, March 19, 1995)	A lot/some: 76 Not much/not at all: 24

Source: Survey data in the table obtained from *Polling the nations.* (n.d.). Topic: Affirmative action. Last accessed 4/25/2022 from https://ptn-infobase-com.exlibris.colgate.edu/topics/VG9waWM6NTI=?aid=14265.

exceptions to this two-decade-long pattern, as captured in the *Washington Post / Kaiser Family Foundation* (2017), *ABC News/Washington Post* (2016), and *Newsweek* (2013) surveys. We gain a clearer look at racial competition from the trend data in figure 3.4. The General Social Survey (GSS) results suggest that for the better part of three decades, a solid majority of the US adult population believes that Whites are hurt most by preferential policies and programs. Fully 65 percent believed in 1990 that Whites were somewhat

Figure 3.4. Whites Hurt by Affirmative Action. *Source*: Davern, M., Bautista, R., Freese, J., Morgan, S. L., & Smith, T. W. (n.d.). *General social surveys, 1972–2021*. NORC, 2021: NORC at the University of Chicago [producer and distributor]. Last accessed 2/16/2021 from the GSS Data Explorer website at gssdataexplorer.norc.org.

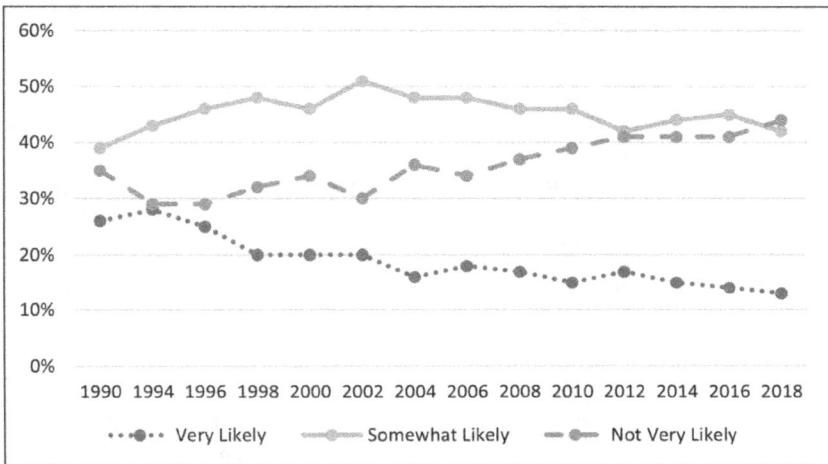

or very likely to be hurt by affirmative action and in 2018 that number remained a sizeable 55 percent of US adults.

Republican and Democratic partisans too are not far from the Court in their praise of ideals. Republicans framed the protection of individual rights in 1992 as "the foundation for opportunity and security."[69] Later, they proclaimed more forcefully that "rights inhere in individuals, not in groups."[70] Recently Republicans vowed to "reaffirm the Constitution's fundamental principles: limited government, separation of powers, individual liberty, and the rule of law." Conservatives' public overtures to individualist ideals extend back to the 1980s when they declared their party "the historical party of Lincoln and individual rights" and pledged to "press for enactment of economic and social policies that promote growth and stress individual initiative of minority Americans."[71] Over the years, Democrats have followed suit. They titled their 1984 plank "Individual Empowerment" to convey that their party's "commitment to full equality is as much a part of prodding individual opportunity as it is part of a program of social justice."[72] Later, Democrats shared their belief that voters "valued Barack Obama's message that alongside Americans' famous individualism, there's another ingredient in the American saga: a belief that we are connected to each other."[73] They went a step further to make known their belief in "the essential American ideal that we are not constrained by the circumstances of birth but can make of our lives what we will."[74]

Presidents too are at one with Supreme Court justices, as evidenced by their constant appeals to American individualism and the principle of equality when laying out their position on race-based preferences—whether for or against them. Under President Obama's administration the Equal Employment Opportunity Commission framed race-conscious policies as a way to help achieve the Title VII congressional purpose of providing equal opportunity.[75] President Reagan also voiced his commitment to "a society in which all men and women have equal opportunities to succeed . . . a society that, in the words of Dr. King, judges people 'not by the color of their skin, but by the content of their character.' "[76] Reagan slammed hard versions of affirmative action, claiming proponents "tell us that the Government should enforce discrimination in favor of some groups through hiring quotas, under which people get or lose particular jobs or promotions solely because of their race or sex."[77] Trump's Executive Order 13950 denigrated racial sensitivity training as rooted in a "vision of America that is grounded in hierarchies based on collective social and political identities rather than in the inherent and equal dignity of every person as an individual."[78] His administration railed against "critical race theory," accusing those who promote it as seeking to "strip individual agency from all Americans and instead relegate them into pre-determined categories of belief based on their racial or sexual identity."

President George H. W. Bush shared the justices' view that racial policies are divisive, stating that such policies "pit one group against another," and "encourage people to think of others as competitors, not colleagues."[79] He thought it important to adopt a different, "more unifying, moral, and noble approach."[80] At a commencement ceremony he described race-neutral affirmative action as follows, "To me, true affirmative action expresses a duty of citizenship: good faith efforts to provide opportunity for individuals based on merit, to reach out and create truly equal opportunity for those who have been left behind, those who have been excluded."[81]

Toeing the line with the Supreme Court, national public opinion, party politics, and presidents are state legislative policy trends that pit individual rights against race-specific policies. Table 3.4 shows that in 2021 alone at least 12 states enacted some form of anti–critical race theory (CRT) policy measure; during the early part of 2022 another six did so, with similar measures pending other states. The Heritage Foundation, a conservative

Table 3.4. Critical Race Theory State Policy Trends, 2021 and 2022

State	Year Enacted	Description
Alabama	2021	Prohibits public K–12 schools from offering any instruction that "indoctrinates students in social or political ideologies or theories that promote one race or sex above another."
Arizona	2021	Bans "instruction that presents any form of blame or judgment on the basis of race, ethnicity or sex."
Arizona	2021	Bans "training, orientation or therapy that presents any form of blame or judgment on the basis of race, ethnicity or sex."
Arkansas	2021	Bans state entities (excluding public schools, charter schools, universities, political subdivisions, and law enforcement) from teaching or training of divisive concepts.
Florida	2021	Prohibits public K–12 schools from including any instructional materials or theories that "distort historical events and are inconsistent with State Board approved standards," including "Critical Race Theory, meaning the theory that racism is not merely the product of prejudice, but that racism is embedded in American society and its legal systems in order to uphold the supremacy of White persons." Prohibits use of the 1619 Project.
Idaho	2021	Bans public schools and institutions of higher education from "direct[ing] or otherwise compel[ling] students to personally affirm, adopt, or adhere" to the outlined "critical race theory" tenets.
Iowa	2021	Requires that any mandatory staff training "does not teach, advocate, act upon, or promote" specific defined concepts.
Kentucky	2022	Requires public K–12 and charter schools to make their instruction and instructional materials "consistent" with certain ideas related to race, sex, and American history and culture.
Mississippi	2022	Bars public K–12 schools and colleges from compelling students to affirm or adopt certain ideas related to race, sex, or other characteristics, nor make "a distinction or classification of students based on account of race."

continued on next page

Table 3.4. Continued.

State	Year Enacted	Description
Montana	2021	Finds that certain educational practices associated with "Critical Race Theory" and "Antiracism" violate the Civil Rights Act and are subject to prosecution.
New Hampshire	2021	Prohibits public schools, government, public employer or contractors from "teach[ing], advocat[ing], instruct[ing], or train[ing] any employee, student, service recipient, contractor, staff member, inmate, or any other individual or group" in certain concepts.
North Dakota	2021	Prohibits the inclusion of any instruction related to critical race theory, defined as "the theory that racism is not merely the product of learned individual bias or prejudice, but that racism is systemically embedded in American society and the American legal system to facilitate racial inequality."
South Carolina	2021	Mandates that funds shall not be used by public schools "to provide instruction in, to teach, instruct, or train any administrator, teacher, staff member, or employee to adopt or believe, or to approve for use, make use of, or carry out standards, curricula, lesson plans, textbooks, instructional materials, or instructional practices that serve to inculcate" certain concepts.
South Dakota	2022	Bans public colleges from compelling students to adopt or affirm certain ideas related to race, sex, and other characteristics, nor require students or employees to attend any training or orientation that teaches these ideas.
South Dakota	2022	Prohibits public K–12 schools from promoting or endorsing certain ideas related to race, color, religion, sex, ethnicity, or national origin.
Tennessee	2021	Bans public schools from including or promoting certain concepts in curriculum. Allows the "impartial discussion of controversial aspects of history."
Tennessee	2022	Bans public colleges and universities from including certain ideas related to race and sex in any "seminars, workshops, trainings, and orientations."

State	Year Enacted	Description
Texas	2021	Bars teachers from being "compelled to discuss a particular current event or widely debated and currently controversial issue." Bars requiring an understanding of the 1619 Project. Bans schools from requiring or making part of a course certain concepts.
Virginia	2022	Prohibits public K–12 schools from directing or compelling students to adopt or affirm certain ideas related to race, skin color, ethnicity, sex, or faith.

Source: PEN America (n.d.). PEN America index of educational gag orders. PEN America: The freedom to write. Last accessed 4/25/2022 from https://docs.google.com/spreadsheets/d/1Tj5 WQVBmB6SQg-zP_M8uZsQQGH09TxmBY73v23zpyr0/edit#gid=1505554870.

think tank, supplied the rationale for such anti-CRT efforts, homing in on the notion that race-based preferences are un-American. Heritage published a 2020 report that decried CRT as an assault on "the liberal order—in the classical sense, referring to Enlightenment ideas and political arrangements in which law protects individuals pursuing their own interests." The report further assailed CRT as "the academic body of work that underpins identity politics, an ongoing effort to reimagine the United States as a nation not of individuals and local communities united under common purposes, but as one riven by groups based on sex, race, national origin, or gender—each with specific claims on victimization."[82]

SECTION SUMMARY

To recap, affirmative action case law echoes two common refrains in national racial politics—that the American political tradition values *individual* and not group rights and that the 1960s civil rights tradition condemns racial preference. It is the rights of individual Whites in particular that most concern average citizens. Three decades of Gallup data show an overwhelming majority believes that Whites are hurt most by preferential policies. Complementing this public consensus is a durable bipartisan consensus around the notion that individualism is a central feature of the American ethos. Even Democrats have resolved that "we are not constrained by the circumstances of birth." Presidents' positioning around affirmative action too is partly anchored in individualist ideology. President Trump was no more fervent than his predecessors Presidents Reagan and Bush in decrying the harmfulness of race-aware government action. All invoked Dr. Martin L. King's call to judge people "not by the color of their skin, but by the content of their character." Meanwhile, conservative think tanks crafted a theoretical framework to galvanize a dozen states to enact anti–critical race theory measures in 2021 alone, which measures the Heritage Foundation decried as a "ceaseless assault on all American institutions and norms." In sum and substance, Supreme Court affirmative action judgments give voice to ideals that most consider foundational to not only American political identity, but to the American principle of equality as well.

Racial Preference Is Racial Prejudice

Most affirmative action rulings posit racial preference as discriminatory against Blacks as well as Whites. Affirmative action is said to implicitly stereotype Blacks as unqualified, undeserving, uniformly disadvantaged, and prone to groupthink. It is also construed as burdensome and harmful to Whites. And while some burden-sharing is permissible and at times mandatory, the Supreme Court insists that White rights are to be carefully guarded by lower courts. Court claims of reverse discrimination and racial stereotyping resonate with everyday Americans, a long line of presidents, and with Republicans more than Democrats.

COURT OPINION ON PREJUDICE AND DISCRIMINATION

Students for Fair Admissions (*SFFA*, 2023) bolstered the notion that racial preferences operate like a double-edged sword. Chief Justice Roberts cited earlier precedent as he cautioned race awareness could devolve into illegitimate stereotyping and discrimination against racial groups that were not designated beneficiaries.[83] He concluded that Harvard and the University of North Carolina failed to comply with the "twin commands of the Equal Protection Clause that race may never be used as a 'negative' and that it may not operate as a stereotype." *SFFA* was not the first but instead the latest in a long line of affirmative action rulings to contest the cornerstone idea behind affirmative action—that it benefits racial minorities. Others suggest that racial preferences reinforce negative stereotypes, lumped all Blacks together as disadvantaged, and assume that they all think alike.

"Serious problems of justice connected with the idea of preference itself" were highlighted in the first ruling on affirmative action in *Regents v. Bakke* (1978). Justice Powell wrote that one such problem is that "preferential programs may only reinforce common stereotypes holding that certain groups are unable to achieve success without special protection based on a factor having no relationship to individual worth." *Croson* (1989) continued this line of reasoning, warning that racial classifications carry a "danger of stigmatic harm" and that without guidance "they may in fact promote notions of racial inferiority and lead to a politics of racial hostility." As a case in point, *Croson* additionally claimed that the set-aside in the Small Business Administration Act "is perceived by many as resting on an assumption that those who are granted this special preference are less qualified in some respect that is identified purely by their race." Justice O'Connor's opinion in *Adarand* (1995) also warned about the potential for stigmatic harm, suggesting that, compared to the impact on Whites, racial preference "actually imposes a greater stigma on its supposed beneficiaries." Elaborating further on this point in *Parents Involved* (2007) Chief Justice Roberts contended the "principal reasons race is treated as a forbidden classification is that it demeans the dignity and worth of a person to be judged by ancestry instead of by his or her own merit and essential qualities."

Supreme Court case law not only questions whether race-specific programs are a net benefit to Blacks, but also whether Blacks are even systematically disadvantaged and thus in need of special considerations. Here too the first step was taken by Justice Powell who complained in *Bakke* that no formal definition of "disadvantaged" was ever produced by the special admissions program in that case. He faulted the blanket designation of racial minorities as "disadvantaged," but not low-income White applicants. When the question of what constitutes racial disadvantage was squarely before the Court two years later, the majority sidestepped it. Plaintiffs in *Fullilove* (1980) argued that the minority business enterprise (MBE) program authorized by the Public Works Employment Act of 1977 was unconstitutional under the Fourteenth and Fifteenth Amendments partly because it was overinclusive. The program required that 10 percent of federal public works grants to state and local governments go to contract services from minority-owned businesses (MBEs), even if their bid was not the lowest, as long as the bid covered costs inflated by "the present effects of prior disadvantage and discrimination." Several predominantly White contractor associations sued, alleging that the MBE program benefited minority-owned businesses that were not proven victims of discrimination. However, Chief Justice Burger was satisfied that the "congressional assumptions" about disadvantage were "assumptions [that] may be rebutted in the administrative process."

By 2014 the Court would settle the matter and embrace the *Fullilove* (1980) challengers' view that minorities should have to prove their disadvantage. *Stotts* (1984) set the stage and declared that "mere membership in the disadvantaged class is insufficient to warrant a seniority award" and that "each individual must prove that the discriminatory practice had an impact on him." *Richmond v. Croson* (1989) criticized the fact that special privileges were accorded to all "citizens of the United States who are Blacks, Spanish-speaking, Orientals, Indians, Eskimos, or Aleuts," despite the fact that, as Justice O'Connor put it, "there is *absolutely no evidence* [*sic*] of past discrimination against Spanish-speaking, Oriental, Indian, Eskimo, or Aleut persons in any aspect of the Richmond construction industry." Absent such findings O'Connor argued that "our history will adequately support a legislative preference for almost any ethnic, religious, or racial group with the political strength to negotiate 'a piece of the action' for its members." And given that the Richmond set-aside policy was adopted by a majority-Black city council, it was arguable that, in that case, it was actually Blacks that held an advantage over Whites. O'Connor pushed back against the notion of systematic racial disadvantage again in *Adarand* (1995), where "Black Americans, Hispanic Americans, Native Americans, Asian Pacific Americans, and other minorities" were presumed socially and economically disadvantaged under federal regulations. The lawsuit in *Adarand* (1995) alleged that "the race-based presumptions involved in the use of subcontracting compensation clauses violate[d] Adarand's right to equal protection." Because the justices deemed it important to know whether the minority contractor provisions required an individualized showing of economic disadvantage and whether the "presumptions of disadvantage" were rebuttable, the case was remanded.

The presumption of systematic racial disadvantage was effectively laid to rest in 2014 by Justice Kennedy. *Schuette v. BAMN* took the Sixth Circuit to task for invalidating a Michigan state constitutional amendment that banned racial considerations in public universities, contracting, and employment. The danger Justice Kennedy saw was that courts lacked reliable means of determining which racial groups were disadvantaged and which were not. "That undertaking, again without guidance from any accepted legal standards, would risk, in turn, the creation of incentives for those who support or oppose certain policies to cast the debate in terms of racial advantage or disadvantage." He believed the possibilities for racial disadvantage allegations were limitless and potentially tied to everything from "tax policy, housing subsidies, wage regulations, and even the naming of public schools, highways, and monuments."

Students for Fair Admissions (2023) called out assumptions about groupthink. Chief Justice Roberts wrote, "Respondents admit as much," that "Harvard's admissions process rests on the pernicious stereotype that 'a Black student can usually bring something that a White person cannot offer' . . . UNC is much the same. It argues that race in itself 'says [something] about who you are.' " As Roberts saw it, when a university admits students "on the basis of race, it engages in the offensive and demeaning assumption that [students] of a particular race, because of their race, think alike."[84] The university furthers "stereotypes that treat individuals as the product of their race, evaluating their thoughts and efforts—their very worth as citizens—according to a criterion barred to the Government by history and the Constitution."

In the years leading up to *SFFA*, we see other rulings that problematized the notion that racial minorities think alike, act like, and gravitate toward similar choices. The Court's reasoning stands apart from affirmative action advocates who say that representative workforces, schools, industries, policymaking bodies, and so forth are better equipped to meet the needs of minority communities. For instance, in *Bakke* (1978) the special admissions policy adopted by the University of California Medical School was partly designed to increase the number of physicians in underserved communities. While Justice Powell's principal opinion conceded it may be more likely that minority doctors "will practice in minority communities than the average White doctor," he concluded the university "cannot assure that minority doctors who entered under the program, all of whom expressed an 'interest' in practicing in a disadvantaged community, will actually do so."

There was a more reliable way to identify such applicants besides skin color, such as admitting "an applicant of whatever race who has demonstrated his concern for disadvantaged minorities in the past and who declares that practice in such a community is his primary professional goal," Justice Powell wrote. Either way, "there is no empirical data to demonstrate that any race is more selflessly socially oriented or by contrast that another is more selfishly acquisitive." In a similar vein a decade later *Richmond v. Croson* (1989) observed that "the set-aside of subcontracting dollars seems to rest on the unsupported assumption that White prime contractors simply will not hire minority firms." For O'Connor it was "completely unrealistic to assume that individuals of one race will gravitate with mathematical exactitude to each employer or union absent unlawful discrimination."

Even liberal justices treat the relation between race and behavior as a "complex empirical question," such as in *Metro Broadcasting, Inc. v. Federal Communications Commission* (1990), where two FCC policies linked minority ownership to programming diversity. Writing for the five-person majority that approved both policies, Justice Brennan commended Congress and the FCC's reliance on research. He reported on studies that showed African American–owned radio stations hire African Americans in top management and other job categories at "far higher rates than have White-owned stations, even those with Afro-American-oriented formats." He also noted a Congressional Research Service study that found a strong correlation between minority ownership and diversity of programming. In light of these studies, the Supreme Court found that "congressional policy does not assume that in every case minority ownership and management will lead to more minority-oriented programming or to the expression of a discrete 'minority viewpoint' on the airwaves." "Neither does it pretend that all programming that appeals to minority audiences can be labeled 'minority programming' or that programming that might be described as 'minority' does not appeal to nonminorities."

According to swing-vote Justice Kennedy too, prior precedent rejected the assumption that "members of the same racial group—regardless of their age, education, economic status, or the community in which they live—think alike, share the same political interests, and will prefer the same candidates at the polls," as expressed in his opinion for the 6–2–1 judgment in *Schuette v. BAMN* (2014). *Schuette* upheld a Michigan state constitutional amendment that prohibits the use of race-based preferences in state college admissions, public employment, and public contracting. The appeals court for the Sixth Circuit invalidated the state ban based on the theory that strict scrutiny must be applied to state action that makes it harder for racial minorities to secure legislation of special interest to them. But, Kennedy criticized what he termed "impermissible racial stereotypes" in the Court of Appeals opinion. He insisted that ascribing "minority views" to defined racial groups was both "demeaning" and complex. And, even if a court could manage to discern "how some races define their own interest in political matters," it would have to also assume "that all individuals of the same race think alike."

Favorable as well as unfavorable affirmative action rulings urging reliance on personal experience and background—instead of skin color—is the best way to ascertain one's viewpoints and trajectory. Under this precept the 5–4 panel in *Grutter v. Bollinger* (2003) found that the assumptions behind the race-conscious admissions policy in that case were not unreasonable. O'Connor admitted, "Just as growing up in a particular region or having particular professional experiences is likely to affect an individual's views, so too is one's own, unique experience of being a racial minority in a society, like our own, in which race unfortunately still matters." Still, the University of Michigan Law School did not proceed on "any belief that minority students always (or even consistently) express some characteristic minority viewpoint on any issue."

Gratz v. Bollinger (2003) also adjudged personal background and experience as more reliable predictors. Chief Justice Rehnquist's majority opinion remarked that preferring a racial minority because they are likely to provide a "distinct perspective" impermissibly values individuals based on a presumption that "persons think in a manner associated with their race." In more carefully devised plans, "the critical criteria are often individual qualities or experience *not dependent upon race but sometimes associated with it* [*sic*]." Rehnquist instanced a scenario that involved the child of a Black physician from a good school (Student A), a Black student who grew up in an inner-city ghetto of semi-literate parents but with great energy and leadership (Student B), and a White student (Student C) with extraordinary artistic talents. The problem he found was that, "instead of considering how the differing backgrounds, experiences, and characteristics of students A, B, and C might benefit the University, admissions counselors reviewing LSA applications would simply award both A and B 20 points because their applications indicate that they are African-American, and student C would receive up to 5 points for his extraordinary talent."

Beside the Court's position that racial preferences impermissibly stereotype minorities is the position taking in *Students for Fair Admissions* (*SFFA*, 2023), that they are harmful also to Whites. *SFFA* criticized the principal dissent by Justice Sonia Sotomayor (joined by Justices Kagan and Jackson) for expecting the Supreme Court to "tell state actors when they have picked the right races to benefit" and, thus, pick winners and losers based on the color of their skin. Contrarily, Roberts concluded Harvard and the University of North Carolina's race-based admissions constituted reverse discrimination because they worked to benefit some applicants and not others and, in doing so, advantaged the former at the expense of the latter. By this reasoning Chief Justice Roberts's opinion for the 6–3 majority labeled race-conscious college admissions a "zero-sum" game wherein applicants from different racial groups are directly pitted against one another. As support, Roberts pointed to the First Circuit finding that racial considerations led to an 11.1 percent decrease in the number of Asian Americans admitted to Harvard. The district court also noted fewer Asian American and White students admitted due to the policy of considering applicants' race. But for racial preferences that favored Blacks and Latinos, Roberts observed, Asians would have been admitted in greater numbers than they were.

SFFA's construction of racial preferences as discriminatory against Whites and Asians is one to which liberal as well as conservative justices ascribed over the years, in both favorable and unfavorable decisions. Their exclusionary impact was first red-flagged in *Bakke*. The University of California Medical School special admissions program admitted "disadvantaged" minority applicants, but not disadvantaged Whites. Of the 100 seats in the entering class, White applicants could compete only for 84, whereas all 100 were open to minority applicants. *Bakke* concluded that "because of that foreclosure, some individuals are excluded from enjoyment of a state-provided benefit—admission to the Medical School—they otherwise would receive." Powell cautioned, "One should not lightly dismiss the inherent unfairness of, and the perception of mistreatment that accompanies, a system of allocating benefits and privileges on the basis of skin color and ethnic origin." He added that racial inequality was not the responsibility of individual Whites, insofar as "nothing in the Constitution supports the notion that individuals may be asked to suffer otherwise impermissible burdens in order to enhance the societal standing of their ethnic groups." *Grutter* (2003) looked approvingly upon the fact that the University of Michigan Law School special admissions policy had minimal impact on Whites. In upholding the policy, Justice O'Connor's opinion stressed "the Law School's race-conscious admissions program does not unduly harm nonminority applicants." Meanwhile the school's undergraduate plan was struck down because it excluded nonminorities.

The Court acknowledges that not all exclusionary set-asides are illegal, given that White privilege has at times precluded Black opportunity. Chief Justice Burger explained in *Fullilove* (1980) that the federal minority business enterprise contracting set-aside was disappointing to nonminority firms, but that a "sharing of the burden" by innocent parties was permissible for two reasons. One was that Congress could "act on the assumption that in the past some nonminority business may have reaped competitive benefits over the years from the virtual exclusion of minority firms from these contracting opportunities." The other, wrote Burger, is that "failure of nonminority firms to receive certain contracts is . . . an incidental consequence of the program, not part of its objective."

Evidence of "White privilege" was particularized in cases where affirmative action plans were upheld.[85] White plaintiffs in *Firefighters v. Cleveland* (1986) were found to have directly benefited from past discrimination against minorities. Black and Hispanic litigants filed a class action suit in 1980, accusing the city of Cleveland of intentional discrimination in the hiring, assignment, and promotion of firefighters in violation of Title VII, the Thirteenth and Fourteenth Amendments, and other civil rights statutes. Having lost a similar lawsuit brought by Black police officers in 1972, the city voluntarily entered into a consent decree in 1981 that established race-based hiring and promotion goals. When the predominantly White Local Number 93 chapter of the International Association of Firefighters, AFL-CIO, C.L.C. sued, the federal district court held that "it is neither unreasonable nor unfair to require non-minority firefighters who, although they committed no wrong, benefited from the effects of the discrimination to bear some of the burden of the remedy." Supreme Court Justices Brennan, joined by Marshall, Blackmun, Powell, Stevens, and O'Connor, upheld the district court ruling.

Specific evidence of White privilege was used to justify White burdening in *Paradise* (1987). According to the Eleventh Circuit, Whites promoted over a 15-year period in the Alabama Department of Public Safety "were the specific beneficiaries of an official policy that systematically excluded all Blacks." Accordingly, it upheld the racial quotas imposed by the district court. The Supreme Court affirmed. Justice Brennan's majority opinion in *Paradise* detailed the proof showing that the high attrition rate among Blacks was due to preferential treatment of Whites in training and testing, along with the selection of lesser qualified Blacks, discrimination against Blacks at the trooper training academy, and harsher discipline of Black troopers. Brennan agreed also with the appeals court's conclusion that the "use of unvalidated selection procedures that disproportionately excluded Blacks precluded any argument that 'quota hiring produces unconstitutional "reverse" discrimination, or a lowering of employment standards, or the appointment of less or unqualified persons.'" The bottom line in *Paradise* was that the court-ordered quotas were a "necessary remedy for an intolerable wrong."

Supreme Court justices have long valued strict scrutiny as the best way to distinguish between reverse discrimination and permissible burden-sharing. In *Adarand Constructors, Inc. v. Pena* (1995) Justice O'Connor's opinion for the Court stipulated that "whenever the government treats any person unequally because of his or her race, that person has suffered an injury. . . . The application of strict scrutiny . . . determines whether a compelling governmental interest justifies the infliction of that injury." *Adarand* (1995) further explained that a program unduly burdens innocent nonminorities whenever it is not narrowly tailored to promote permissible goals. *Bakke* was first to explain decades ago that, when political judgments "touch upon an individual's race or ethnic background, he is entitled to a judicial determination that the burden he is asked to bear on that basis is precisely tailored to serve a compelling governmental interest."

Some affirmative action plans have survived strict scrutiny largely because of their minimal impact on Whites. Justice Brennan and four other justices ruled that the union membership goal in *Sheet Metal* (1986) did not "unnecessarily trammel[s] the interests of White employees" because it did not disadvantage existing union members or applicants for membership. Similarly, the plan in *U.S. v. Paradise* (1987) did not "impose an unacceptable burden on innocent third parties," but instead "involved a delicate calibration of the rights and interests of the plaintiff class, the Department, and the White troopers." Also *Wygant* (1986) found that, because "denial of a future employment opportunity is not as intrusive as loss of an existing job," the "burden to be borne by innocent individuals" in connection with hiring goals is less onerous than that associated with layoff goals.

That the Supreme Court judges affirmative action policy with a special sensitivity to reverse discrimination claims is revealed in the wide latitude given to those who legally challenge the policy. Whites' right to challenge an affirmative action programs after the fact and even when they have sustained no injury was articulated in *Martin v. Wilks* (1989). Several Black prospective firefighters and the National Association for the Advancement of Colored People (NAACP) brought suit in 1974 against the city of Birmingham, Alabama, and the Jefferson County Personnel Board, alleging discriminatory practices in violation of Title VII and other federal law. Consent decrees were entered that included goals for hiring and promoting Blacks as firefighters. Robert K. Wilks and other White members of the Birmingham Firefighters Association brought suit, alleging they were denied promotions in favor of less qualified Blacks in violation of federal law. The question taken up by the Supreme Court was whether White plaintiffs could challenge decisions taken pursuant to affirmative action consent decrees, even if the decrees were publicized in local newspapers well before the fact. A 5–4 majority said "yes." Chief Justice Rehnquist wrote, "A voluntary settlement in the form of a consent decree between one group of employees and their employer cannot possibly 'settle,' voluntarily or otherwise, the conflicting claims of another group of employees who do not join in the agreement."

Northeastern v. Florida (1993) held that Whites do not have to prove that they have been individually harmed in order to establish that an affirmative action plan *could* be harmful to them. The city of Jacksonville, Florida, enacted a Minority Business Enterprise Participation ordinance in 1984 that set aside 10 percent of the budget for city contracts to hire minority-owned businesses. The Northeastern Florida Chapter of the Associated General Contractors of America filed suit claiming that the ordinance violated the equal protection rights of Whites. The trial court sided with the association, but the Eleventh Circuit reversed for lack of standing. On appeal Justice Clarence Thomas wrote for the 7–2 majority, "When the government erects a barrier that makes it more difficult for members of one group to obtain a benefit than it is for members of another group, a member of the former group seeking to challenge the barrier need not allege that he would have obtained the benefit for the barrier in order to establish standing. . . . The 'injury in fact' element of standing in such an equal protection case is the denial of equal treatment resulting from the imposition of the barrier."[86] Following the lead of prior precedent, Chief Justice Roberts's opinion for the 6–3 majority in *Students for Fair Admissions* (2023) went to great lengths to establish the petitioner organization's standing to challenge Harvard and the University of North Carolina's race-aware admissions policies. Roberts wrote, "Because SFFA complies with the standing requirements demanded of organizational plaintiffs in *Hunt*, its obligations under Article III are satisfied."[87] Specifically, Students for Fair Admissions suffered an injury, the injury is traceable to the challenged conduct, and is likely to be compensated by a favorable judicial decision.

To close, Supreme Court racial preference rulings have always been attuned to reverse discrimination claims and to protecting White rights as *White* rights, which means *SFFA* assumed the same posture and, in effect, extended White rights to Asian Americans.

POLITICS OF PREJUDICE

In the political arena also racial preference is widely seen as a form of racial prejudice against both Blacks and Whites, even as scholars red-flag the myriad ways in which it is more likely manipulated as a tool to divide. Schmidt reports that affirmative action is used to "politically pit members of the working class against each other, clearing the way for the government to adopt policies that clearly favor the haves over the have-nots," whether Black, White, or Hispanic.[88] In this way opposition to it serves also as a key force holding White America together and preventing popular uprisings among the White poor. Meanwhile, Gray explains that affirmative action

advocacy is animated by one way of thinking, namely the "organizing principle . . . that the African American race has undergone a long and unique
experience since its arrival in America."[89] Contrarily, affirmative action
skeptics reject the idea that racial characteristics embody or represent in any
essential way the intellectual and cultural qualities by which diversity may
be advanced. So do some of its supporters. In defense of affirmative action
Butler argues against assuming a "minority" viewpoint, agreeing that it reinforces stereotypes and skirts the nuances of life experience. Butler urges, "Any
reconceptualization of the defense of affirmative action must make clear the
radical incommensurability between the determination of the social category
to which a person belongs and the determination of what contribution such
a person may make. . . . Any strict derivation would amount to a form of
essentialism which presupposes that viewpoints inhere in positionalities, and
such a view would override the complex ways in which differing viewpoints
remain incommensurable with and irreducible to such categories."[90] As for
the perspective held by the working class and Americans at large, like Justice
O'Connor, they too see the "danger of stigmatic harm" to Blacks. A national
consensus is coalesced around belief in affirmative action's stigmatizing impacts
on Blacks. A notable point of difference is that, where the Court asserts that
racial preferences *potentially* stigmatize Blacks, the public sees more than a
potentiality and instead a reality. The multi-sourced survey data in table
3.5 show that during the 1990s the overwhelming majority of US adults
believed that under affirmative action, either oftentimes or sometimes, less
qualified individuals are hired for a job, promoted, or admitted to college.
The national YouGov survey commissioned for this study shows that as of
2021 a majority of 56 percent still believe that less qualified people are hired,
promoted, and admitted to college as a result of affirmative action.

Mass attitudes about reverse discrimination are very much in step with
the Supreme Court's basic sense that Whites are excluded, even if at times
permissibly excluded. Single surveys suggest a more complex dynamic. As
to the question whether affirmative action constitutes discrimination against
Whites, the data in table 3.6 indicate that from the 1990s until 2023 belief
in reverse discrimination is shared by about half of the country. In the 2021
Moore/YouGov survey a plurality of 40 percent agrees with the question
whether "affirmative action programs for Blacks and other racial minorities
often result in reverse discrimination against Whites." The 2023 Reuters/
Ipsos poll shows a larger 49 percent. On the other hand, the more definitive
University of Chicago's General Social Survey trend data in figure 3.4 show
that the overwhelming majority believes that Whites are either "Very Likely"
or "Somewhat Likely" to be hurt by affirmative action.

Table 3.5. Affirmative Action as Stigmatizing, US, 1991–2021, Select Years

Year	Survey Question	Select Responses (%)
2021	How often do you think less qualified people are hired, promoted, and admitted to college as a result of affirmative action?[a]	Often/sometimes: 56 Hardly ever/never: 27
2003	As a result of affirmative action for Blacks and Hispanics in college admissions, do you think less qualified applicants are accepted often, sometimes, hardly ever, or never? (*Newsweek*, January 18, 2003)	Often/sometimes: 70
1997	How often do you think less qualified people are hired, promoted, and admitted to college as a result of affirmative action—often, sometimes, hardly ever, or never? (*New York Times*/CBS News, December 13, 1997)	Often/sometimes: 79
1997	When this happens (less qualified people are hired, promoted, and admitted to college as a result of affirmative action), do you think the less qualified people are far less qualified or only slightly less qualified? (*New York Times*/CBS News, December 13, 1997)	Far less: 14 Slightly less: 65 (Don't think this happens: 8)
1997	How often do you think unqualified people are hired and promoted as a result of affirmative action—often, sometimes, hardly ever, or never? (*New York Times*/CBS News, December 13, 1997)	Often/sometimes: 78
1995	Right now, how often do you think affirmative action programs designed to help women and minorities get better jobs and education end up causing businesses or universities to hire or admit unqualified persons—does that happen almost always, quite a lot, only occasionally, or almost never? (*Los Angeles Times*, March 22, 1995)	Almost always/quite a lot: 38 Only occasionally: 47
1991	Do you agree or disagree: When Black people have good jobs, White people often think they're in these positions because of affirmative action and not because they deserve it? (*Time*/CNN/Yankelovich, April 29, 1991)	Agree: 75

Sources: Except where indicated, survey data in the table were obtained from *Polling the nations.* (n.d.). Topic: Affirmative action. Last accessed 4/25/2022 from https://ptn-infobase-com.exlibris.colgate.edu/topics/VG9waWM6NTI=?aid=14265.

[a]Moore, N./YouGov. (2021, May 18–20). *Affirmative Action Omnibus.*

Table 3.6. Affirmative Action as Discrimination, US, 1995–2023, Select Years

Year	Survey Question	Select Responses (%)
2023	Social policies, such as affirmative action, discriminate unfairly against White people.[a]	Strongly/tend to agree: 49 Strongly/tend to disagree: 37
2021	Do you agree or disagree that affirmative action programs for Blacks and other racial minorities often result in reverse discrimination against Whites?[b]	Agree: 40 Disagree: 36
2009	Which comes closer to your point of view—affirmative action programs seek out qualified minorities and do not disadvantage members of other groups, or affirmative action programs result in members of some minority groups being advantaged at the expense of other groups? (Quinnipiac University Poll, June 3, 2009)	At the expense of others: 46 No disadvantage: 44
2008	Do affirmative action programs discriminate against White men? (Rasmussen Reports, July 30, 2008)	Yes: 46 No: 31
2003	All in all, do you think affirmative action programs designed to increase the number of Black and minority students on college campuses are fair, or unfair? (Pew Research Center, May 14, 2003)	Fair: 47 Unfair: 42
2003	Right now, how often do you think affirmative action programs designed to help women and minorities get better jobs and education end up depriving someone else of their rights—does that happen almost always, quite a lot, only occasionally, or almost never? (*Los Angeles Times*, February 2003)	Almost always, quite a lot: 34 Occasionally: 47
1995	Do you think that affirmative action programs for minorities and women sometimes discriminate against White men? (*Time*/CNN/Yankelovich, March 28, 1995)	Yes: 62

Year	Survey Question	Select Responses (%)
1995	Do you think that affirmative action programs for Blacks sometimes discriminate against Whites? If yes, do you think this happens a lot or only sometimes? (*Time/CNN/Yankelovich*, January 30, 1995)	Yes, a lot: 26 Yes, sometimes: 48

Source: Except where indicated, survey data in the table were obtained from *Polling the nations*. (n.d.). Topic: Affirmative action. Last accessed 4/25/2022 from https://ptn-infobase-com. exlibris.colgate.edu/topics/VG9waWM6NTI=?aid=14265.

[a]Reuters/Ipsos Poll: 2024 Primary Election, Debt Ceiling, Ukraine, University Admissions. Accessed 3/13/2024 from https://www.ipsos.com/sites . . . pdf.

[b]Moore, N./YouGov. (2021, May 18–20). *Affirmative Action Omnibus*.

What we hear from political parties concerning reverse discrimination—especially the Republican Party—lines up with Supreme Court declarations. In the year that the landmark Civil Rights Act of 1964 was adopted, the Democratic Platform stated, "True democracy of opportunity will not be served by establishing quotas based on the same false distinctions we seek to erase, nor can the effects of prejudice be neutralized by the expedience of preferential practices." Beyond 1964, the Democratic Party switched to silence mode in regard to the racial harm purportedly wrought by affirmative action and is, therefore, arguably complicit. The Republican Party, on the other hand, has always decried racial set-asides as harmful to Whites. Messaging along these lines began during the peak of the 1960s civil rights movement, when conservatives denounced so-called federally sponsored "inverse discrimination." As the country geared up for the decades-long national battle over affirmative action, Republicans pledged federal support of Proposition 209, the 1995 California Civil Rights Initiative "to restore to law the original meaning of civil rights"[91] by outlawing affirmative action. The drumbeat about harmful effects picked up during the 2000s when conservatives announced, "Because we are opposed to discrimination, we reject preferences, quotas, and set-asides based on skin color, ethnicity, or gender, which perpetuate divisions."[92] Their disapproval of preferential policies "in education or in corporate boardrooms" was spelled out in 2008.[93] Again shining a light on the notion of unfairness to Whites in 2016, Republicans announced that they "reject unfair preferences, quotas, and set-asides as forms of discrimination."[94] Like court opinions that warn preferential policies potentially reinforce negative stereotypes, Republicans warned during the 2000s that they "can lead people to question the accomplishments of successful minorities and women"[95] and that such Democratic Party policies "treat those in the ghetto as if their interests were somehow different from our own."[96]

Supreme Court admonitions concerning stereotyping are channeled equally by presidents. Donald Trump's Executive Order 13950 that banned race-based diversity training echoed the justices' reasoning. The text of the September 2020 EO stated that its purpose was to "combat offensive and anti-American race and sex stereotyping and scapegoating" and that "blame-focused diversity training reinforces biases and decreases opportunities for minorities."[97] Decades before Trump, Ronald Reagan's high-profile opposition to racial quotas was also anchored partly in the view that they were harmful to Blacks, insisting that "quotas . . . cast a shadow on the real achievements of minorities."[98] It was actually Nixon who jumpstarted presidential claims about racial stereotyping. At the same time that the Section 8(a) Program built out by his administration stipulated that racial minorities are presumed "socially disadvantaged" under the program, it also permitted challenges to that presumption with "credible evidence to the contrary."[99] Going further, Nixon dispelled the notion that "Black" and "poor" are synonymous. In his view, "To equate 'poor' with 'Black' does a disservice to the truth."[100] "Many of the worst slums are Black; many are White. And by the same token, the skilled trades, the businesses, and professions increasingly are populated by affluent Blacks whose children go to the best schools."[101]

Presidential agreement with Court reasoning is stronger on the subject of White rights and reverse discrimination. President Trump ratcheted up the reverse discrimination critique. Asked in 2020 by Fox News debate moderator Chris Wallace why his administration "directed federal agencies to end racial sensitivity training that addresses White privilege or critical race theory," Trump replied, "I ended it because it's racist. I ended it because a lot of people were complaining that they were asked to do things that were absolutely insane. That it was a radical revolution that was taking place in our military, in our schools, all over the place. And you know it, and so does everybody else."[102] The Obama administration straddled the fence by supporting race-conscious efforts while simultaneously warning against policies that disadvantage Whites. The 2011 *Guidance on Voluntary Use of Race to Achieve Diversity and Avoid Racial Isolation in Elementary and Secondary Schools* advised that "no student applicant to a school or program should be insulated—based on his or her race—from an assessment or comparison to all other student applicants, to ensure that the district minimizes the impact of its program on those students."[103]

Well before the Trump and Obama presidencies, Reagan's ire comparably rested on the belief that they unfairly excluded Whites. He said, "The truth is, quotas deny jobs to many who would have gotten them otherwise, but who weren't born a specified race or sex. That's discrimination pure and simple and is exactly what the civil rights laws were designed to stop."[104] As well, one of George H. W. Bush's main objections to initial versions of the 1991 civil rights act were that the act failed to protect "innocent non-parties" by not allowing Whites to pursue legal action.[105]

Supreme Court justices' reverse discrimination script was recited by President Bill Clinton more earnestly than any other president. Clinton repeatedly voiced his commitment to preserving White rights and his empathy for White angst over affirmative action. He explained, "This is psychologically a difficult time for a lot of White males, the so-called angry White males. Why? Because those who don't have great educations and who aren't in jobs which are growing, even though they may have started out ahead of those of you who are female and of different races, most of them are working harder for less money than they were making 15 years ago."[106] Asked how he would address White discontent, Clinton said that he would tell those workers about his efforts on their behalf.[107] Putting words into action, Clinton ordered federal agencies to implement the requirements of the 1995 *Adarand* ruling not just "as a matter of constitutional law," but as "a set of basic policy principles."[108] The comprehensive review that he ordered stressed that the "wrong way" to implement affirmative action was to prefer an unqualified person over a qualified person.[109] In the longest ever speech on affirmative action (nearly 50 pages) Clinton explained that the main purpose of the comprehensive review was to address "fair questions" about the effectiveness or justness of particular affirmative action programs.[110]

The idea that racial classifications reinforce negative stereotypes of Blacks as unqualified and undeserving gained a lot of traction in American politics at the start of formal federal affirmative action during the 1960s, then picked up steam during the 1990s. Black conservatives led the fight to ban it, most notably lead proponent of California's Proposition 209 Ward Connerly, who insisted that preferences reinforce feelings of inferiority in Black youth.[111] The broader political undercurrents that run against the idea that Blacks are an undifferentiated monolith or that they think and act alike surfaced in plain view in the 2016 and 2020 election cycles. Both cycles amplified the fact that Americans are disinclined to characterize the

Black population in a uniform way, including liberals. Intense recriminations followed former President Donald J. Trump's infamous query "What do you have to lose?"[112] Trump was aiming to convey that Blacks were faring badly enough in 2016—economically—that a vote for him could not make them any worse off. But liberals took President Trump to task for suggesting that all Blacks are disadvantaged.

Just as the Court evinces a mindfulness of *White* rights and *White* burdens as such, so too the rest of the body politic arbitrates White interests as *White*. This can be seen partly in the critical acclaim and market success of *The New York Times* bestseller *Hillbilly Elegy*,[113] a memoir centered on the woes of the White working class. Author turned politician J. D. Vance was featured on major mainstream and online news platforms as the voice of rural White America. Also considered code for expressing the belief that Whites are losing ground to minorities and women was South Carolina Republican Senator Lindsey Graham's complaint during the Brett Kavanaugh Senate confirmation hearings that he was a "single White male from South Carolina" told he "should just shut up."[114]

Politicians of all stripes sang the anthem of the White working class on the heels of Donald J. Trump's surprise success in the polls in 2015 and ultimately the ballot box in 2016. National conversations emphasized the need to pay more attention to their plight and all the ways that their interests were long ignored by Beltway politicians. The idea that White privilege and wealth were passed down from one generation to the next was caricatured as far-fetched and easily disproved. The dominant narrative in more recent national and state elections is that the White working class's future prospects for success are increasingly dim, that they are the forgotten, deprived of their slice of the American pie, so to speak. In the background of these developments are major demographic shifts that chip away at both the size of the White majority in the US and the viability of White privilege.

SECTION SUMMARY

In short, as in Supreme Court opinions also in the national political arena the core premise of race-based preferences never gained a firm footing. Mass opinion surveys show that, since the 1990s, a clear majority of US adults believe that affirmative action entails hiring less qualified Blacks. Trend survey data show that the overwhelming majority also believes that Whites are hurt by affirmative action. The party system is split. Democrats avoid confronting either the anti-White or anti-Black claim head-on. Republicans rarely miss an opportunity to do so. In presidential politics, however, there is clearer alignment with the Court on both subjects. Trump, Reagan, and Nixon boldly trumpeted the racial stereotyping and anti-White bias claims. Clinton urged empathy with "the so-called angry White males." The Obama administration cautioned against assessing students chiefly in racial terms. Highly publicized developments in 2016 and 2020 confirm just how widely the Supreme Court's concern for *White* interests and Black stereotyping was shared throughout the country. All serves as clear evidence that affirmative action jurisprudence toes the line of racial politics in the way that it too centers the interests of the White working class and argues against negative racial stereotyping.

Chapter Four

Judicial Policy Restraints on Racial Reform

What Can and Cannot Be Done

The formalized policy proscriptions and prescriptions set down from *Bakke* (1978) through *Students for Fair Admissions* (*SFFA*, 2023) present a more complex relationship between the Supreme Court and the rest of America, as compared to the themes discussed in earlier chapters. On the core question whether race can ever justifiably influence formal policymaking, the Court is on the same page as political parties and presidents, but at odds with the general public and a growing number of states. The latter prefer colorblind policies, while the former continues to approve race-based considerations in certain contexts. On the other hand, there is a broad national consensus that supports use of race-specific policies to correct identified instances of discrimination, a consensus that matches the justices' stance on remedial affirmative action. The same goes for the Court's aversion to specific features of affirmative action programming, most of all quotas and permanency. Both are rejected across the political spectrum. A national consensus complements also the ban on using race awareness to accomplish most of the original aims, namely to redress broad societal discrimination, correct racial disparities, help underserved communities, and to supply role models to minority youth.

To this list of impermissible goals set down from 1978 through 2016, *SFFA* (2003) added another: attainment of a racially diverse student body. This particular feature of the holding in *SFFA* represents a major departure from 40 years of precedent, but movement toward the public preferences. Aside from this issue, however, the latest Supreme Court ruling is in step with every other policy-related component of the preceding decades of affirmative action jurisprudence and its politics.

Race and the Colorblind Policy Standard

COURT OPINION ON COLORBLIND POLICY

Affirmative action case law continues to permit race awareness, but in an even more restrictive fashion than in years past. *Students for Fair Admissions* (*SFFA*, 2023) ratcheted up the Court's embrace of colorblindness as the core principle of the equal protection clause. The constitutional question in *SFFA* was "whether a university may make admissions decisions that turn on an applicant's race." The final ruling banned race-aware college admissions programs, but not on the basis of a blanket colorblind ideology. It hinged instead on the argument that the Harvard and University of North Carolina programs lacked measurable objectives, employed race improperly, and lacked meaningful end points.[1] The *SFFA* majority stopped short of mandating colorblindness across the board. It left the door open to other race-conscious policies in military academies, prisons, applicant essays, as well as in the workplace and educational settings where remedial action is necessary (as explained later).[2]

Notwithstanding its limited approval of race-aware policies, the 6–3 majority in *SFFA* underscored the impropriety of race awareness as a matter of principle. Employing stronger language than its predecessors, *SFFA* projected a "marked discomfort with the use of race," according to Chief Justice Roberts. He cited a long list of major civil rights decisions as proof that the "core purpose" of the equal protection clause is that of doing away with "all governmentally imposed discrimination based on race." In his words, "Eliminating racial discrimination means eliminating all of it," except where racial classifications "survive a daunting two-step examination known in our cases as 'strict scrutiny.'" To drive home the point, Roberts hearkened back to Justice Harlan's dissent in *Plessy v. Ferguson* (1896) and repeated the signature line in that case, that "in view of the Constitution, in the eye of the law, there is in this country no superior, dominant, ruling class of citizens. There is no cast here. Our Constitution is color-blind, and neither knows nor tolerates classes among citizens." Although prior to *SFFA* (2023) race-sensitive policies and programs were given the stamp of approval across four decades, dozens of challenges, and from the Burger

Court to the Roberts Court, such policies were always kept on a short leash, so to speak. The Court's timidity was partly at the behest of interest group litigation, according to Perry.[3] However, there are several reasons why the Supreme Court never responded to such demands by way of fully adopting the colorblind doctrine. Former law clerk to Chief Justice Earl Warren and former Assistant to the US Solicitor General Earl Pollock lays them out in *Race and the Supreme Court*.[4] First was belief that the equal protection clause (EPC) and federal civil rights laws do not prohibit all explicit race considerations, only certain types. Second, the EPC and civil rights statutes were never understood as premised on a colorblind principle. Third, laws that do no more than prohibit discrimination are often inadequate to the task of dismantling racial barriers and their effects. Finally, the Supreme Court has recognized that certain compelling interests justify and, at times, compel race consciousness.

Critical for our purposes is that Supreme Court approval of benign race consciousness stretches back to *Bakke* (1978), where Justice Powell's principal opinion was the first to endorse the use of race to serve compelling interests. *Bakke*'s endorsement was reaffirmed multiple times afterward. Writing for seven justices in *Minnick v. California Dept. of Corrections* (1981), Justice Stevens underscored that five members of the *Bakke* panel rejected plaintiffs' legal theory that "the hiring or promotion of a person based in whole or in part on sex or racial background or ancestry is unconstitutional and void." Stevens wrote that *Bakke* "unequivocally stated that race may be used as a factor in the admissions process in some circumstances." In *Wygant v. Jackson Board of Education* (1986) a plurality composed of liberal, conservative, and moderate Justices Powell, Rehnquist, O'Connor, and then–Chief Justice Burger rebuffed plaintiffs' claim that racial considerations violate the equal protection clause. Writing for the panel, Powell stipulated that "in order to remedy the effects of prior discrimination it may be *necessary* [emphasis added] to take race into account."

Again at the 25-year anniversary of *Bakke*, *Grutter* noted that "the only holding for the Court in *Bakke*" was that validating the use of race. The plaintiff, Barbara Grutter, a White Michigan resident who applied to the University of Michigan Law School, argued the law school "had no compelling interest to justify their use of race in the admissions process." Grutter had a 3.8 GPA and 161 LSAT score and alleged that she was rejected because the law school used race as a "predominant" factor, giving minority applicants with similar credentials an unfair advantage, in violation of the Fourteenth Amendment, Title VI of the Civil Rights Act of 1964, and other federal laws. Grutter's argument was rejected by Justice O'Connor along with four other justices who explained that "although all governmental uses of race are subject to strict scrutiny, not all are invalidated by it." *Gratz v. Bollinger* (2003) likewise rejected petitioners' claim that there is never a compelling justification for racial classifications.

At the 35-year anniversary of *Bakke* too Justice Kennedy and six other justices in *Fisher v. University of Texas at Austin I* (2013) reaffirmed that racial considerations are lawful under certain circumstances. Along with Chief Justice Roberts and Justices Scalia, Thomas, Breyer, Alito, and Sotomayor, Justice Kennedy agreed that "the University's use of race in the admissions process violated the Equal Protection Clause of the Fourteenth Amendment." However and importantly, Kennedy maintained that there are conditions in which race may be considered as long as "the admissions process can withstand strict scrutiny." In a second challenge brought by Abigail Fisher in 2016 in *Fisher v. University of Texas at Austin II*[5] a plurality of justices once again validated the University of Texas at Austin admissions plan that expressly considers racial identity "as one of the many ways in which [an] academically qualified individual might contribute to, and benefit from, the rich, diverse, and challenging educational environment of the University."

A key point made across the various cases upholding racial preference prior to *SFFA* is that neither the Constitution nor modern civil rights laws are properly understood as colorblind. Arguments to the contrary often turn to the lone dissent in the infamous 1896 *Plessy v. Ferguson* decision. Objecting to state-enforced racial segregation, Justice John Marshall Harlan wrote in his dissent, "Our Constitution is color-blind, and neither knows nor tolerates classes among citizens."[6] But Randall Kennedy emphasizes that Harlan offered no support for the colorblind thesis in *Plessy*.[7] Indeed Kennedy details how racial selectivity arose during the framing of the Fourteenth Amendment and was not rejected.[8]

Lawsuits that point to federal civil rights legislation as support for the colorblind thesis have met little success too. Powell admitted in *Bakke* (1978) that the Civil Rights Act of 1964 is "susceptible of varying interpretations" and that "isolated statements of various legislators" during congressional proceedings could be taken out of context to support the proposition that the bill "enacted a purely colorblind scheme." Powell conceded, nonetheless, such a reading would be flawed and not "read against the background of both the problem that Congress was addressing and the broader view of the statute that emerges from a full examination of the legislative debates. . . . The problem confronting Congress was discrimination against Negro citizens at the hands of recipients of federal moneys." Furthermore, "there simply was no reason for Congress to consider the validity of hypothetical preferences that might be accorded minority citizens; the legislators were dealing with the real and pressing problem of how to guarantee those citizens equal treatment."

Congress's special authority to enact racial preferences was an important consideration for Chief Justice Warren Burger in his opinion for the 6–3 panel in *Fullilove* (1980). He forthrightly stated, "We reject the contention that in the remedial context the Congress must act in a wholly 'color-blind' fashion." As observed in school desegregation decisions, "just as the race of students must be considered in determining whether a constitutional violation has occurred, so also must race be considered in formulating a remedy." Later, *Sheet Metal Workers v. EEOC* (1986) held that "Congress deliberately gave the district courts broad authority under Title VII to fashion the most complete relief possible to eliminate 'the last vestiges of an unfortunate and ignominious page in this country's history.'" Notably, "a court may have to resort to race-conscious affirmative action when confronted with an employer or labor union that has engaged in persistent or egregious discrimination. Or such relief may be necessary to dissipate the lingering effects of pervasive discrimination." And while *Adarand* (1995)[9] later abandoned *Fullilove*'s deferential posture toward congressional power, it did not disturb the basic precept that civil rights laws permit Congress as well as state and local governments and private entities to employ race when they have a compelling interest to do so.

Despite consistently approving it in the years leading up to the *Students for Fair Admissions* ruling in 2023, the Supreme Court always displayed the same unease with race awareness as that exhibited in *SFFA*. We see this in several developments over the years, most of all the many caveats tied to its approval, the number of plans invalidated, and the proportion of cases decided by slim margins. Almost all of the justices prefer a measured policy approach. None have ever endorsed carte blanche use of racial classifications. Alternatively, in the words of *Grutter* (2003), "context matters when reviewing race-based governmental action under the Equal Protection Clause." Under certain circumstances it is warranted; in others, it is not. The general rule articulated by Chief Justice Roberts's majority opinion in *SFFA* kept with this tradition of conditional support, that "racial discrimination [is] invidious in all contexts," that race-specific policies are the exception to the rule, that the equality principle "cannot be overridden except in the most extraordinary case," and that the Court's "acceptance of race-based state action has been rare for a reason."

Another indication of the Supreme Court's long-term unease with race-specific policies is the fact that it always demanded holistically designed affirmative action policies, namely, those in which race constitutes a *plus* factor that is weighed along with other nonracial factors such as residency, legacy, special skills, and so on. Race may not be considered exclusive of other factors or serve as the determining factor in a preferential scheme. One of the criticisms that Chief Justice Roberts made in *Students for Fair Admissions* (2023) about the Harvard admissions process is that "'race is a determinative tip for' a significant percentage 'of all admitted African American and Hispanic applicants.'" He rejected Justice Ketanji Jackson's suggestion that race was only a plus in the University of Carolina admissions process. For Roberts, neither admissions plan was "genuinely holistic." A third sign that the Court was never fully onboard with race-based decision-making is that it always held that the less race is relied upon in a preferential scheme, the better. Justice Kennedy's *Fisher v. Texas* (2016) opinion commented approvingly on the University of Texas's measured approach and especially "the fact that race consciousness played a role in only a small portion of admissions decisions."

The fact is, Supreme Court justices have regarded race considerations as so thorny in the judicial process that they repeatedly highlight how such considerations work at cross-purposes and that, at some point, their use must come to an end. *Fisher II* (2016) intimated as much by requiring periodic assessments to determine "whether changing demographics have undermined the need for a race-conscious policy." As well, Justice Powell wrote in *Wygant* (1986) that the "core purpose of the Fourteenth Amendment" was to "do away with all governmentally imposed discriminations based on race." *Croson* (1989) warned, "The dream of a Nation of equal citizens in a society where race is irrelevant to personal opportunity and achievement would be lost in a mosaic of shifting preferences based on inherently unmeasurable claims of past wrongs." Justice O'Connor criticized the dissenting opinion by liberal Justices Marshall, Brennan, and Blackmun for embracing an interpretation of equal protection that, she said, "effectively assures that race will always be relevant in American life" and that the ultimate goal of eliminating "entirely from governmental decision-making such irrelevant factors as a human being's race" will never be achieved.

Liberal justices, too, have expressed their belief that preferential policies should eventually end. The fact that the Federal Communication Commission's (FCC) affirmative action plan in *Metro* (1990) contained the "seed of its own termination" was redeeming, in Justice Brennan's view. The

FCC legislation adopted by Congress empowered the agency to implement a minority ownership policy for granting and transferring broadcasting licenses in 1978,[10] in order to correct the underrepresentation of racial minorities in the broadcast media. The 5-4 Supreme Court judgment upholding the plan envisaged the minority ownership policy as a means of achieving greater programming diversity. Brennan wrote, "Such a goal carries its own natural limit, for there will be no need for further minority preferences once sufficient diversity has been achieved." This ambition was articulated plainly in *Grutter v. Bollinger* (2003), where at least five justices projected the year 2028 as the probable end date for all affirmative action. Among these five were liberal justices Stevens, Ginsburg, and Breyer, along with Justice Souter. For this 5–4 panel in *Grutter* Justice O'Connor wrote: "It has been 25 years since Justice Powell first approved the use of race to further an interest in student body diversity in the context of public higher education. Since that time, the number of minority applicants with high grades and test scores has indeed increased. . . . We expect that 25 years from now, the use of racial preferences will no longer be necessary to further the interest approved today."

The upshot of Chief Justice John Roberts's opinion in *Parents Involved* (2007) was that not only is race consciousness harmful per se, but to merely think in racial terms perpetuates the racism that necessitated special policies in the first place. *Parents Involved* and *Meredith* are arguably odd cases for Roberts to lay out this thinking. Up against plaintiffs' personal concerns, both school districts were beset with entrenched school segregation for decades. The Jefferson County school district in Louisville, Kentucky, was found liable in 1973 for having maintained a segregated school system and was placed under a court-ordered desegregation decree that was dissolved in 2001. The Seattle, Washington, school district struggled also with school segregation. Both districts adopted the race-sensitive plans in an effort to "reduce racial concentration in schools and to ensure that racially concentrated housing patterns do not prevent nonwhite students from having access to the most desirable schools." Meanwhile, the lead plaintiff in *Parents Involved*, a Seattle school district ninth-grader (Andy Meeks) who suffered from attention deficit hyperactivity disorder and dyslexia, was accepted into a small biotechnology program but denied assignment because his enrollment contributed to seg-regation. In *Meredith* the lead plaintiff, Crystal Meredith, was the mother of a kindergartener who recently moved to the district, lived within a mile of the nearest school, but assigned to a school 10 miles away under the Jefferson County plan. Together with Justices Scalia, Thomas, and Kennedy, the chief justice was unconvinced by the rationale for the desegregation plans. The panel voted to invalidate both on several grounds.

Significant at the moment is that Chief Justice Roberts complained in 2007 *Parents Involved* about the same issue that he objected to in 2023 in *Students for Fair Admissions*. He believed that the 2007 plans "effectively assure[d] that race will always be relevant in American life, and that the 'ultimate goal' of 'eliminating entirely from governmental decision-making such irrelevant factors as a human being's race' will never be achieved." The chief justice drilled down on this point in *Students for Fair Admissions* (2023), where he placed heavy emphasis on the requirement that race-specific policies be temporary in nature. An end point was important, he explained, because "it was the reason the Court was willing to dispense temporarily with the Constitution's unambiguous guarantee of equal protection." As proof, he recounted *Grutter*'s (2003) conclusion that racial preferences would no longer be necessary in 25 years. Roberts was less charitable, asserting, "Twenty years later, no end is in sight." In this case, the chief justice pushed back to say, "The 25-year mark articulated in *Grutter*, however, reflected only that Court's view that race-based preferences would, by 2028, be unnecessary to ensure a requisite level of racial diversity in college campuses. . . . That expectation was oversold."

A final piece of evidence of the precarity of Supreme Court support over the years is the frequency with which preferential plans are invalidated and the narrow margins by which race-based plans are upheld. Table 4.1 shows a breakdown of votes in cases where the validity of race-conscious planning was addressed.[11] It shows the Court is just as likely to uphold racial preference, as to invalidate it. Of the 29 cases listed, 13 resulted in favorable judgments, 13 unfavorable, and in the remaining three there was no official vote. In cases where a favorable judgment was rendered, slim majorities carry the day; in most instances, either five or six justices approved the plan. In one of the two most recent cases, *Fisher v. University of Texas II* (2016), only four justices did so because the vacancy created by Justice Antonin Scalia's death had not yet been filled and Justice Elena Kagan did not participate.[12] The only exceptions to the trend of tenuous support are the two 9–0 rulings, both of which involved unique circumstances atypical of affirmative action policymaking—one pertained to the Bureau of Indian Affairs with extremely limited jurisdiction, the other a military base in the Philippines.

The tenuous nature of Supreme Court approval of affirmative action is evident from the very start of its work on this front, something that lead

Table 4.1. Affirmative Action Cases: Final Vote, Disposition, and Opinion Author, 1974–2023

Year	Case	Vote	Final Disposition of Race-Conscious Plan/ Planning	Main Opinion Author
1974	DeFunis v. Odegaard	5–4	No ruling	Per curiam
1974	Morton v. Mancari	9–0	Favorable	Blackmun
1978	Regents California v. Bakke	5–4	Unfavorable	Powell
1979	U.S. Steel Workers v. Weber	5–2	Favorable	Brennan
1980	Fullilove v. Klutznick	6–3	Favorable	Burger
1981	Minnick v. California Dept. of Corrections	8–1	No ruling	Stevens
1982	Weinberger v. Rossi	9–0	Favorable	Rehnquist
1984	Firefighters Local 1784 v. Stotts	6–3	Unfavorable	White
1986	Wygant v. Jackson	5–4	Unfavorable	Powell
1986	Sheet Metal Workers v. EEOC	5–4	Favorable	Brennan
1986	Firefighters v. City of Cleveland	6–3	Favorable	Brennan
1987	U.S. v. Paradise	5–4	Favorable	Brennan
1987	Johnson v. Transportation Agency	6–3	Favorable	Brennan
1989	Richmond v. Croson	6–3	Unfavorable	O'Connor
1989	Martin v. Wilks	5–4	Unfavorable	Rehnquist
1990	Metro v. FCC	5–4	Favorable	Brennan
1993	Northeastern v. Florida	7–2	Unfavorable	Thomas
1995	Adarand Constructors v. Pena	5–4	Unfavorable	O'Connor
2000	Adarand Constructors v. Slater	n/a	Unfavorable	Per curiam
2001	Adarand Constructors v. Mineta	n/a	No ruling	Per curiam
1999	Texas v. Lesage and U.S.	n/a	Favorable	Per curiam
2003	Gratz v. Bollinger	6–3	Unfavorable	Rehnquist
2003	Grutter v. Bollinger	5–4	Favorable	O'Connor
2007	Parents Involved v. Seattle, Meredith v. Jefferson County	5–4	Unfavorable	Roberts
2009	Ricci v. DeStefano	5–4	Unfavorable	Kennedy

continued on next page

Table 4.1. Continued.

Year	Case	Vote	Final Disposition of Race-Conscious Plan/ Planning	Main Opinion Author
2013	*Fisher v. University of Texas*	7–1	Favorable	Kennedy
2014	*Schuette v. Coalition to Defend AA*	6–2	Unfavorable	Kennedy
2016	*Fisher v. University of Texas II*	4–3	Favorable	Kennedy
2023	*Students for Fair Admissions v. Harvard*	6–3	Unfavorable	Roberts

Source: Created by the author.

authors of its main opinions have pointed out. Justice O'Connor's *Grutter* (2003) opinion characterized the 1978 *Bakke* ruling that first permitted race-based affirmative action as "fractured," in that it produced six separate opinions, none of which commanded a majority. Justice Powell wrote the principal opinion in *Bakke*, cast the fifth vote that resulted in invalidation of the set-aside program, but reversed the lower court's injunction against all racial considerations. As described by *Grutter* (2003), the remaining justices in *Bakke* were evenly split. Four voted to uphold the racial set-aside program in that case against "all attack," while four voted to invalidate. Roberts's *Students for Fair Admissions* opinion made note of the shaky support behind the foundational ruling in *Bakke*, describing it as "deeply splintered." As for the principal opinion, Roberts highlighted that "no other Member of the Court joined Justice Powell's opinion." According to the chief justice, in the years to follow *Bakke* lower courts struggled for clarity on whether *Bakke* was binding precedent up until *Grutter* (2003), when Justice O'Connor endorsed Powell's justification for race-based admissions. This too, Roberts wrote, represented "another sharply divided decision."

COLORBLINDNESS IN POLICYMAKING

Whereas the Supreme Court has consistently but narrowly approved racial preferences for decades, the same is not true in all corners of the public square. Democrats have long embraced race-conscious policies on a regular basis. So have Republicans, but in a more circumspect fashion. Also in the

Oval Office we observe a long history of support for race-sensitive decision-making. On the other hand, the average American has virtually always been on a different page. We learned in chapter 3 that the overwhelming majority of Americans embrace meritocracy and colorblindness as a matter of principle. Here, we probe the extent to which the public wants colorblindness put into practice. From table 4.2 we learn that indeed the overwhelming majority wants the formal policy process to operate in a colorblind fashion and rejects race-based affirmative action policy. Some scholars contend that the public's embrace of colorblind policymaking is the result of organized efforts to mobilize sentiment against affirmative action.

For example, Mark Golub argues that colorblind constitutionalism has been "transformed into a powerful conservative rights-based attack on legislative efforts to minimize racial inequality."[13] A number of analysts attribute the opposition to racism and sexism, while others point to different life experiences and perspectives. Offering a more layered explanation for lay citizens' "limited acceptance to affirmative action," Faye J. Crosby concludes that "there are many reasons, not a single reason, why Americans have stumbled so much in their support."[14] Some think it is unfair. Some don't understand it. Others believe that it doesn't work. Still others see affirmative action as harming its intended beneficiaries.

Whatever the reason, the time series data in figure 4.1 on page 156 sourced by the NORC's General Social Survey (GSS) paint a clear picture of public opposition to race-based policies. They establish that roughly three out of four Americans oppose preferential hiring and promotion of Blacks, and that the opposition is intense and persistent. Of the 76 percent of US adults shown as opposed fully 45 percent report being strongly opposed. The mix of single surveys in table 4.2 suggests that race-based affirmative action policy has never won steady support from a majority, but instead a degree of public equivocation for a period of time. We see this in the back-and-forth from the 61 percent that favored the policy in 2018 to the 63–70 percent and the 58 percent that more recently opposed it as of 2023 and 2022, respectively. We also see in table 4.2 more intense negative attitudes toward "preference" as compared to "assistance." The Pew surveys that reference "preferential treatment" yielded larger opposition majorities, 62 and 65 percent, respectively. Likewise, the Columbia University polls reveal 50 percent opposition to "affirmative action programs that give *preference* to racial minorities" versus "affirmative action programs that give *assistance*." On this evidence we can say that *Students for Fair Admissions* (2023) brought the Supreme Court closer to the public's side of the affirmative action controversy.

Table 4.2. Support for Colorblindness in the Formal Policymaking Process, US, 1987–2023, Select Years

Year	Survey Question	Select Responses (%)
2023	Do you think college should or should not be allowed to consider an applicant's race, among other factors, when making decisions on admissions?[a]	Should: 25 Should not: 65 Not sure: 10
2023	As you may know, the US Supreme Court may soon decide whether colleges can continue to consider an applicant's race as part of their admissions policies. What should the Supreme Court do regarding colleges considering race in admissions? Should college be . . .[b]	Allowed to consider race: 30 Not allowed to consider race: 70
2023	The US Supreme Court is weighing whether colleges and universities can consider race and ethnicity as part of their admissions decisions, a practice commonly known as affirmative action. Do you think the Supreme Court should or should not prohibit the consideration of race and ethnicity in admissions?[c]	Should: 35 Should not: 63
2018	Do you generally favor or oppose affirmative action programs for racial minorities?[d]	Favor: 61 Oppose: 30 No opinion: 9
2016	Do you generally favor or oppose affirmative action programs for racial minorities? (*Economist*/YouGov, June 28, 2016)	Favor: 34 Oppose: 38 Not sure: 28
2016	Do you generally favor or oppose affirmative action programs for racial minorities?[d]	Favor: 54 Oppose: 40 No opinion: 6
2015	Do you generally favor or oppose affirmative action programs for racial minorities?[d]	Favor: 50 Oppose: 42 No opinion: 8
2013	Are you in favor of affirmative action programs for racial and ethnic minorities? (*Economist*/YouGov, June 24, 2013)	Favor: 36 Oppose: 41 Not sure: 23

Year	Survey Question	Select Responses (%)
2013	Do you favor or oppose affirmative action programs for minorities in hiring, promoting, and college admissions? (CBS News/*New York Times* Poll, June 6, 2013)	Favor: 53 Oppose: 38
2012	We should make every effort to improve the position of Blacks and minorities, even if it means giving preferential treatment.[c]	Agree: 33 Disagree: 62
2009	Are you in favor of affirmative action programs for racial and ethnic minorities? (*Economist*/YouGov, July 24, 2009)	Favor: 26 Oppose: 41 Not sure: 33
2009	Are you in favor of affirmative action? (*Economist*/YouGov, July 29, 2009)	Favor: 25 Oppose: 39 Not sure: 36
2009	We should make every effort to improve the position of Blacks and minorities, even if it means giving preferential treatment.[c]	Agree: 31 Disagree: 65
2008	Do you support or oppose affirmative action programs that give preference to racial minorities in areas such as hiring, promotions, and college admissions? (ABC News/*USA Today*/Columbia University Poll, September 23, 2008)	Support: 44 Oppose: 50
2008	What about affirmative action programs that give assistance but not *preference* to racial minorities in areas such as hiring, promotions, and college admissions—would you support or oppose this? (ABC News/ *USA Today*/Columbia University Poll, September 23, 2008)	Support: 67 Oppose: 28
2008	Do you favor or oppose affirmative action programs? (Rasmussen Reports, July 30, 2008)	Favor: 28 Oppose: 46
2004	Do you generally favor or oppose affirmative action programs for *Blacks*? (Leadership Conference on Civil Rights, January 2004)	Favor: 57 Oppose: 36

continued on next page

Table 4.2. Continued.

Year	Survey Question	Select Responses (%)
2004	Do you generally favor or oppose affirmative action programs for *Hispanics*? (Leadership Conference on Civil Rights, January 2004)	Favor: 57 Oppose: 35
2003	Do you generally favor or oppose affirmative action programs for racial minorities? (Gallup Poll, June 24, 2003)	Favor: 49 Oppose: 43
2002	Do you support or oppose affirmative action programs that give preferences to Blacks and other minorities? (*Washington Post*/Kaiser Family Foundation/Harvard University, October 2002)	Support: 38 Oppose: 55
2002	We should make every effort to improve the position of Blacks and minorities, even if it means giving preferential treatment.[c]	Agree: 24 Disagree: 72
2001	Do you generally favor or oppose affirmative action programs for racial minorities?[d]	Favor: 47 Oppose: 44 No opinion: 9
1997	Now I'm going to read you some proposals concerning social issues that were discussed during this year's presidential and congressional campaigns. As I read each one, tell me if you generally favor it or oppose it. Do you favor or oppose limiting affirmative action efforts in hiring, contracts, and college admissions? (Kaiser Family Foundation, January 15, 1997)	Favor: 47 Oppose: 39
1995	Generally speaking, are you in favor of affirmative action programs designed to help minorities get better jobs and education, or are you opposed to them—or haven't you heard enough to say? Is that (favor/ oppose) strongly or (favor/oppose) somewhat? (*Los Angeles Times*, March 22, 1995)	Favor strongly/somewhat: 52 Oppose strongly/ somewhat: 28
1995	All in all, do you favor or oppose affirmative action programs for Blacks and other minority groups? (NBC News/*Wall Street Journal* Poll, 1995)	Favor: 46 Oppose: 41

Year	Survey Question	Select Responses (%)
1993	We should make every effort to improve the position of Blacks and minorities, even if it means giving preferential treatment.[e]	Agree: 34 Disagree: 63
1987	We should make every effort to improve the position of Blacks and minorities, even if it means giving preferential treatment.[e]	Agree: 24 Disagree: 71

Sources: Except where indicated, survey data in the table were obtained from *Polling the nations.* (n.d.). Topic: Affirmative action. Last accessed 4/25/2022 from https://ptn-infobase-com.exlibris.colgate.edu/topics/VG9waWM6NTI=?aid=14265.

[a]*Economist*/YouGov Poll (2023, June 17–20). Last accessed 2/12/2025 from https://docs.cdn.yougov.com/1ts4uenkci/econTabReport.pdf.

[b]CBS News/YouGov Poll (2023, June 14–17). Last accessed 2/12/2025 from https://docs.cdn.yougov.com/rkdvnuctms/cbsnews_20230618_abortion_2.pdf.

[c]Most oppose banning consideration of race and ethnicity in college and university admissions. (2023, May 11–15). AP/NORC. https://apnorc.org/projects/most-oppose-banning-the-consideration-of-race-and-ethnicity-in-college-and-university-admissions.

[d]Gallup, Inc. (n.d.). *Race relations.* Last accessed 4/25/2022 from https://news.gallup.com/poll/1687/race-relations.aspx.

[e]Rosentiel, T. (2009, June 2). Public backs affirmative action, but not minority preferences. Pew Research Center. https://www.pewresearch.org/2009/06/02/public-backs-affirmative-action-but-not-minority-preferences/.

Note: This table excludes surveys with "women" or "gender" in the question excluded, so as to have a straight comparison between race-based and other forms of affirmative action.

In contrast, *SFFA* enlarged the divide between the Court and political leaders, inasmuch as it fortified the role of the colorblind principle in the formal policymaking process. Anderson's *The Pursuit of Fairness* offers a deep dive into how both Democrats and Republicans advanced color-conscious policies during the late 1960s.[15] But, the Republican Party position is two-sided. On one side, it touts the virtues of race neutrality, notably in regard to elementary and secondary schooling. Republicans launched a full-on attack of racial busing during the 1970s and in 1984, insisting, "No child should be assigned to, or barred from, a school because of race."[16] When it comes to federal funding, on the other hand, Republicans have the longer record of advancing race-specific policy initiatives. They bragged in 1972 that they "provided more support to predominantly Black colleges than ever before—twice the amount being spent when President Nixon took office."[17] In the early 2000s they touted how "Republicans have made Historically

Figure 4.1. Support for Race-Based Preferential Policies. *Source*: Davern, M., Bautista, R., Freese, J., Morgan, S. L., Smith, T. W. (n.d.). *General social surveys, 1972–2021*. NORC, 2021: NORC at the University of Chicago [producer and distributor]. Last accessed 2/16/2021 from the GSS Data Explorer website at gssdataexplorer.norc.org.

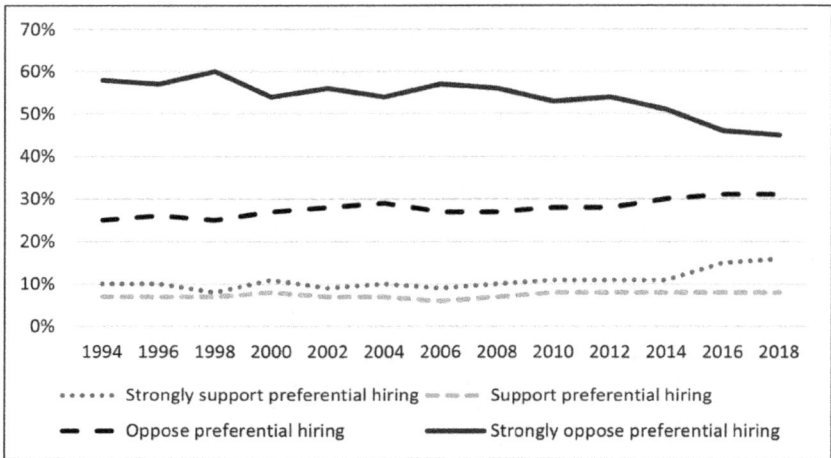

Black Colleges and Universities" a priority and applauded the 30 percent increase in funding for HBCUs.[18] Notwithstanding the conservative politics of the 1970s and 1980s Republicans pledged to "place minority citizens in responsible positions," which efforts yielded a record 20 percent increase of minority federal employees.[19] The Left similarly stressed in 1980 that "particular attention should be given to substantially increasing the share of funding Black colleges receive."[20] Decades later Democrats promised a robust and historic dedicated fund for HBCUs, and other minority-serving institutions.[21] They regularly point to their success in diversifying government, starting in 1980 when they bragged that more Blacks and Hispanics were appointed federal judgeships and senior government positions under their leadership.[22]

It was the Political Right that instituted large-scale race-conscious economic policies years before the 1978 *Bakke* decision deemed racial classifications permissible. Conservatives boasted about "unprecedented progress in strengthening minority participation in American business," and having "created the Office of Minority Business Enterprise in March 1969 to coordinate the Federal programs assisting members of minority groups who seek to establish or expand businesses."[23] They highlighted commitment of 16 percent of the Small Business Administration dollar to minority businesses and increased minority bank deposits in 1972, then "new opportunities for Black men and women to begin small businesses of their own" in 1980, and "increasing the number of minority owners by at least 5.5 million families by the end of the decade" in 2004.[24]

Democrats too pushed increased minority business ownership, targeted assistance for minority firms, and set-asides for minority businesses starting in 1980.[25] They maintained emphasis on the importance of small business to people of color and pledged to "work to help nurture entrepreneurship"[26] into the 2000s, surging their public support during the 2020 election season to declare that "race-neutral policies are insufficient to rectify race-based disparities." Accordingly, liberals promised a comprehensive approach to embed racial justice in every element of their governing agenda, including in jobs and job creation, workforce and economic development, small business and entrepreneurship, eliminating poverty and closing the racial wealth gap, promoting asset building and homeownership, education, health care, criminal justice reform, environmental justice, and voting rights.[27] The 2020 promise was an expanded version of their 1972 promise to "develop affirmative programs in universities and colleges for recruitment of minorities and women for administrative and teaching positions and as students."[28]

The Supreme Court's layered conception of race awareness as problematical yet permissible is reflected in presidential politics and policies across several decades. The lone exception is the Trump administration. President Trump bragged during his first term about supporting historically Black colleges and universities (HBCUs) in Executive Order 13779 and in a presidential proclamation.[29] But, in connection with macro public policy, he championed the colorblind mantra as much as Chief Justice Roberts. Trump's EO 13950 of September 22, 2020, insisted that equal protection principles demand colorblindness and that the principles governing the federal civil service system did as well. He maintained that these principles, codified at 5 U.S.C. 2301, call for all employees to "receive fair and equitable treatment in all aspects of personnel management without regard to" race or sex "and with proper regard for their . . . constitutional rights."[30] Trump's Departments of Justice and Education rescinded all of the Obama administration's "Dear Colleague" guidance for race-conscious education policy, a move that *The New York Times* tied to the administration's press for race-blind admissions policies.[31] Trump also rescinded the Affirmatively Furthering Fair Housing rule that informed a longstanding practice of Housing and Urban Development (HUD) to require that funding recipients do more than just passive nondiscrimination.[32] Going a step further, his Department of Justice Civil Rights Division announced plans for "investigations and possible litigation related to intentional race-based discrimination in college and university admissions."[33]

The fact that, historically, the Executive Branch and the Supreme Court are otherwise in sync with one another is evident in public endorsements of race awareness by Trump's predecessors and successors. A series of "Dear Colleague" letters jointly issued by the Departments of Justice and Education during the Obama years propounded broad interpretations of affirmative action rulings. The guidance endeavored to preserve voluntary use of race-based affirmative action by strategically steering primary, secondary, and higher education institutions to maintain diversity programs. The administration explained, "The Departments of Education and Justice stand ready to support colleges and universities in pursuing a racially and ethnically diverse student body in a lawful manner"[34] and, significantly, the new guidance "reiterates the Departments' position on the voluntary use of race to achieve diversity in higher education."[35] Furthermore on the housing front Obama policies synced with the Supreme Court's support of race awareness. His administration codified the Affirmatively Furthering Fair Housing rule (AFFH), a regulation that defined the funding recipient's duty as "taking meaningful actions that, taken together, address significant disparities in housing needs and in access to opportunity, replacing segregated living patterns with racially balanced living patterns."[36]

Many years before *Bakke* (1978) Presidents John F. Kennedy and Lyndon B. Johnson established race-aware affirmative action. Kennedy first formalized it in 1961 in Executive Order 10925,[37] which mandated that federal agencies take "affirmative steps" to ensure nondiscrimination within the Executive Branch, that contractors take "affirmative action" to ensure nondiscriminatory employment practices, and that labor unions "affirmatively cooperate" in policy implementation.[38] President Johnson's 1965 EO 11246 added specificity to Kennedy's, requiring that all government contractors submit compliance reports. Johnson's order also committed the federal government to "the full realization of equal employment opportunity through a positive, continuing program in each executive department and agency" and in federal construction projects.[39] Widening its scope beyond the federal government, the Johnson administration created the President's Test Cities Program (PTCP) to promote African American employment and minority business ownership in a select number of test cities.[40]

Randall Kennedy contends that "Nixon went further than any previous president toward advancing policies that reached beyond mere antidiscrimination norms."[41] Melvin I. Urofsky agrees, adding that President Nixon "set up an expansive affirmative action program that Johnson had failed to do during his tenure."[42] For Terry H. Anderson the reasoning behind Nixon's active support of the Philadelphia Plan "remains somewhat of a mystery," but that most chalk it up to him being a realist elected on a small margin and seeking liberal support for his foreign policy agenda.[43] His Executive Order 11478 (1969) was but the first step in building out Johnson's affirmative action agenda, especially Executive Order 11246's call for affirmative action in federal contracts and employment.[44] Nixon's Office of Federal Contracts Order No. 4 added teeth to affirmative action in 1970. Where Johnson's EO 11246 required a written plan, Order No. 4 promulgated regulations that added specificity to the requirement, namely that plans include flexible goals and a timetable aimed at correcting "underutilization" of minorities by federal contractors. Where Johnson's President's Test Cities Program (PTCP) did not require small businesses to be minority-owned in order to receive subcontracts, the Nixon administration's Section 8(a) program was "larger and focused more specifically on minority-owned small businesses."[45] The same can be said of Nixon's Philadelphia Plan.

The Departments of Labor and Justice under President Nixon fought for the administration's Philadelphia Plan that imposed minority hiring goals on federal construction projects. Nixon went so far as to threaten a veto to defend his "Philadelphia Plan" against congressional opposition. The plan required that federal contractors make good faith efforts to achieve certain "goals" of minority employment on federal construction projects.[46] It was announced[47] by Nixon's Department of Labor on June 27, 1969, implemented on September 23, 1969, for all federal contractors in Philadelphia, then extended on September 29, 1969, to New York, Seattle, Boston, Los Angeles, San Francisco, St. Louis, Detroit, Pittsburgh, and Chicago. When US Comptroller General Elmer B. Staats worked with members of Congress to declare the plan invalid and to include in the 1970 supplemental appropriations bill (HR 15209) a ban on federal funding for the Philadelphia Plan, Nixon threatened to veto the bill unless the amendment was removed.[48] His key role is further documented in the Clinton 1995 review by then–Senior Adviser George Stephanopoulos and Special Counsel Christopher Edley Jr. The report explains that Nixon's sense of the "need for hiring minority group workers in the construction industry" and his belief that the construction industry posed special problems for minorities is why the Department of Labor established what is known as the Philadelphia Plan.[49] Nixon himself explained, "We would not impose quotas, but would require federal contractors to show 'affirmative action' to meet the goals of increasing minority employment."[50]

The Section 8(a) program inaugurated by Nixon became the largest race-based federal affirmative action program. The Small Business Administration's initial plan for Section 8(a) was to "assist small firms owned by disadvantaged persons to become self-sufficient, viable businesses capable of competing effectively in the marketplace." But, a 1973 Nixon administration regulation confined 8(a)'s subcontracting authority to businesses owned by the "socially and economically disadvantaged" and defined "disadvantaged persons" to include, among others, "Black Americans, Spanish-Americans, oriental Americans, Eskimos, and Aleuts." Statutory authority for the 8(a) program's[51] focus on minority-owned businesses would not come until 1978, but the Nixon administration began doing so years before.[52] This evolved out of Executive Order 11518 (1970), which required that the Small Business Administration devote special attention to "the needs and interests of minority-owned small business concerns and of members of minority groups seeking entry into the business community."[53] The most impactful Nixon-initiated program was housed in the Office of Minority Business Enterprise (MBE), established by EO 11458 (1969) to coordinate federal affirmative action programs and promote it in the private sector.[54] Under Nixon, implementation of the MBE program was stealthy, with huge increases in funding for MBEs.[55] This was in addition to increased licensing of minority businesses by the Small Business Administration and a surge of in-kind resources from the federal government.[56] Nixon's Executive Order 11625 later required federal agencies to develop comprehensive plans and specific program goals for a national MBE contracting program.[57]

When asked about the *Croson* (1989) ruling that tightened the reins on set-asides, President George H. W. Bush stated, "It didn't kill all set-asides, and it didn't kill off affirmative action. I have been committed to affirmative action. I want to see a reinvigorated Office of Minority Business in Commerce. I want to see our SBA [Small Business Administration] program go forward vigorously."[58] Regarding other restrictive rulings handed down in 1989, Bush I indicated his support for a legislative reversal, promising that "if the decisions actually turn out to hamper civil rights enforcement along the lines you're talking about, obviously I would want to take steps to remedy the situation."[59] Later, George W. Bush made known his belief that "the benches ought to reflect as best as possible the diversity of our

country." He felt a "responsibility to work for diversity as well in the administration," claimed to have met that obligation, and offered as proof a list of
minorities in his administration in high-level positions.[60] In Bush II's view
"race-neutral admissions policies ought to be tried," but "if they don't work
to achieve an objective, which is diversification, race ought to be a factor."[61]

President George W. Bush spoke favorably of race-conscious affirmative
action too. In an exchange at the Journalists of Color Convention in 2004,
Bush II rebuffed the claim that his opposition to the University of Michigan
special admissions policies under challenge in *Grutter* (2003) and *Gratz* (2003)
meant that he was opposed to affirmative action. The following snippet from
the exchange[62] evidences his public support for affirmative action:

Q: Mr. President, you say, quote, "Quotas are an unfair system
for all," with regards to your opposition to affirmative action.

THE PRESIDENT: No, no, no, whoa, whoa, whoa—with regard
to my opposition to quota systems . . .

Q: So the colleges should get rid of legacy.

THE PRESIDENT: Well, I think so, yes. I think it ought to be based
upon merit. And I think it also ought to be based upon—and
I think colleges need to work hard for diversity. Don't get
me wrong—don't get me wrong. You said "against affirmative
action," is what you said. You put words in my mouth. What
I am for is——

Q: I just read the speech, Mr. President.

THE PRESIDENT: What speech?

Q: In terms of when you came out against the Michigan affirmative action policy, and—

THE PRESIDENT: No, I said was I against quotas.

Q: So you support affirmative action but not quotas.

THE PRESIDENT: I support colleges affirmatively taking action to
get more minorities in their school.

The conventional wisdom that restrictive Supreme Court rulings were on par with President Ronald Reagan's strong opposition is not borne out by statements that he made to the public. Reagan extolled the virtues of a colorblind society; he did not embrace a colorblind conception of the US Constitution or federal laws. He bragged about the number of minorities that he appointed to state government posts when he was governor of California, the number of Blacks and Hispanics in top executive positions in his presidential administration, and about his Justice Department and the Equal Employment Opportunity Commission having "broken all records in the history of the National Government [*sic*]" in regard to civil rights prosecutions.[63] Reagan's speechmaking was supportive of race-based affirmative action, but against quotas. He offered at a February 11, 1986, news conference that "we want affirmative action to continue." The statement fit with earlier proclamations, going back to a January 19, 1982, news conference where he stated, "But I am for affirmative action; I am against quotas."[64] Reagan frequently clarified his criticism as tied to the prospect of "some affirmative action programs becoming quota systems."[65] Explaining why his Solicitor General's amicus brief in a First Circuit Court ruling[66] did not constitute "an attack on affirmative action," Reagan said, "An image has been created of me, I know, that I do not support these antidiscrimination measures. The record, on the other hand, proves the reverse."[67] When asked specifically about the pro-affirmative action judgment in *Weber* (1988), he replied that "if this is something that simply allows the training and the bringing up so there are more opportunities for them . . . I can't see any fault with that. I'm for that."[68]

Most significant is that affirmative action remained very much intact while he was in office and after his departure. Randall Kennedy reports that Reagan declined to sign a draft executive order that would have outlawed affirmative action.[69] In fact, he boasted about an order he signed on December 18, 1982, "to increase the amount of procurement that the Federal Government buys from minority-owned business."[70] His July 14, 1983, Executive Order directed federal agencies to develop a minority business enterprise (MBE) development plan of their own. He supported the 8(a) program, noting that it "provides greater access for minorities to government contracts."[71] In those same remarks he added, "I've directed the Small Business Administration and the Minority Business Development Agency to assist in creating 60,000 new minority businesses and in expanding an additional 60,000 over the next 10 years. I've established a goal of $15 billion in Federal contract and subcontract awards to minority business over the next 3 years."[72] Anderson helpfully summarizes Reagan's impact on this front as follows, "Amid all the tough talk the president did not sign the executive order to end affirmative action programs in the government and with federal contractors."[73]

SECTION SUMMARY

In all, the 2023 ruling in *Students for Fair Admissions* (*SFFA*) that disallows race-based college admissions closely parallels the public's disposition, but not that of parties and presidents. Time-series data demonstrate that the public is overwhelmingly opposed to race-based decision-making and that the opposition is intense and persistent. For their part, conservative and liberal partisans act within the policy process in ways that are supportive of race consciousness, though Republicans engage in double-speak. They decry racial busing and school assignments at the same time that they brag about their hefty funding for historically Black colleges and universities (HBCUs). It was the Political Right that instituted the largest and most robust federal affirmative action policies to date and generously funded them from the late 1960s onward. In word and deed, a long line of presidents likewise endorsed race-specific affirmative action, including Ronald Reagan, whom many inaccurately label as anti–affirmative action rather than anti-quota. Richard Nixon went farther than any other to not only establish but also build out the infrastructure of the minority business enterprise and the Small Business Administration's 8(a) subcontracting program. The sole outlier, to date, is Donald Trump, who trumpeted the colorblind mantra with fervor equal to Chief Justice Roberts's. Yet, even Donald Trump bragged during his first term about the funding that his administration channeled to HBCUs.

Taking everything into account, it is clear that colorblindness is an ideal that the general public embraces, that the Court inched closer to with *SFFA* (2023), but an ideal that national political parties and the White house have yet to fully embrace.

Policy Restraints: What Cannot Be Done in the Name of Racial Equity and Justice

The arc of *Students for Fair Admissions* (*SFFA*, 2023) bends in the same direction as earlier affirmative action rulings, all of which pronounced ever-restrictive guidelines for race-specific policies. Among the restrictions set down long before *SFFA* are the ban on use of race-based affirmative action to ameliorate systemic racism, to reduce racial imbalance, to target the needs of minority communities, or supply role models to minority youth. *SFFA*'s contribution was to also effectively bar race-based college admissions, by way of contesting the evidence proffered in years past as justification. Spann argues that in imposing these types of constraints the Supreme Court operates as a veiled majoritarian institution.[74] In what follows we learn that Spann's sense of the Supreme Court's majoritarian character is borne out by the fact that presidents also lean toward curtailment of affirmative action, as do national political parties and a growing number of states. In a similar vein, the lay public does not consider racial minority disadvantage exceptional enough to warrant special treatment. Nor does the public see a need for pro-minority policies designed to compensate for the past or to achieve racial proportionality.

THE LIMITED PROMISE OF AMERICA

Chief Justice Roberts's majority opinion in *Students for Fair Admissions* (2023) criticized the dissents for endorsing the view that the Fourteenth Amendment permits race-based measures to be used to remedy the effects of societal discrimination. Explaining that "this Court has long rejected their core thesis," Roberts recounted how Justice Powell's principal opinion in *Bakke* (1978) "firmly rejected the notion that societal discrimination constituted a compelling interest," after which the Court adopted Powell's analysis as its own in *Hunt* (1977) and *Croson* (1989). The signature line in Powell's *Bakke* opinion characterized "societal discrimination" as "an amorphous concept of injury that may be ageless in its reach into the past." It encapsulated the fact that, instead of widespread discrimination, a finding of individualized discrimination must form the basis for race-specific remedial policies.[75] The goal of reform, Powell insisted, must be "far more focused than the remedying of the effects of 'societal discrimination.'" Hoang Vu Tran explains that, "in constructing and narrowing the definition of discrimination as only express forms of racial practices, the Court not only constructed its own rules on how to adjudicate 'colorblind' policies, but most importantly, it articulated the parameters for affirmative action cases."[76] Much more broadly, it is arguable too that the Court's stance on correcting systemic racism carries enormous consequences for racial reform. It guts the original rationale for affirmative action, as laid out in President Lyndon Johnson's "shackled runner" speech.

In *Bakke* the University of California cited school desegregation and employment discrimination cases to support its societywide remediation defense. Powell countered that plaintiffs in those cases "had been the victims of discrimination—not just by society at large, but by the respondent in that case." Further, the judgments "emphasized the existence of previous discrimination as a predicate for the imposition of a preferential remedy." A major weakness of the university's position was that there had been "no determination by the legislature or a responsible administrative agency that the University engaged in a discriminatory practice requiring remedial efforts." Powell asserted, "We have never approved a [racial] classification . . . in the absence of judicial, legislative, or administrative findings of constitutional or statutory violations."

Wygant (1986) was equally emphatic that the Court "never has held that societal discrimination alone is sufficient to justify a racial classification." Here too the Court doubled down on the warning in *Bakke* (1978) that, "in the absence of particularized findings, a court could uphold remedies that are ageless in their reach into the past, and timeless in their ability to affect the future." Continuing along these lines, *Croson* (1989) found the Richmond City Council's declaration "that there had been widespread racial discrimination in the local, state, and national construction industries" an insufficient defense for the set-aside policy in that case. Justice O'Connor reasoned that to do otherwise and accept broad societal discrimination as justification "would be to open the door to competing claims for 'remedial relief' for every disadvantaged group." Her opinion for the 5–4 judgment explained that "a generalized assertion that there has been past discrimination in an entire industry provides no guidance for a legislative body to determine the precise scope of the injury it seeks to remedy." As for Richmond, Virginia, the capital of the Confederacy, she wrote that the record contained "nothing approaching a prima facie case of a constitutional or statutory violation by *anyone* [*sic*] in the Richmond construction industry."

Chief Justice Roberts's first affirmative action opinion declared in 2007 what was previously stipulated in *Bakke* (1978), that "an effort to alleviate the effects of societal discrimination is not a compelling interest." In *Parents Involved v. Seattle School District* and the companion case *Meredith v. Jefferson County* (2007) the chief justice observed that, unlike the Jefferson County, Kentucky, plan challenged in *Meredith*, Seattle never operated segregated schools. Its use of race-based school assignments was "an attempt to address the effects of racially identifiable housing patterns on school assignments." Invalidating this as a permissible goal Roberts argued, "The sweep of the mandate claimed by the district is contrary to our rulings that remedying past societal discrimination does not justify race-conscious government action."

The demand for a finding of individualized discrimination is found not only in cases where affirmative action plans were invalidated, but also in a five-person majority ruling that upheld it in *Local 28 of Sheet Metal Workers' International Association v. Equal Employment Opportunity Commission* (1986). *Sheet Metal* was the culmination of 20+ years of effort by the City of New York, the New York State Commission for Human Rights, the US Solicitor General for the Nixon administration, the US Equal Employment Opportunity Commission (EEOC), a federal district court–appointed administrator, and the Second Circuit Court of Appeals. The efforts stemmed from the union's repeated defiance of "cease and desist" government mandates from 1964 through 1983. The back and forth led to multiple court-ordered relief plans from 1975 through 1983, including an amended 1983 plan that established a 29.23 percent nonwhite membership goal to be met by August 1987.

It was particularized evidence of discrimination that led to the pro–affirmative action judgment in *Sheet Metal*. The Supreme Court observed that the district court–ordered plan was based on four judicial determinations, each grounded in extensive and detailed factual evidence. First, the union adopted discriminatory procedures for admission into its apprenticeship program. It restricted the size of its membership to deny access to non-Whites. It organized mostly White nonunion sheet metal shops and admitted to membership only White employees from those shops. And, it discriminated in favor of White applicants seeking to transfer from sister locals.[77] Interleaved throughout Justice Brennan's opinion for the Court were other facts specific to Local 28 and that Local 28 refused to admit Blacks until 1969. A 1964 state investigation showed that "Local 28 had never had any Black members or apprentices," due to admissions practices that created "an impenetrable barrier for nonwhite applicants." After 1964 there was additional "direct and overwhelming evidence of purposeful racial discrimination over a period of many years." Court records show too that the Sheet Metal Workers' International Union was formed in 1888 for the establishment of "White local unions."[78]

Concrete proof of "a historical pattern of racial discrimination in the promotions in the City of Cleveland Fire Department" grounded the pro–affirmative action ruling in *Local Number 93, International Association of Firefighters, AFL-CIO, C.L.C. v. Cleveland* (1986). The district court found that the discrimination was "effectuated by a number of intentional practices by the City." The US Court of Appeals for the Sixth Circuit agreed that the race-conscious relief ordered by the district court was "justified by the statistical evidence presented to the District Court and the City's express admission that it had engaged in discrimination." A 6–3 ruling of the US Supreme Court affirmed.

Until 1995 the US Supreme Court had carved out exceptions for Congress. In *Fullilove* (1980) Chief Justice Burger wrote that "Congress . . . may legislate without compiling the kind of 'record' appropriate with respect to judicial or administrative proceedings." In the case at hand "it is not necessary that these prime contractors be shown responsible for any violation of antidiscrimination laws." That Congress was uniquely empowered to act on evidence of a "nationwide history of past discrimination" emanated also from *Croson* (1989). There, Justice O'Connor wrote that because "Congress may identify and redress the effects of society-wide discrimination does not mean that, *a fortiori*, the States and their political subdivisions are free to decide that such remedies are appropriate." *Metro* (1990) furthermore endorsed an exception for Congress and echoed *Fullilove's* key point that "deference was appropriate in light of Congress' institutional competence as the National Legislature." Not until *Adarand Constructors, Inc. v. Pena* (1995) did the Supreme Court eliminate the exception and hold Congress to the same evidentiary standards as those imposed on state and local governments, educational institutions, employers, and nongovernmental entities. Justice O'Connor found that the equal protection component of the Fifth Amendment demanded the same searching judicial inquiry of race-conscious measures that is demanded of states under the Fourteenth Amendment.

In addition to prohibiting racial preferences designed to remedy societywide discrimination, moreover, Chief Justice Roberts contended in *Students for Fair Admissions* (2023) that racial balancing likewise violates the US Constitution. It was the second occasion on which Roberts himself declared as much. In *Parents Involved* (2007) where the Court struck down two school desegregation plans, Roberts wrote that, "however closely related race-based assignments may be to achieving racial balance, that itself cannot be the goal, whether labeled 'racial diversity' or anything else." Otherwise, "accepting racial balancing as a compelling state interest would justify imposing racial proportionality throughout American society, contrary to the Court's repeated admonitions that this is unconstitutional." For the 5–4 majority, Roberts concluded that, "in design and operation, the plans are directed only to racial balance, pure and simple, an objective this Court has repeatedly condemned as illegitimate."

The ban on racial balancing extends back decades to 1978. The Court's first favorable affirmative action judgment, *Bakke*, rejected the University of California's goal of "reducing the historic deficit of traditionally disfavored minorities in medical schools and in the medical profession." Writing for the plurality and as the swing vote in the two-part 5–4 ruling, Justice Powell stated that if the purpose of the special admissions process was to "assure within its student body some specified percentage of a particular group merely because of its race or ethnic origin," then such a "preferential purpose must be rejected not as insubstantial but as facially invalid. Preferring members of any one group for no reason other than race or ethnic origin is discrimination for its own sake. This the Constitution forbids." After *Bakke* the Court went on to disallow racial balancing on multiple occasions from 1978 through 2013. Justice Kennedy's *Fisher* (2013) opinion cited *Bakke* (1978), *Grutter* (2003), and *Parents Involved* (2007) to reinforce the point. Kennedy quoted *Bakke* to stipulate that "a university is not permitted to define diversity as 'some specified percentage of a particular group merely because of its race or ethnic origin' and that as much 'would amount to outright racial balancing, which is patently unconstitutional.'"

Not only the US Constitution but several decisions held that racial proportioning additionally violates Title VII of the landmark Civil Rights Act of 1964, including cases where affirmative action policies were upheld. A collective bargaining agreement supplied occasion to judge racial balancing in light of the original intent behind the 1964 act. The plan in *Steelworkers v. Weber* (1979) reserved 50 percent of the openings in an in-plant craft-training program for Black employees until the percentage of Black craftworkers in the plant matched Blacks' share of the local labor force. In an opinion by Justice Brennan, joined by Justices Stewart, White, Marshall, and Blackmun, the "question for decision" was framed as whether "Title VII of the Civil Rights Act of 1964 . . . left employers and unions in the private sector free to take such race-conscious steps to eliminate manifest racial imbalances in traditionally segregated job categories." Although the panel concluded that "Title VII does not prohibit such race-conscious affirmative action plans," it was careful to also stress that the plan was "a temporary measure" and "not intended to maintain racial balance, but simply to eliminate a manifest racial imbalance."

A more definitive analysis of racial balancing and Title VII came from Justice Brennan in *Sheet Metal Workers v. EEOC* (1986), where he gave a detailed account of congressional debate and proceedings on the 1964 act. Brennan homed in on language in the bill that explicitly prohibits the

US Equal Employment Opportunity Commission and federal courts from requiring employers to maintain racially balanced workforces. The "specter of 'racial balancing'" was raised repeatedly by opponents, Brennan observed. In response, bill advocates "insisted repeatedly that Title VII would not require employers or unions to implement hiring or promotional quotas in order to achieve racial balance." Accordingly the 5–4 majority in *Sheet Metal* ruled that a court may order preferential relief under Title VII to remedy past discrimination but "should exercise its discretion with an eye toward Congress' concern that affirmative race-conscious measures not be invoked simply to create a racially balanced work force."

The only circumstance in which an employer may use preferences to eliminate racial disparity is when the workplace practice that caused it can be presumed discriminatory because it is not job related, according to *Ricci v. DeStefano* (2009). Lead plaintiff Frank Ricci and several White and Hispanic firefighters brought suit against the city of New Haven, Connecticut. They alleged that the city discarded promotion exam results because they adversely impacted Black and Hispanic firefighters. The captain exam pass rate for White candidates was 64 percent, but only 37.5 percent for Black and Hispanic candidates. The lieutenant exam pass rate was 58.1 percent, 31.6 percent, and 20 percent for White, Black, and Hispanic candidates, respectively. As "guidance to employers and courts" in cases where disparate treatment and disparate impact collide, Justice Kennedy explained that in order for the city of New Haven to lawfully discard the exam results due to disparate outcomes, it had to first show that the exam was not job related and consistent with business necessity. Either that, or, the city had to show there was an equally valid, less discriminatory alternative that could have served the city's needs, but that it declined to adopt for cause. The mere fact that minorities were half as likely as nonminorities to pass the promotion exams was not enough. An employer cannot discard the test in order "to achieve a more desirable racial distribution of promotion-eligible candidates," Kennedy wrote. Such racial balancing is "antithetical to the notion of a workplace where individuals are guaranteed equal opportunity regardless of race."

Despite the fact that seniority systems are known to widen the various gaps between White and Black employees, affirmative action rulings continually shield seniority. *Teamsters v. U.S.* (1977)[79] involved a Title VII challenge to a union seniority plan that forced mostly minority city drivers or servicepersons that transferred to mostly White line drivers positions to forfeit the seniority they accumulated as a driver or serviceperson. While the Supreme Court found that the government met its burden of proving the company had engaged in discrimination, it held that the union seniority system was protected and did not violate Title VII. Seven years later the 6–3 majority in *Firefighters Local 1784 Stotts* (1984) reaffirmed that "Title VII protects bona fide seniority systems." Specifically, *Stotts*'s majority opinion by Justice Byron White concluded that, before courts can impose the kind of "make whole relief" that overrides a seniority system, individual members of a class suit must each show that they have been "actual victims of the discriminatory practice," meaning each individual must prove the practice "had an impact" on him. Much the same was again conveyed again later in *Sheet Metal Workers v. EEOC* (1986).

The Supreme Court's protection of seniority plans is bottomed on the special value accorded to seniority, as expounded in *Wygant v. Jackson* (1986). The ruling disposed of a challenge to a 1972 collective-bargaining agreement between the Board of Education in Jackson, Michigan, and the Jackson Education Association. The agreement instituted a new procedure, such that, if layoffs became necessary, seniority rules will prevail "except that at no time will there be a greater percentage of minority personnel laid off than the current percentage of minority personnel employed at the time of the layoff." After initially failing to comply with the provision in 1974, the board eventually laid off nonminority teachers with more seniority in 1976 and 1981, and retained minority teachers with less seniority. The laid-off nonminority teachers filed suit in federal district court alleging that they were laid off due to their race, in violation of the equal protection clause, Title VII, and other federal and state statutes. The district court and circuit court sided with the board. However, the US Supreme Court ruled in favor of the nonminority teachers. Justice Powell's plurality opinion for Chief Justice Burger and Justices Rehnquist and O'Connor set forth the reason for protecting seniority systems despite their racially disparate impacts. He explained, "A worker may invest many productive years in one job and one city with the expectation of earning the stability and security of seniority. At that point, the rights and expectations surrounding seniority make up what is probably the most valuable capital asset that the worker 'owns,' worth even more than the current equity in his home."

Against this backdrop, it is clear that *Students for Fair Admissions* (2023) was in keeping with one of the two main constitutional-legal criticisms that earlier decisions lodged against racial balancing. In the same spirit as authors of earlier opinions, Roberts argued in *SFFA* that the goal of achieving racial proportionality remained "patently unconstitutional" because the guarantee of equal protection requires that citizens be treated as individuals. Part of the downfall of the Harvard and University of North Carolina admissions plans in *SFFA*, he wrote, was that, "by promising to terminate their use of race only when some rough percentage of various racial groups is admitted, respondents turn that principle on its head." The other major criticism articulated over the years was voiced by Justice O'Connor's majority opinion in *Richmond v. Croson* (1989), namely, that racial balancing risks a slippery slope. The disparity between the number of city contracts awarded to minority businesses and the city's minority population prompted the city of Richmond, Virginia, to adopt a 30 percent minority contractor set-aside. The 6–3 panel in *Croson* found that the city population-to-contractor imbalance did not meet the required threshold of "identified discrimination." O'Connor stipulated a proper statistical analysis must compare the percent of qualified minority business enterprises in the relevant market to the percent of total city construction dollars awarded to minority subcontractors. Otherwise, a generalized assertion about racial inequality and industrywide discrimination has "no logical stopping point."

The slippery slope warning first set forth in *Croson* was again voiced in *Parents Involved* (2007). There, Chief Justice Roberts observed that "an interest 'linked to nothing other than proportional representation of various races . . . would support indefinite use of racial classifications, employed first to obtain the appropriate mixture of racial views and then to ensure that the [program] continues to reflect that mixture.'" To drive home his claim concerning "no logical stopping point," the chief justice highlighted "the degree to which the districts tie their racial guidelines to their demographics" and surmised that as the "districts' demographics shift, so too will their definition of racial diversity."

Also like its predecessors, *SFFA* (2023) reinforced the bar on using racial preferences purposed to meet the needs of underserved minority communities, a ban first established in *Bakke* (1978). Chief Justice Roberts recounted in *SFFA* how *Bakke* found "virtually no evidence in the record" indicating that the school's special admissions program would accomplish that end. One of the stated goals of the medical school's special admissions policy was that of "increasing the number of physicians who will practice in communities currently underserved." Justice Powell's opinion for the 5–4 judgment in *Bakke* admitted that a state's interest in the health care of its citizens is compelling enough to justify a racial classification, but that the university had not proven that its special admissions program was needed or properly designed to promote that goal. It wasn't simply that the university had "not carried its burden of demonstrating that it must prefer members of particular ethnic groups over all other individuals in order to promote better health-care delivery to deprived citizens." Rather, "the University concedes it cannot assure that minority doctors who entered under the program, all of whom expressed an 'interest' in practicing in a disadvantaged community, will actually do so." Hence, instead of reliance on racial identity, there were "more precise and reliable ways to identify applicants who are genuinely interested in the medical problems of minorities."

Partly due to "the unsupported assumption that White prime contractors simply will not hire minority firms," the majority struck the setaside in *Richmond v. Croson* (1989) and demanded concrete proof instead of assumptions. *Metro Broadcasting, Inc. v. FCC* (1990) later upheld the plan in that case, based on similar reasoning. In *Metro* and its companion case[80] the Federal Communications Commission's (FCC) preferential policies were challenged under the Fifth Amendment equal protection guarantee. The FCC policies were purposed to "compensate for a dearth of minority broadcasting experience." One awarded an enhancement to minority applications for new radio or television broadcast licenses. The other allowed a distressed broadcaster to transfer its license outside of FCC proceedings, if the recipient was a minority enterprise. A 19.8 percent minority-owned broadcaster, Metro Broadcasting, was denied a license to operate a new television station in Orlando, Florida, in 1984. The license was granted instead to a 90 percent Hispanic-owned broadcaster, Rainbow Broadcasting, Inc. Metro filed suit in the DC Circuit Court and lost. Meanwhile, the same year Faith Center, Inc., in Hartford, Connecticut, was granted permission by the FCC to assign its television broadcast license to a minority-controlled buyer, instead of Shurberg Broadcasting of Hartford, Inc. The White owner Alan Shurberg filed suit in the DC Circuit Court, challenging the FCC distress sale policy, and won.

The Supreme Court upheld both FCC policies on appeal. Especially pertinent to this discussion is that the judgment was rested on hard evidence, such as a Congressional Research Service analysis of 8,720 FCC-licensed radio and television stations that found a strong correlation between minority ownership and diversity programming. Brennan additionally cited University of Wisconsin, Howard University, and University of Massachusetts studies that found statistically significant differences in race-ethnicity of ownership and minority audience targeting, minority images, and treatment of news events. In sum, *Metro* held that the FCC did not proceed on the basis of presumptions about minority broadcasters, but rather proof.[81]

A fourth original goal of affirmative action—to provide role models for youth in marginalized minority communities—was long ago prohibited. Justice Powell identified role modeling as one of the "subgoals" of the University of California Medical School's rubric of "compensation for past discrimination" in *Bakke* (1978). "Role model theory," he wrote, centers on the idea that "by providing examples of success whom other members of the group will emulate," preferential policies can advance "the group's interest and society's interest in encouraging new generations to overcome the barriers and frustrations of the past." His opinion for the 5–4 judgment rejected role model theory. It was again rejected in a more explicit fashion in *Wygant v. Jackson* (1986). The Jackson, Michigan, Board of Education sought to provide role models for minority students as part of a larger plan to alleviate the effects of societal discrimination. The effort led to a collective-bargaining agreement between teachers and the board that called for preferential treatment of minority teachers if and when layoffs became necessary. Detailing the reasons the agreement was invalidated, Justice Powell's plurality opinion argued that "the role model theory employed . . . has no logical stopping point" in that it "allows the Board to engage in discriminatory hiring and layoff practices long past the point required by any legitimate remedial purpose." Furthermore, role model theory could have the unintended effect of reinforcing tokenism and racial inequality. Worse, "it actually could be used to escape the obligation to remedy such practices by justifying the small percentage of Black teachers by reference to the small percentage of Black students."

Students for Fair Admissions' (2023) most notable feat was to effectively ban college admissions policies that consider race in order to advance student diversity learning. To demonstrate how *SFFA* is and is not distinguishable from its predecessors, it bears highlighting, first, that student diversity was never approved as a compelling use of race in the elementary and secondary school setting. The school district briefs in *Parents Involved* and *Meredith* of 2007 articulated diversity goals to justify race-based school assignments. Besides their aim to reduce racial concentration in schools and the impact of housing segregation on minority access to top schools, the districts argued as well that educational and socialization benefits flow from a racially diverse learning environment. Chief Justice Roberts declared instead that the school plans were "directed only to racial balance, pure and simple." Roberts's opinion for the 5–4 majority in *Parents Involved* observed that "prior cases . . . have recognized two interests." In addition to the remedial goal, he wrote, "the second government interest we have recognized as compelling for purposes of strict scrutiny is the interest in diversity in higher education upheld in *Grutter*."

The line of cases in which the interest in diversity in higher education was recognized as compelling stretch back to 1978 in the Court's first affirmative action ruling. *Bakke* declared that "the interest of diversity is compelling in the context of a university's admissions program." In his principal opinion that announced a split judgment, Justice Powell explained that the University of California's goal of "attainment of a diverse student body . . . clearly is a constitutionally permissible goal for an institution of higher education" because such diversity contributes to a robust exchange of ideas. Years after *Bakke*, *Grutter v. Bollinger* (2003) set out "to resolve the disagreement among the Courts of Appeals on a question of national importance: Whether diversity is a compelling interest that can justify the narrowly tailored use of race in selecting applicants for admission to public universities." The district court in *Grutter* had deemed the law school's use of race unlawful, reasoning that "assembling a diverse student body" was not compelling because "the attainment of a racially diverse class . . . was not recognized as such by *Bakke* and is not a remedy for past discrimination." Conversely, the federal appeals court concluded that *Bakke* did establish diversity as a compelling interest. The Supreme Court agreed. O'Connor put the matter plainly, "Today we endorse Justice Powell's view that student body diversity is a compelling state interest that can justify the use of race in university admissions."

The opinion by the late Chief Justice Rehnquist in *Grutter*'s companion case, *Gratz* (2003), likewise held that student diversity was a compelling goal, even though the plan itself was struck down. Two White applicants to the University of Michigan College of Literature, Science and the Arts (LSA), Jennifer Gratz and Patrick Hamacher, directly challenged race-conscious diversity policies. Gratz was denied admission to LSA in 1995 after the university determined that she was "well qualified" but "less competitive" than the students who were admitted. Hamacher was initially waitlisted, then later denied admission in 1997 after it was determined that his academic credentials were in the qualified range but "not at the level needed for first review admission." Both filed a federal class-action suit in 1997 against the university, the LSA, and the university president.[82] The petitioners objected to "*any* use of race by the University in undergraduate admissions" and sought an injunction prohibiting the university from "continuing to discriminate on the basis of race in violation of the Fourteenth

Amendment." They charged that "diversity as a basis for employing racial preferences is simply too open-ended, ill-defined, and indefinite to constitute a compelling interest." Joined by Justices O'Connor, Scalia, Kennedy, Thomas, and Breyer, Chief Justice Rehnquist wrote, "The Court has rejected these arguments of petitioners." Finally, Justice Kennedy delineated the list of "diversity" goals pursued by the University of Texas at Austin in *Fisher v. Texas* (2016) and concluded, "All of these objectives, as a general matter, mirror the 'compelling interest' this Court has approved in its prior cases." The petitioner, Abigail Fisher, wanted the university to change the weight given to academic scores versus socioeconomic factors. Her proposal, Justice Kennedy replied, "ignores this Court's precedent making clear that the Equal Protection Clause does not force universities to choose between a diverse student body and a reputation for academic excellence."

In *Students for Fair Admissions* (2023) Roberts landed on a different conclusion than all of these earlier decisions, finding instead that student diversity learning is not a permissible goal for race-based affirmative action. It must be stressed that the chief justice did not deem race-aware diversity learning an unworthy goal, or a noncompelling goal, or one barred by the equal protection clause. On the contrary, *Students for Fair Admissions* (*SFFA*, 2023) characterized Harvard and the University of North Carolina's (UNC) interest in producing engaged and productive citizens; enhancing appreciation, respect, and empathy; or training further leaders as "plainly worthy" goals. The gravamen of Roberts's analysis in *SFFA* was that they could not be meaningfully reviewed by courts. He wrote:

> The interests they view as compelling cannot be subjected to meaningful judicial review. Harvard identifies the following educational benefits that it is pursuing: (1) "training future leaders in the public and private sectors"; (2) preparing graduates to "adapt to an increasingly pluralistic society"; (3) "better educating its students through diversity"; and (4) producing new knowledge stemming from diverse outlooks." . . . Although these are commendable goals, they are not sufficiently coherent for purposes of strict scrutiny. . . . It is unclear how courts are supposed to measure any of these goals.

In sum and substance, the Roberts Court's ban on student diversity learning is evidently a departure from the Supreme Court's prior validation of diversity learning from *Bakke* (1978) through *Fisher II* (2016). It is equally clear that in 2023 *SFFA* added another policy restriction to the already-lengthy list of restrictions crafted by prior courts.

POLITICAL RESTRAINTS

With one exception,[83] the restrictions imposed by the Supreme Court concerning affirmative action goals are in step with the prevailing views of American society at large, most notably the prohibition on remedying systemic racism and on correcting racial unevenness. Concerning the latter, constitutional law scholar Ronald J. Fiscus makes the case for "proportional quotas" that are tied to population ratio. Fiscus asks, "Let us assume a society without racism; departures from the initial racial proportions in that society can only be attributed to racism; how would we go about fixing them?"[84] On the other hand, William M. Leiter and Samuel Leiter point up the fact that Congress did not incorporate language in federal civil rights legislation that explicitly endorses voluntary racial balancing plans in the private sector.[85]

Significant for our purposes is that the lay public's dual positioning around racism in the US squares with the Supreme Court's blurred lines around proof of discrimination; so does its disinterest in further government action to reduce racial inequality. To the first point, in the same way that racial preference rulings ignore the unique barriers that structural racism poses for Blacks, a large swath of the country is as likely to believe that racism against Whites is as serious a problem as racism against Blacks. Concerns about anti-White racism have actually grown in recent years. As of 2023 nearly half of all US adults believe that there is "a lot" or "some" discrimination in America today against Whites. Fully 40 percent believed as much in the preceding years according to the Pew survey in table 4.3. The 2016 *Vox* survey shows that number takes in a 57 percent majority of Whites. And while survey respondents are two times more likely to identify Blacks and Hispanics as the target of discrimination, the belief in anti-Black racism is not hitched to a belief in White privilege. The 2020 Pew survey reveals that 59 percent of Americans believe that "White people benefit from advantages in society that Black people do not have." But that is only 20 percent lower than the number that believes there is widespread discrimination against Black people in 2021.

The Gallup survey data in table 4.4 reveal that the overwhelming majority of Americans do not believe that additional laws are needed to reduce racial discrimination and have believed as much for several decades. A slight shift, perhaps more aptly, an exception, is observed in the immediate

Table 4.3. Views of Widespread Discrimination and White Privilege, US, 1991–2023, Select Years

Year	Survey Question	Select Responses (%)
2023	In America today, how much discrimination do you think there is against the following groups:	Percent answering "A lot" or "Some" against . . . Black people: 83 White people: 46
2021	Please tell us how much discrimination there is against each of these groups in society:[b]	Percent answering "A lot" or "Some" against . . . Black people: 79 Hispanic people: 76 White people: 40
2020	In general, how much do White people benefit from advantages in society that Black people do not have?[c]	A great deal: 33 A fair amount: 26
2020	How much more difficult, if at all, is it to be a Black person in this country than it is to be a White person?[c]	A lot more difficult: 34 A little more difficult: 35 No more difficult: 28
2018	In your opinion, how well do you think Blacks are treated in your community?[d]	The same as Whites are: 53
2017	Please tell us how much discrimination there is against each of these groups in society: Black people, Hispanic, people, White people . . .[b]	Percent answering "A lot" or "Some" against . . . Black people: 81 Hispanic people: 77 White people: 40
2016	In general, how much do White people benefit from advantages in society that Black people do not have?[c]	A great deal/fair amount: 53
2016	Today discrimination against Whites has become as big a problem as discrimination against Blacks and other minorities.[e]	Percent "Agree" • US total: 49 • Whites (non-H): 57 ○ White working class: 66 ○ White college educated: 43 • Blacks (non-H): 29 • Hispanics: 38

continued on next page

Table 4.3. Continued.

Year	Survey Question	Select Responses (%)
1995	Do you think schools and businesses would or would not provide Blacks and other racial minorities with equal opportunities if the government dropped all affirmative action programs? (*USA Today*, March 24, 1995)[f]	Would: 46 Would not: 45
1991	Do you feel that there should be affirmative action laws on hiring of women and minorities, or do you think most companies such as yours would hire and train and give women and minorities the opportunities to get ahead without such laws? (*Business Week*/Harris Poll, July 8, 1991)[f]	Need affirmative action: 31 Business will do by itself: 65

Sources:

[a]CBS News Poll/YouGov. (2023, June 14–17). https://docs.cdn.yougov.com/iaqktpkrma/cbsnews_20230618_aff_action_1.pdf.

[b]Daniller, A. (2021, March 18). Majorities of Americans see at least some discrimination against Black, Hispanic and Asian people in the U.S. Pew Research Center. https://www.pewresearch.org/fact-tank/2021/03/18/majorities-of-americans-see-at-least-some-discrimination-against-Black-hispanic-and-asian-people-in-the-u-s/.

[c]Pew Research Center. (2020, July 27–August 2). *American Trends Panel Wave 71*. Final topline. file:///C:/Users/nmoore/Downloads/PP_2020.09.10_Voter-Attitudes-Race-Gender_TOPLINE%20(1).pdf.

[d]Associated Press–NORC Center for Public Affairs Research. (2018, March). *50 years after Martin Luther King's assassination: Assessing progress of the civil rights movement.* https://apnorc.org/wp-content/uploads/2020/02/50-years-after-Martin-Luther-King%E2%80%99s-Assassination.pdf.

[e]Massie, V. M. (2016, June 29). Americans are split on "reverse racism." That still doesn't mean it exists. *Vox.* https://www.vox.com/2016/6/29/12045772/reverse-racism-affirmative-action.

[f]*Polling the nations.* (n.d.). Topic: Affirmative action. Last accessed 4/25/2022 from https://ptn-infobase-com.exlibris.colgate.edu/topics/VG9waWM6NTI=?aid=14265.

aftermath of the George Floyd and Black Lives Matter movements, such that in 2020 more believed that new civil rights legislation was needed. Otherwise, from *Fisher v. Texas* of 2016 through *Students for Fair Admissions* of 2023 the justices have proceeded in the same direction as longstanding mass attitudes about racism.

Table 4.4. Perceived Need for Laws to Reduce Discrimination, US, 1993–2020, Select Years

Responses given as percentages in response to the question "Do you think new civil rights laws are needed to reduce discrimination against Black people or not?"

	Yes	No
2020	61	39
2015	40	58
2013	27	71
2011	21	76
2003	26	70
1993	38	58

Source: Gallup, Inc. (n.d.). Race relations. Last accessed 4/25/2022 from https://news.gallup.com/poll/1687/race-relations.aspx.

Public sentiment is in striking accord also with Supreme Court rules concerning racial imbalance. Asked in a 2009 Quinnipiac University survey (not shown in the table) whether members of some racial groups should get preference for government jobs so that the workforce has the same racial makeup as its community, fully 70 percent of respondents said "no," including 45 percent of Blacks who said "no" versus 49 percent of Blacks who said "yes."[86] Especially telling is that the Quinnipiac survey asked specifically about the *Ricci* Supreme Court case. The questionnaire informed respondents that the US Supreme Court would be deciding a case involving New Haven, Connecticut's, use of promotion tests for firefighters, and that because no Blacks scored high enough to qualify for promotion, the city decided to throw the test out. The question was posed, "Do you think the Supreme Court should uphold the city or order the city to promote the 14 White and one Hispanic firefighter who scored high enough for promotion?" Fully 71 percent said "promote the firefighters" and only 19 percent said "uphold the city."[87]

For many years both the Republican and Democratic Parties were in sync with the Court's devaluation of racial balancing, usually negotiated in terms of equal opportunity versus equal results. Republicans champion equal opportunity and oppose racial proportioning. Their praise for racial opportunity goes back to 1952 when they declared, "All American citizens are entitled to full, impartial enforcement of Federal laws relating to their civil rights" and called for "Federal legislation to further just and equitable treatment" in employment.[88] The 1960s brought Republicans' opportunity rhetoric into sharper focus, when they explained that "equality under law . . . becomes a reality only when all persons have equal opportunity, without distinction of race, religion, color or national origin, to acquire the essentials of life."[89]

More strident conservative opposition to outcomes-based policies came after the '60s. They were "irrevocably opposed to busing for racial balance," on the reasoning that the "racial composition of many schools results from decisions by people about where they choose to live." They turned up the volume in 1980, proclaiming "forced busing of school children to achieve arbitrary racial quotas" as disastrous, divisive, and a failure.[90] Their repudiation of racial balancing was eventually fused with anti-quota pronouncements. They argued that "equal opportunity should not be jeopardized by bureaucratic regulations and decisions which rely on quotas, ratios, and numerical requirements to exclude some individuals in favor of others."[91] A fuller elaboration came in 1984 when they insisted, "Just as we must guarantee opportunity, we oppose attempts to dictate results," and, "We must always remember that, in a free society, different individual goals will yield different results."[92] Much the same continued into the 2000s when the "Republican banner" was self-described as fulfillment of Lincoln's vision of a country in which "all people are guaranteed equal rights and opportunity to pursue their dream."[93] The "principle of affirmative access," as they characterized it, means "taking steps to ensure that disadvantaged individuals of all colors and ethnic backgrounds have the opportunity to compete economically and that no child is left behind educationally."[94] Prior to the 1960s, Democrats emphasized opportunity instead of outcomes, but later changed positions. Their 1952 agenda stressed the "right to safety and security of the person, the right to all the privileges of citizenship, the right to equality of opportunity in employment, and the right to public services and accommodations and housing."[95]

By the 1960s, however, liberals began to inch toward a results-oriented agenda, arguing that ending discrimination "demands not only equal opportunity but the opportunity to be equal."[96] The 1970s, 1980s, and later saw further demand for "a more equal distribution of power, income and wealth" and "compensatory efforts" were advanced.[97] Today's Democrats strongly reject the Supreme Court's position on racial balancing and advocate instead for results-oriented policies. The 2020 platform pledged to vigorously enforce federal housing policies through reliance on the "disparate impact standard," whereby outcomes assessment determines policy direction. Toward this end they promised that federal data collection and analysis would be adequately funded and designed to allow for "disaggregation by race" so that "disparities can be better understood and addressed."[98] Before this Democrats promised in 2016 to mandate that colleges and universities "take quantifiable, affirmative steps in increasing the percentages of racial and ethnic minority, low-income, and first-generation students they enroll and graduate." They also called for charter schools to reflect their communities and "retain proportionate numbers of students of color."[99]

The Left is at odds also with Supreme Court rulings on other affirmative action goals. Opposite the doubts expressed in *Bakke* about the distinctive needs of underserved minority communities, Democrats argue "the need for a significant increase in the number of minority and women health care professionals" and for "placing greater emphasis on enrollment and retention of minorities and women in medical schools and related health educational professional programs."[100] Also in contrast with the Court's denunciation of targeted role modeling for minority students, Democrats pledged special efforts to recruit minority teachers toward that end.[101]

We see more symmetry between the Court and presidential politics concerning remediation of systemic racism. President Barack Obama continually signaled his desire to tackle it through large-scale remedial policies, but he stopped short of implementing such policies. Much of his administration's stance was detailed in guidance for compliance with the latest affirmative action rulings. "Dear Colleague" letters from the Departments of Education and Justice to school districts and colleges across the country stipulated that, while they "recognize[d] the compelling interest in remedying the vestiges of past racial discrimination," the guidance was not aimed at that goal.[102] The departments pushed the envelope by mapping out various types of interests that institutions might articulate as justification for race-conscious school policies. Also during Obama's tenure the Equal Employment Opportunity Commission (EEOC) issued 2012 regulations that pledged legal support to employers in the event that their policies were challenged in court.[103] In the end, the Obama White House did not implement or advocate for race-specific policies expressly designed to rectify systemic racism.

Every modern president has propagated the same equal opportunity versus equal results mantra as the Supreme Court. Only two were equally interested in outcomes, most of all President Johnson, who believed it was insufficient "just to open the gates of opportunity"[104] and that it is necessary to "seek not just legal equity but human ability, not just equality as a right and a theory but equality as a fact and equality as a result."[105] Although the 1995 review by the Clinton administration stressed that "the goal of any affirmative action program must be to promote equal opportunity," it also remarked that "increases in the numbers of employees, or students or entrepreneurs from historically underrepresented groups are a measure of increased opportunity."[106] And further federal government enforcement "action is triggered by manifest underrepresentation of minorities and women."[107] Yet, the guidance also stated in blunt terms that federal agencies may not use race or gender to override bona fide seniority systems.[108]At one point even Donald J. Trump seemed of two minds concerning measurable outcomes when he declared at a 2018 Young Black Leadership Conference, "We are focused on results. . . . We want results."[109] He went on to boast about "the amazing results that we've all achieved, you've achieved—you've helped us so much in your communities," declaring that "the results speak for themselves." Trump often highlighted that the unemployment and the poverty rate for African Americans reached record lows, while minority business ownership was growing at a faster rate than any other.

The Supreme Court's call for equal access as opposed to equal outcomes was echoed by presidents sympathetic to racial reform, including Presidents Barack Obama, John F. Kennedy, and Richard M. Nixon. Obama was direct on this point, declaring, "We are not a country that guarantees equal outcomes."[110] Under his administration the Equal Employment Opportunity Commission (EEOC) regulations highlighted the problematic nature of racial imbalances, but merely encouraged Title VII employers to steer away from practices that produce imbalance, except when doing so was unavoidable due to business necessity.[111] Even the executive order that originated affirmative action centered on opportunity and access. John F. Kennedy's Executive Order 10925 mandated that contractors take affirmative action to ensure that minority applicants are employed and treated during employment without regard to their race. It wasn't until later that statistical goals and timetables were folded into federal preferential policies by Nixon's Office of Federal Contract Compliance. This, while Nixon himself railed against "any compulsory busing of pupils beyond normal geographic zones for the purpose of achieving racial balance."[112] Nixon's rationale was that "racial balance has been discovered to be neither a static nor a finite condition; in many cases it has turned out to be only a way station on the road to resegregation."[113]

Few White House occupants matched Supreme Court endorsement of opportunity over and above outcomes more than Presidents Ronald Reagan and George H. W. Bush, both of whom insisted that public policy is properly aimed at rectifying disparate treatment, not disparate impact. At the same time that Bush I supported legislative reversal of a series of Supreme Court decisions that required evidence of disparate treatment (discriminatory intent) to prove allegations, he opposed "disparate impact" as a guide for gauging constitutionality. Accordingly, Bush threatened to veto an initial version of the Civil Rights Restoration Act of 1991, claiming, among other things, that it placed too much emphasis on racial balancing. He complained,

"Unless an employer's bottom-line numbers are 'correct,' he or she will face the almost certain prospect of lawsuits in which a successful defense will be virtually impossible."[114] For Bush, "government's responsibility is to enhance, not redistribute, opportunity to ensure that all people get a fair chance to achieve their dreams."[115] Under Reagan the Equal Employment Opportunity Commission (EEOC) eliminated the requirement that agencies set goals and directed them to instead focus on the removal of barriers and on flexible plans to improve representativeness.[116] (The use of goals and timetables was not resumed until the Clinton years.) Reagan went to great lengths in his speeches to defend seniority systems in particular.[117]

Also running parallel to policy restrictions imposed by the Supreme Court are state legislative trends on this front. The 28 states that retain some form of affirmative action plans in public employment outnumber the eight states that enacted measures prohibiting preferential treatment in public university admissions, state employment, and state contracting. However, the Century Foundation reports that the eight states that ban race considerations account for almost one-third of all US high school students.[118] And, according to a source that tracks ballot measures and policies,[119] Ballotpedia, only 109 of 577 public four-year universities report that they consider race in admissions. In addition to these state-level trends affecting education are others aimed at blocking the collection of racial data in a wide range of policy spaces from corporate employment to police departments, federal and state grant agencies, and the US Census Bureau. Such efforts represent a broader strategy that cites the same constitutional and civil rights ideals as those invoked in strategies to curtail affirmative action. A *Washington Post* op-ed by Frank J. Cirillo details how White politicians in southern states deployed colorblindness as a way to adapt their messaging to a post–civil rights movement era. Cirillo explains that colorblind arguments selectively "appropriate the dream of Rev. Martin L. King, Jr. for a future post-race society by pretending it was already reality."[120]

Anti–affirmative action state referenda are uniquely indicative of the country's disposition toward race-based preferences because they represent actual policy and political choices made by the voters. Barbara Perry reports that "public universities were rethinking affirmative action not as a result of adverse court decisions but because of grassroots efforts to abolish racial preferences."[121] Breaking down the referenda data, we can see that six of the eight anti–affirmative action bans emerged out of grassroots mobilization.[122] Millions of dollars were poured into drumming up support and getting out the vote. Millions of voters turned out to formally register opposition.[123] While more recent bans target sexual orientation, table 4.5 shows that most are directed at racial, ethnic, and gender preferences.

Table 4.5. Anti–Affirmative Action Voter Referenda, Executive Orders, and State Legislation, 1996–2010

State	Year Adopted	Election Result (%)	Title of Ballot Initiative	Ballot or Policy Provisions
Arizona	2010	59.5	Arizona Civil Rights Amendment (Proposition 107)	Amended state constitution to ban preferential treatment on the basis of "race, sex, color, ethnicity, or national origin" in public education, employment, and contracting.
California	1996	54.6	Prohibition Against Discrimination or Preferential Treatment by State and Other Public Entities (Proposition 209)	Amended state constitution to prohibit preferential treatment on the basis of "race, sex, color, ethnicity, or national origin" in public employment, education, and contracting.
Colorado	2008	50.8	Colorado Discrimination and Preferential Treatment by Governments (Colorado Initiative 46)	Proposed amendment to state constitution to ban preferential treatment on the basis of "race, sex, color, ethnicity, or national origin" in public employment, education, and contracting.
Florida	1999	n/a	Executive Order 99-281	Prohibits the use of race, gender, creed, color, and national origin preferences in public employment, contracting, and education.
Michigan	2006	57.9	Michigan Civil Rights Amendment (Michigan Proposal 2)	Amended state constitution to prohibit preferential treatment on the basis of "race, sex, color, ethnicity or national origin" in public employment, education, and contracting.

State	Year Adopted	Election Result (%)	Title of Ballot Initiative	Ballot or Policy Provisions
Nebraska	2008	57.6	Nebraska Civil Rights Initiative (Nebraska Measure 424)	Amended state constitution to prohibit preferential treatment on the basis of "race, sex, color, ethnicity or national origin" in public employment, education, or contracting.
New Hampshire	2011	n/a	House Bill 0623 https://www.gencourt.state.nh.us/legislation/2011/HB0623.html	State law prohibits preferential treatment on the basis of "race, sex, national origin, religion, or sexual orientation" by state agencies and public colleges and universities.
Oklahoma	2012	59.2	Oklahoma Affirmative Action Ban Amendment (Oklahoma State Question 759)	Amended state constitution to ban preferential treatment on the basis of "race, color, sex, ethnicity or national origin" in public employment, education, and contracting.
Texas	1996/1997	n/a	Top Ten Percent Rule (Texas House Bill 588)	The Fifth Circuit banned affirmative action in 1996 but was effectively overturned by the US Supreme Court in 2003. The "Top Ten Percent Plan" is a partial replacement that automatically admits the top 10 percent of high school students to state-funded universities.
Washington	1998	58.22	Washington Initiative 200	Prohibits preferential treatment on the basis of "race, sex, color, ethnicity or national origin" in public employment, education, and contracting.

Source: Information obtained from state government websites and from Ballotpedia. (n.d.). Affirmative action. Last accessed 4/25/2022 from https://ballotpedia.org/Affirmative_action#State_bans.

SECTION SUMMARY

The bottom line here is that the Supreme Court's steady disapproval of all but two of the original stated goals of affirmative action jives with the policy preferences of US citizens, presidents, national political parties, and a growing number of states. We see this in connection with the bar on remedial policies that tackle systemic racism. Most US citizens do not believe more government action is needed to help Blacks. A majority of White citizens believe that Whites are increasingly the victims of race discrimination. We see a matchup also in connection with racial balancing. More than two-thirds of Americans reject the idea that employment test results should be ignored because of racial unevenness. Likewise on the political front, Republicans have long decried racial balancing. As Democrats merged their demands for access with equity, conservative opposition amped up during the same time period.

Presidents too side with the Court's stance on equal outcomes, all of whom champion opportunity more than results. Under President Obama the Equal Employment Opportunity Commission offered only tepid guidance regarding race-based outcomes-oriented policies. Meanwhile, several states codified the Court's takedown of traditional affirmative action goals. Citizen-driven ballot initiatives are why fewer than one out of five public four-year universities employ race-based admissions and roughly one-third of all US high school students are beyond the reach of racial preferences. In short, the legal restraints imposed by the Court on the use of race are buoyed as well by a broad coalition. A growing share of the American electorate and politicians are quite literally *actively* opposed to race-based affirmative action policy.

Anti-Racism Policy Options:
What Can Be Done in the Name of Racial Equity

Although it abandoned a long line of precedents when it banned race-based admissions, *Students for Fair Admissions* (*SFFA*, 2023) left intact remedial affirmative action—one of the other two types of race-based policies originally approved by the Court, plus it articulated other permissible race-aware policies as well. Altogether in *SFFA*, Chief Justice Roberts cited individualized discrimination, prison safety, military academy admissions, and student college application essays as situations where race awareness may still pass constitutional muster under the strict scrutiny standard. At least to date, affirmative action case law furthermore approves broadcast diversity as a compelling interest that justifies race-based decision-making. As for the politics of these judicial policies, the Court's continued approval of race-specific remedial policy matches the general public's sense of restorative justice. A decisive public consensus is coalesced around the precept that racial exclusion is contrary to American identity. There is like-mindedness too around the value of diversity, specifically the idea that American national identity is bound up in a tapestry of races, colors, creeds, religions, and national origins. Add to this that both national parties have long condemned racism and praised the virtues of diversity and inclusion, as have presidents, and a picture of alignment between the Court and the rest of America emerges.

LEGAL OPTIONS

Chief Justice Roberts wrote in *Students for Fair Admissions* (2023) that, of the compelling interests identified in prior precedents, "one is remediating specific, identified instances of past discrimination that violated the Constitution or a statute." Roberts explained that, unlike student diversity learning, workplace discrimination and school segregation are situations where courts can determine on their own whether race-based remedial action will make litigants whole or produce a racial composition commensurate to what would have existed in the absence of a constitutional violation. The Court's continuing approval of race-conscious remediation is rooted in precedent that extends back to *Bakke* (1978), the case in which guidance for remedial plans or "liability affirmative action" was first set down. The special admissions program in that case had articulated four goals. Upon striking down three,[124] Powell held that race-conscious policies derived from specific "judicial, legislative, or administrative findings of constitutional or statutory violations" are allowable. Five justices in *Bakke* invalidated the program in that case, because it was not narrowly tailored to serve the otherwise compelling goal of correcting individually identified discrimination. *Fullilove* (1980) later approved the minority business enterprise (MBE) provision of the Public Works Employment Act that was challenged there because "Congress enacted the program as a strictly remedial measure." Again in *Sheet Metal* (1986) a court-ordered plan was upheld due to lower courts' power to remedy identified discrimination through race-conscious means.

After 10 years of fleshing out what is and isn't a permissible use of race Justice Brennan announced for the 5–4 majority in *U.S. v. Paradise* (1987),

"It is now well established that government bodies, including courts, may constitutionally employ racial classifications essential to remedy unlawful treatment of racial or ethnic groups subject to discrimination." Based on the extensive evidentiary record before it in *Paradise* (1987) the Alabama Department of Public Safety was found by the federal district court to have excluded Blacks from every position for more than four decades, with the result that the discrimination was deemed "long term, open, and pervasive." The court ordered affirmative action on the reasoning that "without promotional quotas the continuing effects of this discrimination cannot be eliminated." When Alabama defied the order, the court mandated that at least 50 percent of those promoted must be Black, if qualified Black candidates were available. The Court of Appeals for the Eleventh Circuit affirmed, observing that "the relief at issue was designed to remedy the present effects of past discrimination, effects which, as the history of this case amply demonstrates, 'will not wither away of their own accord.'"

The US Supreme Court affirmed, persuaded by evidence of a long history of intentional exclusion. That record led Brennan to conclude, "The race-conscious relief at issue here is justified by a compelling interest in remedying the discrimination that permeated entry-level hiring practices and the promotional process alike." He detailed how the court-ordered quotas were a response to a National Association for the Advancement of Colored People (NAACP) lawsuit that alleged a "blatant and continuous pattern and practice of discrimination." The NAACP sought relief from the department's attempts to evade the order by reducing the size of the trooper force and the number of new troopers hired.[125] Again in 1977 the organization petitioned the court, so that it approved a consent decree in 1979. Another was approved in 1981, followed by further noncompliance, then another petition in 1983 for enforcement of the first two consent decrees.

A mere declaration of acting in a remedial capacity is not enough, even when accompanied by on-the-record admissions of past discrimination. *Wygant*'s (1986) plurality opinion insisted that, if prior discrimination is the factual predicate for race-based state action, then trial courts must inquire whether the action is indeed justifiable as a remedial plan. Those who employ affirmative action cannot "unilaterally insulate themselves from this key constitutional question by conceding that they have discriminated in the past." Having failed to establish proof of its own past discrimination, the school board's layoff plan in *Wygant* was invalidated in a 5–4 ruling. Justice Sandra Day O'Connor further stated for the 6–3 majority in *Richmond v. Croson* (1989) that "blind judicial deference to legislative or executive pronouncements," whether on the part of Congress, states, or others, will not do. And, to "accept Richmond's claim that past societal discrimination alone can serve as the basis for rigid racial preferences—would be to open the door to competing claims for 'remedial relief' for every disadvantaged group."

Students for Fair Admissions (2023) identified additional compelling interests—besides remediation—that warrant race-specific policies. One is avoiding the risks to safety in prisons posed by race riots. Chief Justice Roberts cited *Johnson v. California* (2005) as support, a case in which a prisoner challenged racial segregation in prisons as a violation of the equal protection clause.[126] Roberts first explained that courts can inquire whether race-based cell assignments will prevent harm to those in prison. Second, *SFFA* intimated that US military academies may have a compelling interest in race-based admissions programs, as argued by the US Solicitor General's amicus brief. Roberts clarified that a military academy was not involved in *SFFA* and that the issue was not addressed in the lower courts, but he nonetheless noted "the potentially distinct interests that military academies may present." Third, *SFFA* leaves college admissions applicants free to discuss and admissions counselors free to consider "how race affected his or her life, be it through discrimination, inspiration or otherwise." The chief justice was emphatic that universities may not use application essays to establish the kind of race-based admissions deemed unlawful in *SFFA*, that any benefit to a student who overcame racial discrimination or whose heritage motivated him or her "must be tied to *that student's*" courage and ability.

It remains to be seen whether the Roberts Court will adhere to precedents that permit race-based diversity programming in media broadcasting. Addressing the federal set-aside in *Metro Broadcasting, Inc. v. FCC* (1990), Brennan stressed that "Congress and the Commission do not justify the minority ownership policies strictly as remedies for victims of this discrimination. . . . Rather, Congress and the FCC have selected the minority ownership policies primarily to promote programming diversity." Furthermore, "the interest in enhancing broadcast diversity is, at the very least, an important governmental objective and is therefore a sufficient basis for the Commission's minority ownership policies."[127] Writing for the majority, Brennan concluded that, "just as a 'diverse student body' that contributes to a 'robust exchange of ideas' is a 'constitutionally permissible goal' on which a race-conscious university admissions program may be predicated, the diversity of views and information on the airwaves serve important First Amendment values."

Politics of Anti-Racism and Diversity

In its first and most recent affirmative action decision—*Bakke* (1978) and *Students for Fair Admissions* (2023), respectively—the Supreme Court channeled America's basic sense of racial justice and inclusivity. Like the justices, average Americans express the belief that the "legal rights of victims must be vindicated." More will be said in the next chapter about the body politic's attitudes toward diversity. At the moment we observe, simply, that much of the country supports the diversity goal that is bolstered by Supreme Court precedents from 1978 through 2016. General Social Survey trend data in figure 4.2 show that a supermajority of the adult population supported racial inclusion when last asked in 2002. Support strengthened over the years to 63 percent of respondents who disagreed with the statement "Blacks shouldn't push themselves where they're not wanted." GSS surveys that probe respondents' support for a housing law that bars property owners from discriminating further show that 79 percent supports such a ban.[128]

As to Supreme Court pronouncements about correcting identified discrimination, here as well we observe alignment between affirmative action case law and citizens, parties, and presidents. Survey data show that, conceptually, a majority of US adults believe that victims of identified discrimination should

Figure 4.2. Support for Inclusivity. *Source*: Davern, M., Bautista, R., Freese, J., Morgan, S. L., & Smith, T. W. (n.d.). *General social surveys, 1972–2021*. NORC, 2021: NORC at the University of Chicago [producer and distributor]. Last accessed 2/16/2021 from the GSS Data Explorer website at gssdataexplorer.norc.org

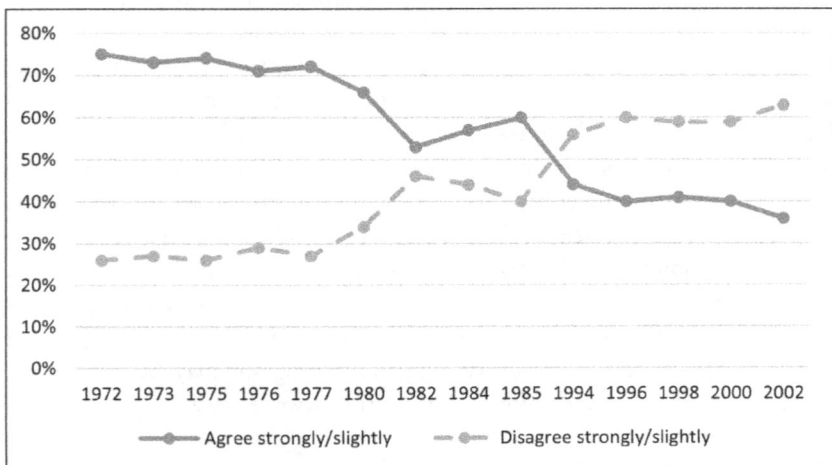

be compensated. A *Washington Post*/ABC News Poll taken on the heels of *Adarand v. Pena* (1995) asked about the use of compensatory affirmative action programs. The prompt was "The Supreme Court has also ruled that federal affirmative action programs cannot give preference to all minority contractors, but only to those who can prove their company has been discriminated against in the past. Do you approve or disapprove of this ruling?" A 55 percent majority approve this grounded use, while 41 percent disapprove.[129] The catch is, Americans' beliefs about the need for remedial justice don't line up with their policy priorities. The data in table 4.6 reveal that the country is divided over the extent to which affirmative action should be prioritized

Table 4.6. Affirmative Action as a Priority for Policymakers, US, 1999–2021, Select Years

Year	Survey Questions	Select Responses (%)
2021	Please tell me what kind of priority affirmative action should receive in the current Joe Biden presidential administration?[a]	Highest/somewhat high priority: 50 Somewhat low/low priority: 50
2008	For each item I name, please tell me what kind of priority it should receive in the next administration in Washington—the highest priority, a high priority but not the highest, or a lower priority than that? Affirmative action programs. (ABC News/*USA Today*/Columbia University Poll, September 23, 2008)	Highest priority: 56 High priority: 40 Low priority: 39
2005	Please tell me whether you think that Congress should be active and pass legislation and be directly involved in discrimination and affirmative action, or whether Congress should not be active and not pass legislation and should not be directly involved in this area? (NBC News/*Wall Street Journal* Poll, April 6, 2006)	Should pass legislation: 76

continued on next page

Table 4.6. Continued.

Year	Survey Questions	Select Responses (%)
2002	As I read you some things the new Congress might do over the next two years, please tell me if you think each should be one of their top priorities, a lower priority, or shouldn't be done at all. What about limiting or eliminating affirmative action preferences for minorities and women? Should this be one of their top priorities, a lower priority, or should this not be done at all? (*Newsweek*, November 9, 2002)	Top: 28 Lower: 35 Not be done: 30
1999	I'm going to read you a list of some different things the president and the new Congress might try to do in the next year. As I read each one, tell me if you think it should be one of their top priorities, important but a lower priority, not too important, or should not be done. What about this—limiting affirmative action that affects hiring, promotions, government contracts, and school admissions? Should this be one of their top priorities, important but a lower priority, not too important, or should this not be done? (Kaiser Family Foundation, January 1999)	Top priority: 22 Important but lower priority: 38

Sources: Except where indicated, survey data in the table were obtained from *Polling the nations*. (n.d.). Topic: Affirmative action. Last accessed 4/25/2022 from https://ptn-infobase-com.exlibris.colgate.edu/topics/VG9waWM6NTI=?aid=14265.

[a]Moore, N./YouGov. (2021, May 18–20). *Affirmative Action Omnibus.*

by policymakers. The national survey fielded by YouGov for this study shows the public is split 50/50 on whether lawmakers should make it a priority. Not only where formal lawmaking is concerned but also at the ballot box affirmative action does not register high on the list of priorities. All but a couple of data points in table 4.7 indicate that the policy does not influence voters' choice of one candidate for office over another. Nor is it the kind of

Table 4.7. Affirmative Action as a Priority for Respondents, US, 1995–2018, Select Years

Year	Survey Question	Select Responses (%)
2018	How important is it to you that the next Supreme Court justice agrees with your position on affirmative action? (*Economist/* YouGov, July 10, 2018)	Very/somewhat important: 66
2013	Thinking about some cases the Supreme Court will decide on next week (June 2013) . . . How interested are you in the court's decision on . . . affirmative action in college admissions—very interested, fairly interested, not too interested, or not at all interested?[a]	Very/fairly interested: 62
2009	As I read some issues the Supreme Court may rule on over the coming years, please tell me how important each issue is to you personally. Are court decisions on . . . affirmative action . . . very important, fairly important, not too important, or not at all important to you? (June 15, 2009)	Very/fairly important: 72
2008	How important is each of the following issues to you personally? Affirmative Action (Associated Press/Yahoo, June 23, 2008)	Not at all/slightly important: 39 Moderately important: 27 Very/extremely important: 34
2005	As I read some issues the Supreme Court may rule on over the coming years, please tell me how important each issue is to you personally. Are court decisions on . . . affirmative action . . . very important, fairly important, not too important, or not at all important to you? (Pew Research Center, November 8, 2005)	Very/fairly important: 75
2004	On a scale from 0 to 10, where "10" is "extremely important" and "0" is "not at all important" how important would you say the issue of laws eliminating affirmative action is to you? (NBC News/*Wall Street Journal* Poll, March 10, 2004)	Extremely important, 10: 19 8–9: 19 Less important, 0–7: 56

continued on next page

Table 4.7. Continued.

Year	Survey Question	Select Responses (%)
2003	I will read a list of some stories covered by news organizations this past month. As I read each item, tell me if you happened to follow this news story very closely, fairly closely, not too closely, or not at all closely. Debate over eliminating affirmative action programs. (Pew Research Center, May 14, 2003)	Not at all/not too closely: 62
1996	Bill Clinton has said that he is in favor of some types of affirmative action programs, as long as they don't use quotas. Bob Dole has said that he would eliminate most federal affirmative action programs. Would you be more likely to vote for Clinton because of his views on affirmative action, or would you be more likely to vote for Dole because of his views on affirmative action, or would neither of their views on affirmative action make a difference for your vote? (*Los Angeles Times*, April 16, 1996)	More likely Clinton: 32 More likely Dole: 35 No difference: 27
1995	If a candidate for president were committed to eliminating all government affirmative action programs that give preferences to minorities and women, would that make you more likely to vote for that candidate, less likely to vote for that candidate, or would that not affect your vote? (NBC News/*Wall Street Journal* Poll, September 1995)	More likely to vote for candidate: 18 Less likely to vote for candidate: 33 Would not affect my vote: 45
1995	Now I will read a list of some stories covered by news organizations this past month. As I read each item, tell me if you happened to follow this news story very closely, fairly closely, not too closely, or not at all closely? Proposals to eliminate affirmative action programs. (*Times Mirror*, August 24, 1995)	Very/fairly closely: 52 Not too/not at all closely: 47

Sources: Except where indicated, survey data in the table were obtained from *Polling the nations*. (n.d.). Topic: Affirmative action. Last accessed 4/25/2022 from https://ptn-infobase-com. exlibris.colgate.edu/topics/VG9waWM6NTI=?aid=14265; Pew Research Center. (2013, June 24). Final court rulings: Public equally interested in voting rights, gay marriage. https://www. pewresearch.org/wp-content/uploads/sites/4/legacy-pdf/06-24-13-Supreme-Court-release.pdf.

policy subject that most see as important enough to follow closely in the news. In fact, as far as the general population is concerned, there is scarce interest in governmental policies that do more to help Blacks. As depicted in figure 4.3, for all but two of the years during 1984–2014, less than one-third of Americans believed too little was being done to assist Blacks.

Turning to national political parties and their positioning around anti-racist policies, our multi-decade analysis of platforms reveals that a bipartisan consensus was formed decades before the Court first approved remedial affirmative action in 1978. The fact that bipartisan vows to actively combat racial discrimination started long before *Bakke* serves as additional proof that Supreme Court policy pronouncements sometimes follow, and do not lead, national political trends. In its 1940 "Negroes" plank the Democratic Party promised "to strive for complete legislative safeguards against discrimination in government service and benefits, and in the national defenses."[130] Republicans' 1940 "Negro" plank demanded that "discrimination in the civil service, the army, navy, and all other branches of the Government cease." They also opposed poll taxes and called for anti-lynching legislation as well as an "immediate Congressional inquiry" into mistreatment, segregation, and discrimination against Blacks in the armed forces.[131]

Figure 4.3. Assistance to Blacks. *Source*: Davern, M., Bautista, R., Freese, J., Morgan, S. L., & Smith, T. W. (n.d.). *General social surveys, 1972–2021*. NORC, 2021: NORC at the University of Chicago [producer and distributor]. Last accessed 2/16/2021 from the GSS Data Explorer website at gssdataexplorer.norc.org.

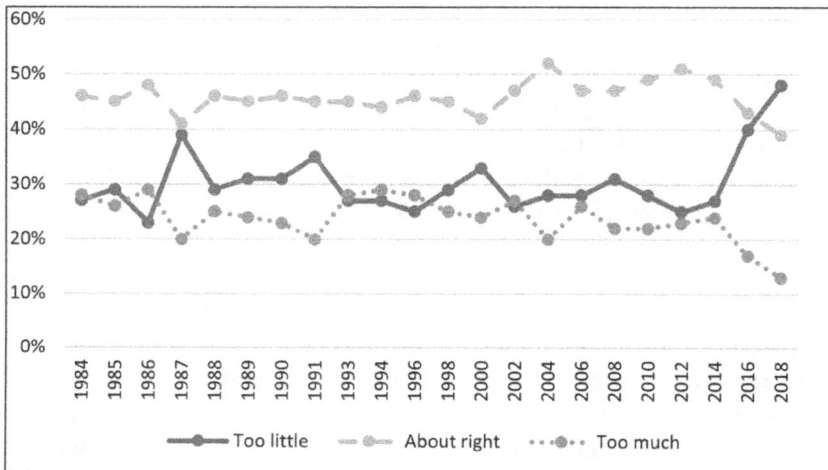

National political parties' mutual, longstanding interest in actively fighting does not extend to the question of whether to deploy race-conscious policies in that fight. Democrats' support of corrective racial preferences has closely matched the Court's, but Republicans anti-racism stance has not translated into support for race-aware remedial policies. Enforcement of statutes against ongoing illegal discrimination was as far as Republicans are willing to go.[132] Even conservative messaging on nondiscrimination became more measured as of 2004, as it advocated "aggressive, proactive measures to ensure that no individual is discriminated against," with the caveat that the best qualified individuals are encouraged to apply for jobs, contracts, and university admissions."[133]

Neither does American presidents' interest in anti-discrimination policies entail societywide racial preferences and instead centers on anti-discrimination action. Executive Branch action on this front stretches back decades and it, too, predates the Supreme Court's. Every modern president mapped out an agenda specifically to guard racial minorities' rights, except President Donald J. Trump. Trump's emphasis was instead on anti-racist teachings, as reflected in Proclamation 10110's denunciation of critical race theory and similar "theoretical frameworks"[134] and Executive Order 13950's ban on diversity training for federal agencies and contractors.[135] Trump's politics and policies are an outlier to the otherwise striking symmetry between the Supreme Court and the White House in regard to reparative justice. As an example, years before the Court's first preferential policy case, Nixon issued Executive Order 11478 in 1969; it mandated that "the Civil Service Commission shall provide for the prompt, fair, and impartial consideration of all complaints of discrimination in Federal employment on the basis of race, color, religion, sex, or national origin."[136]

Presidents Reagan and Clinton each made similar public commitments to redressing specific instances of civil rights violations. Reagan backed his promises by signing the Fair Housing Amendments Act of 1988 that expanded the reach of the original 1968 housing act. When signing the bill he remarked, "I joined with Members of Congress on both sides of the aisle in vowing that 'We will work to strengthen enforcement of fair housing laws for all Americans,' and now we've achieved that goal."[137] Before this Reagan bragged about his administration's efforts to confront civil rights infractions, asserting, "Our record on enforcing minority voting rights is at the top of the list. And we've increased to an all-time high the number of criminal civil rights cases filed."[138] He added, "If you'll look at the Justice Department and the Equal Employment Opportunity Commission, you will find that we've broken all records in the history of the National Government with regard to hearings on violations of civil rights, on trials, and on successful convictions of violations of those civil rights."[139] Finally, President Clinton made a pointed argument about the need for corrective action to redress specific instances of discrimination, as follows, "The primary justification for the use of race- and gender-conscious measures is to eradicate discrimination, root and branch. Affirmative action, therefore, is used first and foremost to remedy specific past and current discrimination or the lingering effects of past discrimination—used sometimes by court order or settlement, but more often used voluntarily by private parties or by governments."[140]

SECTION SUMMARY

Students for Fair Admissions (*SFFA*) did not disturb the Supreme Court's support of one of the two policy goals approved by decades of affirmative action case law and by the country as a whole. That remedial affirmative action is supported by the public is evidenced by the fact that most Americans believe that victims of race discrimination should be made whole. Despite citizens' support for remedial affirmative action, however, it has never been a priority for them. Another caveat is that, consistent with the Supreme Court's demand for individualized proof of discrimination are survey data that show 55 percent approve of the *Adarand* ruling mandating that only identified victims should be compensated for a company's past discrimination. As for major national parties, they too consistently rally against illegal discrimination and have done so since the 1940s. Correcting the effects of racial discrimination is another matter, one that has never achieved bipartisan support. Democrats traditionally embrace corrective measures; Republicans do not. On the presidential front, except for Donald J. Trump, every president has launched some form of anti-discrimination policy, including Ronald Reagan. Every president implemented their own brand of diversity programming as well, including George H. W. Bush. All told, to the extent that it undermines the diversity principle, *SFFA* moves the Court farther away from the body politic.

Rules of Engagement

The multi-prong constitutional test crafted by the Supreme Court severely diminishes affirmative action's capacity to improve the racial status quo in the US. The strict scrutiny test requires that race-aware policies: be narrowly tailored to fit a constitutionally permissible goal; be adopted only after race-neutral options are first considered; employ race as but one of several diversity identifiers; be applied flexibly to ensure individualized consideration; be minimally impactful on nonminorities; be devoid of hard measures like quotas and set-asides; and be temporary. While these restraints on implementation were front and center in *Students for Fair Admissions* (*SFFA*, 2023), they were originally established decades ago. In *SFFA* Chief Justice Roberts dismissed what he described as Harvard and the University of North Carolina's "trust us" response and the dissents call to "leav[e] well enough alone" and defer to universities and "experts" in determining who should be discriminated against. If any distinction is to be read into Chief Justice Roberts's 2023 opinion, it's that he doubled-down on longstanding rules of engagement by placing emphasis on the strictness of strict scrutiny.

In what follows we unpack the test of constitutionality applied in *SFFA* and its predecessors.

Court Requirements

The most critical component of the Supreme Court's multi-prong test is the requirement that race-aware plans must be narrowly tailored, meaning closely tethered to a permissible policy goal. Among the reasons that *Students for Fair Admissions* (*SFFA*, 2023) invalidated the Harvard and University of North Carolina (UNC) special admissions policies was that both failed the narrow-tailoring prong. According to Roberts, neither articulated a meaningful connection between the means they employed and the goals they pursued. He stated, "It is far from evident . . . how assigning students to these racial categories and making admissions decisions based on them furthers the educational benefits that the universities claim to pursue." He deemed the racial categories used in the plans "imprecise" and further claimed that use of "opaque racial categories undermines, instead of promotes, respondents' goals."

The narrow-tailoring requirement that proved decisive in *SFFA* was first applied to affirmative action in 1978 in *Bakke*, after which the requirement was reaffirmed time and again. Specifically in higher education cases, it demands that courts ascertain whether it is "necessary" for a university to use race to achieve the educational benefits of a diverse student body. *SFFA*'s most immediate predecessors involved the Court stressing its importance. The plan in *Fisher v. Texas* (2013) was vacated and remanded based on the Fifth Circuit's failure to apply strict scrutiny to assess whether the University of Texas offered sufficient evidence to prove that its race-based admissions program was narrowly tailored to achieve the student diversity learning goal.[141] Although *Fisher I* endorsed race-based admissions policies in principle, it was adamant about the narrow-tailoring requirement. Justice

Kennedy's opinion for the seven-person majority—which included Justices Sonia Sotomayor and Stephen Breyer—stressed that the university "must prove that the means chosen by the University to attain diversity are narrowly tailored to that goal. On this point, the University receives no deference." When the University of Texas's admissions plan was revisited three years later in *Fisher v. Texas* (2016),[142] the Court again speaking through Justice Kennedy was no less insistent on the narrow-tailoring mandate.

A second requirement for implementation was also reinforced in *SFFA*, that race-specific options must be considered before race-based policies are adopted. Chief Justice Roberts emphasized that there was no way to know whether the Harvard and University of North Carolina student diversity learning "goals would adequately be met in the absence of race-based admissions programs." His opinion followed earlier precedents that likewise stressed the need to consider race-neutral alternatives. Justice O'Connor's opinion for the *Richmond v. Croson* (1989) judgment against Richmond's set-aside program hinged partly on the fact that the city could have used race-neutral means, but chose not to. Conversely, upon determining that nonracial means were tried first, but with little success, five justices approved the Federal Communication Commission's broadcast licensing preference in *Metro Broadcasting* (1990). And, while *Grutter* (2003) clarified that it is not necessary to weigh every conceivable race-neutral alternative, the obligation to consider alternatives was pointed up again in 2016 in Justice Kennedy's opinion for the 4–3 plurality, which included Justices Ruth Bader Ginsburg, Stephen Breyer, and Sonia Sotomayor. Kennedy wrote that "when determining whether the use of race is narrowly tailored to achieve the university's permissible goals, the school bears the burden of demonstrating that available and workable race-neutral alternatives do not suffice."

A third precept governing implementation of race-specific policies is the requirement of individualized consideration. Applicants must be treated as individuals, not as part of a racial group. Roberts's complaint against the plans in *Students for Fair Admissions* (2023) turned partly on this obligation. Citing a racial gerrymandering case, *Miller v. Johnson*,[143] Roberts asserted, "We have repeatedly explained. . . . At the heart of the Constitution's guarantee of equal protection lies the simple command that the Government must treat citizens as individuals, not as simply components of a racial, religious, sexual or national class." His first treatment of this issue was in *Parents Involved* (2007), where he insisted on individualized consideration partly on the reasoning that impermissible stereotypes serve to bolster assessments that are based on racial-ethnic group membership. For the 5–4 majority the chief justice insisted, "Like the University of Michigan undergraduate plan struck down in *Gratz* . . . the plans here 'do not provide for a meaningful individualized review of applicants' but instead rely on racial classifications in a 'nonindividualized, mechanical' way."

Rigidity was proscribed throughout the years leading up to *Students for Fair Admissions* (*SFFA*, 2023), whether in the form of "inflexible quotas," "set asides," "numerical goals," or other concrete targets. The undergraduate admissions program in *Gratz* (2003) was rejected chiefly because it automatically awarded 20 points to every minority applicant. That, the Court held, was violative of the equal protection clause because it precluded equal treatment of White applicants. On the other hand, the law school plan in the companion case, *Grutter* (2003), survived scrutiny because it was more flexible. The bar on rigidity was echoed also in *Metro* (1990) and *Adarand* (1995). As well, earlier judgments in *Sheet Metal Workers* (1986) and *Croson* (1989) demanded flexibility in the form of waivers or multi-stage review to complement plans that incorporate targets. In fact, the plan in *Bakke* (1978) was invalidated due to its rigidity; it set aside 10 out of the 100 seats in the incoming class for racial-ethnic minorities.

Rejecting the college admissions plans in *SFFA* Roberts denounced what he termed Harvard and UNC's "numerical commitment." He recalled that, under Justice Powell's *Bakke* opinion, "a university could not employ a quota system." Nor could it impose a "multitrack program with a prescribed number of seats set aside for each identifiable category of applicants." In response to the universities' claims that the "metric of meaningful representation" did not involve numerical benchmarks or specified percentages, Roberts wrote that it amounted to "numbers all the same."[144] Specifically addressing UNC's admissions policy, he contended, "The racial preferences at issue here in fact operate like clockwork."

Chief Justice Roberts devoted special attention in *SFFA* to the requirement that affirmative action plans treat race as a plus factor, and not a determining factor. A lack of holistic review is another reason that the two special admissions programs in *SFFA* were struck down. Referring to Justice Sotomayor's dissent, Roberts claimed that "even the dissent acknowledges that race—and race alone—explains the admissions decisions for hundreds if not thousands of applicants to UNC each year." Again he held up *Bakke* (1978) as support, highlighting how in that case "the role of race had to be cabined, that it could operate only as a 'plus' in a particular applicant's file." Citing Harvard's amicus brief in *Bakke*, Roberts added that "the race of an applicant may tip the balance in his favor just as geographic origin or a life [experience] may tip the balance in other candidates' cases."

Not only in *SFFA* and *Bakke*, but in wholly favorable decisions too comprehensive review is in play. For instance, the plan approved in *Fisher v. Texas* (2016) filled 75 percent of the incoming freshman class through the Texas Top Ten Percent Law; it guaranteed students in the top 10 percent of their high school class admission to a Texas public university. The remaining 25 percent was admitted on the basis of a combination of Academic Index (AI) and Personal Achievement Index (PAI) scores, with race weighted as a subfactor within the PAI. Since she was not in the top 10 percent of her high school class Abigail Fisher was evaluated through the University of Texas's holistic review process. Rejected, Fisher filed suit in federal court, alleging the university's consideration of race in admissions violated the equal protection clause. Both the district court and the Fifth Circuit Court of Appeals disagreed; so did the Supreme Court. Justice Kennedy's majority opinion in *Fisher II* praised the fact that race consciousness played a role in "only a small portion of admissions decisions."

In regard to affirmative action policy as a whole, moreover, *Grutter v. Bollinger* (2003) proclaimed, "The Court expects that 25 years from now, the use of racial preferences will no longer be necessary to further the interest approved today." Other rulings insisted that race-aware diversity plans incorporate a sunset clause. This requirement has been in place since *Weber* (1979), the first to offer commentary on the importance of temporariness. Several years later the plan in *Sheet Metal Workers v. EEOC* (1986) was approved partly because it was temporary. That an end date is not as important as an end point was observed in *Johnson v. Transportation Agency* (1987). The Santa Clara County Transportation Agency voluntarily adopted a race- and gender-based plan in December 1978. It was invalidated by a federal district court on the conclusion that it failed *Weber*'s temporariness test. The Ninth Circuit Appeals Court reversed, holding that "the absence of an express termination date in the Plan was not dispositive, since the Plan repeatedly expressed its objective as the attainment, rather than the maintenance of a work force mirroring the labor force in the County." Supreme Court approval also turned on the temporariness issue.

Whatever "administrative inconvenience" may result from its multi-prong test is of little concern to the Court. The plans in *Croson* (1989), *Gratz* (2003), and *Parents Involved* (2007) were invalidated due to faults in their execution. Representing what the Court deemed a well-devised execution is the plan in the second Abigail Fisher lawsuit. A variety of adjustments and readjustments were tried over several years by architects of the University of Texas special admissions program to satisfy the multi-prong test. In the years preceding the *Fisher I* (2013) lawsuit, the university adjusted its admissions policy multiple times in light of new Supreme Court rulings or newly enacted state legislation. Prior to 1996, admission to the university was based on an academic index (AI) that combined test scores and high school grade point averages, with preference given to racial minorities. In 1997 and after the Fifth Circuit ruling in *Hopwood v. Texas*[145] (1996) deemed the use of "any consideration of race in college admissions" a violation of the equal protection clause, a new policy was adopted in 1997. It combined an applicant's AI with their "personal achievement index" (PAI), without consideration of race in the calculation of either index. This policy was replaced in 1998 after the Texas Legislature reacted to *Hopwood* by enacting the Top Ten Percent Law. The law guarantees college admission to students who graduate from a Texas high school in the top 10 percent of their class. The University of Texas at Austin again changed its system after the Supreme Court upheld the use of race in college admissions in *Grutter v. Bollinger* in 2003. Justice Kennedy's opinion in *Fisher II* dove into the details of the school's changing policies, laying out how they came to be, what they entailed, the particulars of their implementation, and so on. Along the way, Kennedy commented approvingly on the compelling interest goal, narrow tailoring, individualized consideration, and temporariness of the plan. The university's 20-year effort to survive Supreme Court review proved successful in 2013[146] and 2016, but, clearly, not without considerable back-and-forth.

POLITICS OF IMPLEMENTATION

In national racial politics we find marked parallels to Supreme Court strictures concerning how, when, where, and why race awareness may be used. Under Stephen C. Halpern's framing, the limitations of affirmative action reform are rooted not so much in political process as they are in legal processes. Halpern concludes in his book *On the Limits of the Law: The Ironic Legacy of Title VI of the 1964 Civil Rights Act*, "On matters of race and education we have routinely come to rely on laws, law enforcement, and litigation to resolve problems perhaps better dealt with by other means. Indeed, in the nearly three decades since Congress enacted Title VI, legal reforms and litigation have become increasingly futile, irrelevant, and symbolic surrogates for real solutions to our racial problems—in schools and elsewhere."[147] Yet, such limitations are not without a political footing. Neither is the way that Court decisions hamstring racial preferences. Both are in accord with public sentiment. Take, for example, the temporariness standard articulated in Court opinions. A majority of America wants affirmative action policy changed; many want it ended altogether. According to the Reuters/Ipsos 2023 poll in table 4.8, nearly half

Table 4.8. Public Opinion on Ending Affirmative Action, US, 1995–2023, Select Years

Year	Survey Question	Select Responses (%)
2023	In general, do you think affirmative action programs in hiring, promoting, and college admissions should be continued, or do you think these affirmative action programs should be abolished?[a]	Abolished: 47 Continued: 53
2023	Do you think affirmative action programs in hiring, promoting, and college admissions should be continued?[b]	Should be continued: 57 Should be abolished: 38
2023	Due to racial discrimination, programs such as affirmative action are necessary to help create equality. (Reuters/Ipsos, February 6–13, 2023)[c]	Strongly/tend to agree: 49 Strongly/tend to disagree: 37
2016	Do you think affirmative action programs for racial minorities were never needed, were needed once but not anymore, are still needed, but eventually will not be needed, or will always be needed? (*Economist*/YouGov, June 28, 2016)	Needed once, but not anymore: 29 Needed, eventually not needed: 25 Were never needed: 11
2009	Do you think affirmative action programs that give preferences to Blacks and other minorities in hiring, promotion, and college admissions should be continued, or do you think these affirmative action programs should be abolished? (Quinnipiac University Poll, June 3, 2009)	Abolished: 55 Continued: 36
2008	Should affirmative action programs be continued or are they no longer necessary? (Rasmussen Reports, July 31, 2008)	No longer necessary: 46 Continued: 32
2006	What do you think should happen to affirmative action programs? Should they be ended now, should they be phased out over the next few years, or should affirmative action programs be continued for the foreseeable future? (CBS News, January 9, 2006)	Ended now: 12 Phased out: 33 Continued: 36
2003	Do you think affirmative action programs that provide advantages or preferences for Blacks, Hispanics, and other minorities in hiring, promoting, and college admissions should be continued, or do you think these affirmative action programs should be abolished? (Associated Press, March 12, 2003)	Abolished: 35 Continued: 53

continued on next page

Table 4.8. Continued.

Year	Survey Question	Select Responses (%)
2003	Do you think affirmative action programs in hiring, promoting, and college admissions should be continued, or do you think these affirmative action programs should be abolished? (CBS News/*New York Times*, January 23, 2003)	Abolished: 37 Continued:54
2000	Should affirmative action policies be continued or eliminated? (Portrait of America, January 18, 2000)	Eliminated: 44 Continued: 28
1999	Should affirmative action programs be continued or eliminated? (Portrait of America, January 22, 1999)	Eliminated: 44 Continued: 30
1997	What if abolishing affirmative action programs meant there would be far fewer minority doctors, lawyers, and other minority professionals? Then, would you say affirmative action programs should be continued or should be abolished? (*New York Times*/CBS News Poll, December 13, 1997)	Abolished: 57 Continued: 31
1995	There is a proposal to eliminate all affirmative action criteria—such as race or gender—in deciding admissions to state universities, hiring for government jobs, and awarding of government contracts. Do you strongly favor, somewhat favor, somewhat oppose, or strongly oppose this proposal? (NBC News/*Wall Street Journal* Poll, March 1995)	Strongly/somewhat oppose: 33 Strongly/somewhat favor: 57

Source: Except where indicated all data obtained from: *Polling the nations.* (n.d.). Topic: Affirmative action. Last accessed 4/25/2022 from https://ptn-infobase-com.exlibris.colgate.edu/topics/VG9waWM6NTI=?aid=14265.

[a]Reuters/Ipsos Poll. (2023, February 6–13). 2024 primary election, debt ceiling, Ukraine, university admissions. Accessed 3/13/2024 from https://www.ipsos.com/sites . . . pdf.

[b]NPR/PBS NewsHour/Marist Poll. (2023, June 12–14). Majority of Americans say it was wrong for the Supreme Court to overturn Roe. https://www.npr.org/2023/06/21/1183253121/roe-dobbs-abortion-affirmative-action-gender-supreme-court.

[c]CBS News Poll/YouGov. (2023, June 14–17). https://docs.cdn.yougov.com/iaqktpkrma/cbsnews_20230618_aff_action_1.pdf.

of Americans believe formalized affirmative action programs should be ended, though more (53%) believe they should be continued. In 2016 a 54 percent majority believed that affirmative action programs were needed once but not anymore or they believe that it is needed now, but not indefinitely. If we add to these numbers the 11 percent that believe such programs were never needed in the first place, it is safe to say that three-quarters of America are disinclined to sanction any sort of permanency for affirmative action programs.

Meanwhile, coinciding with affirmative action case law's insistence on continual reassessment is survey respondents' brand of "Mend It, Don't End It." In the backdrop of national conversations about *Grutter* and *Gratz* in 2003, the 1995 upset over California Proposition 209, and the Clinton administration's "Mend It, Don't End It" 1995 policy was a desire on the part of most for some kind of change. As shown in table 4.9, of the 54 percent desirous of change, those that felt "affirmative action programs designed to help Blacks and other minorities get better jobs and education" went too far were double the number that felt it did not go far enough. When asked at the start of anti-affirmative action mobilization in the 1990s whether such programs should be mended, changed, or ended altogether, 65 percent of adults in the US in 1995 said that they should be mended.

Survey data show that the Supreme Court's distaste for rigidity from *Bakke* (1978) to *Fisher II* (2016) is shared by the American electorate. As of 2023 a majority of voters expressed disapproval of racial quotas, and most of those who disapprove feel strongly about it. We see this in the data shown in table 4.10. Of special note are the results of the NBC News series data. Respondents were given two prompts, one of which was "affirmative action programs are still needed to counteract the effects of discrimination against minorities, and are a good thing as long as there are no rigid quotas." The results of the NBC News series show that public opposition to quotas extends back to the early 1990, when affirmative action first came under attack nationally. In addition to the NBC News data, the other polls in the table show too that the public was decidedly opposed to quotas, around 60 percent.

The Supreme Court's nullification of rigidity was preceded by Congress's efforts to preemptively achieve the same result. Moore details the record-setting floor proceedings on the landmark Civil Rights Act of 1964, the need to win two-thirds support to break southerners' filibuster, and the huge compromises needed to win over moderate Republicans most especially for the equal employment provisions in Title VII.[148] Accordingly, Section

Table 4.9. Public Opinion on Amending Affirmative Action, US, 1991–2003, Select Years

Year	Survey Question	Select Responses (%)
2003	Do you think affirmative action programs designed to help Blacks and other minorities get better jobs and education go too far these days, or don't they go far enough, or are they just about adequate now? (*Los Angeles Times*, February 2003)	Go too far: 36 Not far enough: 18
1997	What's the best thing to do with affirmative action programs giving preference to some minorities—leave the programs as they are, change the programs, or do away with the programs entirely? (*New York Times*/CBS News, December 13, 1997)	Change them: 43 Do away with them entirely: 25
1997	I would like to read you some pairs of statements. For each one, please tell me which of the statements you agree with more. Which is closer to your view—affirmative action programs are needed to promote diversity and to ensure that minorities have access to college, job promotions, and government contracts; or, affirmative action programs are no longer necessary and are a form of reverse discrimination that should be ended? (Democratic Leadership Council, July 27, 1997)	Affirmative action programs are no longer needed: 50 Affirmative action programs are needed: 43
1995	If you had to choose, would you rather see the federal government's affirmative action programs mended—that is, changed in certain ways—or ended altogether? (*Time*/CNN/Yankelovich, July 21, 1995)	Mended: 65 Ended altogether: 24
1995	What's the best thing to do with affirmative action programs giving preference to some minorities—leave them as they are, change them, or do away with them entirely? (*Washington Post*/ABC News, March 19, 1995)	Change them: 47 Do away with them entirely: 28
1991	Do you think affirmative action goes too far, or not far enough? (*Los Angeles Times*, September 25, 1992)	Too far: 24 Not far enough: 27

Source: Polling the nations. (n.d.). Topic: Affirmative action. Last accessed 4/25/2022 from https://ptn-infobase-com.exlibris.colgate.edu/topics/VG9waWM6NTI=?aid=14265.

Table 4.10. Public Attitudes Toward Racial Quotas, US, 1991, 1995, 2021

Year	Survey Question	Select Responses (%)
2023	Affirmative action programs are still needed to counteract the effects of discrimination against minorities, and are a good thing as long as there are no rigid quotas.[a]	Strongly agree: 37 Agree, not strongly: 16 Not sure: 5
2021	Do you favor or oppose affirmative action programs that promote employment and college access for Blacks by requiring businesses and colleges to hire and admit a specific number or quota of Blacks?[b]	Oppose: 50 Favor: 50
2013	Affirmative action programs are still needed to counteract the effects of discrimination against minorities and are a good thing as long as there are no rigid quotas.[a]	Strongly agree: 29 Agree, not strongly: 16 Not sure: 10
2010	Affirmative action programs are still needed to counteract the effects of discrimination against minorities and are a good thing as long as there are no rigid quotas.[a]	Strongly agree: 31 Agree, not strongly: 18 Not sure: 8
2003	Affirmative action programs are still needed to counteract the effects of discrimination against minorities and are a good thing as long as there are no rigid quotas.[a]	Strongly agree: 32 Agree, not strongly: 17 Not sure: 8
2000	Affirmative action programs are still needed to counteract the effects of discrimination against minorities and are a good thing as long as there are no rigid quotas.[a]	Strongly agree: 33 Agree, not strongly: 21 Not sure: 9
1995	Affirmative action programs are still needed to counteract the effects of discrimination against minorities and are a good thing as long as there are no rigid quotas.[a]	Strongly agree: 33 Agree, not strongly: 17 Not sure: 7
1995	Should businesses establish affirmative action quotas? (*USA Today*, March 24, 1995)	Oppose: 63
1995	Here are some specific affirmative action programs. For each one, please tell me if you strongly favor, somewhat favor, somewhat oppose, or strongly oppose that program . . . set-aside programs that guarantee a certain percentage of government contracts to minority-owned firms? (NBC News/*Wall Street Journal* Poll, March 1995)	Somewhat/strongly oppose: 59

continued on next page

Table 4.10. Continued.

Year	Survey Question	Select Responses (%)
1995	Do you favor or oppose affirmative action programs that promote Black employment by requiring businesses to hire a specific number or quota of Blacks? (*Time*/CNN/ Yankelovich, January 30, 1995)	Oppose: 61
1991	Affirmative action programs are still needed to counteract the effects of discrimination against minorities and are a good thing as long as there are no rigid quotas.[a]	Strongly agree: 40 Agree, not strongly: 21 Not sure: 11
1991	Do you favor or oppose affirmative action programs that promote Black employment by requiring businesses to hire a specific number or quota of Blacks? (*Time*/CNN/ Yankelovich, April 29, 1991)	Oppose, Whites: 63 Oppose: Blacks: 22

Source: Except where indicated, survey data in the table were obtained from *Polling the nations*. (n.d.). Topic: Affirmative action. Last accessed 4/25/2022 from https://ptn-infobase-com. exlibris.colgate.edu/topics/VG9waWM6NTI=?aid=14265.

[a]NBC News/Hart Research Associates. (2023, Apr 14–18). NBC News Survey. Accessed 3/3/2025 from https://acrobat.adobe.com/id/urn:aaid:sc:VA6C2:bd94d0b7-8925-4871-a89b-05 797a0e488d.

[b]Moore, N./YouGov. (2021, May 18–20). *Affirmative Action Omnibus.*

703 of Title VII was amended by a bipartisan vote to provide that "nothing contained in this title shall be interpreted to require any employer . . . to grant preferential treatment to any individual or to any group because of the race, color, religion, sex, or national origin of such individual or group on account of an imbalance which may exist with respect to the total number or percentage of persons of any race, color, religion, sex, or national origin employed by any employer."

Section 406 of the 1964 act additionally stipulates that "nothing herein shall empower any official or court of the United States to issue any order seeking to achieve a racial balance in any school by requiring the transportation of pupils or students from one school to another or one school district to another in order to achieve such racial balance, or otherwise enlarge the existing power of the court to insure compliance with constitutional standards." A similar legislative consensus was forged during congressional proceedings on the 1966 Elementary and Secondary

Education Act (ESEA), which provides that "nothing contained in this Act shall . . . require the assignment or transportation of students or teachers in order to overcome racial imbalance."

Opposition to rigidity is more prominent and enduring in presidential politics. The "Mend It, Don't End It" mantra signaled President Clinton's disapproval of quotas. Asked at a news conference about Americans who felt they were punished by affirmative action he replied, "First of all, our administration is against quotas and guaranteed results, and I have been throughout my public career."[149] Clinton later boasted that his administration had "done more than the last two to reform affirmative action."[150] He ordered the comprehensive review of affirmative action for the precise purpose of deciding whether federal programs should be reformed. Upon completion of the review by White House advisors and staff, Clinton gave the longest ever presidential speech on affirmative action, where he set forth his perspective. He shared that he believed it was good for America, but not perfect, that "we should reaffirm the principle of affirmative action and fix the practices. We should have a simple slogan: mend it, but don't end it."[151] A memorandum signed the same day directed federal agencies to eliminate or reform any program that created or utilized quotas.

Ronald Reagan's forceful rhetoric around affirmative action during his time in office mainly targeted quotas. Reagan proclaimed on many occasions, "I am against quotas,"[152] and that he was opposed to "some affirmative action programs becoming quota systems."[153] He instanced the history of racial quotas in the US as proof,[154] detailing how they were used against Jewish Americans.[155] Deriding advocates of racial quotas he said, "They couldn't be more wrong," that "when the Civil Rights Act of 1964 was being debated in the Congress, Senator Hubert Humphrey, one of its leading advocates, said he'd start eating the pages of the act if it contained any language which provides that an employer will have to hire on the basis of percentage or quota . . . [and] . . . if Senator Humphrey saw how some people today are interpreting that act, he'd get a severe case of indigestion."[156] Reagan believed that quotas were discriminatory against White men, that they denied jobs to otherwise qualified White men, were expressly barred by the Civil Rights Act of 1964, and constituted "the easy course" to racial reform.

Both Bush administrations in like manner channeled their criticisms toward racial quotas. George H. W. Bush threatened to veto early versions of the 1991 civil rights restoration act on the argument that it called for quotas and racial balancing.[157] His administration drafted regulations that would have barred the use of quotas but then walked the plan back.[158]

George H. W. Bush's critique of quotas zeroed in on Asian American students and what he termed "arbitrary discrimination" against them.[159] At an event hosted by the Asian-Pacific Community he spoke of "quotas that harm talented Americans like the thousands of Asian students in our universities" and of how "quotas penalize achievers" and "slam shut opportunity's door." Bush clarified, "Our administration does believe in affirmative action, in offering a hand, in opening the door of opportunity. But we don't believe in an America by the numbers. We do not believe in discriminating by quotas or by the numbers."

Bush II offered much the same when announcing that he directed the solicitor general to oppose the University of Michigan's race-based admissions policies. He announced, "I strongly support diversity of all kinds, including racial diversity in higher education. But the method used by the University of Michigan to achieve this important goal is fundamentally flawed. At their core, the Michigan policies amount to a quota system that unfairly rewards or penalizes prospective students, based solely on their race."[160] Accordingly, his administration filed "a brief with the Court arguing that the University of Michigan's admissions policies, which award students a significant number of extra points based solely on their race and establishes numerical targets for incoming minority students, are unconstitutional."[161] After the Court struck down the numerical measures in *Grutter* (2003), Bush II told the Journalists of Color Convention that he "agreed with the Court in saying that we ought to reject quotas."

Although the Nixon administration originated hard versions of affirmative action, Nixon himself was adamantly opposed to racial quotas. From the outset he noted the distinctions of his plan, clarifying that "the Philadelphia Plan does not set quotas; it points to goals. It does not presume automatic violation of law if the goals are not met," but instead required "affirmative action if a review of the totality of a contractor's employment practices shows that he is not affording equal employment opportunity."[162] Nixon's memoir elaborated his own thinking about the Philadelphia Plan devised by his secretary of labor, George Schultz. Nixon wrote, "I felt that the plan Schultz devised, which would require such [affirmative] action by law, was both necessary and right. We would not impose quotas, but would require federal contractors to show *affirmative* action to meet the goals of increasing minority employment."[163]

Presidents have aligned with the Court on other aspects of affirmative action implementation besides quotas and rigidity. Concerning the temporariness standard, for instance, Clinton insisted that "affirmative action should not go on forever . . . it should be retired when its job is done."[164] His July 19, 1995, Memorandum on Affirmative Action ordered federal agencies to eliminate any affirmative action program whose "equal opportunity purposes have been achieved."[165] Regarding the narrow tailoring requirement, moreover, the Trump administration's rescission of 24 policy guidance documents originally issued by the Obama administration was based on Trump's Attorney General Jeff Sessions's claim that the guidance went too far. Sessions decried them as bureaucratic rule run amok, asserting that "federal agencies must abide by constitutional principles and follow the rules set forth by Congress and the President."[166]

In short, by the time *Bakke* (1978) came onto the scene to delineate the do's and don'ts of affirmative action implementation, the stage was already set by a bipartisan vote in Congress that prohibited enforcement of numerical targets, by Nixon and presidents to follow, and by the American people.

SECTION SUMMARY

To recap, the Supreme Court's multi-prong constitutional test that substantially handicaps implementation of race-based programming, crafted long before *Students for Fair Admissions* (2023), is in accord with the policy preferences of not only the masses but also elected officials on both sides of the aisle. Three-quarters of survey respondents anticipate affirmative action will eventually end or express that they want it to end, and up to 65 percent believed that it should be mended. Lawmakers believe the same. The "Mend It, Don't End It" policy was the making of Democratic President Bill Clinton, who was emphatic that he was "against quotas and guaranteed results," and that his administration did more to reform affirmative action than his predecessors Presidents Reagan and Bush. The anti-quota agenda pushed by Reagan, Bush I, and Bush II were on par with that of Richard M. Nixon. Even as Nixon and his Secretary of Labor George Schultz expanded Johnson's Philadelphia Plan, Nixon stressed that the "Philadelphia Plan does not set quotas." When all is said and done, the rules of engagement for affirmative action implementation as set down by Supreme Court justices are tacitly endorsed by everyday citizens and politicians alike.

Chapter Five

All Lives Matter

DEI and the Death of Affirmative Action

Forty-five years before the 2023 *Students for Fair Admissions* (*SFFA*) ruling that banned race-based admissions, the Supreme Court had already defined diversity affirmative action in a way that directly counterbalanced *racial* minority interests. Under the Court's longstanding definition racial-ethnic identity is mediated as but one of countless types of diversity. Anyone considered "different" by traditional societal standards or that contributes to heterogeneity in a particular setting is a viable beneficiary of preferential policies and programs. Whether owing to mutable or immutable character-istics, the entire range of human differentiation counts—all shapes, sizes, and colors. Affirmative action case law thus evinces its own variant of "All Lives Matter,"[1] a framework in which Blacks and other racial minorities are decentered—albeit, due to otherwise good intentions. In all of its rulings and opinions leading up to *SFFA* the Supreme Court never hitched preferential policy to opportunity expansion for racial minorities or to the original goal of correcting the generational effects of slavery. Prior to *SFFA*, one of the two primary aims approved to justify race-aware diversity policies was that of helping nonminorities better understand an increasingly diverse society. The other was preserving the nation's future by training leaders who could discover truth "out of a multitude of tongues." Neither of these aims had to do with opening doors of opportunity for Blacks and other racial minorities once shut out, by law.

By banning race-based college admissions policies geared toward learning through diversity, *SFFA* effectively ended a policy that was hollowed out long ago not only by the Supreme Court but also the body politic's own "All Lives Matter" framing. In other words, the "All Lives Matter" conception of diversity advanced by the Supreme Court mirrors the thinking that drives diversity, equity, and inclusion (DEI) politics. Contemporary DEI politics are not now, nor have they ever been, chiefly about Blacks and other racial minorities or experiences under slavery, Jim Crow, and structural racism. Like affirmative action rulings, DEI politics are oriented to protect and advance any and every iteration of human differentiation that lays claim to marginalization in a given setting. In the political realm too, certain conceptions are tied to mutable characteristics such as "caregivers" "religion," and "first-generation" professionals and students, as well as other immutable characteristics besides race and ethnicity (e.g., gender, sexual orientation, physical disability, immigrant background, etc.). To the extent that today's DEI politics revolve around the idea that everyone is entitled to construct their own identity experience, the DEI brand of diversity is also not a function of objective experience with marginalization but rather one's psychological experience, perception, and discontent. As in judicial process, also scarcely prioritized within the larger political arena is the original aim of affirmative action, namely remediation of past discrimination against racial minorities at large, and descendants of formerly enslaved Blacks in particular.

The "Diversity" in DEI

COURT OPINION ON DEI

The 2023 ruling in *Students for Fair Admissions* rejected the rationale that was used for 40+ years in *Bakke* (1978) and its progeny to permit race-conscious diversity policies, most notably in higher education. It is important to understand, however, that the fundamental premise from which *SFFA* launched was established long ago. Universities were always directed to define diversity in a way that takes in the kaleidoscope of racial-ethnic minority groups. Furthermore, race and ethnicity was never allowed as the center point of diversity programming and instead had to be situated alongside other factors, in addition to being assigned the least weight of all. Under the Court's longstanding catchall conception, an Italian American contributes to a higher education institution's diversity profile as much as an African American. The same for academically challenged athletes, a student who struggles in biology, an underperforming high school freshman, or a student who has an "ability to communicate with the poor."[2] The Court's definition of "diversity" now takes in almost three-quarters of the US population, necessarily offsetting the political capital of uniquely racial minority concerns.

The first step toward establishing catchall diversity was to upend the Black-White paradigm for mediating racial matters and, in the same stroke, decenter Black interests. Justice Roberts finally made this explicit in 2007 when he remarked, "Classifying and assigning schoolchildren according to a binary conception of race is an extreme approach in light of our precedents and our Nation's history of using race in public schools." Partly for this reason the plans adopted by the Seattle, Washington, school district and the Jefferson County school district in Louisville, Kentucky, were struck down in *Parents Involved Comm. v. Seattle School District*.[3] Among the problems that Roberts saw with defining "diversity" in binary terms were inconsistencies in how the race-based assignment plans distinguished a racially balanced school from one that is not. He explained, "Under the Seattle plan, a school with 50 percent Asian-American students and 50 percent White students but no African-American, Native-American, or Latino students would qualify as balanced." Alternatively, "a school with 30 percent Asian-American, 25 percent African-American, 25 percent Latino, and 20 percent White students would not." It was hard for him to understand how a plan that could allow such results could be viewed as achieving enrollment that is "broadly diverse."

As prelude to *Parents Involved* the landmark civil rights cases of the 1950s and early 1960s dismantled legally sanctioned racial barriers, but without requiring desegregation in a way that placed Black interests front-and-center. Nor did the Court ever settle on a Black-White template. Rather, it consistently defined "racial" and "ethnic" diversity to take in a wide assortment of racial-ethnic minority groups. *Bakke* first wrestled with the meaning of "race" and "ethnicity" as it jumpstarted affirmative action rulemaking in 1978. Powell's principal opinion questioned the inclusion of "only the four favored groups—Negroes, Mexican-Americans, American Indians, and Asians—for preferential treatment" in the special admissions program of the University of California Medical School. It was Powell who maintained in *Bakke* that an Italian American could "count" just as much as an African American in furthering the kind of compelling interest in diversity that justifies race consciousness. Elaborating, Powell wrote, "The file of a particular Black applicant may be examined for his potential contribution to diversity without the factor of race being decisive when compared, for example, with that of an applicant identified as an Italian-American if the latter is thought to exhibit qualities more likely to promote beneficial educational pluralism."

In a similar vein *Fullilove* (1980) and other pro–affirmative action rulings expressed concern about future "misapplications of the racial and ethnic criteria." The plaintiffs in *Fullilove* charged that the minority business enterprise (MBE) provision of the congressionally enacted Public Works Employment Act of 1977 was overinclusive. The Court disagreed and validated the MBE program. But, while the opinion sustained Congress's selection of "citizens of the United States who are Negroes, Spanish-speaking, Orientals, Indians, Eskimos and Aleuts" for preferential treatment, it did so because the door was left open for other groups. Chief Justice Burger's opinion for the Court highlighted that "on very special facts a case might be made to challenge the congressional decision to limit MBE eligibility to the particular minority groups identified in the Act." Subsequent to this, the Court approved the Federal Communication Commission's special broadcast licensing program in *Metro* (1990), which defined "minority" to include not just Blacks, but "those of Black, Hispanic Surnamed, American Eskimo, Aleut, American Indian and Asian American extraction." The same is true of the multi-racial plan upheld in *Fisher II* (2016), where the University of Texas at Austin asked students to classify themselves among five predefined racial categories on its application listing.

The opinion in *Students for Fair Admissions* joined this line of rulings that scrutinized the racial categories used to designate beneficiaries of affirmative action. In addition to the reasoning detailed in chapter 4 Roberts also wrote for the 6–3 majority that the designations used in Harvard and UNC's admissions process were "imprecise in many ways." Some were overly inclusive; some underinclusive. Some were unclear, such as a class with 15 percent of students from Mexico being preferred over a class with 10 percent of students from several Latin American countries. He wondered, as well, why all Asian students were grouped together and why applicants from Middle Eastern countries were classified as they were. The end result, he concluded, was that "the use of these opaque racial categories undermines, instead of promotes, respondents' goals."

Above and beyond binary versus nonbinary conceptions of race the Court has always frowned upon diversity designations anchored in racial-ethnic criteria of any kind. To this point, Justice Kennedy's opinion for the Court in *Fisher v. Texas II* (2016) warned, "Formalistic racial classifications may sometimes fail to capture diversity in all of its dimensions." Kennedy applauded the fact that "race is but a 'factor of a factor of a factor' in the holistic-review calculus" employed by the University of Texas admissions plan. It incorporated "the many ways in which [an] academically qualified individual might contribute to, and benefit from, the rich, diverse, and challenging educational environment of the University." In *Fisher II* admissions decisions for about 25 percent[4] of applicants were based on a combination of the applicant's Academic Index (AI) score and Personal Achievement Index (PAI) score. Race was a subfactor within the Personal Achievement Index, which consisted of an essay score and a "Personal Achievement Score" (PAS) that weighed various supplemental items such as letters of recommendation, student activities, honors, and "special circumstances." Race was folded into the "special circumstances" category, alongside socioeconomic status, family responsibilities, family structure, and home language. Hence, Kennedy's characterization of race counting as but a "factor of a factor of a factor."

Years before *Fisher II* Justice O'Connor had urged that when using race as a "plus," university admissions must ensure that each applicant is not evaluated "in a way that makes an applicant's race or ethnicity the defining feature of his or her application." She concluded of the plan in *Grutter* (2003), "The policy does not define diversity 'solely in terms of racial and ethnic status.'" Rather, the law school "actually gives substantial weight to diversity factors besides race," in that it frequently accepted nonminority applicants with grades and test scores that were lower than minority applicants who were rejected. The justices's pushback against diversity policies centered on racial-ethnic criteria stretches back to *Bakke* (1978). Powell's plurality opinion explained that approval of racial considerations in the University of California Medical School's admissions process program was grounded in the precept that "ethnic diversity . . . is only one element in a range of factors a university properly may consider in attaining the goal of a heterogeneous student body." He criticized as "seriously flawed" the university's argument that ethnic diversity is the only effective means of serving the interest of diversity. For Powell, "the diversity that furthers a compelling state interest encompasses a far broader array of qualifications and characteristics of which racial or ethnic origin is but a single though important element." In fact, he wrote that a "special admissions program, focused *solely* [sic] on ethnic diversity, would hinder rather than further attainment of genuine diversity." Chief Justice John Roberts pushed the envelope further in *Parents Involved* to suggest that plans that aim for racial diversity may not promote cross-cultural understanding at all. He juxtaposed the Court's broad conception against the race-centric notion in the school assignment plans at issue in *Parents Involved* (2007). Striking down both, Roberts found that "under each plan when race comes into play, it is decisive by itself" and that "race [was] not considered as part of a broader effort to achieve 'exposure to widely diverse people, cultures, ideas, and viewpoints.' "

The conception of "diversity" embraced by Supreme Court justices over the years is one that encompasses a potentially infinite number of factors, most of them unrelated to race/ethnicity. Rejecting plaintiff's contention that class rank should be the sole deciding factor in admissions, *Fisher II* (2016) urged that the University of Texas at Austin "should remain mindful that diversity takes many forms." Among the "other aspects of diversity" that Justice Kennedy believed should not be sacrificed were "the star athlete or musician whose grades suffered because of daily practices and training . . . a talented young biologist who struggled to maintain above-average grades in humanities classes . . . a student whose freshman-year grades were poor because of a family crisis but who got herself back on track in her last three years of school."

Fisher II's race-neutral take on "diversity" adheres to a long line of precedents. Justice Powell's *Bakke* (1978) opinion featured a lengthy list of what he termed "pertinent elements of diversity" that included "exceptional personal talents, unique work or service experience, leadership potential, maturity, demonstrated compassion, a history of overcoming disadvantage, ability to communicate with the poor, or other qualifications." *Bakke*'s reasoning that "diversity" effectively means almost anything was suggested by Justice O'Connor in the first case to review racial preference in public higher education following a 25-year hiatus. She observed in *Grutter* (2003) that the special admissions policy in that case reaffirmed the University of Michigan Law School's longstanding commitment to "one particular type of diversity," namely "racial and ethnic diversity with special reference to the inclusion of students from groups which have been historically discriminated against, like African-Americans, Hispanics and Native Americans." At the same time, however, the policy did "not restrict the types of diversity contributions eligible for 'substantial weight' in the admissions process" and instead recognized "many possible bases for diversity admissions." Among the types of diversity showcased in the law school's 1992 written policy were "admittees who have lived or traveled widely abroad, are fluent in several languages, have overcome personal adversity and family hardship, have exceptional records of extensive community service, and have had successful careers in other fields."

In all, the Roberts Court's demand for all-inclusive diversity in 2023 in *Students for Fair Admissions* tracked an earlier Court's stance in 1978 in

All Lives Matter | 219

Bakke, in 2003 in *Grutter*, in 2007 in *Parents Involved*, and *Fisher II* of 2016. We learn next that the Court's "All Lives Matter" approach is markedly different from what was originally intended by the early architects of affirmative action during the 1960s and 1970s, yet very much in sync with today's DEI politics.

POLITICS AND BENEFICIARIES

The decentering of Blacks within affirmative action jurisprudence from 1978 to 2023 emulates developments in the national political arena. Most Americans prefer that the benefits and beneficiaries of diversity policies not hinge on skin color at all. In fact, the public is more open to preferences for the poor and developmentally disabled than for racial-ethnic minorities. Among the types of ascriptive characteristics for preferential treatment, the 2023 Associated Press/NORC survey data in table 5.1 show that demographic characteristics such as race are less supported, and gender least supported. From 1995 to 2023 Americans primarily supported diversity programs based on socioeconomic disadvantage or disability. As of 2023 almost half support economic-based compared to one-third that support race-based affirmative action. The same is captured by the 2009 Quinnipiac University data. They show that one-third support programs that increase diversity by giving preferences to Blacks (33%) and Hispanics (29%) or White women (32%), whereas a higher 55 percent endorse diversity programs that give preferences to people with disabilities. An even larger 63 percent endorse affirmative action programs based on income, according to the ABC News poll. These data too show more support for "assistance" (78%) than for "preferences."

National parties have long embraced a catchall understanding of diversity as well. The 2020 Democratic National Party platform cast a wide net. It declared, "Federal contractors should be required to develop and disclose plans to recruit and promote people of color, women, LGBTQ people, people with disabilities, and veterans."[5] The platform called for more vigorous "enforcement of laws that prohibit discrimination in the workplace and other settings" on the basis of "race, ethnicity, national origin, language, religion, gender, sexual orientation, gender identity, [and] disability status."[6] During the 1980s too, Democrats expressed that "government has a special responsibility to those whom society has historically prevented from enjoying the benefits of full citizenship for reasons of race, religion, sex, age, national origin and ethnic heritage, sexual orientation, or disability."[7]

Table 5.1. Preferred Beneficiaries of Diversity Affirmative Action, US, 1995–2023, Select Years

Year	Survey Question	Select Responses (%)
2023	How important should each of the following be when colleges and universities make decisions about admitting students?[a]	Percent say extremely/very important . . . Test scores: 62 Able to afford tution: 47 Race-ethnicity: 34 Athletic ability: 9 Gender: 9
2022	How much should colleges consider the following factors when deciding which students to admit?[b]	Percent say a lot/a little . . . Grade point average: 90 Test scores: 83 Athletic activities: 54 Socioeconomic background: 46 Race-ethnicity: 38 Gender: 35
2019	Here are some factors colleges and universities may consider when making decisions about student admissions. Do you think each of the following should be a major factor, minor factor, or not a factor in college admissions?[c]	Should be major/minor factor . . . Community service: 69 First in family to college: 47 Athletic ability: 42 Legacy: 32 Race-ethnicity: 26 Gender: 19
2009	In order to increase diversity, do you support or oppose affirmative action programs that give preferences in hiring, promotions, and college admissions . . . ? (Quinnipiac University, June 3, 2009)	Support preferences for . . . Handicapped: 55 Blacks: 33 White women: 32 Hispanics: 29 Gays and lesbians: 27
2008	Say such programs (affirmative action programs) were based on income, not race. Would you support or oppose affirmative action programs that give preference to *poor people* in areas such as hiring, promotions, and college admissions, regardless of race? (ABC News/*USA Today*/Columbia University Poll, September 23, 2008)	Support: 63 Oppose: 32

Year	Survey Question	Select Responses (%)
2008	What about affirmative action programs that give assistance but not preference to poor people in areas such as hiring, promotions, and college admissions. Would you support or oppose this? (ABC News/*USA Today*/Columbia University Poll, September 23, 2008)	Support: 78 Oppose: 18
2003	Would you favor or oppose an affirmative action program that gives preference in jobs and education to people who come from an *economically disadvantaged* background, regardless of their gender or ethnicity? (*Los Angeles Times*, February 2003)	Favor strongly/somewhat: 59 Oppose somewhat/strongly: 31
2003	Would you approve or disapprove of affirmative action based on income instead of race, that is, giving preferences for college admissions to people from low-income families, regardless of their race or ethnic background? (*Newsweek*, January 18, 2003)	Approve: 65 Disapprove: 28
1997	Suppose that affirmative action programs to help minorities and women were ended and new programs were created to help poor people regardless of their race or sex. Do you believe that preference in hiring or promotion should be given to people from poor families today, or not? (CBS News/ *New York Times*, December 13, 1997)	Yes: 53 No: 37
1997	Should affirmative action preferences be targeted to companies owned by minorities or to companies that operate in poor and inner city communities, regardless of who owns them? (Democratic Leadership Conference, July 27, 1997)	Minority-owned companies: 16 Operate in poor/inner city: 65

continued on next page

Table 5.1. Continued.

Year	Survey Question	Select Responses (%)
1995	Which one of the following comes closest to your own views? 1) I think federal affirmative action programs should be available to all poor Americans, regardless of race or gender. 2) I support federal affirmative action programs for minorities and women, but only if they are meant to address specific cases of discrimination. 3) I oppose all federal affirmative action programs. 4) I support federal affirmative action programs for minorities and women and believe they should not be changed at all. (*Time*/CNN/Yankelovich, July 21, 1995)	Poor: 43 Specific cases of discrimination: 24 Oppose all: 16 Support with no changes: 6

Sources: Except where indicated, survey data in the table were obtained from *Polling the nations*. (n.d.). Topic: Affirmative action. Last accessed 4/25/2022 from https://ptn-infobase-com.exlibris.colgate.edu/topics/VG9waWM6NTI=?aid=14265.

[a]Associated Press/NORC. (2023, May 11–15). *Most oppose banning consideration of race and ethnicity in college and university admissions.* https://apnorc.org/projects/most-oppose-banning-the-consideration-of-race-and-ethnicity-in-college-and-university-admissions.

[b]YouGov. (2022, April 12–18). Last accessed 2/12/2025 from https://today.yougov.com/politics/articles/42233-affirmative-action-yougov-poll-april-12-18-2022.

[c]Graf, N. (2019, February 25). Most Americans say colleges should not consider race or ethnicity in admissions. Pew Research Center. Accessed 4/2021 from https://www.pewresearch.org/short-reads/2019/02/25/most-americans-say-colleges-should-not-consider-race-or-ethnicity-in-admissions/.

Parties' enlargement of the tent preceded the Court's, something that further proves that the latter is toeing the line of national politics in its wide-reaching conceptualization of diversity. A universal diversity approach on both sides of the aisle crystallized over the course of several decades and before *Bakke* (1978) raised questions about the inclusion of "only the four favored groups—Negroes, Mexican-Americans, American Indians, and Asians—for preferential treatment" in the special admissions program in that case. As of the 1940s race and religion were the main guideposts for federal civil rights policy, in that Blacks and Jews garnered the lion's share of national party attention on this front. Democrats dedicated its first-ever civil rights plank to "Negroes" in 1940 and stressed the importance of equal rights for "racial and religious minorities" in 1944 and 1948.[8] In lockstep fashion Republicans offered their own dedicated plank titled "Negro" in 1940 and used the "Immigration" plank to emphasize the problem of "racial and religious intolerance" and the need to "give refuge to millions of distressed Jewish men, women and children driven from their homes by tyranny."[9] A full-court press on Black issues came in 1948, with Republicans turning their attention to lynching, the poll tax, racial segregation in the armed services, and "equality of educational opportunity for all and the promotion of education and educational facilities."[10]

Democrats eventually expanded their social justice agenda to encompass migrant workers, having dedicated planks in 1952 to "Migratory Workers" and the "Children of Migratory Workers." In 1965 a Democrat-controlled Congress enacted immigration reform that overhauled the makeup of the immigrant population.[11] They also took on the cause of nondiscrimination in immigration and refugee policies. Republicans followed suit, as they continued to advocate for racial and religious minorities in the 1950s, with special attention to "Negroes," along with "thousands of refugees, expellees and displaced persons" under the Refugee Relief Act of 1953.[12] But conservatives' economic agenda was more wide-reaching than Democrats' by the late 1950s, highlighting "special employment problems" of "older workers, handicapped workers, members of minority groups and migratory workers."[13]

Soon those on the right were more plainspoken in conveying that their civil rights politics no longer centered on Blacks. Their platforms maintained a special focus on Jewish refugees[14] and the "Civil Rights" plank singled out "Negro citizens," calling for an end to segregation, voting discrimination, and the discriminatory employment practices of government and government contractors. But the same platform also declared that racial problems were not confined to the South, "Nor is discrimination confined to the discrimination against Negroes."[15] Rather, "discrimination in many, if not all, areas of the country on the basis of creed or national origin is equally insidious."[16]

Liberals' abandonment of Black and White politics came in 1968, a time of considerable racial turmoil against the backdrop of the 1967 nationwide race riots. Democrats' platform steered away from the elephant in the room, avoiding altogether references to "Blacks" and "Negroes"—only to "ghetto dwellers."[17] Contrarily, they delved at length into the benefits of eliminating the national origins quota system to make room for a more diverse pool of migrants. As opposed to Blacks, the next platform declared that the "American Indian has the oldest claim on our national conscience"[18] and labeled "America's migrant farm workers" as "the poorest of the poor in our country."[19] "Difference" and "heterogeneity" figured prominently enough in Democrats' agenda that Whites too were soon explicitly recognized as part of that agenda. Their 1972 plank, "The Right to Be Different," declared that "diversity" pertained to every conceivable group in the US, including Whites. In their words, "Recognition and support of the cultural identity and pride of Black people are generations overdue. The American Indians, the Spanish-speaking, the Asian Americans—the cultural and linguistic heritage of these groups is too often ignored. . . . So, too, are the backgrounds, traditions and contributions of White national, ethnic, religious and regional communities ignored." Further enlargement of the Democratic tent continued from 1984 to 2020 when the party took up the fight against discrimination on the basis of sexual orientation and for same-sex marriage.

The reach of the Republican Party diversity agenda continued to broaden too, as it renewed commitment to opportunity for groups "originating from all sectors of the world, from Asia to Africa to Europe to Latin America."[20] Albeit, as compared to Democrats, Republicans talked more about race-ethnicity and about Blacks specifically during the 1980s, as their "Black Americans" plank claimed that "the Carter Administration entered office with a pledge to 'all minorities' of a brighter economic future," yet ended with "more Black Americans unemployed than on the day Mr. Carter became President." LTBTQ+ individuals were the only demographic excluded by way of the party's consistent opposition to same-sex marriage from 1980 through 2016. Starting in the 1980s conservatives switched gears on the immigration front to warn that the "hospitality" of the American people was severely tested by emerging immigration controversies.[21] Up through the 2000s their immigration policy interests continued to coalesce around border control as opposed to accommodation and inclusivity."[22] But, a decade later the party's civil rights agenda was reoriented to a pledge "to protect the most vulnerable of our people: children, the elderly, the disabled" relative to health care.[23]

Like the public and political parties, the executive branch shares the Supreme Court's conception of diversity. While the language used in the nondiscrimination policies of Roosevelt through Kennedy encompassed all racial-ethnic groups, initially, Blacks were the main focus. President Lyndon B. Johnson spotlighted the effects of slavery and the "shackled runner thesis" in his 1965 Howard University speech. But Johnson was also the first president to extend federal affirmative action policy beyond the "race, creed, color or national origin" criteria that were the focus of his foundational

Executive Order 11246 (1965). In 1967 EO 11375 amended 11246 to "expressly embrace discrimination on account of sex."[24] An inflection point came during the Nixon administration in connection with a battle over the regulations promulgated in 1973 for the Small Business Administration's (SBA) centerpiece 8(a) program. A founding member and then-chair of the Congressional Black Caucus (CBC) Representative Parren J. Mitchell fought to restrict the category of racial and ethnic minorities deemed "socially disadvantaged" under 8(a) to only African Americans and Native Americans or, as some described, "those who did not come to the United States seeking the 'American dream.' "[25] Rejecting the CBC's preference, the program instead defined "disadvantaged persons" as including, but not limited to "Black Americans, Spanish-Americans, Oriental Americans, Eskimos, and Aleuts."[26]

At Nixon's urging Congress later codified an even longer list of at least 40 racial-ethnic groups[27] to be presumed socially disadvantaged for 8(a) eligibility purposes. The list included: Black Americans; Hispanic Americans; Native Americans (including American Indians, Eskimos, Aleuts, Native Hawaiians); Asian Pacific Americans originating from Burma, Thailand, Malaysia, Indonesia, Singapore, Brunei, Japan, China (including Hong Kong), Taiwan, Laos, Cambodia, Vietnam, Korea, the Philippines, US Trust Territory of the Pacific Islands (Republic of Palau), Republic of the Marshall Islands, Federated States of Micronesia, Commonwealth of the Northern Mariana Islands, Guam, Samoa, Macao, Fiji, Tonga, Kiribati, Tuvalu, and Nauru; and Subcontinent Asian Americans originating from India, Pakistan, Bangladesh, Sri Lanka, Bhutan, the Maldives Islands, and Nepal.[28] The minority business enterprise policies that Nixon originated were expanded further to take in gender, as did a 1971 change to Order No. 4 that required federal contractors' goals, timetables, and underutilization analyses incorporate opportunities for women as well.

Not only policies, but the language of civil rights politics too became increasingly deracialized from one president to the next. President George H. W. Bush framed disability access as a civil rights issue. In a 1989 speech commemorating the 25th anniversary of the Civil Rights Act of 1964, Bush remarked that "the time-tested laws that give civil rights protections can and ought to be extended to persons with disabilities."[29] Casting the net wider he urged that it was time "to move forward on a broader front, to move forward into the century's final decade with a civil rights mission that fully embraces every deserving American, regardless of race—whether women, children, or the aged; whether the disabled, the unemployed, or the homeless."[30] Later President George W. Bush's 2002 Executive Order

13279 amended the foundational affirmative action order (EO 11246) to include faith-based organizations.[31]

The Clinton administration likewise opted for an across-the-board conception of diversity. Executive Order 13160 was issued in June 2000 to "ensure nondiscrimination on the basis of race, sex, color, national origin, disability, religion, age, sexual orientation, and status as a parent in federally conducted education and training programs" as well as participants in military programs.[32] In Clinton's view, historical arguments on behalf of preferential policies were just as applicable to women, Hispanic Americans, and Asian Americans as to African Americans. His administration's affirmative action review placed them on equal footing, asserting, "For much of this century, racial and ethnic minorities and women have confronted legal and social exclusion. African Americans and Hispanic Americans were segregated into low wage jobs, usually agricultural. Asian Americans, who were forbidden by law from owning land, worked fields to which they could not hold title. Women were barred by laws in many states from entering entire occupations, such as mining, fire-fighting, bartending, law, and medicine."[33]

By far, Presidents Obama and Biden advanced the most sweeping conceptions of diversity. Obama's Executive Order 13672 (2014) extended affirmative action coverage to lesbian, gay, bisexual, and transgender employees of federal contractors. He did so mindful of a shift in racial politics. In an interview with best-selling author Ta-Nehisi Coates, Obama said of the Reparations movement, "This is not just a Black/White society, and it is becoming less so every year. So how do Latinos feel if there's a big investment just in the African American community, and they're looking around and saying, 'We're poor as well. What kind of help are we getting?' Or Asian Americans who say, 'Look, I'm a first-generation immigrant, and clearly I didn't have anything to do with what was taking place.'"[34]

The Biden administration handling outstripped the Supreme Court's "All Lives Matter" diversity. His Executive Order 14035 on Diversity, Equity, Inclusion, and Accessibility in the Federal Workforce defined "diversity" to incorporate "beliefs," and more specifically the "many communities, identities, races, ethnicities, backgrounds, abilities, cultures, and beliefs of the American people, including underserved communities."[35] The EO designated those "who have been systematically denied a full opportunity to participate in aspects of economic, social, and civic life" to include individuals who are:

- Black and African American

- Hispanic and Latino

- Native American

- Alaska Native and Indigenous

- Asian American

- Native Hawaiian and Pacific Islander

- Middle Eastern

- North African

- Face discrimination based on . . .

  o Sex

  o Sexual orientation

  o Gender identity (including lesbian, gay, bisexual, transgender, queer, gender nonconforming, and nonbinary [LGBTQ+] persons)

  o Pregnancy or pregnancy-related conditions

  o Parents

  o Caregivers

  o Religion

  o Disability

  o First-generation professionals

  o First-generation college students

  o Individuals with limited English proficiency

  o Immigrants

  o Older age

  o Former incarceration

  o Live in rural areas

  o Veterans and military spouses

- Otherwise adversely affected by persistent poverty, discrimination, or inequality. Individuals may belong to more than one underserved community and face intersecting barriers

In concert with national public opinion, political parties, and presidents, moreover, the liberalized diversity ideal set down in *Bakke* (1978), *Grutter* (2003), *Parents Involved* (2007), *Fisher I* (2013), and *Fisher II* (2016) is mirrored in grassroots politics, especially on the left. There, Blacks and racial-ethnic minorities who were the original intended beneficiaries of affirmative action have been decentered. The yardstick of left-leaning DEI politics is heterogeneity, with emphasis on the experience of being "othered." The metrics of precisely who "counts" fluctuates sometimes according to emotion. In "An Affirmative View" Judith Butler worries that, "as a result of recovery psychology's influence over identity politics, the status of 'deserving' victim can be granted to anyone who *feels* that his or her pain is caused by a traumatizing abuse, provided that this feeling elicits enough empathy and support."[36] She continues, adding, "Such privilege granted to subjective experience . . . makes it impossible to establish an objective hierarchy among different plights. Consequently, victims of racism and, say, of a smoking parent have an equal opportunity to advance their identity politics."[37] By this reasoning conservative leaders can "present their constituency as the real victims of the federal government and its proteges—that is, women and minorities."[38] Butler's worries are arguably bolstered by the fact that White and heterosexual males of middle- to upper-class Anglo Saxon background constitute the bulk of what falls outside the DEI ambit.

The Supreme Court's praise for policies that prioritize nonracial factors over racial ones is in sync with DEI politics that impute equivalency between the lived experience of marginalized racial-ethnic minority groups and that of other disfavored groups. The driving concern is not structural disadvantage caused by centuries of violence and exclusionary laws, but rather devaluation within America's cultural mainstream. This mode of negotiating diversity diminishes the potential impact of race-based affirmative action upon access and opportunities for descendants of the enslaved. Hence, the way in which the politics of racial-ethnic diversification have evolved over the years in the US serves to not only deprioritize but to also dematerialize the Black American experience. As Stephen C. Halpern put it, "The expansion of the civil rights movement, fueled by people inspired by the Black struggle and hoping to emulate its success, blurred the distinction between Blacks and members of other groups claiming that they, like Blacks, had been treated unjustly in American society. Moreover, those groups, whether they were women, the disabled, the aged, or more recently, homosexuals [*sic*], were overwhelmingly White."[39] Halpern adds, "The lumping together of the injustices suffered by the various mistreated groups, and of their respective moral and legal claims, make it more tenuous to assert . . . that America's treatment of its Black population was a singular historic evil that produced continuing, incomparable harm deserving paramount attention and priority."[40]

All this is true specifically in regard to the Court's dismantling of the Black-White paradigm as well. Although civil rights politics in the US never revolved exclusively around a Black-White template, Black interests dominated the civil rights agenda up until the 1960s. This was owed largely to political activism and pressure, but also the fact that Blacks were the largest racial minority for much of American history.[41] Evidence of the prominence of Black concerns is found partly in the Kerner Commission Report that declared in 1967 that the nation was "moving toward two societies, one Black, one White—separate and unequal."[42] Data from the US Census Bureau captures the transformative changes in the demographic landscape that helped to edge Blacks away from its center.[43] This is why, according to Earl E. Pollock, NAACP leader Julian Bond opposed inclusion of a multi-racial category for government counting purposes. Pollock traced the Census Bureau's growing list of racial-ethnic categories for census-taking purposes, a list that began in 1790 with "White, Black and Indian," then expanded to four by 1977.[44] By the late 1990s a nondescript multi-racial category was included. It was in response to this that Bond announced his opposition to effectively "diluting the power and the strength of numbers as they affect legal decisions about race in this country."[45]

The Black population itself is increasingly composed of varied ethnic and national identities, given the growing number of people who identify as Black are foreign-born Blacks.[46] This stands apart from a time when 90 percent of Blacks were born and lived in the South and subject to Jim Crow laws and traditions. In addition to the traditional assumption of a collective lived experience that goes with having Black skin, such changes also bump up against Black claims of systematically rooted victimization that stems from slavery, southern segregation, and the racial caste system in the US. As between American-born and foreign-born blacks, work by Massey and colleagues indicate that the latter have an edge over the former, not because of differences in social preparation, academic preparation, psychological readiness, and the like; rather, they are liked more. More aptly, they exhibit the "traits and characteristics valued by admissions committees."[47]

The weight of Black social and political capital was further counterbalanced by the politics that accompanied the Latino population's emergence as the largest racial-ethnic minority in the US in 2000. McClain and colleagues offered the first probe of racial tension between Black and

Latino immigrants. Similar examinations followed,[48] including Corral's 2020 meta-analysis that summarizes how "political science research has consistently found perceptions of competition between Blacks and Latinos."[49] Growing racial-ethnic diversification and competition marginalizes Blacks most notably in the workplace and higher education.[50] For example, the preponderant share of racial-ethnic minority students and faculty at American colleges and universities are foreign-born.

The college campus has played a pivotal role in advancing the kind of omnibus diversity that decenters Blacks. The impact of the college campus is significant because, according to Harvard University Law Professor Randall Kennedy, higher education was the locus of affirmative action controversy and development. Kennedy explains that "the struggles at these sites have given rise to the most significant judicial rulings, the most influential writings in the affirmative action literature, and the most important of the electoral campaigns against so-called reverse discrimination."[51] In *Color and Money: How Rich White Kids Are Winning the War over College Affirmative Action*, Peter Schmidt reports that colleges have worked to bolster their own view of "how campus diversity benefits particular institutions, or career fields, or society as a whole."[52] The gravamen of the college campus conflict "involves the allocation of benefit between, on the one hand, the offspring of American-born Black parents and, on the other, the offspring of interracial couples and foreign-born Blacks," according to Kennedy.[53] As Harvard Law School Professor the late Lani Guinier remarked, "If you look around Harvard College today, how many young people will you find who grew up in urban environments and went to public high schools and public junior high schools? . . . I don't think, in the name of affirmative action, we should be admitting people because they look like us, but then they don't identify with us."[54]

Powell's principal opinion in *Bakke* (1978) lauded the Harvard University special admissions program as a model program precisely because of its liberalized approach to diversity. Quoting the amicus brief jointly submitted by Columbia University, Harvard University, and Stanford University, Powell wrote:

> In recent years Harvard College has expanded the concept of diversity to include students from disadvantaged economic, racial and ethnic groups. . . . In practice, this new definition of diversity has meant that race has been a factor in some admission decisions. When the Committee on Admissions reviews

the large middle group of applicants who are "admissible" and deemed capable of doing good work in their courses, the race of an applicant may tip the balance in his favor just as geographic origin or a life spent on a farm may tip the balance in other candidates' cases. A farm boy from Idaho can bring something to Harvard College that a Bostonian cannot offer. Similarly, a Black student can usually bring something that a White person cannot offer.[55]

Thus, it was the product of college campus governance and politics, a Harvard University program, that laid the foundation for the "All Lives Matter" version of affirmative action, a version that the Supreme Court in turn adopted as its own.

SECTION SUMMARY

From *Bakke* (1978) through *SFFA* (2023) the justices mediated diversity-oriented affirmative action policy along two continuums, one that deemed race-centered diversity too constricted and another that defined diversity to encompass any form of human differentiation. The resultant "All Lives Matter" approach to diversity syncs with the mindset of the general population. Together, survey data from the Pew Research Center and Quinnipiac University show that Americans prefer income- and disability-based diversity to race-based diversity. Over time both national political parties too shifted from positions that focused on Blacks and Jews to an agenda that focused equally on immigrants, women, older workers, disabled workers, LGBTQ+, and "White communities." And, over the objections of Congressional Black Caucus leaders and the NAACP, presidents from Lyndon B. Johnson through Joseph R. Biden embraced a similarly expansive conception, a trend that began in earnest with Nixon's designation of 40 racial-ethnic groups as eligible for the 8(a) minority funding program. The Biden administration outran them all, defining "diversity" to include traditionally marginalized groups alongside those with pregnancy-related conditions, first-generation professionals and college students, the elderly, formerly incarcerated persons, residents of rural areas, and all who are "adversely affected by persistent poverty, discrimination, or inequality." Compared to the policy consequences of identity politics elsewhere in the country, the college campus led the way to blurring the political distinction between the "singular historic evil" against Blacks, on the one hand, and the injustices suffered by mistreated groups, on the other.

Diversity Is for the Good of America

COURT OPINION ON AMERICA'S DIVERSITY

Chief Justice John Roberts's opinion in *Students for Fair Admissions* (2023) thrust aside what little remained of the rationale that enabled race-based diversity admissions to survive strict judicial scrutiny for more than 40 years. It is critical to recognize, however, that the original purpose behind affirmative action was cast aside by the Supreme Court decades before *SFFA*. Formal affirmative action policy was originated by Presidents Kennedy, Johnson, and Nixon chiefly to benefit racial-ethnic minorities, to remove racial barriers, and to compensate for past societal discrimination. But, even liberal justices of the Supreme Court had never validated affirmative action due to its potential to level the playing field for Blacks and other racial minorities. Rather, the primary reason racial preferences were upheld in college admissions rulings from 1978 to 2016 is that the Court framed the diversity goal as beneficial to the educational process and to the future of America *as a whole*. Diversity, equity, and inclusion were not the end goal but a means to what Powell's opinion in *Bakke* regarded as a grander mission tied to the "transcendent value of academic freedom."

The stipulation that a racially diverse student body cannot be an end in itself but must be geared instead to the educational needs of the whole student body and the well-being of the nation was first set forth in *Bakke* (1978). Thirty-five years after the fact *Fisher v. Texas I* (2013) reinforced this holding in *Bakke*, noting that "Justice Powell identified one compelling interest that could justify the consideration of race: the interest in the educational benefits that flow from a diverse student body." Again in 2016 *Fisher II* remarked, "As this Court's cases have made clear . . . the compelling interest that justifies consideration of race in college admissions is not an interest in enrolling a certain number of minority students. Rather, a university may institute a race-conscious admissions program as a means of obtaining the "the educational benefits that flow from student body diversity."

At the outset of affirmative action jurisprudence, as opposed to minority interests, the rights of educational institutions were front and center in special admissions rulings, namely the university's right to decide that diversity is an important part of its educational mission. Powell explained that the "four essential freedoms" of a university that are folded under the First Amendment's protection of academic freedom are the right "to determine for itself on academic grounds who may teach, what may be taught, how it shall be taught, and who may be admitted to study." In pursuing a diverse student body by way of its special admissions program, the University of California was "seeking to achieve a goal that is of paramount importance in the fulfillment of its mission," he wrote. The preeminent importance of university rights was reinforced in *Grutter* (2003), a ruling that also rested on First Amendment academic freedom protections and the university's right to compose a diverse student body. Finding that the law school had a compelling interest in student diversity, Justice O'Connor asserted the judgment was "informed by our view that attaining a diverse student body is at the heart of the Law School's proper institutional mission" and that a university's "educational judgment that such diversity is essential to its educational mission is one to which we defer." Likewise Justice Kennedy's opinion in *Fisher II* (2016) elaborated on how the academic mission of a university is "a special concern of the First Amendment," how the business of a university is to provide an atmosphere that is conducive to speculation, and that "this in turn leads to the question of 'who may be admitted to study.'"

To help explain the mechanisms by which a diverse student body promotes classroom learning, Powell's principal opinion in *Bakke* (1978) quoted a then–Princeton University president, who testified that

> A great deal of learning occurs informally. It occurs through interactions among students of both sexes; of different races, religions, and backgrounds; who come from cities and rural areas, from various states and countries; who have a wide variety of interests, talents, and perspectives; and who are able, directly or indirectly, to learn from their differences and to stimulate one another to reexamine even their most deeply held assumptions about themselves and their world. As a wise graduate of ours observed in commenting on this aspect of the educational process, "People do not learn very much when they are surrounded only by the likes of themselves."

The seven-person majority in the 2013 *Fisher I* case expanded this list of benefits, finding that "the attainment of a diverse student body . . . serves values beyond race alone, including enhanced classroom dialogue and the lessening of racial isolation and stereotypes."

As for the nexus between the "nation's future" and race-aware diversity learning, that too was first illuminated in *Bakke*. The main opinion proclaimed, "The Nation's future depends upon leaders trained through wide exposure to that robust exchange of ideas which discovers truth 'out of a multitude of tongues, [rather] than through any kind of authoritative selection.'" Twenty-five years later *Grutter* (2003) grounded its validation of the law school's special admissions program partly on studies that "show that student body diversity promotes learning outcomes" and "better prepares students for an increasingly diverse workforce and society, and better prepares them as professionals." The majority of justices in *Grutter* were especially attuned to the nation's future and its leaders, for which they believed "universities, and in particular, law schools, represent the training ground." Indeed, for Justice O'Connor, preparing students for work and citizenship and "sustaining our political and cultural heritage" was of "overriding importance."

Equal access and opportunity for racial minorities were never at the top of the list of benefits said to "flow from student body diversity," something we glean from the Court and the university's conclusions about the concept of "critical mass." Universities' pursuit of a critical mass of minority students was significant only insofar as it helped to facilitate the educational benefits that flow from a diverse student body. In simpler terms, critical mass was but a pathway to a diverse student body, the ultimate aim of which was to educate nonminorities. *Bakke* (1978) argued the "relationship between numbers and achieving the benefits to be derived from a diverse student body, and between numbers and providing a reasonable environment for those students admitted." In this case, "those students" referred to minorities admitted through the University of California Medical School special admissions process. *Grutter* (2003) further unpacked the meaning of "critical mass" and its relation to pedagogy.

Under *Grutter* "critical mass" meant enough minorities for them to not feel isolated in the classroom and on campus, in order for universities to achieve the educational benefits that flow from a diverse student body. O'Connor's majority opinion relied on testimony about "critical mass" from architects of the University of Michigan Law School special admissions policy. For them "critical mass" meant "a number that encourages under-represented minority students to participate in the classroom and not feel isolated,"[56] "numbers such that underrepresented minority students do not feel isolated or like spokespersons for their race."[57] Critically, the pedagogic purpose of "critical mass" was laid bare by the admissions director.[58] The director assured that under the school's affirmative action policy, "a critical mass of underrepresented minority students would be reached so as to realize the educational benefits of a diverse student body." O'Connor further clarified that it was the faculty believed that "when a critical mass of underrepresented minority students is present, racial stereotypes lose their force because nonminority students learn there is no 'minority viewpoint' but rather a variety of viewpoints among minority students."

Shortly after *Grutter* (2003) Chief Justice Roberts warned in *Parents Involved* (2007) that when a special admissions plan is not directly tied to the educational mission it runs the risk of being struck down—including desegregation plans. Part of the reason the race-based school assignment plans in *Parents Involved* (2007) was invalidated is that it was "tied to reach districts' specific racial demographics, rather than to any pedagogic concept of the level of diversity needed to obtain the asserted educational benefits." Years after *Parents Involved* the Court again stressed that the purpose of the race-based admissions plan upheld in *Fisher II* (2016) was to provide an "academic environment" that offers a "robust exchange of ideas, exposure to differing cultures, preparation for the challenges of an increasingly diverse workforce, and acquisition of competencies required of future leaders." The ruling turned partly on Justice Kennedy's finding that low numbers translated into limited diversity learning. In his words, "Although demographics alone are by no means dispositive, they do have some value as a gauge of the University's ability to enroll students who can offer underrepresented perspectives."

While *Students for Fair Admissions* reversed the Court's longstanding validation of a racially diverse student body as a compelling interest that warrants race-conscious admissions, the 2023 ruling was not entirely unforeseeable. It came just seven years after approving race-aware college admissions in *Fisher II* (2016), the same 4–3 ruling that arguably foreshadowed its own toppling.[59] There, Kennedy conceded there was a "challenge to our Nation's education system to reconcile the pursuit of diversity with the constitutional promise of equal treatment and dignity." Instead of constitutional principle, however, the focus in *SFFA* was on practicality. Roberts did not believe that the goal of learning through diversity can be subjected to meaningful judicial review, that is, that courts can reliably measure the educational benefits said to flow from a racially diverse student body. A comparison of student diversity learning goals to other compelling interests, the chief justice wrote, "further illustrates their elusive nature." Courts can calibrate the impact of race-based remedies on workplace discrimination and school segregation. On the other hand, while "plainly worthy," "the question whether a particular mix of minority students produces 'engaged and productive citizens,' sufficiently 'enhance[s] appreciation, respect, and empathy,' or effectively 'train[s] future leaders' is standardless."

Hence, *SFFA*'s main point of departure from prior rulings was to dispute the evidence that race-aware admissions policies serve the university's interest in student learning. It was the culmination of a long line of affirmative action rulings that continually undercut the original remedial goals of affirmative action policy. Earlier rulings had already disconnected race-based college admissions policies from the plight of minority students and tethered them instead to the diffuse benefits of diversity intended for the entire college campus and, indeed, all of America.

DEI Politics

The thrust of *Students for Fair Admissions* (2023) does not align with corporate America's endorsement of student diversity learning, but it does align with Mainstreet America's valuation of race-conscious diversity. Peter Schmidt reports that a host of corporations rallied behind the University of Michigan and the contention that race-conscious admissions policies are justified by their educational and societal benefits.[60] Among these were corporations as large and varied as General Motors, Boeing, Texaco, Nationwide Mutual Insurance, and more. Professional groups, too, submitted briefs advancing the same argument, such as the American Bar Association, the Association of American Law Schools, and the Association of American Medical Colleges, along with 30 healthcare associations. According to Schmidt, most influential was a brief signed by 29 former leaders of the US military who suggested that ruling in Michigan's favor was a matter of national security.

It's not that Americans do not value diversity as a matter of principle. They do. In table 5.2 are data that show that average Americans believe race-aware diversity policies are a good thing on the college campus, but not necessarily productive. The 2017 Pew Research Center survey shows that 71 percent said "yes" when asked, "Do you think affirmative action programs designed to increase the number of Black and minority students on college campuses are a good thing or a bad thing?" Additionally, table 5.5 indicates that in 2023 a supermajority of 82 percent believes that diversity makes the US a stronger country. The 2022 YouGov data in the table show that racial diversity is considered either just as or more important than other types of diversity. Likewise, the Pew data similarly show that in 2020 at least 61 percent expressed the belief that the "growing number of newcomers from other countries strengthens American society." The GSS time series data in figure 5.1 further corroborate that diversity is valued on a national scale, as the vast majority reject the idea that immigrants increase

Figure 5.1. Valuing Diversity. *Source*: Davern, M., Bautista, R., Freese, J., Morgan, S. L., & Smith, T. W. (n.d.). *General social surveys, 1972–2021*. NORC, 2021: NORC at the University of Chicago [producer and distributor]. Last accessed 2/16/2021, from the GSS Data Explorer website at gssdataexplorer.norc.org.

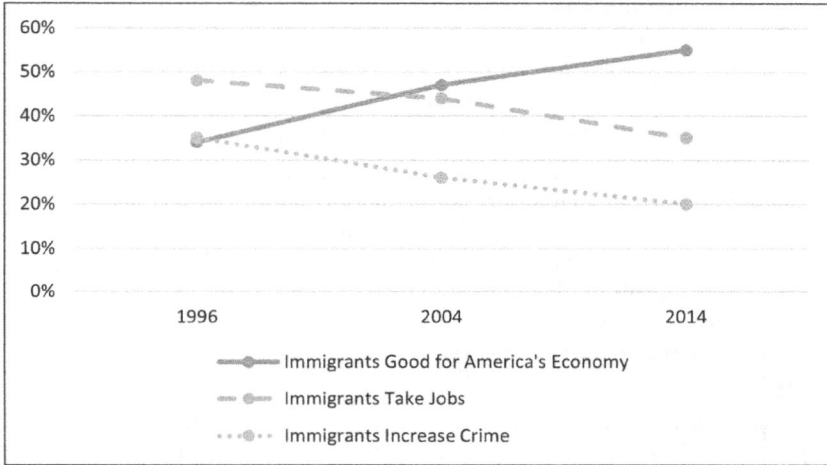

crime or take jobs and the larger share consider immigrants "generally good for America's economy."

But, while they embrace racial-ethnic diversity in the abstract, in the same way that *Students for Fair Admissions* (2023) questions whether diversity actually promotes learning, most Americans are unconvinced of the purported diffuse benefits on the college campus and beyond. When asked whether it improves the quality of education, only 22 percent believe that it does. Meanwhile, the 2023 Pew data in table 5.2 earlier in the chapter show that many more believe that race-based considerations make the admissions process less fair. Of those polled, two times more believe that they actually worsen the learning experience and admit less qualified students. Furthermore, *Students for Fair Admissions* (2023) and prior rulings' limited approval of remedial hiring parallels weak support on the public's part for implementation in the workplace and the country at large. According to table 5.3 nearly half of American citizens believe that affirmative action negatively impacts race relations in the US at large and, therefore, should be ended. A larger 64 percent is hard-pressed to see any impact from affirmative action, in that they rate the programs somewhere between a success and a failure, as opposed to an outright success (11%) or outright failure (22%). It has

Table 5.2. Public Perception of Affirmative Action's Impact on College Campuses, US, 2003–2023, Select Years

Year	Survey Question	Select Responses (%)
2023	When selective colleges and universities consider race and ethnicity as a factor in admissions decisions, in order to increase the racial and ethnic diversity of the school . . . this makes the overall admissions process of these colleges . . .[a]	Much/somewhat less fair: 49 Much/somewhat more fair: 20
2023	When selective colleges and universities consider race and ethnicity as a factor in admissions decisions, in order to increase the racial and ethnic diversity of the school . . . this makes students' overall educational experiences at these colleges . . .[a]	Much/somewhat better: 17 Much/somewhat worse: 26
2023	When selective colleges and universities consider race and ethnicity as a factor in admissions decisions, in order to increase the racial and ethnic diversity of the school . . . this makes the students who are accepted to these colleges . . .[a]	Much/somewhat more qualified: 11 Much/somewhat less qualified: 33
2023	When selective colleges and universities consider race and ethnicity as a factor in admissions decisions, in order to increase the racial and ethnic diversity of the school . . . this is good or bad for ensuring equal educational opportunity for Americans of all racial and ethnic backgrounds?[a]	Very/somewhat good: 36 Very/somewhat bad: 31
2022	Do you agree or disagree that . . . prioritizing diversity benefits students of all races?[b]	Agree: 42 Disagree: 35 Not sure: 24
2022	Do you agree or disagree that . . . affirmative action will result in lower academic standards?[b]	Agree: 35 Disagree: 38 Not sure: 27
2017	In general, do you think affirmative action programs designed to increase the number of Black and minority students on college campuses are a good thing or a bad thing? (Pew Research Center, October 5, 2017)[c]	Good thing: 71 Bad thing: 22

Year	Survey Question	Select Responses (%)
2014	In general, do you think affirmative action programs designed to increase the number of Black and minority students on college campuses are a good thing or a bad thing? (Pew Research Center, April 23, 2014)[c]	Good thing: 63 Bad thing: 30
2003	How do you think affirmative action for Blacks and Hispanics in college admissions affects the overall quality of education? Do you think it improves quality, decreases quality, or doesn't have much effect on quality either way? (*Newsweek*, January 18, 2003)[c]	Not much effect: 53 Improves: 22 Decreases: 14

Source:

[a]Pew Research Center. (2023, June 8). More Americans disapprove than approve of colleges considering race, ethnicity in admissions decisions. https://www.pewresearch.org/politics/2023/06/08/more-americans-disapprove-than-approve-of-colleges-considering-race-ethnicity-in-admissions-decisions.

[b]YouGov. (2022, April 12–18). Last accessed 2/12/2025 from: https://today.yougov.com/politics/articles/42233-affirmative-action-yougov-poll-april-12-18-2022.

[c]*Polling the nations*. (n.d.). Topic: Affirmative action. Last accessed 4/25/2022 from https://ptn-infobase-com.exlibris.colgate.edu/topics/VG9waWM6NTI=?aid=14265.

been decades since a preponderant share was prepared to reject the claim that preferences lower the country's moral standards and pose problems in the workplace.

Alongside public doubts about whether race-aware diversity enhances the college classroom and beyond, most question too whether affirmative action helps Blacks and other minorities. In *Mismatch: How Affirmative Action Hurts Students It's Intended to Help, and Why Universities Won't Admit It*, authors Richard H. Sander and Stuart Taylor Jr. argue that affirmative action hurts minorities more than it helps them because they are often mismatched to colleges and universities where they struggle to keep up.[61] For different reasons, most Americans also report that they do not consider affirmative action helpful to Blacks and other racial-ethnic minorities. The surveys in table 5.4 reveal that, more often than not, they believe that it makes little difference. The most generous assessments date back to 1999, when a slim majority felt it helped Blacks and to 1991 when 61 percent believed affirmative action provided necessary help to women and minorities.

Table 5.3. Public Perception of Affirmative Action's Impact Beyond College Campuses, US, 1991–2012, Select Years

Year	Survey Question	Select Responses (%)
2012	Many ideas have been suggested for improving relations between racial and ethnic groups in the United States. Please indicate if you think each of the following ideas would be helpful, unhelpful, or would make no difference in improving racial and ethnic relations: ending affirmative action. (*Economist*/YouGov, May 21, 2012)	Very/somewhat helpful: 48 Would make no difference: 19 Very/somewhat unhelpful: 17
2008	Have affirmative action programs been a success, a failure, or somewhere in-between? (Rasmussen Reports, July 30, 2008)	Somewhere in-between: 64 Failure: 22 Success: 11
1997	Percentage of respondents who felt affirmative action has had a positive effect on worker's own company. (*Wall Street Journal*, September 19, 1997)	Positive effect: 25
1996	I am going to read you a list of reasons some people have given for why the economy is not doing better than it is. For each one, please tell me if you think it is a major reason the economy is not doing better than it is, a minor reason, or not a reason at all. The first one is women and minorities get too many advantages under affirmative action. (Kaiser Family Foundation, October 1996)	Major reason: 18 Minor reason: 43 Not a reason: 38
1996	I'm going to read you a list of things that some people think might contribute to lower moral standards in this country. As I read each, please tell me whether you think this contributes to lower moral standards or does not contribute to lower moral standards: affirmative action. (*Time*/CNN/Yankelovich, July 12, 1996)	Does not contribute: 47 Does contribute: 39
1995	Generally speaking, do you think affirmative action is a good thing or a bad thing for the country, or doesn't it affect the country much? (Kaiser Family Foundation, September 1995)	Good thing: 44 Bad thing: 26 Doesn't affect country much: 20

Year	Survey Question	Select Responses (%)
1995	In general, would you say that the federal government's affirmative action programs have been good for the country or bad for the country? (*Time*/CNN, July 21, 1995)	Good for the country: 47 Bad for the country: 33
1991	How much trouble do you feel this whole area of affirmative action has caused your company: a lot of trouble, some but not a lot, or not much trouble? (Harris Poll, July 8, 1991)	A lot of trouble: 6 Some but not a lot: 39 Not much trouble: 53

Source: Polling the nations. (n.d.). Topic: Affirmative action. Last accessed 4/25/2022 from https://ptn-infobase-com.exlibris.colgate.edu/topics/VG9waWM6NTI=?aid=14265.

Turning now to national party politics, equally with the Supreme Court Democrats and Republicans publicly valuate diversity in terms of its worth to America as a whole. Past decisions' framing of diversity as tied to the nation's strength and well-being is recited on both sides of the aisle. Each goes to great lengths to broadcast how cultural diversity is an essential element of what sets America apart from the rest of the world. Republicans declared in 2000, "Our country's ethnic diversity within a shared national culture is unique in all the world."[62] When praising "immigrants seeking a better life" in 2004 they again proclaimed, "Our nation has been enriched by their determination, energy, and diversity."[63] This was in step with conservative positioning in earlier years, such as in 1984 when they averred that, "without the contributions of innumerable ethnic and cultural groups, our country would not be where it is today."[64] Regarding immigrants and diversity, Democrats have asserted the same, insisting in 1992 that "America's special genius has been to forge a community of shared values from people of remarkable and diverse backgrounds."[65] In 2012 it was their belief that "the story of the United States would not be possible without the generations of immigrants who have strengthened our country and contributed to our country."[66] By 2020 Democrats would declare that "diversity is our greatest strength."[67]

The bipartisan message that cultural diversity is a source of strength for the nation goes back to 1964, when Democrats pronounced, "The variety of our people is the source of our strength,"[68] and Republicans embraced the same mantra in 1972, stating, "The cultural diversity of America's heritage groups has always been a source of strength for our society and our party."[69] The drumbeat continued in subsequent decades when Republicans

Table 5.4. Public Opinion of Affirmative Action's Impact on Blacks, US, 1991–2022, Select Years

Year	Survey Question	Select Responses (%)
2022	Do you agree or disagree that . . . affirmative action does more harm than good to racial minorities?[a]	Agree: 37 Disagree: 33 Not sure: 30
2022	Do you agree or disagree that . . . affirmative action helps right past injustices against minorities?[a]	Agree: 34 Disagree: 39 Not sure: 28
2021	How much, if at all, has affirmative action programs improved conditions for Black Americans in recent years?[b]	A lot/some: 39 Only a little: 38 None at all: 13
2003	Without affirmative action for Blacks and Hispanics, do you think Blacks' and Hispanics' representation among college students would get better, get worse, or stay about the same? (*Newsweek*, January 18, 2003)	Stay the same: 47 Get worse: 24 Get better: 20
1999	Please tell me how much, if anything, you think each of the following has done to improve conditions for Black Americans in recent years. What about affirmative action programs—have they done a lot, some, only a little, or nothing to improve conditions for Black Americans? (*Newsweek*, April 19, 1999)	A lot/some: 51 Only a little/nothing: 33
1997	These days, do you think it is necessary to have affirmative action programs to make sure there are more Black doctors, or don't you think it's necessary? (*New York Times*/CBS News, December 13, 1997)	Not necessary: 63 Necessary: 29
1995	Percentage of people who think that without affirmative action Blacks' status in the workplace would . . . (*Newsweek*, April 3, 1995)	Stay about the same: 46 Get worse: 30 Get better: 19

Year	Survey Question	Select Responses (%)
1991	Tell me if you tend to agree or disagree. If there are no affirmative action programs helping women and minorities in employment and education, then these groups will continue to fail to get their share of jobs and higher education, thereby continuing past discrimination in the future. (Harris Poll, June 2, 1991)	Agree: 61 Disagree: 36

Sources: Except where indicated, survey data in the table were obtained from *Polling the nations.* (n.d.). Topic: Affirmative action. Last accessed 4/25/2022 from https://ptn-infobase-com.exlibris.colgate.edu/topics/VG9waWM6NTI=?aid=14265.

[a]YouGov. (2022, April 12–18). Last accessed 2/12/2025 from: https://today.yougov.com/politics/articles/42233-affirmative-action-yougov-poll-april-12-18-2022.

[b]Moore, N./YouGov. (2021, May 18–20). *Affirmative Action Omnibus.*

characterized "the healthy mix of America's ethnic, cultural, and social heritage" has the "backbone of our nation and its progress throughout our history."[70] Supreme Court justices effectively joined a chorus that was mobilized in national party politics well before the first affirmative action judgment was announced in 1978.

Besides contributing to the country's cultural identity and richness, parties have specified also how diversity benefits the economy and innovation. Republicans maintained in 2000 that an "expanded visa program (H1-B) provided much of the highly skilled labor that makes rapid technological progress possible."[71] Decades prior they stressed that "the ethnic, cultural, and regional diversity of our people . . . fosters a dynamism in American society that is the envy of the world"[72] and highlighted the "enrichment of ideas that immigrants have brought with them."[73] Democrats likewise catalog diversity-related contributions, proclaiming in 1984 that spurring innovation in the private sector means paying special attention to the needs of small and minority and women-owned businesses.[74] At other times Democrats have held up "immigrants from every nation and their descendants" as the "backbone of the labor movement and an integral party of the Democratic Party."[75] Years before *Bakke* they bragged that "the new Democratic Administration can help lead America to celebrate the magnificence of the diversity within its population, the racial, national, linguistic

Table 5.5. Public Opinion on Value of Racial-Ethnic Diversity, US, 2018–2024, Select Years

Year	Survey Question	Select Responses (%)
2024	The United States has a diverse population, with people of many different races, ethnicity, religions, and backgrounds. Do you think this diversity makes the country . . .[a]	Much/somewhat stronger: 82 Much/somewhat weaker: 18
2022	In your opinion, how important are each of the following when it comes to colleges?	Very/somewhat important . . . Racial diversity: 59 Socioeconomic diversity: 59 Gender diversity: 55 Ideological diversity: 58
2020	Which statement comes closer to your own views—even if neither is exactly right? The growing number of newcomers from other countries strengthens American society? (Or, threatens traditional American customs and values)[c]	Strengthens: 61 Threatens: 37
2019	The U.S. population is made up of people of many different races and ethnicities. Overall, do you think this is . . .	Very good/somewhat good for the country: 77 Somewhat bad/very bad for the country: 6 Neither good nor bad for the country: 17
2019	In general, do you think the fact that the U.S. population is made up of people of many different races makes it . . .	Easier for policymakers to solve the country's problems: 7 Harder for policymakers to solve the country's problems: 47 Doesn't make much difference: 45
2019	In general, do you think the fact that the U.S. population is made up of people of many different races and ethnicities has . . .	A positive impact on the country's culture: 64 A negative impact on the country's culture: 12 Doesn't make much difference: 23

Year	Survey Question	Select Responses (%)
2019	How important, if at all, would you say it is for companies and organizations to promote racial and ethnic diversity in their workplace?	Very/somewhat important: 75 Not too/not at all important: 24
2018	The United States has a diverse population, with people of many different races, ethnicities, religions, and backgrounds. Do you think this diversity makes the country . . .[d]	Much/moderately stronger: 60 Neither stronger nor weaker: 28 Much/moderately weaker: 12

Sources: Except where indicated, survey data in the table were obtained from Pew Research Center. (2019, January 22-February 5). *American Trends Panel Wave 43.* Final topline. file:///C:/Users/nmoore/Downloads/W43-topline_final_diversity_report%20(1).pdf.

[a]Marist National Poll. (2024, January 29–Feb 01). Diversity, equity, and inclusion in the United States. https://maristpoll.marist.edu/wp-content/uploads/2024/02/Marist-Poll_USA-NOS-and-Tables_RR_202402021601.pdf.

[b]YouGov (2022, April 12-18). Last accessed February 12, 2025, from: https://today.yougov.com/politics/articles/42233-affirmative-action-yougov-poll-april-12-18-2022.

[c]Pew Research Center. (2020, July 27-August 2). *American Trends Panel Wave 71.* Final topline. file:///C:/Users/nmoore/Downloads/PP_2020.09.10_Voter-Attitudes-Race-Gender_TOPLINE%20(1).pdf.

[d]Associated Press/NORC. (n.d.). *Diversity and immigration in America.* https://apnorc.org/projects/diversity-and-immigration-in-america/.

and religious groups which have contributed so much to the vitality and richness of our national life."[76]

Presidential pronouncements about the nation-state benefits of diversity emphasize what is best, not only for minorities but also for the nation as a whole. For Clinton diversity was important to a strong economy and to individual access and opportunity. In a major affirmative action speech, Clinton offered that "most economists who study it agree that affirmative action has also been an important part of closing gaps in economic opportunity in our society, thereby strengthening the entire economy," and that "managing diversity and individual opportunity and being fair to everybody is the key to our future economic success in the global marketplace."[77] The Obama administration likewise highlighted the impact of race-based diversity on individual opportunity in a way that was melded to broader impacts. President Obama linked diversity to a strong economy, insisting

that immigrant diversity helps to "revitalize and renew America."[78] His proof
was that "many of the Fortune 500 companies in this country were founded
by immigrants or their children. Many of the tech startups in Silicon Valley
have at least one immigrant founder."[79] Additionally, the diversity guidance
jointly issued by Attorney General Eric Holder and Secretary of Education
Arne Duncan emphasized that, where schools lack a diverse student body
or are racially isolated (i.e., are composed overwhelmingly of students of
one race), they may fail to provide the full panoply of benefits that K–12
schools can offer. The academic achievement of students at racially isolated
schools often lags behind that of their peers at more diverse schools.

The same goes for Clinton and Obama's predecessors. For Nixon the
most worrisome damage to society wrought by housing segregation was that
such racial isolation "readily engenders unwarranted mistrust, hostility, and
fear" and results in the kind of "waste of human resources" that is ultimately
costly to the nation as a whole.[80] President Jimmy Carter gave an impas-
sioned speech at the National Italian-American Bicentennial Tribute Dinner
about how "our diversity of language, heritage, and religion is the key to
the American unity and to the American strength."[81] Reagan proclaimed at
the National Conference of Christians and Jews that "diversity should be
one of our greatest prides."[82]

The way in which President Trump situated diversity interests within
a large frame of America First from 2016 to 2020 was not all that different from the Supreme Court's valuation of affirmative action as a function
of what is best for America. His vision of diversity and immigration was
folded into the Make America Great Again (MAGA) agenda. Titled the
"Bold Immigration Plan for the 21st Century," Trump's immigrant diversity plan plotted out how immigrants would be assimilated into America
in ways that would contribute to "our society." The document stipulated,
"The President's plan is designed to attract immigrants who are ready to
integrate into America's melting pot. Before being able to apply, green card
applicants must pass a US civics exam and demonstrate English proficiency.
The plan also gives priority to young applicants who are likely to build long-
term ties and contribute to our society over their lifetimes."[83] In essence,
Trump's conservative vision of immigration and diversity was a matter of
what immigrants can do for America, more so than what America was
poised to do for immigrants.

Various on-the-ground developments reflect widespread embrace of
the idea that diversity is in service to the greater good. Several studies
outline how diversity is good for business and for American capitalism

more broadly. Gartner, Inc., a technological research and consulting firm, reported that through the year 2022, 75 percent of "organizations with frontline decision-making teams reflecting a diverse and inclusive culture will exceed their financial targets."[84] Also the difference in employee performance between "nondiverse and diverse organizations is 12 percent." A McKinsey report showed that companies in the top quartile for racial-ethnic diversity are 35 percent more likely to realize above-average financial returns.[85] It reported a strong correlation across the board between increased racial-ethnic diversity and earnings. Significantly, moreover, a series of studies published in the *Harvard Business Review* "found that the vast majority of organizations—approximately 80%—used the business case to justify the importance of diversity. In contrast, less than 5% used the fairness case."[86]

It would seem, then, that DEI policies are working precisely as Supreme Court decisions from 1978 to 2016 would have them: for the benefit of the bottom line in America, and not necessarily for Blacks and racial-ethnic minorities. It remains to be seen whether *Students for Fair Admissions'* (2023) progeny will demand concrete evidence that race-aware diversity policies are beneficial to corporations' bottom line and to the country as a whole.

Epilogue

The data and analysis presented in this book detail the extent to which the logic and argumentation in Supreme Court affirmative action opinions are echoed in national racial politics. Intellectual alignment between the Court and the body politic stretches from 1978 up to and including the most recent controversial *Students for Fair Admissions v. Harvard University* (*SFFA*) ruling of 2023. It is true that *SFFA* is a departure from one aspect of prior precedent, in that it invalidated race-based college admission policies whereas earlier decisions upheld such policies. However, it is also true that in regard to the other 12 running themes in affirmative action case law *SFFA* is unexceptional. It follows the same script as that followed by earlier Supreme Court rulings, which, more to the main point of this study, is the same script followed by the body politic as a whole.

Of the many explanations for Supreme Court treatment of racial preference that have gained traction, one that is notably counterfactual is the claim that it is the making of a runaway tribunal. What the justices do, reason, and write in these particular opinions is closely aligned with how the rest of America thinks and talks about these issues. The evidence of alignment offered in this study consists of an in-depth probe of 200+ public opinion surveys from 1991 to 2023, Democratic and Republican National Party platforms from 1940 to 2020, and presidential positioning from FDR through Biden, plus supplementary insights on grassroots happenings. When analyzed side by side with jurisprudential developments, these political trend data help to establish that there is considerable correspondence across several decades between judicial policy and politics on this front.

Unless we probe the reasoning behind preferential rulings, it is impossible to fully grasp the breadth and depth of the Court's countermajoritarian impulse vis-à-vis racial matters or, as it turns out, the lack thereof. As important and decisive as final votes are for the litigants directly involved, knowing how each justice voted does not tell us why the justices voted as they did, the ins and outs of the policy edicts set down in the case, or the resultant benefits and costs to affected industries and the rest of society. For these insights, we must delve into the opinions. The following summary table (table E.1) contains an overview of the evidence in this study that captures the convergence between Supreme Court affirmative action opinions and national racial politics. The table is intended to synopsize the main takeaway from this study, that on all thirteen critical race themes or "flashpoints" in America's racial politics the Supreme Court is at one with major fronts in national race politics.

The evidence of ideational symmetry in the preceding chapters also gives pause for more careful thought about the adequacy of a conservative-liberal paradigm for explaining affirmative action jurisprudential developments, including the 2023 decision rendered by a 6–3 conservative majority. There is little doubt that, alongside other factors, ideology is bound up in the constitutional-legal constraints imposed on affirmative action, just as ideology is implicated in the fact that affirmative action managed to survive judicial review all these years. It is the case, nonetheless, that the institution of the Supreme Court, *as a whole*, has exhibited a marked unease with race-aware policies for as long as it has wrestled with them. Liberal justices such as Thurgood Marshall and William Brennan treaded just as carefully as conservative justices on the question whether racial classifications demand the most exacting judicial scrutiny and whether particularized proof of discrimination is needed to justify remedial affirmative action policies. In cases like *Sheet Metal* (1986) where affirmative action was upheld as well as in cases like *Adarand* (1995) where it was invalidated, we observe the same precepts applied in like measure. Despite the blunt language in the opinions penned by Chief Justice John Roberts for the negative rulings in *Parents Involved* (2007) and *SFFA* (2023), the underlying principles and reasoning parallel those in Chief Justice Burger's favorable opinion for the 6–3 majority in *Fullilove v. Klutznick* (1980).

Inasmuch as the public is conceptually committed to the colorblind ideal, *Students for Fair Admissions* moved the Court, as an institution, closer to majority preferences—closer than prior rulings that had approved race-based college admissions. Chief Justice Roberts stopped short of a full embrace of colorblind constitutionalism in his *SFFA* opinion, insofar as it contemplates permissible use of race awareness in military academy

Table E.1. Summary Table: Toeing the Line

Supreme Court Opinion	Public Opinion	Political Parties	Modern Presidents	Grassroots Politics
History: The history of societywide racial exclusion does not dictate racial preferences.	✓	✓	✓	✓
Critical race theory: Racism is not the root cause of racial inequality.	✓	✓	✓	✓
Equivalency: White ethnics once experienced the same barriers as Blacks.	✓	✓	✓	✓
Colorblind principle: Race awareness is unavoidably problematic.	✓	Republicans ✓ Democrats X	✓	✓
Disparity: Racial disparity does not constitute racial discrimination.	✓	✓	✓	✓

continued on next page

Table E.1. Continued.

Supreme Court Opinion	Public Opinion	Political Parties	Modern Presidents	Grassroots Politics
Ideals: Affirmative action betrays individualist and civil rights ideals.	✓	✓	✓	✓
Harmfulness: Affirmative action policies hurt Whites and Blacks.	✓	✓	✓	✓
Racial policy: The US Constitution and civil rights laws do not require colorblind policies.	X	✓	✓	
Opportunity: The promise of America is equal opportunity, not equal outcomes.	✓	Republicans ✓ Democrats X	✓	✓
Anti-racism: Proven race discrimination may be corrected by racial preference.	✓	Republicans X Democrats ✓	✓	
Racial quotas: Quotas may not be implemented.	✓	✓	✓	

Supreme Court Opinion	Public Opinion	Political Parties	Modern Presidents	Grassroots Politics
"Diversity" defined: Everyone is a candidate for diversity affirmative action, not just minorities.	✓	✓	✓	✓
Purpose: DEI is about Americanism, not minority access.	✓	✓	✓	✓

Source: Created by the author.

admissions, prisoner assignments, college application essays, and at least for now, broadcast diversity programming. Otherwise, the chief finding in *SFFA* that felled race-based college admissions logically emerged from that which grounded earlier decisions: a demand for evidence. Roberts invalidated the Harvard University and University of North Carolina special admissions policies because, as he saw it, neither university proved that use of a suspect classification was necessary to achieve what Roberts deemed the otherwise "worthy" goal of student diversity learning. According to Roberts, under prior precedents, courts lacks means to independently gauge the narrow-tailoring requirement of strict scrutiny because the metrics to do so were elusive, leaving judges to essentially take universities at their word and, thus, abdicate their constitutional responsibility.

However controversial and disconcerting the 2023 decision may be to some, the fact is, the original goal of affirmative action policy was abandoned over 45 years ago in the first preferential ruling, *Bakke v. Regents of California* (1978). From the very outset, that ruling severely diluted the "race" part of racial preferences. There, Justice Powell's principal opinion concluded that the equal protection clause (EPC) of the US Constitution does not permit institutions to tackle societywide racism against Blacks and other minorities through race-specific policies. Nor does the EPC permit private and public bodies to remediate the effects of slavery and past discrimination by way of policies designed only for Blacks and other racial minorities. This precept is the opposite of what guided the original architects and supporters of affirmative action. President John F. Kennedy's Executive Order 10925 was solely concerned with redressing race discrimination. The "shackled runner" thesis detailed in President Lyndon B. Johnson's 1965 speech at Howard University envisaged Blacks—descendants of the enslaved—as the beneficiaries of affirmative action. Dr. Martin L. King approved of compensatory measures as settlement of the appropriation of the labor of one human being by another.[1] In 1973 founding member and then-chair of the Congressional Black Caucus worked to restrict racial preferences to Blacks and Native Americans and to "those who did not come to the United States seeking the 'American Dream.'"

Yet, the Supreme Court rejected the underpinning rationalizations for reparative affirmative action—that all Blacks are disadvantaged, that persistent racial disparities are traceable to slavery and systemic racism, that the EPC of the Fourteenth Amendment is for the protection of minority interests, even the notion that there is a White majority and racial minority in America, and so on. In sum and substance, Supreme Court decisions from 1978 to 2016 hollowed out the foundational aims of race-aware policymaking decades before the *SFFA* ruling in 2023.

The kind of affirmative action policymaking approved by the Court as "compelling" for strict scrutiny purposes is not and never was about opening doors of opportunity for Black, Red, or Brown people; and the college campus is largely to thank for that. Preferential rulings involving higher education always demanded more holistic policies that take into account a wide and varied spectrum of ascriptive and behavioral characteristics—such as, for instance, playing the violin to understanding poor people to being pregnant to living in a rural area. This all-encompassing conception of diversity-oriented affirmative action was not originated by the Supreme Court, though it is the only kind of race-aware diversity ever approved by the Court. The race-aware diversity plan lauded as the model to follow in *Bakke* (1978) as well as its progeny was adopted and implemented before Justice Powell penned the principal opinion in *Bakke*, obviously. Perhaps ironically, it was a Harvard University plan. The point here is that, when it comes to racial matters, nowhere is the convergence between happenings within the courthouse and happenings outside the courthouse clearer than in the symmetry between college campus politics and Supreme Court adjudication of diversity. The tent-enlarging Progressivism of the college campus enormously facilitated the justices' and the country's deracialization of affirmative action and the decentering of Black, Red, and Brown Americans.

The prospects for restoring policies originated for the benefit of socio-economically disadvantaged racial minorities are limited in today's political environment. This is partly because no singular culprit is to blame. It will not be enough to simply change the makeup or lifetime tenure of those who serve on the highest court. Fundamentally, the diminished probabilities for reform are a function not merely of Court dictates but rather the fact that those dictates have a firm footing in America's macro racial politics. Even if a whole new panel of justices were appointed, they would be drawn from society and thus arrive at the courthouse already groomed by prevailing societal norms. Nowadays, the belief system of lay citizens, political parties, and occupants of the Oval Office is at odds with the thinking behind preferential policies. This broad-based disconnect defies conventional civil rights framing also. Consider, for example, that Democratic President Bill Clinton's "Mend It, Don't End It" policy and rhetoric helped to legitimate the 1990s assault on racial preference, an assault launched by a Black activist, who hailed from the uber liberal state of California, which passed the nation's first anti–affirmative action ballot initiative. Years later the first Black president, Barack Obama, spoke to the power of the "theoretical" argument for targeted aid, yet also conceded the political perils of earmarking benefits to one racial group in a country composed of many racial-ethnic groups, and still diversifying.

Notwithstanding the less than optimal prospects, knowing the mainstay flashpoints of affirmative action jurisprudence and politics is a starting point for a pathway forward. These flashpoints are durable and consequential in that they emerge time and again in judicial and political discourses, as documented extensively in this study. Racial reformers would do well to lean into them, to develop a political strategy that is laser-focused on them, and to address head-on the questions and objections around these hot spots. Is the legacy of slavery impactful still now, all these centuries later? How are we to reconcile the Fourteenth Amendment guarantee of equal treatment and the aspirational vision of Dr. Martin L. King's "I Have a Dream" speech with a policy scheme that privileges one race over others? Is the American dream geared toward equal opportunity or equal outcomes, and if the latter, then when, if ever, does race awareness end? Does racial disparity per se constitute proof of discrimination or are disparate outcomes just a fact of American life? Does the US Constitution bestow rights and privileges solely on individuals or does it envisage racial-ethnic groups as such? And more.

To some, these questions require little thought to resolve in favor of race-based affirmative action. However, to most—namely, the majority of the population, the Democratic and Republican party leadership, and presidents from FDR through Biden—these questions are hardly self-explanatory or well understood. As this project wraps, President Donald Trump is deploying executive orders and the administrative state to dismantle diversity, equity, and inclusion (DEI) programs in all federal agencies, in cities and states across the country, and in virtually every American institution. It is highly probable that DEI programs will be just as quickly reinstituted with the stroke of a pen if and when a Democratic presidential administration is reelected in 2028 or later. Even so, the original version of affirmative action advanced in the 1960s and 1970s by Kennedy, Johnson, King, and the Congressional Black Caucus will remain lifeless unless and until the body politic is spurred to breathe new life into it, and to do so by way of actual legislative enactments. It will not be enough to just elect a brand-new president.

This study's examination of national party positioning and presidential policies from 1940 to 2020 carefully documents how Democratic Party stances on all but two of the 13 flashpoints are just as closely aligned with the US Supreme Court's as is Republican Party positioning. On this point, their words speak for themselves. For example, the equivalency between Black and White history that is imputed by Supreme Court justices has been parroted by Democratic leaders. President Jimmy Carter spoke of how "all of us have known the pain associated with discrimination," given the prejudice and suffering in the South and the fact that "we haven't had a President elected from the deep South since 1848."[2] Akin to how preferential rulings question whether skin color remains a determinative force in American society, Democrats proclaimed in 2008 "the essential American ideal that we are not constrained by the circumstances of birth but can make of our lives what we will."[3] An often overlooked part of affirmative action policy history is that a Democrat-controlled Congress spearheaded the bipartisan vote to amend the landmark Civil Rights Act of 1964 so as to expressly bar government from mandating racial evenness in the workplace, government contracting, schools, and so on.

Resurrecting the original affirmative action policy goal of remediating slavery and past societal race discrimination will require more than a new panel of justices, a sympathetic occupant in the Oval Office, or more power to dedicated racial reformers within the ecosystem of the Democratic Party. It will require outreach to the as-yet-unpersuaded American who does not grasp that colorblindness is appealing in principle but, in practice, a means of freezing the status quo that privileges Whites. To facilitate a better understanding of the inextricable tie between race and class, someone will have to explain to average Americans how 300 years of state-enforced racial degradation and exclusion render bootstraps admonitions poorly tailored to the Black experience. It is incomparable to the Italian, Irish, and Jewish American experience with much, much shorter-lived and less dehumanizing, destructive and deadly bigotry in the United States. It will not be easy to rationalize racial preferences to those who were once poor, maligned, and marginalized and now convinced that sheer hard work and determination saved the day, and to the exclusion of built-in privilege. It will be hard to build a national consensus around racial minority issues at a time when the White working class is headlining its own grievances and flexing considerable political muscle within the Make America Great Again movement (MAGA).

Few developments are as challenging as the fact that the national discourse on race was dramatically changed in the 1980s by scholarly research that credibly claims that one's socioeconomic class is more significant than skin color in determining life outcomes. This strain of literature published by a multi-disciplinary cadre of mostly liberal-leaning academics constitutes—in effect if not intent—a formidable counternarrative to any agenda that continues to treat race as the main determinant of how much Black, Red, and Brown lives matter. Being poor matters more than race in a mostly service-producing economy, they say. Not only in light of *Students for Fair Admissions'* embrace of the colorblind principle but also due to this well-received body of research, civil rights policy leaders must be poised to make public declarations that will be jolting for some allies. Among these is that of what affirmative action was originally designed to address, what it has since become, and what it ought to be going forward. Should it redress cultural, economic, and social marginalization too? Or, is it simply to make society more inclusive of all, including first-generation professionals, as in Biden's diversity executive order, right alongside the descendants of the enslaved as in Kennedy and Johnson's executive orders? If race is to continue as a focal point of affirmative action advocacy, it is important to say so.

A 21st-century racial reform movement is needed to overcome these countervailing forces in affirmative action politics and jurisprudence, a movement that is primarily and purposely geared to build a lawmaking majority within the electorate. As in any democratic policy process, so in regard to affirmative action, the change that is sought within policy institutions must be initiated from without. The most basic of democratic principles is that voters must be persuaded to get behind race-based affirmative action if they are to, in turn, elect policymakers that do the same and that, eventually, nominate and confirm likeminded federal judges. The preeminence of the electoral connection is well established by political science research. Its importance supersedes the influence of party, money, and the media. *Students for Fair Admissions* (2023), its predecessors, and successors are not forged in a political vacuum but instead a broad political consensus.

The end goal of the persuasion strategy must be to change minds and to do so through persuasion and factual information, in the tradition of the public awareness-raising campaign that buoyed the 1960s Black civil rights movement. The end goal of that movement, the protests, marches, demonstrations, and all was to secure legislative enactments, specifically by presenting to those outside the South a raw look at the harm and degradation wrought by Jim Crow. This strategic goal was intentional and is elaborated in the writings of Dr. Martin L. King as well as other scholarly accounts of the movement. Strengthening the lay public's grasp of the realities of racial segregation and southern violence laid a critical foundation for the ground-breaking legislative reforms that followed. It was a movement to explain the true nature of race in America, to the rest of America. The movement achieved its legislative goals by first procuring a national political consensus.

Conversations about race nowadays are increasingly charged and emotional. This is to be expected given that such conversations touch on America's original sin, the one from which it has never been fully redeemed or restored. Many are uncomfortable discussing race; many are fatigued. Some resort to rhetorical devices to demonize racial matters as the machinations of race-baiters, race hustlers, and the like, often in an effort to quash change before it begins. At the other end of the political spectrum, progressive racial discourses too often devolve into parochial battles over words, labels, symbols, personality defects, past transgressions, and other issues that are but tangentially related to the lived, material experience of racial minorities. At times racial advocacy is reactionary, diverting limited bandwidth to controversies that are of far less policy consequence than the durable flashpoints—elevating the minor above the major. Some political actors use race for gaslighting purposes.

Frequently, racial discourses and advocacy are co-opted, merged together with, or leveraged by other causes trained on different aims. The tendency to treat the problems facing Blacks and other minorities as add-ons or cousins to other policy agendas—such as gun control, marijuana legalization, environmental policy, abortion rights, saving democracy, opposing Trump, and so on—dilutes the "racial" dimensions of racial matters. These other causes are unquestionably worthy. Nevertheless, they are still *other* causes. An effective strategy of persuasion must anticipate this pattern of diversion and navigate it effectively. There are no other social issues in the US with histories that parallel the nation's long, brutal, and deadly racial history, regardless of whether that history is traced to 1619, 1776, 1865, or 1896.

The more frank the messaging of a 21st-century racial reform movement, the better. It is imperative to acknowledge what most Blacks and Latinos and race studies scholars already know: that the primary beneficiaries of government contracting and college admissions under today's affirmative action are White women and foreign-born minorities. Harvard Law Professor Lani Guinier and Secretary of State Colin Powell lamented the latter years ago. The concerns that they expressed were validated by methodologically rigorous research that reveals that foreign-born Blacks are preferred over American-born Blacks in college admissions, not due to stronger academic credentials (such as grades, test scores, extracurriculars, etc.), but because the former exhibit traits and characteristics preferred by admissions counselors. Moreover, a mass consensus-building strategy must openly concede too that racism does not explain everything, that race-neutral factors help to account for disparities. These include behavioral pathologies such as those well documented by sociologists and neatly packaged for public consumption by the evening news (namely, racially disparate criminality, drug addiction, single-headed households, low academic achievement, etc.). It will be important to squarely address the layered, complicated, and sometimes thorny truth about race. It is already apparent to much of America that all Blacks are not victimized, or disadvantaged, or in need of preferential treatment. These and other complicated truths must be addressed head-on.

Chief Justice Roberts's opinion in *Students for Fair Admissions* was rested on a demand for evidence—for concrete, measurable proof that race-aware admissions policies promoted student diversity learning. Whether Roberts's demand for proof was merely cover for a ploy to upend racial preference is beside the point. American society at large is bombarded with selective facts about the flashpoints in affirmative action politics, and too often through profit-driven social and mainstream media. These facts must not be ignored or summarily dismissed as racist but instead reinterpreted and reexplained through an informed, empirically grounded lens.

Serious, action-oriented discussions about racial matters must ultimately take place on the floor of legislatures and in the halls of government. Hopefully, serious debate about racial matters is not limited to the heat of election season, then relegated to the back shelf, until it again becomes politically expedient in the next election season. It is preferable that those leading and advocating on behalf of the cause are armed with a deep understanding of the historical and contemporary dynamics of race in the US, of what works and doesn't work, of what is and is not true, and most of all, what is a major problem and what is a minor problem. It is even better if the lead advocates are not the moonlighters or the occasional self-appointed spokespersons, but instead those with skin in the game. Those setting the terms of debate and leading the way should have a proven record of commitment and dedication to the cause in spaces where it matters, and even when racial reform is not trending. The overriding objective must be to build and mobilize a sympathetic lawmaking majority outside the courthouse—to, in effect, change America's mind.

Although this study does not assert that lay citizens and elected officials are the driving causal forces behind affirmative action decision-making, it is nonetheless mindful of what we know from empirical studies of judicial behavior and from common sense—that justices of the US Supreme Court are molded by American society and chosen by policymakers who are elected by American society. America, as a whole, has settled on certain conclusions about race. Whatever the precise pathways of extrajudicial influences—whether ideology, other political factors, the threat of nonenforcement, or the looming shadow of Congress's Article III powers—preferential rulings reflect what the country at large believes about race. The Supreme Court has always toed the line of America's racial politics. The bottom-line takeaway of this study is that—no less than during the Civil War era and the '60s—there is always opportunity to move that line, first and foremost at the point where the line begins. Change America's mind, and the rest will follow.

Notes

Introduction

1. Stein, C., & Walters, J. (2023, June 29). "This is not a normal court": Joe Biden condemns affirmative action ruling. *Guardian*. Accessed 1/18/2024 from https://www.theguardian.com/us-news/2023/jun/29/joe-biden-affirmative-action-supreme-court-reaction; Guo, K. (2023, June 29). In Congress, Democrats denounced and Republicans celebrated the ruling on affirmative action. *New York Times*. Accessed 1/18/2024 from https://www.nytimes.com/live/2023/06/29/us/affirmative-action-supreme-court?unlocked_article_code=1.Ok0.GH1G.cMQp81KoVfoB&smid=url-share#in-congress-democrats-denounced-and-republicans-celebrated-the-ruling-on-affirmative-action.

2. Sheer, M. D. (2023, June 29). "This is not a normal court": Biden denounces affirmative action-ruling. *New York Times*. Accessed 1/18/2024 from https://www.nytimes.com/2023/06/29/us/politics/biden-supreme-court-affirmative-action.html.

3. *Students for Fair Admissions v. Harvard*, 600 U.S. ___ (2023).

4. *Dobbs v. Jackson Women's Health Organization*, 597 U.S. ___ (2022).

5. Saad, L. (2022, June 2). "Pro-choice" identification rises to near record high in U.S. Gallup.com. Accessed 1/17/2024 from https://news.gallup.com/poll/393104/pro-choice-identification-rises-near-record-high.aspx.

6. *Masterpiece Cakeshop v. Colorado Civil Rights Commission*, 584 U.S. ___ (2018); *303 Creative LLC v. Elenis*, 600 U.S. ___ (2023).

7. LGBTQ+ Rights. (n.d.). Gallup.com. Accessed 1/17/2024 from https://news.gallup.com/poll/1651/gay-lesbian-rights.aspx.

8. Greve, J. E. (2023, July 9). "Democracy is at risk": Inside the fight for Supreme Court reform. *Guardian*. Accessed 1/18/2024 from https://www.theguardian.com/law/2023/jul/09/supreme-court-reform-conservative-justices.

9. Rosenberg, G. N. (2008). *The hollow hope: Can courts bring about change?* 2nd ed. University of Chicago Press.

10. Spann, G. A. (1993). *Race against the Court: The Supreme Court and minorities in contemporary America.* New York University Press, 13.

11. *Brown v. Board of Education,* 347 U.S. 483 (1954).

12. Spann labels it the "*Marbury*-based model of judicial review," in light of the *Marbury v. Madison* decision that enhanced judicial independence.

13. Guinier, L. (1994). *Tyranny of the majority: Fundamental fairness in representative democracy.* Free Press.

14. See, for example, *U.S. v. Windsor* (2013), *Obergefell v. Hodges* (2015), *Bostock v. Clayton County* (2020), *Altitude Express, Inc. v. Zarda* (2020), *R. G. & G. R. Harris Funeral Homes Inc., v. EEOC* (2020).

15. See, for example, *Moore v. Harper,* 600 U.S. ___ (2023) and *Allen v. Milligan,* 599 U.S. ___ (2023).

16. https://docs.cdn.yougov.com/1ts4uenkci/econTabReport.pdf. Accessed 3/13/2024.

17. https://docs.cdn.yougov.com/iaqktpkrma/cbsnews_20230618_aff_action_1.pdf. Accessed 3/13/2024.

18. Gramlich, J. (2023, June 16). Americans and affirmative action: How the public sees the consideration of race in college admissions, hiring. Pew Research Center. Accessed 1/17/2024 from https://www.pewresearch.org/short-reads/2023/06/16/americans-and-affirmative-action-how-the-public-sees-the-consideration-of-race-in-college-admissions-hiring/.

19. Borter, G. (2023, February 15). Most Americans think college admissions should not consider race—Reuters/Ipsos poll. Accessed 1/17/2024 from https://www.reuters.com/world/us/most-americans-think-college-admissions-should-not-consider-race-reutersipsos-2023-02-15/.

20. *Fisher v. Texas* (Docket No. 14–981, 2016).

21. Luskin, R. C., McIver, J. P., & Carmines, E. G. (1989). Issues and the transmission of partisanship. *American Journal of Political Science, 33*: 440–458. https://doi.org/10.2307/2111155.

22. See, for example: Urofsky, M. I. (2020). *The affirmative action puzzle: A living history from Reconstruction to today.* Pantheon Books; Vu Tran, H. (2020). *Race, law, and higher education in the colorblind era: Critical investigations into race-related Supreme Court disputes.* Routledge; Kennedy, R. (2013). *For discrimination: Race, affirmative action, and the law.* Vintage Books; Schmidt, P. (2007). *Color and money: How rich White kids are winning the war over college affirmative action.* Palgrave Macmillan; Crosby, F. J. (2004). *Affirmative action is dead; Long live affirmative action.* Yale University Press; Spann, G. A. (2000). *The law of affirmative action: Twenty-five years of Supreme Court decisions on race and remedies.* New York University Press; Fiscus, R. J. (1992). *The constitutional logic of affirmative action* (ed. S. L. Wasby). Duke University Press.

23. I extend my sincere thanks to the following student research assistants who were enormously helpful in gathering data for this study, listed in chronological order: Adrielle Jefferson, Stacy Silnik, Danielle Dillon, Anthony DeRose, Lauren Henske, Cassidy Murphy, Izabel Melgoza, Nam Nguyen, Fiona Saunders,

Boen Bevers, and Brianna Wright. I am grateful also for the thoughtful editorial guidance of Michael Rinella and Robert Spitzer at State University of New York Press and the invaluable insights of external reviewers. Grants from the Colgate Research Council under Dominka Koter and Ahmet Ay helped fund the Moore/YouGov survey. The financial support and time off for reflection facilitated by Dean of the Faculty Lesleigh Cushing and Associate Dean of the Faculty Krista Ingram were indispensable to the book's completion.

1. Affirmative Action Jurisprudence in Institutional, Political, and Historical Context

1. O'Brien, D. M. (2014). *Storm center: The Supreme Court in American politics*. 10th edition. W. W. Norton, 33.

2. For more research on the politics of presidential nominations to the Supreme Court, see: Black, R. C., & Owens, R. J. (2016). Courting the president: How circuit court judges alter their behavior for promotion to the Supreme Court. *American Journal of Political Science*, *60*(1), 30–43; Kahn, M. A. (1992). Shattering the myth about President Eisenhower's Supreme Court appointments. *Presidential Studies Quarterly*, *22*(1): 47–56; Whittington, K. E. (2006). Presidents, Senates, and failed Supreme Court nominations. *Supreme Court Review*, *2006*(1): 401–438. https://doi-org.exlibris.colgate.edu/10.1086/655178.

3. O'Brien, D. M. (2014). *Storm center: The Supreme Court in American politics*. 10th edition. W. W. Norton, 44.

4. Abraham, H. S. (1992). *Justices and presidents: A political history of appointments to the Supreme Court*. Oxford University Press.

5. For evidence on ideological drift, see: Epstein, L., Martin, A. D., Quinn, I. M., & Segal, J. A. (2007). Ideological drift among Supreme Court justices: Who, when, and how important? *Northwestern University Law Review* 101: 1483–1542.

6. Epstein and Posner note the Obama administration's experience as the exception to this trend. See: Epstein, L., & Posner, E. A. (2018). The decline of Supreme Court deference to the President. *University of Pennsylvania Law Review*, *166*(4): 829–860, 845; Epstein, L., & Posner, E. A. (2016). Supreme Court justices' loyalty to the president. *Journal of Legal Studies*, *45*(2): 401–436. For evidence on ideological drift, see: Epstein, L., Martin, A. D., Quinn, I. M., & Segal, J. A. (2007). Ideological drift among Supreme Court justices: Who, when, and how important? *Northwestern University Law Review*, *101*: 1483–1542.

7. Mishler, W., & Sheehan, R. W. (1996). Public opinion, the attitudinal model, and Supreme Court decision making: A micro-analytic perspective. *Journal of Politics*, *58*(1): 169–200; Cardozo, B. (1921). *The nature of the judicial process*. Yale University Press.

8. Moraski, B. J., & Shipan, C. R. (1999). The politics of Supreme Court nominations: A theory of institutional constraints and choices. *American Journal of*

Political Science, 43(4): 1069–1095. See also: U.S. Senate. (n.d.). Supreme Court nominations (1789–present). Last accessed 4/27/2022 from https://www.senate.gov/legislative/nominations/SupremeCourtNominations1789present.htm.

9. Epstein, L., Segal, J. A., Spaeth, H. J., & Walker, T. G. (2007). *The Supreme Court compendium: Data, decisions & developments.* CQ Press, table 7-15, 691; Baum, L. (2001). *American courts: Process and policy.* Houghton Mifflin, 262; Meinhold, S. S., & Shull, S. A. (1998). Policy congruence between the president and the solicitor general. *Political Research Quarterly, 51*: 527–537; Caldeira, G. A., & Wright, J. R. (1988). Organized interests and agenda setting in the U.S. Supreme Court. *American Political Science Review, 82*(4): 1109–1127. https://doi.org/10.2307/1961752; Caplan, L. (1987). *The tenth justice: The solicitor general and the rule of law.* Vintage Books.

10. Overby, L. M., Henschen, B. M., Walsh, M. H., & Strauss, J. (1992). Courting constituents? An analysis of the Senate confirmation vote on Justice Clarence Thomas. *American Political Science Review, 86*: 997–1006; Ruckman, P. S., Jr. (1993). The Supreme Court, critical nominations, and the Senate confirmation process. *Journal of Politics, 55*: 793–805.

11. Overby, L. M., Henschen, B. M., Walsh, M. H., & Strauss, J. (1992). Courting constituents? An analysis of the Senate confirmation vote on Justice Clarence Thomas. *American Political Science Review, 86*: 997–1006.

12. Kastellec, J. P., Lax, J. R., & Phillips, J. H. (2010). Public opinion and Senate confirmation of Supreme Court nominees. *Journal of Politics, 72*(3): 767–784. https://doi.org/10.1017/s0022381610000150.

13. Cameron, C. M., Cover, A. D., & Segal, J. A. (1990). Senate voting on Supreme Court nominations: A neo-institutional model. *American Political Science Review, 84*(2): 525–34, 527.

14. For more information, go to: Administrative Office of the United States Courts. (n.d.). United States courts. Last accessed 5/01/2022 from https://www.uscourts.gov/statistics-reports/funding-and-budget-annual-report-2021.

15. More on the Court's rulemaking power can be found here: 28 U.S.C. §2071: https://www.govinfo.gov/content/pkg/USCODE-2011-title28/pdf/USCODE-2011-title28-partV-chap131-sec2071.pdf.

16. Codes managing buildings and grounds are detailed at http://supremecourt.gov, under "Buildings Regulations" and also here: https://uscode.house.gov/view.xhtml?path=/prelim@title40/subtitle2/partC/chapter61&edition=prelim.

17. More on federal regulations concerning the Court's calendar is found under "The Term and Caseload" subsection here: https://www.supremecourt.gov/about/courtatwork.aspx.

18. For excellent summary treatment of the episode, see: O'Brien, D. M. (2014). *Storm center: The Supreme Court in American politics.* 10th edition. W. W. Norton.

19. Epstein, L., Segal, J. A., Spaeth, H. J., & Walker, T. G. (2007). *The Supreme Court compendium: Data, decisions & developments.* CQ Press, table 1-1.

20. CQ Press. (1964). First federal pay bill rejected; compromise enacted. *Congressional Quarterly Almanac 1964*. CQ Press, a division of Sage. https://library. cqpress.com/cqalmanac/document.php?id=cqal64-1304735#H2_2.

21. O'Brien, D. M. (2014). *Storm center: The Supreme Court in American politics*. 10th edition. W. W. Norton, 95.

22. Stanley, H. W., & Niemi, R. G. (2015). *Vital statistics on American politics 2015–2016*. CQ Press, tables 7-8 and 7-9, 287–288.

23. United States Courts. (2001, March 14). Judicial conference adopts strategy to improve pay for top government officials. https://www.uscourts.gov/news/2001/03/14/ judicial-conference-adopts-strategy-improve-pay-top-government-officials.

24. Stanley, H. W., & Niemi, R. G. (2015). *Vital statistics on American politics 2015–2016*. CQ Press, figure 7-4, 292, based on personal communication from Professor Lawrence Baum; Baum, L. (2001). *The Supreme Court*. 7th edition. CQ Press, table 5-2, 192.

25. Baum, L. (2001). *The Supreme Court*. 7th edition. CQ Press, table 5-2, 192.

26. McCloskey, R. G. (2016). *The American Supreme Court*. 6th edition. Revised by S. Levinson. University of Chicago Press, 73; O'Brien, D. M. (2014). *Storm center: The Supreme Court in American politics*. 10th edition. W. W. Norton, 358.

27. Epstein, L., Knight, J. L., & Martin, A. D. (2001). The Supreme Court as a strategic national policymaker. *Emory Law Review*, *55*: 583–611.

28. Casillas, C. J., Enns, P. K., & Wohlfarth, P. C. (2011). How public opinion constrains the U.S. Supreme Court. *American Journal of Political Science*, *55*(1): 74–88, 76.

29. Segal, J. A., Westerland, C., & Lindquist, S. A. (2011). Congress, the Supreme Court, and judicial review: Testing a constitutional separation of powers model. *American Journal of Political Science*, *55*(1): 89–104, 102.

30. Caldeira, G. A., & Gibson, J. L. (1992). The etiology of public support for the Supreme Court. *American Journal of Political Science*, *36*(3): 635–664. https:// doi.org/10.2307/2111585.

31. Gibson, J. L., & Caldeira, G. A. (2011). Has legal realism damaged the legitimacy of the U.S. Supreme Court? *Law & Society Review*, *45*(1): 195–219; Gibson, J. L., Caldeira, G. A., & Spence, L. K. (2003). The Supreme Court and the U.S. presidential election of 2000: Wounds, self-inflicted or otherwise? *British Journal of Political Science*, *33*: 535–556.

32. Executive Order 14023.

33. Min Kim, S., & Barnes, R. (2021, December 28). Supreme Court term limits are popular—and appear to be going nowhere. *Washington Post*. https://www. washingtonpost.com/nation/2021/12/28/supreme-court-term-limits/.

34. Root, D., & Berger, S. (2019, May 8). Structural reforms to the federal judiciary: Restoring independence and fairness to the courts. Center for American Progress. https://www.americanprogress.org/article/structural-reforms-federal-judiciary/.

35. Casillas, C. J., Enns, P. K., & Wohlfarth, P. C. (2011). How public opinion constrains the U.S. Supreme Court. *American Journal of Political Science*, 55(1): 74–88.

36. Hall, M. E. K. (2011). *The nature of Supreme Court power.* Cambridge University Press; Halpern, S. C. (1995). *On the limits of the law: The ironic legacy of Title VI of the 1864 Civil Rights Act.* Johns Hopkins University Press.

37. Owens, R. J. (2010). The separation of powers and Supreme Court agenda setting. *American Journal of Political Science*, 54: 412–427; Cross, F. B., & Nelson, B. J. (2001). Strategic institutional effects on Supreme Court decision making. *Northwestern University Law Review*, 95: 1437–1493; Baum, L. (2003). The Supreme Court in American politics. *Annual Review of Political Science*, 6: 161–180.

38. McGuire, K. T., & Stimson, J. A. (2004). The least dangerous branch revisited: New evidence on Supreme Court responsiveness to public preferences. *Journal of Politics*, 66(4): 1018–1035, 1019. https://doi.org/10.1111/j.1468-2508.2004.00288.x.

39. McGuire, K. T., & Stimson, J. A. (2004). The least dangerous branch revisited: New evidence on Supreme Court responsiveness to public preferences. *Journal of Politics*, 66(4): 1018–1035, 1019. https://doi.org/10.1111/j.1468-2508.2004.00288.x.

40. CBS News Poll. (2006, January 9). *Polling the nations.* (n.d.). Topic: Affirmative action. Last accessed 4/25/2022 from https://ptn-infobase-com.exlibris.colgate.edu/topics/VG9waWM6NTI=?aid=14265.

41. Quinnipiac University. (2010, May 29). *Polling the nations.* (n.d.). Topic: Affirmative action. Last accessed 4/25/2022 from https://ptn-infobase-com.exlibris.colgate.edu/topics/VG9waWM6NTI=?aid=14265.

42. Carmines, E. G., & Stimson, J. A. (1989). *Issue evolution: Race and the transformation of American politics.* Princeton University Press.

43. CBS News. (2005, September 14). Obtained from *Polling the nations.* (n.d.). Topic: Affirmative action. Last accessed 4/25/2022 from https://ptn-infobase-com.exlibris.colgate.edu/topics/VG9waWM6NTI=?aid=14265.

44. ABC News. (2004, December 22). Obtained from *Polling the nations.* (n.d.). Topic: Affirmative action. Last accessed 4/25/2022 from https://ptn-infobase-com.exlibris.colgate.edu/topics/VG9waWM6NTI=?aid=14265.

45. The Eleventh Amendment reversed *Chisolm v. Georgia* (1793); the Thirteenth Amendment, *Scott v. Sanford* (1857); Fourteenth Amendment, *Scott v. Sanford* (1857); Sixteenth Amendment, *Pollock v. Farmer's Loan and Trust Col.* (1895); and, Twenty-Sixth Amendment, *Oregon v. Mitchell* (1970) from: Epstein, L., Segal, J. A., Spaeth, H. J., & Walker, T. G. (2007). *The Supreme Court compendium: Data, decisions & developments.* CQ Press, table 7-1, 663.

46. https://constitution.congress.gov/resources/decisions-overruled/.

47. O'Brien, D. M. (2014). *Storm center: The Supreme Court in American politics.* 10th edition. W. W. Norton, 30,

48. Original Text of Civil Rights Restoration Act of 1991.

49. *Richmond v. J. A. Croson* (488 U.S. 469, 1989); *Patterson v. McLean Credit Union* (491 U.S. 164, 1989); *Wards Cove Packing Co. v. Atonio* (490 U.S. 642, 1989);

Price Waterhouse v. Hopkins (490 U.S. 228, 1989); *Martin v. Wilks* (490 U.S. 755, 1989); *United Automobile Workers v. Johnson Controls, Inc.* (499 U.S. 187, 1991).

50. Rosenberg, G. N. (2008). *The hollow hope: Can courts bring about change?* 2nd edition. University of Chicago Press. For an alternative view, see: Hall, M. E. K. (2011). *The nature of Supreme Court power.* Cambridge University Press.

51. Boyd, C. L., Ringhand, L. A., & Collins, P. M. (2018). The role of nominee gender and race at U.S. Supreme Court confirmation hearings. *Law & Society Review, 52:* 871–890.

52. Segal, J. A., & Spaeth, H. J. (1993). *The Supreme Court and the attitudinal model.* Cambridge University Press; Segal, J. A., & Spaeth, H. J. (2002). *The Supreme Court and the attitudinal model revisited.* Cambridge University Press.

53. Ulmer, S. S. (1970). Dissent behavior and the social background of Supreme Court justices. *Journal of Politics, 32:* 580–598, 580.

54. Rehnquist, W. H. (1986). Constitutional law and public opinion. *Suffolk University Law Review, 20:* 751–769.

55. Stanley, H. W., & Niemi, R. G. (2015). *Vital statistics on American politics 2015–2016.* CQ Press, figure 7-4, 292, based on personal communication from Professor Lawrence Baum; Baum, L. (2001). *The Supreme Court.* 7th edition. CQ Press, table 5-2, 192.

56. Giles, M. W., Blackstone, B., & Vining, R. L. (2008). The Supreme Court in American democracy: Unraveling the linkages between public opinion and judicial decision making. *Journal of Politics, 70:* 293–306; Marshall, T. R. (2008). *Public opinion and the Rehnquist Court.* State University of New York Press; McGuire, K. T., & Stimson, J. A. (2004). The least dangerous branch revisited: New evidence on Supreme Court responsiveness to public preferences. *Journal of Politics, 66:* 1018–1035; Flemming, R. B., Bohte, J., & Wood, B. D. (1997). One voice among many: The Supreme Court's influence on attentiveness to issues in the United States, 1947–92. *American Journal of Political Science, 41:*1224–1250; Mishler, W., & Sheehan, R. S. (1993). The Supreme Court as a countermajoritarian institution? The impact of public opinion on Supreme Court decisions. *American Political Science Review, 87:* 87–101; Mishler, W., & Sheehan, R. S. (1994). Popular influence on Supreme Court decisions. *American Political Science Review, 88:* 716–724; Mishler, W., & Sheehan, R. S. (1996). Public opinion, the attitudinal model, and Supreme Court decision making: A micro-analytic perspective. *Journal of Politics, 58:* 169–200; Link, M. W. (1995). Tracking public mood in the Supreme Court: Cross-time analyses of criminal procedure and civil rights cases. *Political Research Quarterly, 48:* 61–78; Stimson, J. A., MacKuen, M. B., & Erikson, R. S. (1995). Dynamic representation. *American Political Science Review, 89:* 543–565.

57. Gibson, J. L. (1990). Review of *Public Opinion and the Court,* Thomas R. Marshall. *Public Opinion Quarterly* (54): 289–290, 90.

58. Casillas, C. J., Enns, P. K., & Wohlfarth, P. C. (2011). How public opinion constrains the U.S. Supreme Court. *American Journal of Political Science, 55*(1): 74–88, 79.

59. Baum, L., & Devins, N. (2010). Why the Supreme Court cares about elites, not the American people. *Georgetown Law Journal, 98*: 1515–1581.

60. Giles, M. W., Blackstone, B., & Vining, R. L. (2008). The Supreme Court in American democracy: Unraveling the linkages between public opinion and judicial decision making. *Journal of Politics, 70*: 293–306, 293.

61. McGuire, K. D., & Stimson, J. A. (2004). The least dangerous branch revisited: New evidence on Supreme Court responsiveness to public preferences. *Journal of Politics, 66*: 1018–1035, 1020.

62. McGuire, K. D., & Stimson, J. A. (2004). The least dangerous branch revisited: New evidence on Supreme Court responsiveness to public preferences. *Journal of Politics, 66*: 1018–1035, 1020.

63. Stanley, H. W., & Niemi, R. G. (2015). *Vital statistics on American politics 2015–2016.* CQ Press, table 7-12, 291; Keck, T. M. (2004). *The most activist Supreme Court in history: The road to modern judicial conservatism.* University of Chicago Press.

64. Bickel, A. M. (1986). *The least dangerous branch: The Supreme Court at the bar of politics.* 2nd edition. Yale University Press.

65. Chemerinsky, E. (2014). *The case against the Supreme Court.* Penguin Books.

66. Chemerinsky, E. (2014). *The case against the Supreme Court.* Penguin Books.

67. Spann, G. A. (2000). *The law of affirmative action: Twenty-five years of Supreme Court decisions on race and remedies.* New York University Press.

68. Perry, B. (2007). *The Michigan affirmative action cases.* University Press of Kansas, preface.

69. Spann, G. A. (1993). *Race against the Court: The Supreme Court and minorities in contemporary America.* New York University Press, 27.

70. Spann, G. A. (1993). *Race against the Court: The Supreme Court and minorities in contemporary America.* New York University Press, 2.

71. Golub, M. (2018). *Is racial equality unconstitutional?* Oxford University Press, 66.

72. Golub, M. (2018). *Is racial equality unconstitutional?* Oxford University Press, 66.

73. Goldstone, L. (2020). *On account of race.* Counterpoint Press, 235.

74. Dahl, R. A. (1957). Decision-making in a democracy: The Supreme Court as a national policy maker. *Journal of Public Law, 6*: 279–295, 292.

75. Dahl, R. A. (1957). Decision-making in a democracy: The Supreme Court as a national policy maker. *Journal of Public Law, 6*: 279–295, 292–293.

76. Dahl, R. A. (1957). Decision-making in a democracy: The Supreme Court as a national policy maker. *Journal of Public Law, 6*: 279–295, 293.

77. Dahl, R. A. (1957). Decision-making in a democracy: The Supreme Court as a national policy maker. *Journal of Public Law, 6*: 279–295, 285.

78. Kennedy, R. (2013). *For discrimination: Race, affirmative action, and the law.* Pantheon Books, 182.

79. Kennedy, R. (2013). *For discrimination: Race, affirmative action, and the law*. Pantheon Books, 182.

80. Klarman, M. J. (2004). *From Jim Crow to civil rights: The Supreme Court and the struggle for racial equality*. Oxford University Press, 5.

81. Davis, A. L., & Graham, B. L. (1995). *The Supreme Court, race, and civil rights*. Sage.

82. Sunstein, C. R. (1998). Casuistry. In R. Post & M. Rogin (Eds.), *Race and representation: Affirmative action*. Zone Books, 309.

83. For excellent discussions of these approaches, see: McGuire, K. T., Vanberg, G., Smith, C. E., & Caldeira, G. A. (2009). Measuring policy content on the U.S. Supreme Court. *Journal of Politics, 71*: 1305–1321. https://doi.org/10.1017/s0022381609990107; Kidd, Q. (2008). The real (lack of) difference between Republicans and Democrats: A computer word score analysis of party platforms, 1996–2004. *PS: Political Science and Politics, 41*: 519–525; Baum, L. (1988). Measuring policy change in the U.S. Supreme Court. *American Political Science Review, 82*: 905–912. https://doi.org/10.2307/1962497.

84. Hansford, T. G., & Spriggs, J. F., II (2006). *The politics of precedent on the U.S. Supreme Court*. Oxford University Press, 4 and 124.

85. Hansford, T. G., & Spriggs, J. F., II (2006). *The politics of precedent on the U.S. Supreme Court*. Oxford University Press.

86. Carr, M. K. (2018). Prudential Supreme Court opinion writing. In *The rhetorical invention of diversity: Supreme Court opinions, public arguments, and affirmative action*. Michigan State University Press, 142. https://doi.org/10.14321/j.ctt21kk1fv.8.

87. Black, R. C., Wedeking, J., Owens, R. J., & Wohlfarth, P. C. (2016). The influence of public sentiment on Supreme Court opinion clarity. *Law & Society Review, 50*: 703–732; Wedeking, J., & Zilis, M. A. (2018). Disagreeable rhetoric and the prospect of public opposition: Opinion moderation on the U.S. Supreme Court. *Political Research Quarterly, 71*: 380–394.

88. Sunstein, C. R. (1998). Casuistry. In R. Post & M. Rogin (Eds.), *Race and Representation: Affirmative action*. Zone Books, 327.

89. *Students for Fair Admissions v. Harvard*, 600 U.S. ___ (2023), 39.

90. *Grutter v. Bollinger*, 539 U.S. 306, 325 (2003).

91. For more on the Supreme Court's review process, see: O'Brien, D. M. (2014). *Storm center: The Supreme Court in American politics*. 10th edition. W. W. Norton.

92. Mere citation of an affirmative action precedent or replication dicta did not qualify a case.

93. Spann, G. A. (2000). *The law of affirmative action: Twenty-five years of Supreme Court decisions on race and remedies*. New York University Press. See table at 162–163.

94. Spann, G. A. (2000). *The law of affirmative action: Twenty-five years of Supreme Court decisions on race and remedies*. New York University Press.

95. *Grutter* (2003), 323.

96. Sunstein, C. R. (1998). Casuistry. In R. Post & M. Rogin (Eds.), *Race and Representation: Affirmative action*. Zone Books, 313–314.

97. Sunstein, C. R. (1998). Casuistry. In R. Post & M. Rogin (Eds.), *Race and Representation: Affirmative action*. Zone Books, 311.

98. Ekins, E., & Gygi, J. (2023, August 8). Americans say they like "affirmative action" yet oppose racial preferences in college admissions. Cato Institute. Accessed 3/02/2025 from https://www.cato.org/blog/americans-say-they-affirmative-action-yet-oppose-racial-preferences-college-admissions.

99. Simmons, A. D., & Bobo, L. D. (2015). Can non-full-probability internet surveys yield useful data? A comparison with full-probability face-to-face surveys in the domain of race and social inequality attitudes. *Sociological Methodology, 45*: 357–387; Bobo, L. D., & Fox, C. (2003). Race, racism, and discrimination: Bridging problems, methods, and theory in social psychological research. *Social Psychology Quarterly, 66*: 319–332. https://doi.org/10.2307/1519832; Bobo, L. (1997). Race, public opinion, and the social sphere. *Public Opinion Quarterly, 61*: 1–15; Bobo, L., & Hutchings, V. L. (1996). Perceptions of racial group competition: Extending Blumer's theory of group position to a multiracial social context. *American Sociological Review, 61*: 951–972. https://doi.org/10.2307/2096302.

100. Kidd, Q. (2008). The real (lack of) difference between Republicans and Democrats: A computer word score analysis of party platforms, 1996–2004. *PS: Political Science and Politics, 41*: 519–525, abstract.

101. Fagan, E. J. (2018). Marching orders? U.S. party platforms and legislative agenda setting 1948–2014. *Political Research Quarterly, 71*: 949–959.

102. Ginsberg, B. (1976). Elections and public policy. *American Political Science Review, 70*: 41–49; Monroe, A. D. (1983). American party platforms and public opinion. *American Journal of Political Science, 27*: 27–42.

103. Simas, E. N., & Evans, K. A. (2011). Linking party platforms to perceptions of presidential candidates' policy positions, 1972–2000. *Political Research Quarterly, 64*: 831–839.

104. For more details, go to: https://www.presidency.ucsb.edu/about.

105. Segal, J. A., Timpone, R. J., & Howard, R. M. (2000). Buyer beware? Presidential success through Supreme Court appointments. *Political Research Quarterly, 53*(3): 557–573. https://doi.org/10.2307/449198, 558.

106. Kennedy, R. (2013). *For discrimination: Race, affirmative action, and the law*. Vintage Books, 80.

107. Lyndon B. Johnson, Commencement Address at Howard University: "To Fulfill These Rights" from Peters, G., & Woolley, J. T. (n.d.). American Presidency Project. https://www.presidency.ucsb.edu/node/241312.

108. Urofsky, M. I. (2020). *The affirmative action puzzle: A living history from Reconstruction to today*. Pantheon Books.

109. Anderson, T. H. (2004). *The pursuit of fairness: A history of affirmative action*. Oxford University Press.

110. Urofsky, M. I. (2020). *The affirmative action puzzle: A living history from Reconstruction to today*. Pantheon Books, see chapter 1, "Affirmative Action before Kennedy"; Leiter, W. M., & Leiter, S. (2010). *Affirmative action in antidiscrimination law and policy*. 2nd edition. State University of New York Press.

111. Kennedy, R. (2013). *For discrimination: Race, affirmative action, and the law*. Vintage Books, 22 et sequi.

112. Congressional Research Service. (2022, March 9). *SBA's "8(a) Program": Overview, history, and current issues*. https://sgp.fas.org/crs/misc/R44844.pdf, 4.

113. Congressional Research Service. (2022, March 9). *SBA's "8(a) Program": Overview, history, and current issues*. https://sgp.fas.org/crs/misc/R44844.pdf, 4.

114. Kennedy, R. (2013). *For discrimination: Race, affirmative action, and the law*. Vintage Books, 20–21.

115. For a thorough treatment of these different applications, see: Leiter, W. M., & Leiter, S. (2010). *Affirmative action in antidiscrimination law and policy*. 2nd edition. State University of New York Press.

116. For further discussion of hard and soft versions, see: Urofsky, M. I. (2020). *The affirmative action puzzle: A living history from Reconstruction to today*. Pantheon Books.

117. Chapter 4 discusses the Supreme Court's rulings on which goals are allowed under the US Constitution and which are banned.

118. Kennedy, R. (2013). *For discrimination: Race, affirmative action, and the law*. Vintage Books; Keiter, W. M., & Leiter, S. (2010). *Affirmative action in antidiscrimination law and policy*. 2nd edition. State University of New York Press.

2. Burying the Past: That Was Then; This Is Now

1. In the next section of this chapter we take up Powell's elaboration of this point.

2. See: Alexander, M. (2020). *The new Jim Crow: Mass incarceration in the age of colorblindness*. 10th anniversary edition. Free Press; Klarman, M. J. (2006). *From Jim Crow to civil rights: The Supreme Court and the struggle for racial equality*. Oxford University Press; Tonry, M. (1995). *Malign neglect: Race, crime, and punishment in America*. Oxford University Press.

3. Justices Powell and Stevens did not take part in the consideration or decisions of this case.

4. Democratic Party platforms for 1940, 1944, and 1948 from Peters, G., & Woolley, J. T. (n.d.). The American Presidency Project. University of California at Santa Barbara. https://www.presidency.ucsb.edu/documents/app-categories/elections-and-transitions/party-platforms.

5. Republican Party platforms for 1940, 1944, and 1948 from Peters, G., & Woolley, J. T. (n.d.). The American Presidency Project. University of California

at Santa Barbara. https://www.presidency.ucsb.edu/documents/app-categories/elections-and-transitions/party-platforms.

6. 1968 Democratic Party platform.

7. 2020 Democratic Party platform.

8. 1960 Democratic Party platform.

9. 1980 through 1996 Republican Party platforms.

10. 1960 Democratic Party platform.

11. 1980 Democratic Party platform.

12. 1976 Republican Party platform.

13. 1980 Republican Party platform.

14. 2004 Republican Party platform.

15. 2000 Democratic Party platform.

16. 2020 Democratic Party platform.

17. This point is further elaborated in chapter 5.

18. 1976 Republican Party platform.

19. Anderson, T. H. (2004). *The pursuit of fairness: A history of affirmative action*. Oxford University Press, 22–24.

20. Franklin D. Roosevelt, Executive Order 8802—Reaffirming Policy of Full Participation in the Defense Program by All Persons, Regardless of Race, Creed, Color, or National Origin, and Directing Certain Action in Furtherance of Said Policy from Peters, G., & Woolley, J. T. (n.d.). The American Presidency Project. https://www.presidency.ucsb.edu/node/209704. The main provision of the order barred discrimination in defense industries.

21. Franklin D. Roosevelt, Executive Order 9346—Establishing a Committee on Fair Employment Practice from Peters, G., & Woolley, J. T. (n.d.). The American Presidency Project. https://www.presidency.ucsb.edu/node/210091.

22. Dwight D. Eisenhower, Executive Order 10590—Establishing the President's Committee on Government Employment Policy from Peters, G., & Woolley, J. T. (n.d.). The American Presidency Project. https://www.presidency.ucsb.edu/node/306902.

23. Stephanopoulos, G., & Edley, C., Jr. (1995, July 19). Affirmative action review. The White House. Last accessed 5/5/2022 from https://clintonWhitehouse4.archives.gov/WH/EOP/OP/html/aa/aa-lett.html.

24. Stephanopoulos, G., & Edley, C., Jr. (1995, July 19). Affirmative action review. The White House. Last accessed 5/5/2022 from https://clintonWhitehouse4.archives.gov/WH/EOP/OP/html/aa/aa-lett.html.

25. Donald J. Trump, Remarks in a Town Hall Meeting with George Stephanopoulos of ABC News at the National Constitution Center in Philadelphia, Pennsylvania, from Peters, G., & Woolley, J. T. (n.d.). The American Presidency Project. https://www.presidency.ucsb.edu/node/345477.

26. Donald J. Trump, Address Accepting the Republican Presidential Nomination from Peters, G., & Woolley, J. T. (n.d.). The American Presidency Project. https://www.presidency.ucsb.edu/node/342196; Donald J. Trump, Proclamation

10123—World AIDS Day, 2020, from Peters, G., & Woolley, J. T. (n.d.). The American Presidency Project. https://www.presidency.ucsb.edu/node/347195.

27. Donald J. Trump, Campaign Press Release—Remarks for Night Four of the Republican National Convention from Peters, G., & Woolley, J. T. (n.d.).The American Presidency Project. https://www.presidency.ucsb.edu/node/345889.

28. Donald J. Trump, Executive Order 13958—Establishing the President's Advisory 1776 Commission from Peters, G., & Woolley, J. T. (n.d.).The American Presidency Project. https://www.presidency.ucsb.edu/node/346695.

29. Ronald Reagan, Radio Address to the Nation on Civil Rights from Peters, G., & Woolley, J. T. (n.d.). The American Presidency Project. https://www.presidency.ucsb.edu/node/260375.

30. Ronald Reagan, Remarks in New York City on Receiving the Charles Evans Hughes Gold Medal of the National Conference of Christians and Jews from Peters, G., & Woolley, J. T. (n.d.). The American Presidency Project. https://www.presidency.ucsb.edu/node/245920.

31. Ronald Reagan, Remarks and a Question-and-Answer Session at the "Choosing a Future" Conference in Chicago, Illinois, from Peters, G., & Woolley, J. T. (n.d.).The American Presidency Project. https://www.presidency.ucsb.edu/node/261060.

32. Ronald Reagan, Address to High School Students on Martin Luther King Jr.'s Birthday from Peters, G., & Woolley, J. T. (n.d.). The American Presidency Project https://www.presidency.ucsb.edu/node/252241.

33. Stephanopoulos, G., & Edley, C., Jr. (1995, July 19). Affirmative action review. The White House. Last accessed 5/5/2022 from https://clintonWhitehouse4.archives.gov/WH/EOP/OP/html/aa/aa-lett.html.

34. George Bush, Remarks at the National Urban League Conference from Peters, G., & Woolley, J. T. (n.d.). The American Presidency Project. https://www.presidency.ucsb.edu/node/263422.

35. Lyndon B. Johnson, Commencement Address at Howard University, "To Fulfill These rights," from Peters, G., & Woolley, J. T. (n.d.). The American Presidency Project. https://www.presidency.ucsb.edu/node/241312.

36. William J. Clinton, Remarks on Affirmative Action at the National Archives and Records Administration from Peters, G., & Woolley, J. T. (n.d.). The American Presidency Project. https://www.presidency.ucsb.edu/node/221889.

37. Rizzo, K. (1997, June 13). Lawmaker calls for apology to Blacks for slavery. AP News. https://timesmachine.nytimes.com/timesmachine/1997/06/14/644722.html?pageNumber=10.

38. Barack Obama, Interview with Ta-Nehisi Coates from Peters, G., & Woolley, J. T. (n.d.). The American Presidency Project. https://www.presidency.ucsb.edu/node/331727.

39. Barack Obama, Interview with Ta-Nehisi Coates from Peters, G., & Woolley, J. T. (n.d.). The American Presidency Project. https://www.presidency.ucsb.edu/node/331727.

40. H.R. 40—Commission to Study and Develop Reparation Proposals for African Americans Act, U.S. House of Representatives, 117th Congress.

41. Joseph R. Biden, pool reports of April 13, 2021, from Peters, G., & Woolley, J. T. (n.d.). The American Presidency Project. https://www.presidency.ucsb.edu/node/349527; Joseph R. Biden, Press Gaggle by Principal Deputy Press Secretary Karine Jean-Pierre en route Portland, Oregon, from Peters, G., & Woolley, J. T. (n.d.). The American Presidency Project. https://www.presidency.ucsb.edu/node/355513.

42. Felton, E. (2022, February 25). Supporters say they have the votes in the House to pass a reparations bill after years of lobbying. *Washington Post*.

43. Jackson Lee, S. (2020, May 22). H.R. 40 is not a symbolic act. It's a path to restorative justice. ACLU. https://www.aclu.org/news/racial-justice/h-r-40-is-not-a-symbolic-act-its-a-path-to-restorative-justice.

44. https://www.hoover.org/research/case-against-reparations-slavery.

45. https://www.hoover.org/research/case-against-reparations-slavery.

46. https://www.theatlantic.com/business/archive/2014/06/the-impossibility-of-reparations/372041/.

47. According to its website, the National Association for the Advancement of Colored People had long advocated for its removal and led a 15-year economic boycott of South Carolina.

48. *New York Times*. (2015, July 8). Excerpts from the Confederate flag debate in the South Carolina House. *New York Times* from https://www.nytimes.com/interactive/2015/07/08/us/09carolinaexcerpts.html.

49. Excerpts from the Confederate flag debate in the South Carolina House. (2015, July 8). *New York Times*. https://www.nytimes.com/interactive/2015/07/08/us/09carolinaexcerpts.html.

50. Lemon, J. (2020, July 21). Majority of Americans now support removing Confederate statues, up 16 points from 2018: Poll. *Newsweek*.

51. Treisman, R. (2021, February 23). Nearly 100 Confederate monuments removed in 2020, report says; More than 700 remain. NPR. https://www.npr.org/2021/02/23/97061048/nearly-100-confederate-monuments-removed-in-2020-report-says-more-than-700-remain.

52. Hannah-Jones, N. (2021). *A new origin story: The 1619 Project*. One World.

53. Donald J. Trump, Executive Order 13958—Establishing the President's Advisory 1776 Commission from Peters, G., & Woolley, J. T. (n.d.). The American Presidency Project. https://www.presidency.ucsb.edu/node/346695.

54. See Taylor, E., Gillborn, D., & Ladson-Billings, G. (2016). *Foundations of critical race theory in education*. Routledge; Delgado, R., & Stefancic, J. (2000). *Critical race theory: The cutting edge*. Temple University Press; Crenshaw, K., Gotanda, N., Peller, G., & Thomas, K. (1995). *Critical race theory: The key writings that formed the movement*. New Press.

55. Fiscus, R. J. (1992). *The constitutional logic of affirmative action* (ed. S. L. Wasby). Duke University Press, 38.

56. *Grutter v. Bollinger*, 539 U.S. 306, 323.

57. 2016 Democratic Party platform from Peters, G., & Woolley, J. T. (n.d.). The American Presidency Project. University of California at Santa Barbara. https://www. presidency.ucsb.edu/documents/app-categories/elections-and-transitions/party-platforms.

58. 2020 Democratic Party platform.

59. 1960 and 1960 Democratic Party platforms.

60. For insights on liberals' role in sidestepping pervasive housing segregation, see: Hannah-Jones, N. (2015, June 25). Living apart: How the government betrayed a landmark civil rights law. *ProPublica*.

61. 1980 Democratic Party platform.

62. 1980 and 1984 Democratic Party platforms.

63. 1992 and 2000 Democratic Party platforms.

64. 2008 Democratic Party platform.

65. 1940 Republican Party platform from Peters, G., & Woolley, J. T. (n.d.). The American Presidency Project. University of California at Santa Barbara. https://www. presidency.ucsb.edu/documents/app-categories/elections-and-transitions/party-platforms.

66. 1968 Republican Party platform.

67. 1980 Republican Party platform.

68. 2000 Republican Party platform.

69. 2004 Republican Party platform.

70. Equal Employment Opportunity Commission (EEOC), affirmative action appropriate under Title VI of the Civil Rights Act of 1964, as amended, 44 F.R. § 4422 (1979).

71. Barack Obama, Interview with Ta-Nehisi Coates from Peters, G., & Woolley, J. T. (n.d.). The American Presidency Project. https://www.presidency. ucsb.edu/node/331727.

72. Barack Obama, Interview with Ta-Nehisi Coates from Peters, G., & Woolley, J. T. (n.d.). The American Presidency Project. https://www.presidency. ucsb.edu/node/331713.

73. Barack Obama, Remarks During a Panel Discussion at the Catholic-Evangelical Leadership Summit on Overcoming Poverty at Georgetown University from Peters, G., & Woolley, J. T. (n.d.). The American Presidency Project. https:// www.presidency.ucsb.edu/node/311020.

74. Office of Policy Planning and Research, U.S. Department of Labor. (1965, March). *The Negro family: The case for national action*. https://www.dol.gov/general/ aboutdol/history/webid-moynihan.

75. Stephanopoulos, G., & Edley, C., Jr. (1995, July 19). Affirmative action review. The White House. Last accessed 5/5/2022 from https://clintonWhitehouse4. archives.gov/WH/EOP/OP/html/aa/aa-lett.html.

76. William J. Clinton, Remarks in a Race Initiative Outreach Meeting with Conservatives from Peters, G., & Woolley, J. T. (n.d.). The American Presidency Project. https://www.presidency.ucsb.edu/node/223535.

77. William J. Clinton, Remarks on Affirmative Action at the National Archives and Records Administration from Peters, G., & Woolley, J. T. (n.d.). The American Presidency Project. https://www.presidency.ucsb.edu/node/221889.

78. William J. Clinton, Remarks on Affirmative Action at the National Archives and Records Administration from Peters, G., & Woolley, J. T. (n.d.). The American Presidency Project. https://www.presidency.ucsb.edu/node/221889.

79. Congressional Research Service. (2022, March 9). *SBA's "8(a) Program": Overview, history, and current issues* R44844. https://sgp.fas.org/crs/misc/R44844.pdf.

80. George Bush, Remarks at the United States Military Academy Commencement Ceremony in West Point, New York, from Peters, G., & Woolley, J. T. (n.d.). The American Presidency Project. https://www.presidency.ucsb.edu/node/265610.

81. George Bush, Remarks at the National Urban League Conference from Peters, G., & Woolley, J. T. (n.d.). The American Presidency Project. https://www.presidency.ucsb.edu/node/263422.

82. Donald J. Trump, Remarks at a "Black Voices for Trump" Rally in Atlanta, Georgia, from Peters, G., & Woolley, J. T. (n.d.). The American Presidency Project. https://www.presidency.ucsb.edu/node/351207.

83. Donald J. Trump, Remarks on Infrastructure and an Exchange with Reporters in New York City from Peters, G., & Woolley, J. T. (n.d.). The American Presidency Project. https://www.presidency.ucsb.edu/node/329623.

84. Donald J. Trump, Remarks in a Town Hall Meeting with George Stephanopoulos of ABC News at the National Constitution Center in Philadelphia, Pennsylvania, from Peters, G., & Woolley, J. T. (n.d.). The American Presidency Project. https://www.presidency.ucsb.edu/node/345477.

85. Order No. 4 was issued by the Office of Federal Contract Compliance (OFCC) under the Nixon administration in 1971. The order required a written plan that established goals based on an underutilization analysis, and a timetable for reaching those goals.

86. Richard Nixon, Statement Urging Senate and House Conferees to Permit Continued Implementation of the Philadelphia Plan from Peters, G., & Woolley, J. T. (n.d.). The American Presidency Project. https://www.presidency.ucsb.edu/node/240433.

87. Richard Nixon, Special Message to the Congress Urging Expansion of the Minority Business Enterprise Program from Peters, G., & Woolley, J. T. (n.d.). The American Presidency Project https://www.presidency.ucsb.edu/node/241056; Richard Nixon, Statement About Federal Policies Relative to Equal Housing Opportunity from Peters, G., & Woolley, J. T. (n.d.). The American Presidency Project. https://www.presidency.ucsb.edu/node/240233.

88. Richard Nixon, Statement About Federal Policies Relative to Equal Housing Opportunity from Peters, G., & Woolley, J. T. (n.d.). The American Presidency Project https://www.presidency.ucsb.edu/node/240233.

89. Richard Nixon, Statement About Federal Policies Relative to Equal Housing Opportunity from Peters, G., & Woolley, J. T. (n.d.). The American Presidency Project. https://www.presidency.ucsb.edu/node/240233.

90. Richard Nixon, Statement About Federal Policies Relative to Equal Housing Opportunity from Peters, G., & Woolley, J. T. (n.d.). The American Presidency Project. https://www.presidency.ucsb.edu/node/240233.

91. Richard Nixon, Statement About Federal Policies Relative to Equal Housing Opportunity from Peters, G., & Woolley, J. T. (n.d.). The American Presidency Project. https://www.presidency.ucsb.edu/node/241065.

92. Richard Nixon, Statement About Federal Policies Relative to Equal Housing Opportunity from Peters, G., & Woolley, J. T. (n.d.). The American Presidency Project. https://www.presidency.ucsb.edu/node/239554.

93. Richard Nixon, Special Message to the Congress Urging Expansion of the Minority Business Enterprise Program from Peters, G., & Woolley, J. T. (n.d.). The American Presidency Project. https://www.presidency.ucsb.edu/node/241056.

94. Minority Business Development Agency, U.S. Department of Commerce. *The history of the MDBA*. Last accessed 5/5/2022 from https://www.mbda.gov/about/history.

95. Garrow, D. J. (1978). *Protest at Selma: Martin Luther King, Jr., and the Voting Rights Act of 1965.* Yale University Press.

96. Wilson, W. J. (2001). *The bridge over the racial divide: Rising inequality and coalition politics.* University of California Press.

97. Murray, C. (1984). *Losing ground: American social policy, 1950–1980.* Basic Books.

98. Wilson, W. J. (1978, 2012). *The declining significance of race: Blacks and changing American institutions.* University of Chicago Press.

99. Kahlenberg, R. D. (1997). *The remedy: Class, race, and affirmative action.* Basic Books.

100. For more on the intersection of race and criminal justice, see: Moore, N. (2015). *The political roots of racial tracking in American criminal justice.* Cambridge University Press.

101. U.S. House of Representatives, 117th Congress, George Floyd Justice in Policing Act of 2021 H.R.1280.

102. Sunstein, C. R. (1998). Casuistry. In R. Post & M. Rogin (Eds.), *Race and representation: Affirmative action.* Zone Books, 319.

103. Sunstein, C. R. (1998). Casuistry. In R. Post & M. Rogin (Eds.), *Race and representation: Affirmative action.* Zone Books, 319.

104. This theme is further unpacked in chapter 5.

105. 1972 Democratic Party platform from Peters, G., & Woolley, J. T. (n.d.). The American Presidency Project. University of California at Santa Barbara. https://www.presidency.ucsb.edu/documents/app-categories/elections-and-transitions/party-platforms.

106. 1976 Republican Party platform from Peters, G., & Woolley, J. T. (n.d.). The American Presidency Project. University of California at Santa Barbara. https://www.presidency.ucsb.edu/documents/app-categories/elections-and-transitions/party-platforms.

107. 1980 Republican Party platform.

108. William J. Clinton, Remarks at the Premiere of *Ragtime* from Peters, G., & Woolley, J. T. (n.d.). The American Presidency Project. https://www.presidency.ucsb.edu/node/225994.

109. Mills, D. (1992, May 13). Sister Souljah's call to arms. *Washington Post*.

110. Edsall, T. B. (1992, June 14). Clinton stuns Rainbow Coalition. *Washington Post*.

111. De Velasco, A. (2010). *Centrist rhetoric: The production of political transcendence in the Clinton presidency*. Lexington Books, 75.

112. Lyndon B. Johnson, Remarks at the Signing of the Columbus Day Proclamation from Peters, G., & Woolley, J. T. (n.d.). The American Presidency Project. https://www.presidency.ucsb.edu/node/238535.

113. Jimmy Carter, Address at the National Italian-American Bicentennial Tribute Dinner in Washington, DC, from Peters, G., & Woolley, J. T. (n.d.). The American Presidency Project. https://www.presidency.ucsb.edu/node/347544.

114. Jimmy Carter, Address at the National Italian-American Bicentennial Tribute Dinner in Washington, DC, from Peters, G., & Woolley, J. T. (n.d.). The American Presidency Project. https://www.presidency.ucsb.edu/node/347544.

115. Lyndon B. Johnson, Commencement Address at Howard University, "To Fulfill These Rights," from Peters, G., & Woolley, J. T. (n.d.). The American Presidency Project. https://www.presidency.ucsb.edu/node/241312.

116. Barack Obama, Remarks at a Naturalization Ceremony at the National Archives and Records Administration from Peters, G., & Woolley, J. T. (n.d.). The American Presidency Project. https://www.presidency.ucsb.edu/node/311427.

117. Richard Nixon, Statement about Federal Policies Relative to Equal Housing Opportunity from Peters, G., & Woolley, J. T. (n.d.). The American Presidency Project. https://www.presidency.ucsb.edu/node/240233; Richard Nixon, Statement about Desegregation of Elementary and Secondary Schools from Peters, G., & Woolley, J. T. (n.d.). The American Presidency Project. https://www.presidency.ucsb.edu/node/241065.

118. Cobb, J. (2017, March 8). Ben Carson, Donald Trump, and the misuse of American history. *New Yorker*. https://www.newyorker.com/news/daily-comment/ben-carson-donald-trump-and-the-misuse-of-american-history. See also: Burton, T. I. (2018, August 30). The insidious cultural history of Kanye West's slavery comments. *Vox*.

119. Donald J. Trump, Remarks on Infrastructure and an Exchange with Reporters in New York City from Peters, G., & Woolley, J. T. (n.d.). The American Presidency Project. https://www.presidency.ucsb.edu/node/329623.

120. See: Knobel, D. T. (1986). *Paddy and the republic*. Wesleyan University Press; Curtis, L. P., Jr. (1971). *Apes and angels: The Irish in Victorian caricature*. Smithsonian Institution Press; Wittke, C. (1956). *The Irish in America*. Louisiana State University Press; Ford, H. J. (1915). *The Scotch-Irish in America*. Princeton University Press.

121. Handlin, O. (1991). *Boston's immigrants, 1780–1880: A study in acculturation*. 50th anniversary edition. Harvard University Press.

122. See for example: Waters, M. C. (1990). *Ethnic options: Choosing identities in America*. University of California Press; and Alba, R., & Abdel-Hady, D. (2005). Galileo's children: Italian Americans' difficult entry into the intellectual elite. *Sociological Quarterly, 46*(1): 3–18.

123. Simon, R. J., & Alexander, S. H. (1993). *The ambivalent welcome: Print media, public opinion, and immigration*. Praeger; Lord, E., Trenor, J. J. D., & Barrows, S. J. (1970). *The Italian in America*. Reprinted edition. R & E Associates; and Brigham, C. C. (1923). *A study of American intelligence*. Princeton University Press.

124. Higham, J. (1975). *Strangers in the land: Patterns of American nativism, 1860–1925*. Revised edition. Atheneum, 48.

125. Chow, K. (2017, April 19). "Model Minority" myth again used as a racial wedge between Asians and Blacks. NPR. https://www.npr.org/sections/codeswitch/2017/04/19/524571669/model-minority-myth-again-used-as-a-racial-wedge-between-asians-and-blacks.

126. https://www.migrationpolicy.org/article/what-immigrants-say-about-life-united-states.

127. https://www.migrationpolicy.org/article/what-immigrants-say-about-life-united-states.

3. The Reconstruction of Race and Racism

1. López, I. H. (2006). *White by law: The legal construction of race*. New York University Press.

2. Quoting *Grutter v. Bollinger*, 539 U.S. 306, 342 (2003).

3. Quoting *Edmonson v. Leesville Concrete Co.*, 500 U.S. 614, 619 (1991).

4. See *Parents Involved in Community Schools v. Seattle School District* (551 U.S. 701, 2007). Reflecting on *Swann v. Charlotte-Mecklenburg Board of Education* (402 U.S. 1, 1971), Chief Justice Roberts wrote, "When *Swann* was decided, this Court had not yet confirmed that strict scrutiny applies to racial classifications like those before us."

5. *Regents of the University of California v. Bakke*, 274.

6. *Bakke*, 274.

7. *Bakke*, 279.

8. Opinion of Justice O'Connor in *Richmond v. Croson* (488 U.S. 469, 496).

9. Rather, "any person, of whatever race, has the right to demand that any governmental actor subject to the Constitution justify any racial classification subjecting that person to unequal treatment under the strictest of judicial scrutiny."

10. O'Connor's third point received more treatment as it pertained to the larger question of whether Congress was subject to the same level of scrutiny as state and local governments and agencies. More is said about this in a moment and also in chapter 4.

11. In the end, *Adarand I* remanded the case back to the Tenth Circuit Court of Appeals. Six years later the Supreme Court was likely poised to ensure enforcement of the *Adarand I* strict scrutiny requirement when it again granted certiorari to the same petitioner, Adarand Constructors, Inc. It did so after an intervening ruling in *Adarand Constructors v. Slater* (2000), in which a per curiam opinion held that the Tenth Circuit had improperly dismissed Adarand's claim on grounds of mootness. However, because the petitioner had essentially changed the focus of its court appeal in *Adarand Constructors, Inc. v. Mineta* (2001) the writ was dismissed as improvidently granted.

12. *Fisher v. University of Texas*, 7.

13. *Parents*, 730.

14. The seven-person majority included: Justices Kennedy, Scalia, Thomas, Breyer, Alito, Sotomayor, and Chief Justice Roberts.

15. *Grutter v. Bollinger*, 539 U.S. 982, 270.

16. Vu Tran, H. (2020). *Race, law, and higher education in the colorblind era: Critical investigations into race-related Supreme Court disputes.* Routledge, 4–5.

17. Crosby, F. J. (2004). *Affirmative action is dead; Long live affirmative action.* Yale University Press, 233.

18. Duster, T. (1998). Individual fairness, group preferences, and the California strategy. In R. Post & M. Rogin (Eds.), *Race and representation: Affirmative action.* Zone Books, 133 n38.

19. Piven, F. F. (1998). Affirmative action. In R. Post & M. Rogin (Eds.), *Race and representation: Affirmative action.* Zone Books, 378.

20. National Advisory Commission on Civil Disorders. (1967). *Report on the causes, events, and aftermaths of the civil disorders of 1967.* United States, Kerner Commission: U.S. G.P.O.

21. 1968 Democratic Party platform from Peters, G., & Woolley, J. T. (n.d.). The American Presidency Project. University of California at Santa Barbara. https://www.presidency.ucsb.edu/documents/app-categories/elections-and-transitions/party-platforms.

22. 1968 Republican Party platform from Peters, G., & Woolley, J. T. (n.d.). The American Presidency Project. University of California at Santa Barbara. https://www.presidency.ucsb.edu/documents/app-categories/elections-and-transitions/party-platforms.

23. 2020 Democratic Party platform.

24. 1992 Republican Party platform.

25. 2008 Republican Party platform.

26. 2012 and 2016 Republican Party platforms.

27. Congressional Research Service. (2022, March 9). *SBA's "8(a) Program":
Overview, history, and current issues.* https://sgp.fas.org/crs/misc/R44844.pdf.

28. See, for instance, William J. Clinton, Remarks and a Question-and-Answer
Session with the College Press Forum from Peters, G., & Woolley, J. T. (n.d.). The
American Presidency Project. https://www.presidency.ucsb.edu/node/221510; and
William J. Clinton, Presidential Debate in San Diego from Peters, G., & Woolley,
J. T. (n.d.). The American Presidency Project. https://www.presidency.ucsb.edu/
node/217289.

29. William J. Clinton, Remarks on the 40th Anniversary of the Desegregation of Central High School in Little Rock, Arkansas, from Peters, G., & Woolley,
J. T. (n.d.). The American Presidency Project. https://www.presidency.ucsb.edu/
node/224968.

30. Donald J. Trump, Proclamation 9642—National Historically Black
Colleges and Universities Week, 2017, from Peters, G., & Woolley, J. T. (n.d.).
The American Presidency Project. https://www.presidency.ucsb.edu/node/330954.

31. Cillizza, C. (2015, August 17). Donald Trump on "Meet the Press,"
annotated. *Washington Post.*

32. Ronald Reagan, Radio Address to the Nation on Martin Luther King,
Jr., and Black Americans from Peters, G., & Woolley, J. T. (n.d.). The American
Presidency Project. https://www.presidency.ucsb.edu/node/259262.

33. Stephanie J. Monroe, Assistant Secretary for Civil Rights, U.S. Department
of Education. (2008, August 28). *Dear Colleague.* https://www2.ed.gov/about/offices/
list/ocr/letters/raceassignmentese.html.

34. George W. Bush, Remarks to the UNITY: Journalists of Color Convention and a Question-and-Answer Session from Peters, G., & Woolley, J. T. (n.d.).
The American Presidency Project. https://www.presidency.ucsb.edu/node/212523.

35. George W. Bush, Remarks to the UNITY: Journalists of Color Convention and a Question-and-Answer Session from Peters, G., & Woolley, J. T. (n.d.).
The American Presidency Project. https://www.presidency.ucsb.edu/node/212523.

36. Donald J. Trump, Executive Order 13950—Combating Race and Sex
Stereotyping from Peters, G., & Woolley, J. T. (n.d.). The American Presidency
Project. https://www.presidency.ucsb.edu/node/343883.

37. Joseph R. Biden, Executive Order 13985—Advancing Racial Equity and
Support for Underserved Communities Through the Federal Government from
Peters, G., & Woolley, J. T. (n.d.)., The American Presidency Project https://www.
presidency.ucsb.edu/node/347813.

38. U.S. Department of Justice. (n.d.). *The compelling interest to remedy the
effects of discrimination in federal contracting: A survey of recent evidence.* https://www.
justice.gov/crt/page/file/1463921/download, 3–4.

39. Barack Obama, Interview with Ta-Nehisi Coates from Peters, G., & Woolley, J. T. (n.d.). The American Presidency Project. https://www.presidency.ucsb.edu/node/331713.

40. U.S. Department of Justice, U.S. Department of Education. (2011, December 2). *Guidance on the voluntary use of race to achieve diversity and avoid racial isolation in elementary and secondary schools.* Last accessed 5/05/2022 from https://www2.ed.gov/about/offices/list/ocr/docs/guidance-ese-201111.pdf.

41. U.S. Department of Justice, U.S. Department of Education. (2011, December 2). *Guidance on the voluntary use of race to achieve diversity and avoid racial isolation in elementary and secondary schools.* Last accessed 5/05/2022 from, https://www2.ed.gov/about/offices/list/ocr/docs/guidance-ese-201111.pdf.

42. Knopp, C. (2005, December 14). Morgan Freeman defies labels. *60 Minutes.* Retrieved on 2/23/2024 from https://www.cbsnews.com/news/morgan-freeman-defies-labels-14-12-2005/. See also: Crugnale, J. (2014, June 5). Morgan Freeman says not to make race a "bigger issue than it needs to be." *The Wrap.* https://www.thewrap.com/morgan-freeman-disputes-race-plays-factor-in-income-inequality-video/.

43. CNN. (2023, May 17). 'Star Trek's' Zoe Saldana on racism: 'I'm not going to talk about it.' https://www.cnn.com/2013/05/17/us/star-treks-zoe-saldana-on-racism-im-not-going-to-talk-about-it.

44. Kennedy, R. (2013). *For discrimination: Race, affirmative action, and the law.* Vintage Books, 34–35.

45. Vu Tran, H. (2020). *Race, law, and higher education in the colorblind era: Critical investigations into race-related Supreme Court disputes.* Routledge, 118.

46. Pollock, E. E. (2012). *Race and the Supreme Court: Defining equality.* Peppertree Press, 2–4.

47. A principal holding in *Croson* was that "where special qualifications are necessary, the relevant statistical pool for purposes of demonstrating discriminatory exclusion must be the number of minorities qualified to undertake the particular task."

48. 426 U.S. 229, 1976.

49. 429 U.S. 252, 1977.

50. Sheeran, T. J. (1976). Title VII and layoffs under the "Last Hired, First Fired" seniority rule: The preservation of equal employment. *Case Western Reserve Law Review, 26*: 409–482.

51. Fiscus, R. J. (1992). *The constitutional logic of affirmative action* (ed. S. L. Wasby). Duke University Press, 107.

52. 1984 Republican Party platform from Peters, G., & Woolley, J. T. (n.d.). The American Presidency Project. University of California at Santa Barbara. https://www.presidency.ucsb.edu/documents/app-categories/elections-and-transitions/party-platforms.

53. 1988 Republican Party platform.

54. 1980 Democratic Party platform.

55. 2000 Democratic Party platform.

56. William J. Clinton, Executive Order 13050—President's Advisory Board on Race from Peters, G., & Woolley, J. T. (n.d.). The American Presidency Project. https://www.presidency.ucsb.edu/node/223913.

57. Fletcher, M. A. (1998, September 19). President accepts report on race. *Washington Post*.

58. Donald J. Trump, Presidential Debate at Belmont University in Nashville, Tennessee, from Peters, G., & Woolley, J. T. (n.d.). The American Presidency Project. https://www.presidency.ucsb.edu/node/345898.

59. Treisman, R. (2021, February 23). Nearly 100 Confederate monuments removed in 2020, report says; More than 700 remain.

60. McAdam, D. (1999). *Political process and the development of Black insurgency, 1930–1970*. University of Chicago Press.

61. Luskin, R. C., McIver, J. P., & Carmines, E. G. (1989). Issues and the transmission of partisanship. *American Journal of Political Science, 33*: 440–458. https://doi.org/10.2307/2111155.

62. Barack Obama, Interview with Ta-Nehisi Coates from Peters, G., & Woolley, J. T. (n.d.). The American Presidency Project. https://www.presidency.ucsb.edu/node/331727.

63. Quoting *Miller v. Johnson*, 515 U.S. 900 (1995), 911.

64. Justices Sonya Sotomayor and Ruth Bader Ginsberg dissented and Justice Elena Kagan abstained.

65. 379 U.S. 184

66. 388 U.S. 1

67. Quoting *Adarand Constructors, Inc. v. Pena*, 515 U.S. 200, 236 (1995).

68. Samson, F. L. (2013). Altering public university admission standards to preserve White group position in the United States: Results from a laboratory experiment. *Comparative Education Review, 57*: 369–396. https://doi.org/10.1086/670664; Norton, M. I., & Sommers, S. R. (2011). Whites see racism as a zero-sum game that they are now losing. *Perspectives on Psychological Science, 6*: 215–218.

69. 1992 Republican Party platform.

70. 1996 Republican Party platform.

71. 1984 Republican Party platform.

72. 1984 Democratic Party platform from Peters, G., & Woolley, J. T. (n.d.). The American Presidency Project. University of California at Santa Barbara. https://www.presidency.ucsb.edu/documents/app-categories/elections-and-transitions/party-platforms.

73. 2008 Democratic Party platform.

74. 2008 Democratic Party platform.

75. Equal Employment Opportunity Commission (EEOC). (1979). Affirmative action appropriate under Title VI of the Civil Rights Act of 1964, as amended, 44 F.R. § 4422.

284 | Notes to Chapter 3

76. Ronald Reagan, Radio Address to the Nation on Martin Luther King, Jr., and Black Americans from Peters, G., & Woolley, J. T. (n.d.). The American Presidency Project. https://www.presidency.ucsb.edu/node/259262.

77. Ronald Reagan, Radio Address to the Nation on Civil Rights from Peters, G., & Woolley, J. T. (n.d.). The American Presidency Project. https://www.presidency.ucsb.edu/node/260375.

78. Donald J. Trump, Executive Order 13950—Combating Race and Sex Stereotyping from Peters, G., & Woolley, J. T. (n.d.). The American Presidency Project. https://www.presidency.ucsb.edu/node/343883.

79. George Bush, Remarks at the United States Military Academy Commencement Ceremony in West Point, New York, from Peters, G., & Woolley, J. T. (n.d.). The American Presidency Project, https://www.presidency.ucsb.edu/node/265610.

80. George Bush, Remarks at the United States Military Academy Commencement Ceremony in West Point, New York, from Peters, G., & Woolley, J. T. (n.d.). The American Presidency Project. https://www.presidency.ucsb.edu/node/265610.

81. George Bush, Remarks at the United States Military Academy Commencement Ceremony in West Point, New York, from Peters, G., & Woolley, J. T. (n.d.). The American Presidency Project. https://www.presidency.ucsb.edu/node/265610.

82. Butcher, J., & Gonzalea, M. (2020, December 7). *Critical race theory, the new intolerance and its grip on America.* The Heritage Foundation. https://www.heritage.org/civil-rights/report/critical-race-theory-the-new-intolerance-and-its-grip-america.

83. *Students for Fair Admissions*, 20, slip opinion.

84. Quoting *Miller v. Johnson*, 515 U.S. 900 (1995), 911–912.

85. Also significant to this analysis is that the six-person majority in *Firefighters v. Cleveland* that affirmed the lower court decision also acknowledged in footnote 11 that Title VII provides protections for nonminorities with respect to private affirmative action plans. Nonetheless, here, the past exclusion of Blacks trumped the exclusionary effect of the consent decree on Whites.

86. *Texas v. Lesage* (1999) later added that if the government can demonstrate that a White graduate student admissions application would have been rejected, even in the absence of race consciousness, then it can defeat liability.

87. *Hunt v. Washington State Apple Advertising Comm'n*, 432 U.S. 333 (1977).

88. Schmidt, P. (2007). *Color and money: How rich White kids are winning the war over college affirmative action.* Palgrave Macmillan, 8–9.

89. Gray, W. R. (2001). *The four faces of affirmative action: Fundamental answers and actions.* Greenwood Press, 30.

90. Butler, J. (1998). An affirmative view. In R. Post & M. Rogin (Eds.), *Race and representation: Affirmative action.* Zone Books, 158.

91. 1996 Republican Party platform from Peters, G., & Woolley, J. T. (n.d.). The American Presidency Project. University of California at Santa Barbara. https://www.presidency.ucsb.edu/documents/app-categories/elections-and-transitions/party-platforms.

92. 2004 Republican Party platform.

93. 2008 Republican Party platform.

94. 2016 Republican Party platform.

95. 2004 Republican Party platform.

96. 1984 Republican Party platform.

97. Donald J. Trump, Executive Order 13950—Combating Race and Sex Stereotyping from Peters, G., & Woolley, J. T. (n.d.). The American Presidency Project. https://www.presidency.ucsb.edu/node/343883.

98. Ronald Reagan, Radio Address to the Nation on Civil Rights from Peters, G., & Woolley, J. T. (n.d.). The American Presidency Project. https://www.presidency.ucsb.edu/node/260375.

99. Congressional Research Service. (2022, March 9). *SBA's "8(a) Program": Overview, history, and current issues.* https://sgp.fas.org/crs/misc/R44844.pdf, 12.

100. Richard Nixon, Statement About Federal Policies Relative to Equal Housing Opportunity from Peters, G., & Woolley, J. T. (n.d.). The American Presidency Project. https://www.presidency.ucsb.edu/node/240233.

101. Richard Nixon, Statement About Federal Policies Relative to Equal Housing Opportunity from Peters, G., & Woolley, J. T. (n.d.). The American Presidency Project. https://www.presidency.ucsb.edu/node/240233.

102. Donald J. Trump, Presidential Debate at Case Western Reserve University in Cleveland, Ohio, from Peters, G., & Woolley, J. T. (n.d.). The American Presidency Project https://www.presidency.ucsb.edu/node/343824.

103. U.S. Department of Justice, U.S. Department of Education. (2011, December 2). *Guidance on the voluntary use of race to achieve diversity and avoid racial isolation in elementary and secondary schools.* Last accessed 5/05/2022 from https://www2.ed.gov/about/offices/list/ocr/docs/guidance-ese-201111.pdf.

104. Ronald Reagan, Radio Address to the Nation on Civil Rights from Peters, G., & Woolley, J. T. (n.d.). The American Presidency Project. https://www.presidency.ucsb.edu/node/260375.

105. George Bush, Statement of Administration Policy: H.R. 4000—Civil Rights Act of 1990 from Peters, G., & Woolley, J. T. (n.d.). The American Presidency Project. https://www.presidency.ucsb.edu/node/328921.

106. William J. Clinton, Remarks to the California Democratic Party in Sacramento from Peters, G., & Woolley, J. T. (n.d.). The American Presidency Project. https://www.presidency.ucsb.edu/node/220671.

107. William J. Clinton, The President's News Conference from Peters, G., & Woolley, J. T. (n.d.). The American Presidency Project. https://www.presidency.ucsb.edu/node/220794.

108. Stephanopoulos, G., & Edley, C., Jr. (1995, July 19). Affirmative action review. The White House. Last accessed 5/05/2022 from https://clintonWhitehouse4.archives.gov/WH/EOP/OP/html/aa/aa-lett.html.

109. Stephanopoulos, G., & Edley, C., Jr. (1995, July 19). Affirmative action review. The White House. Last accessed 5/05/2022 from https://clintonWhitehouse4.archives.gov/WH/EOP/OP/html/aa/aa-lett.html.

110. William J. Clinton, Remarks on Affirmative Action at the National Archives and Records Administration from Peters, G., & Woolley, J. T. (n.d.). The American Presidency Project. https://www.presidency.ucsb.edu/node/221889; William J. Clinton, Remarks at a Clinton/Gore '96 Dinner in Los Angeles, California, from Peters, G., & Woolley, J. T. (n.d.). The American Presidency Project. https://www.presidency.ucsb.edu/node/222006.

111. Bearak, B. (1997, July 27). Questions of race run deep for foe of preferences. *New York Times*.

112. Associated Press. (2016, August 19). "What do you have to lose?" Donald Trump appeals for Black vote. *Guardian*. https:apnews.com/united-states-presidential-election-events-341b104bc5484fad85ca340d537810af

113. Vance, J. D. (2016). *Hillbilly elegy: A memoir of a family and culture in crisis*. Harper.

114. Peters, J. W., & Chira, S. (2018, September 29). Kavanaugh borrows from Trump's playbook on White male anger. *New York Times*.

4. Judicial Policy Restraints on Racial Reform: What Can and Cannot Be Done

1. *SFFA* (2023), 39 (slip opinion).

2. Surprisingly little was said in *SFFA* about civil rights laws and colorblindness, even though the litigant briefs dwelt at length on whether Harvard and the University of North Carolina's race-aware admissions policies violated civil rights statutes.

3. Perry, B. (2007). *The Michigan affirmative action cases*. University Press of Kansas, 44.

4. Pollock, E. E. (2012). *Race and the Supreme Court: Defining equality*. Peppertree Press, 237.

5. Under the Top Ten Percent Plan, every high school student in the top 10 percent of their class is guaranteed admission to a public university.

6. *Plessy v. Ferguson*, 163 U.S. 537, 559 (1896).

7. Kennedy, R. (2013). *For discrimination: Race, affirmative action, and the law*. Vintage Books, 150 et sequi.

8. Kennedy, R. (2013). *For discrimination: Race, affirmative action, and the law*. Vintage Books, 27.

9. Writing for the majority in *Adarand I* (1995), Justice O'Connor stated, "To the extent (if any) that *Fullilove* held federal racial classifications to be subject to a less rigorous standard, it is no longer controlling," 235.

10. Staff, Memorandum on "Lifting voices: Legislation to promote media marketplace diversity." January 9, 2020. Committee on Energy & Commerce, US House of Representatives.

11. It is difficult to classify the cases wholly in one camp or another, as the opinions and the votes are usually much more complicated. Bakke is a prime example of this, where the Court held that racial considerations are permissible under certain circumstances, but it invalidated the special admissions program in that case.

12. Had Kagan participated and voted in favor of the plan, that would still mean only five favorable votes.

13. Golub, M. (2018). *Is racial equality unconstitutional?* Oxford University Press, 133.

14. Crosby, F. J. (2004). *Affirmative action is dead; Long live affirmative action.* Yale University Press, 232.

15. Anderson, T. H. (2004). *The pursuit of fairness: A history of affirmative action.* Oxford University Press, 118.

16. 1984 Republican Party platform.

17. 1972 Republican Party platform from Peters, G., & Woolley, J. T. (n.d.). The American Presidency Project. University of California at Santa Barbara. https://www.presidency.ucsb.edu/documents/app-categories/elections-and-transitions/party-platforms.

18. 2004 Republican Party platform.

19. 1972 Republican Party platform.

20. 1980 Democratic Party platform from Peters, G., & Woolley, J. T. (n.d.). The American Presidency Project. University of California at Santa Barbara. https://www.presidency.ucsb.edu/documents/app-categories/elections-and-transitions/party-platforms.

21. 2016 Democratic Party platform.

22. 1980 Democratic Party platform.

23. 1972 Republican Party platform.

24. 1972, 1980, and 2004 Republican Party platforms.

25. 1980 Democratic Party platform.

26. 2012 Democratic Party platform.

27. 2020 Democratic Party platform.

28. 1972 Democratic Party platform.

29. Donald J. Trump, Executive Order 13779—White House Initiative to Promote Excellence and Innovation at Historically Black Colleges and Universities from Peters, G., & Woolley, J. T. (n.d.). The American Presidency Project. https://www.presidency.ucsb.edu/node/323731; Donald J. Trump, Proclamation 9786—National Historically Black Colleges and Universities Week, 2018, from Peters, G., & Woolley, J. T. (n.d.). The American Presidency Project. https://www.presidency.ucsb.edu/node/333167.

30. Donald J. Trump, Executive Order 13950—Combating Race and Sex Stereotyping from Peters, G., & Woolley, J. T. (n.d.). The American Presidency Project. https://www.presidency.ucsb.edu/node/343883.

31. Green, E. L., Apuzzo, M., & Benner, K. (2018, July 3). Trump officials reverse Obama's policy on affirmative action in schools. *New York Times*.

32. For more on this and its restoration, see Office of Fair Housing and Equal Opportunity, Housing and Urban Development. (2021, June 10). Restoring affirmatively furthering fair housing definitions and certifications. Last accessed 5/5/2022 from https://www.federalregister.gov/documents/2021/06/10/2021-12114/restoring-affirmatively-furthering-fair-housing-definitions-and-certifications.

33. Savage, C. (2017, August 1). Justice Dept. to take on affirmative action in college admissions. *New York Times*.

34. U.S. Department of Justice, U.S. Department of Education. (2013, September 27). *Joint "Dear Colleague" Letter*. Last accessed 5/7/2022 from https://www2.ed.gov/about/offices/list/ocr/letters/colleague-201309.html.

35. U.S. Department of Justice, U.S. Department of Education. (2013, September 27). *Joint "Dear Colleague" Letter*. Last accessed 5/7/2022 from https://www2.ed.gov/about/offices/list/ocr/letters/colleague-201309.html.

36. Office of Fair Housing and Equal Opportunity, Housing and Urban Development. (2021, June 10). Restoring Affirmatively Furthering Fair Housing definitions and certifications. Last accessed 5/5/2022 from https://www.federal-register.gov/documents/2021/06/10/2021-12114/restoring-affirmatively-furthering-fair-housing-definitions-and-certifications.

37. Randall Kennedy reports on a 1945 New York law that first required that employers "take affirmative action." Kennedy, R. (2013). *For discrimination: Race, affirmative action, and the law*. Vintage Books, 17.

38. John F. Kennedy, Executive Order 10925—Establishing the President's Committee on Equal Employment Opportunity from Peters, G., & Woolley, J. T. (n.d.). The American Presidency Project. https://www.presidency.ucsb.edu/node/237176.

39. To date, EO 11246 remains the governing document for federal agencies and federal contractors, which together employ roughly one-fifth of the US labor force. Office of Federal Contract Compliance Programs, U.S. Department of Labor. *History of Executive Order 11246*. Last accessed 5/7/2022 from https://www.dol.gov/agencies/ofccp/about/executive-order-11246-history.

40. Congressional Research Service. (2022, March 9). *SBA's "8(a) Program": Overview, history, and current issues*. https://sgp.fas.org/crs/misc/R44844.pdf.

41. Kennedy, R. (2013). *For discrimination: Race, affirmative action, and the law*. Vintage Books, 47.

42. Urofsky, M. I. (2020). *The affirmative action puzzle: A living history from Reconstruction to today*. Pantheon Books, 82.

43. Anderson, T. H. (2004). *The pursuit of fairness: A history of affirmative action*. Oxford University Press, 118–119.

44. Richard Nixon, Executive Order 11478—Equal Employment Opportunity in the Federal Government from Peters, G., & Woolley, J. T. (n.d.). The American Presidency Project. https://www.presidency.ucsb.edu/node/256661.

45. Congressional Research Service. (2022, March 9). *SBA's "8(a) Program": Overview, history, and current issues*. https://sgp.fas.org/crs/misc/R44844.pdf; Hood, J. L. (1993). The Nixon administration and the revised Philadelphia Plan for Affirmative Action: A study in expanding presidential power and divided government. *Presidential Studies Quarterly, 23*: 145–167.

46. Richard Nixon, Statement Urging Senate and House Conferees to Permit Continued Implementation of the Philadelphia Plan from Peters, G., & Woolley, J. T. (n.d.). The American Presidency Project. https://www.presidency.ucsb.edu/node/240433; "'Philadelphia Plan.'" In *CQ Almanac 1969*, 25th ed., 417–418. Congressional Quarterly, 1970. http://library.cqpress.com/cqalmanac/cqal69-1248312.

47. Schuwerk, R. P. (1972). The Philadelphia Plan: A study in the dynamics of executive power. *University of Chicago Law Review*, 39: 723–760. https://doi.org/10.2307/1599050. Schuwerk reports that the text of the original plan is contained in CCH Employment Practices Guide ¶1708 (1972) and ¶1710 (1972).

48. "'Philadelphia Plan.'" In *CQ Almanac 1969*, 25th ed., 417–418. *Congressional Quarterly*, 1970. http://library.cqpress.com/cqalmanac/cqal69-1248312.

49. Stephanopoulos, G., & Edley, C., Jr. (1995, July 19). Affirmative action review. The White House. Last accessed 5/5/2022 from https://clintonWhitehouse4.archives.gov/WH/EOP/OP/html/aa/aa-lett.html.

50. Stephanopoulos, G., & Edley, C., Jr. (1995, July 19). Affirmative action review. The White House. Last accessed 5/5/2022 from https://clintonWhitehouse4.archives.gov/WH/EOP/OP/html/aa/aa-lett.html.

51. The current Small Business Administration (SBA) was officially created in 1953, when Congress transferred the Small Defense Plants Administration subcontracting authorities, among others, to it. The Small Business Act of 1958 made SBA a permanent agency and folded its subcontracting authority into Section 8(a) of the act. Statutory authority for the SBA's 8(a) Program for minority-owned businesses was granted in 1978 when Congress amended the Small Business Act so that, under the 1978 amendments, the SBA can only subcontract under Section 8(a) to businesses that are "at least 51% owned by one or more socially and economically disadvantaged individuals and whose management and daily operations are controlled by such individual(s)." The 1978 amendments established a basic definition of "socially disadvantaged individuals," which included those who have been "subjected to racial or ethnic prejudice or cultural bias because of their identity as a member of a group without regard to their individual qualities." They also included congressional findings that "Black Americans, Hispanic Americans, Native

Americans, and other minorities" are socially disadvantaged. For more background, see: Congressional Research Service. (2022, March 9). *SBA's "8(a) Program": Overview, history, and current issues.* https://sgp.fas.org/crs/misc/R44844.pdf.

52. Congressional Research Service. (2022, March 9). *SBA's "8(a) Program": Overview, history, and current issues.* https://sgp.fas.org/crs/misc/R44844.pdf.

53. Richard Nixon, Executive Order 11518—Providing for the Increased Representation of the Interests of Small Business Concerns Before Departments and Agencies of the United States Government from Peters, G., & Woolley, J. T. (n.d.). The American Presidency Project. https://www.presidency.ucsb.edu/node/256671.

54. Richard Nixon, Special Message to the Congress Urging Expansion of the Minority Business Enterprise Program from Peters, G., & Woolley, J. T. (n.d.). The American Presidency Project. https://www.presidency.ucsb.edu/node/241056.

55. Specifically, there was a three-fold increase in grants to and purchases from MBEs by federal agencies from 1969 to 1971 and an increase in Nixon's budget for the MBE office from $3.6 million in FY 1972 to $100 million for FY 1973.

56. Richard Nixon, Special Message to the Congress Urging Expansion of the Minority Business Enterprise Program from Peters, G., & Woolley, J. T. (n.d.). The American Presidency Project. https://www.presidency.ucsb.edu/node/241056.

57. Richard Nixon, Executive Order 11625—Prescribing Additional Arrangements for Developing and Coordinating a National Program for Minority Business from Peters, G., & Woolley, J. T. (n.d.). The American Presidency Project. https://www.presidency.ucsb.edu/node/256700.

58. George Bush, The President's News Conference from Peters, G., & Woolley, J. T. (n.d.). The American Presidency Project. https://www.presidency.ucsb.edu/node/247566.

59. George Bush, The President's News Conference from Peters, G., & Woolley, J. T. (n.d.). The American Presidency Project. https://www.presidency.ucsb.edu/node/247566.

60. George W. Bush, Remarks to the UNITY: Journalists of Color Convention and a Question-and-Answer Session from Peters, G., & Woolley, J. T. (n.d.). The American Presidency Project. https://www.presidency.ucsb.edu/node/212523.

61. George W. Bush, Remarks to the UNITY: Journalists of Color Convention and a Question-and-Answer Session from Peters, G., & Woolley, J. T. (n.d.). The American Presidency Project. https://www.presidency.ucsb.edu/node/212523.

62. George W. Bush, Remarks to the UNITY: Journalists of Color Convention and a Question-and-Answer Session from Peters, G., & Woolley, J. T. (n.d.). The American Presidency Project. https://www.presidency.ucsb.edu/node/212523.

63. Ronald Reagan, Remarks in an Interview with Independent Radio Network Correspondents on Domestic and Foreign Policy Issues from Peters, G., & Woolley, J. T. (n.d.). The American Presidency Project https://www.presidency.ucsb.edu/node/244880.

64. Ronald Reagan, The President's News Conference from Peters, G., & Woolley, J. T. (n.d.). The American Presidency Project. https://www.presidency.

ucsb.edu/node/246569; Ronald Reagan, The President's News Conference from Peters, G., & Woolley, J. T. (n.d.). The American Presidency Project. https://www.presidency.ucsb.edu/node/257723.

65. Ronald Reagan, The President's News Conference from Peters, G., & Woolley, J. T. (n.d.). The American Presidency Project. https://www.presidency.ucsb.edu/node/246569.

66. *Boston Firefighters Union Local 718 v. Boston Chapter*, 463 U.S. 1226 (1983). The Supreme Court declined to hear the case.

67. Ronald Reagan, Remarks in an Interview with Independent Radio Network Correspondents on Domestic and Foreign Policy Issues from Peters, G., & Woolley, J. T. (n.d.). The American Presidency Project. https://www.presidency.ucsb.edu/node/244880.

68. Ronald Reagan, The President's News Conference from Peters, G., & Woolley, J. T. (n.d.). The American Presidency Project. https://www.presidency.ucsb.edu/node/246290.

69. Kennedy, R. (2013). *For discrimination: Race, affirmative action, and the law*. Vintage Books, 67.

70. Ronald Reagan, Remarks in an Interview with Independent Radio Network Correspondents on Domestic and Foreign Policy Issues from Peters, G., & Woolley, J. T. (n.d.). The American Presidency Project. https://www.presidency.ucsb.edu/node/244880.

71. Ronald Reagan, Remarks at a White House Ceremony Marking the Observance of Minority Enterprise Development Week from Peters, G., & Woolley, J. T. (n.d.). The American Presidency Project. https://www.presidency.ucsb.edu/node/261409.

72. Ronald Reagan, Remarks at a White House Ceremony Marking the Observance of Minority Enterprise Development Week from Peters, G., & Woolley, J. T. (n.d.). The American Presidency Project. https://www.presidency.ucsb.edu/node/261409.

73. Anderson, T. H. (2004). *The pursuit of fairness: A history of affirmative action*. Oxford University Press, 187; also Shull's work suggests that, on balance and in terms of statistical measures, the Reagan record on civil rights is best understood as strong in some respects (e.g., civil rights investigations) and weak in others (e.g., reduced funding for EEOC and the civil rights division of the Justice Department). See Shull, S. A. (1989). *The president and civil rights policy: Leadership and change*. Greenwood Press.

74. See Spann, G. A. (1993). *Race against the Court: The Supreme Court and minorities in contemporary America*. New York University Press.

75. The restrictions imposed by the Court logically follow from what we learned in chapter 2, namely that the Court deemed it "speculative" and "unprecedented" to assume that racial disparities are the making of systemic racism.

76. Vu Tran, H. (2020). *Race, law, and higher education in the colorblind era: Critical Investigations into race-related Supreme Court disputes*. Routledge, 85.

77. *Sheet Metal Workers v. EEOC* (1986), 440.

78. *Sheet Metal Workers v. EEOC* (1986), footnote 1.

79. 431 U.S. 324.

80. *Shurberg Broadcasting v. Federal Communications Commission, Appellee, Astroline Communications Co., Intervenor*, 876 F.2d 902 (D.C. Cir. 1989).

81. *Adarand* (1995) later overturned *Metro* largely because of its more relaxed standard of review of congressional policies.

82. James Duderstadt was president of the university when Gratz's application was denied and the president at the time that Hamacher's application was rejected was Lee Bollinger.

83. Chapter 5 delves more deeply into the Supreme Court's positioning around diversity, equity, and inclusion (DEI).

84. Fiscus, R. J. (1992). *The constitutional logic of affirmative action* (ed. S. L. Wasby). Duke University Press, x and 83.

85. See chapter 3 of Leiter, W. M., & Leiter, S. (2010, 2nd ed.). *Affirmative action in antidiscrimination law and policy*. State University of New York Press.

86. Quinnipiac University Poll. (2009, June 3). *U.S. voters disagree 3–1 with Sotomayor on key case, Quinnipiac University National Poll finds; most say abolish affirmative action*. https://poll.qu.edu/Poll-Release-Legacy?releaseid=1307.

87. Quinnipiac University Poll. (2009, June 3). *U.S. voters disagree 3–1 with Sotomayor on key case, Quinnipiac University National Poll finds; most say abolish affirmative action*. https://poll.qu.edu/Poll-Release-Legacy?releaseid=1307.

88. 1952 Republican Party platform.

89. 1960 Republican Party platform.

90. 1980 Republican Party platform.

91. 1980 Republican Party platform.

92. 1984 Republican Party platform.

93. 2004 Republican Party platform.

94. 2004 Republican Party platform.

95. 1952 and 1968 Democratic Party platforms.

96. 1964 Democratic Party platform.

97. 1972 and 1980 Democratic Party platforms.

98. 2020 Democratic Party platform from Peters, G., & Woolley, J. T. (n.d.). The American Presidency Project. University of California at Santa Barbara. https://www.presidency.ucsb.edu/documents/app-categories/elections-and-transitions/party-platforms.

99. 2016 Democratic Party platform.

100. 1980 Democratic Party platform.

101. 1988 Democratic Party platform.

102. U.S. Department of Justice, U.S. Department of Education. (2011, December 2). *Guidance on the voluntary use of race to achieve diversity and avoid racial isolation in elementary and secondary schools*. Last accessed 5/5/2022 from https://www2.ed.gov/about/offices/list/ocr/docs/guidance-ese-201111.pdf.

103. Equal Employment Opportunity Commission (EEOC). Affirmative action appropriate under Title VI of the Civil Rights Act of 1964, as amended, 44 F.R. § 4422 (1979).

104. Lyndon B. Johnson, Commencement Address at Howard University, "To Fulfill These Rights," from Peters, G., & Woolley, J. T. (n.d.). The American Presidency Project. https://www.presidency.ucsb.edu/node/241312.

105. Lyndon B. Johnson, Commencement Address at Howard University, "To Fulfill These Rights," from Peters, G., & Woolley, J. T. (n.d.). The American Presidency Project. https://www.presidency.ucsb.edu/node/241312.

106. Stephanopoulos, G., & Edley, C., Jr. (1995, July 19). Affirmative action review. The White House. Last accessed 5/5/2022 from https://clintonWhitehouse4.archives.gov/WH/EOP/OP/html/aa/aa-lett.html.

107. Stephanopoulos, G., & Edley, C., Jr. (1995, July 19). Affirmative action review. The White House. Last accessed 5/5/2022 from https://clintonWhitehouse4.archives.gov/WH/EOP/OP/html/aa/aa-lett.html.

108. Stephanopoulos, G., & Edley, C., Jr. (1995, July 19). Affirmative action review. The White House. Last accessed 5/5/2022 from https://clintonWhitehouse4.archives.gov/WH/EOP/OP/html/aa/aa-lett.html.

109. Donald J. Trump, Remarks at the Young Black Leadership Conference from Peters, G., & Woolley, J. T. (n.d.). The American Presidency Project. https://www.presidency.ucsb.edu/node/332748.

110. Barack Obama, Remarks at a Naturalization Ceremony at the National Archives and Records Administration from Peters, G., & Woolley, J. T. (n.d.). The American Presidency Project. https://www.presidency.ucsb.edu/node/311427.

111. Equal Employment Opportunity Commission (EEOC), affirmative action appropriate under Title VI of the Civil Rights Act of 1964, as amended, 44 F.R. § 4422 (1979); a very similar disposition was displayed in a 2016 Memo on Advancing Pay Equality that required the collection of data on race and gender disparities in pay.

112. Richard Nixon, Statement About Desegregation of Elementary and Secondary Schools from Peters, G., & Woolley, J. T. (n.d.). The American Presidency Project. https://www.presidency.ucsb.edu/node/241065.

113. Richard Nixon, Statement About Desegregation of Elementary and Secondary Schools from Peters, G., & Woolley, J. T. (n.d.). The American Presidency Project. https://www.presidency.ucsb.edu/node/241065; President Gerald Ford's administration followed suit. A statement issued by the Equal Employment Opportunity Coordinating Council on September 13, 1976, called for race-, color-, sex-, or ethnic-conscious policies that ameliorated procedures that have an exclusionary effect. Equal Employment Opportunity Commission (EEOC). Affirmative action appropriate under Title VI of the Civil Rights Act of 1964, as amended, 44 F.R. § 4422 (1979).

114. George Bush, Statement of Administration Policy: H.R. 4000—Civil Rights Act of 1990, from Peters, G., & Woolley, J. T. (n.d.). The American Presidency Project. https://www.presidency.ucsb.edu/node/328921.

115. George Bush, Remarks at the United States Military Academy Commencement Ceremony in West Point, New York, from Peters, G., & Woolley, J. T. (n.d.). The American Presidency Project. https://www.presidency.ucsb.edu/node/265610.

116. Stephanopoulos, G., & Edley, C., Jr. (1995, July 19). Affirmative action review. The White House. Last accessed 5/5/2022, from https://clintonWhitehouse4.archives.gov/WH/EOP/OP/html/aa/aa-lett.html.

117. Ronald Reagan, Remarks in an Interview with Independent Radio Network Correspondents on Domestic and Foreign Policy Issues from Peters, G., & Woolley, J. T. (n.d.). The American Presidency Project. https://www.presidency.ucsb.edu/node/244880.

118. Potter, H. (2014, June 26). What can we learn from states that ban affirmative action. The Century Foundation. https://tcf.org/content/commentary/what-can-we-learn-from-states-that-ban-affirmative-action/.

119. Ballotpedia. (n.d.). State affirmative action information. Last accessed 5/7/2022 from https://ballotpedia.org/State_affirmative_action_information.

120. Cirillo, F. J. (2020, August 7). Colorblindness has become a conservative shield for racial inequality. *Washington Post.* https://www.washingtonpost.com/outlook/2020/08/07/colorblindness-has-become-conservative-shield-racial-inequality/.

121. Perry, B. (2007). *The Michigan affirmative action cases.* University Press of Kansas, 39.

122. Florida is the only state that banned racial preferences by executive order, New Hampshire and Idaho through state legislative enactment, and the other six states approved bans via the ballot box.

123. Colorado is the first and only state where a ballot initiative to ban racial preferences was rejected.

124. See the preceding section of this chapter for a discussion of the other three goals.

125. The district court reaffirmed its 1972 order and enjoined the department from further delay.

126. *Johnson v. California,* 543 U.S. 499 (2005).

127. *Adarand Constructors, Inc. v. Pena* (1995) left intact *Metro's* approval of diversity broadcasting, even though it overruled *Metro's* (1990) relaxed standard for review of congressionally enacted preferential programs (i.e., intermediate scrutiny rather than strict scrutiny).

128. Davern, M., Bautista, R., Freese, J., Morgan, S. L., & Smith, T. W. (n.d.). *General social surveys, 1972–2021.* NORC, 2021: NORC at the University of Chicago [producer and distributor]. Last accessed 2/16/2021 from the GSS Data Explorer website at gssdataexplorer.norc.org and "racopen" variable.

129. *Washington Post* / ABC News Poll (1995, July 1995). *Polling the nations.* (n.d.). Topic: Affirmative action. Last accessed 4/25/2022 from https://ptn-infobase-com.exlibris.colgate.edu/topics/VG9waWM6NTI=?aid=14265.

130. 1940 Democratic Party platform from Peters, G., & Woolley, J. T. (n.d.). The American Presidency Project. University of California at Santa Barbara. https://www.presidency.ucsb.edu/documents/app-categories/elections-and-transitions/party-platforms.

131. 1944 Republican Party platform.

132. 1992 Republican Party platform.

133. 2004 Republican Party platform.

134. Donald J. Trump, Proclamation 10110—National American History and Founders Month, 2020 Online by Gerhard Peters and John T. Woolley, The American Presidency Project https://www.presidency.ucsb.edu/node/346090.

135. Donald J. Trump, Executive Order 13950—Combating Race and Sex Stereotyping from Peters, G., & Woolley, J. T. (n.d.). The American Presidency Project. https://www.presidency.ucsb.edu/node/343883.

136. Richard Nixon, Executive Order 11478—Equal Employment Opportunity in the Federal Government from Peters, G., & Woolley, J. T. (n.d.). The American Presidency Project. https://www.presidency.ucsb.edu/node/256661.

137. Ronald Reagan, Remarks on Signing the Fair Housing Amendments Act of 1988 from Peters, G., & Woolley, J. T. (n.d.). The American Presidency Project. https://www.presidency.ucsb.edu/node/254049.

138. Ronald Reagan, Radio Address to the Nation on Civil Rights from Peters, G., & Woolley, J. T. (n.d.). The American Presidency Project. https://www.presidency.ucsb.edu/node/260375.

139. Ronald Reagan, Remarks in an Interview with Independent Radio Network Correspondents on Domestic and Foreign Policy Issues from Peters, G., & Woolley, J. T. (n.d.). The American Presidency Project. https://www.presidency.ucsb.edu/node/244880.

140. Stephanopoulos, G., & Edley, C., Jr. (1995, July 19). Affirmative action review. The White House. Last accessed 5/5/2022 from https://clintonWhitehouse4.archives.gov/WH/EOP/OP/html/aa/aa-lett.html.

141. The 2013 lawsuit against the University of Texas at Austin was the first of two brought by Abigail Fisher.

142. Abigail Fisher filed two separate lawsuits against the University of Texas at Austin, the first in 2013 and the second in 2016.

143. 515 U.S. 900, 1995.

144. Especially Harvard's process reflected a numerical commitment, Roberts wrote, given that Black students represented a tight band of 10.0–11.7 percent of the admitted pool from 2009 through 2018. The same for other minority groups.

145. *Hopwood v. Texas*, 78 F. 2d 932 (1996).

146. Note that the Fifth Circuit again approved the plan, without it going to the district court.

147. Halpern, S. C. (1995). *On the limits of the law: The ironic legacy of Title VI of the 1964 Civil Rights Act*. Johns Hopkins University Press, 304.

148. Moore, N. (2000). *Governing race: Policy process and the politics of race.* Praeger.

149. William J. Clinton, The President's News Conference from Peters, G., & Woolley, J. T. (n.d.). The American Presidency Project. https://www.presidency.ucsb.edu/node/221045.

150. William J. Clinton, Remarks at a Clinton/Gore '96 Dinner from Peters, G., & Woolley, J. T. (n.d.). The American Presidency Project. https://www.presidency.ucsb.edu/node/221759.

151. William J. Clinton, Remarks on Affirmative Action at the National Archives and Records Administration from Peters, G., & Woolley, J. T. (n.d.). The American Presidency Project. https://www.presidency.ucsb.edu/node/221889.

152. Ronald Reagan, The President's News Conference from Peters, G., & Woolley, J. T. (n.d.). The American Presidency Project. https://www.presidency.ucsb.edu/node/246569; Ronald Reagan, The President's News Conference from Peters, G., & Woolley, J. T. (n.d.). The American Presidency Project. https://www.presidency.ucsb.edu/node/257723.

153. Ronald Reagan, The President's News Conference from Peters, G., & Woolley, J. T. (n.d.). The American Presidency Project. https://www.presidency.ucsb.edu/node/246569.

154. Ronald Reagan, Radio Address to the Nation on Civil Rights from Peters, G., & Woolley, J. T. (n.d.). The American Presidency Project. https://www.presidency.ucsb.edu/node/260375; Ronald Reagan, The President's News Conference from Peters, G., & Woolley, J. T. (n.d.). The American Presidency Project. https://www.presidency.ucsb.edu/node/257723.

155. Ronald Reagan, The President's News Conference from Peters, G., & Woolley, J. T. (n.d.). The American Presidency Project. https://www.presidency.ucsb.edu/node/257723.

156. Ronald Reagan, Radio Address to the Nation on Civil Rights from Peters, G., & Woolley, J. T. (n.d.). The American Presidency Project. https://www.presidency.ucsb.edu/node/260375.

157. George Bush, Statement of Administration Policy: H.R. 1—Civil Rights and Women's Equity in Employment Act of 1991, from Peters, G., & Woolley, J. T. (n.d.). The American Presidency Project. https://www.presidency.ucsb.edu/node/330668; George Bush, Statement of Administration Policy: H.R. 4000—Civil Rights Act of 1990, from Peters, G., & Woolley, J. T. (n.d.). The American Presidency Project. https://www.presidency.ucsb.edu/node/328921.

158. Gerstenzang, J. (1991, November 22). Bush drops repeal of anti-bias rules: Legislation: Rights bill is signed after fierce protests halt a plan to scuttle guidelines authorizing affirmative action. Incident is seen as exacerbating racial tensions. *Los Angeles Times.* Accessed 3/2/2025 from https://www.latimes.com/archives/la-xpm-1991-11-22-mn-46-story.html.

159. George Bush, Remarks to the Asian-Pacific Community in Fountain Valley, California, from Peters, G., & Woolley, J. T. (n.d.). The American Presidency Project. https://www.presidency.ucsb.edu/node/266059.

160. George W. Bush, Remarks on the Michigan Affirmative Action Case from Peters, G., & Woolley, J. T. (n.d.). The American Presidency Project. https://www.presidency.ucsb.edu/node/215818.

161. George W. Bush, Remarks on the Michigan Affirmative Action Case from Peters, G., & Woolley, J. T. (n.d.). The American Presidency Project. https://www.presidency.ucsb.edu/node/215818.

162. Richard Nixon, Statement Urging Senate and House Conferees to Permit Continued Implementation of the Philadelphia Plan from Peters, G., & Woolley, J. T. (n.d.). The American Presidency Project. https://www.presidency.ucsb.edu/node/240433.

163. Nixon, R. M. (1978). *RN: The memoirs of Richard Nixon*. Grosset & Dunlap, 437.

164. William J. Clinton, Remarks on Affirmative Action at the National Archives and Records Administration from Peters, G., & Woolley, J. T. (n.d.). The American Presidency Project. https://www.presidency.ucsb.edu/node/221889.

165. William J. Clinton, Memorandum on Affirmative Action from Peters, G., & Woolley, J. T. (n.d.). The American Presidency Project. https://www.presidency.ucsb.edu/node/221894.

166. Office of Public Affairs, Department of Justice. (2018, July 3). *Attorney General Jeff Sessions rescinds 24 guidance documents*. Last accessed 5/7/2022 from https://www.justice.gov/opa/pr/attorney-general-jeff-sessions-rescinds-24-guidance-documents.

5. All Lives Matter: DEI and the Death of Affirmative Action

1. This terminology is typically used derisively in American politics. It is a useful rhetorical device in this context for conveying the way in which the substantive elements of otherwise opposing politics yield the same marginalizing policy result, even though they spring from different intentions.

2. *Regents California v. Bakke*, 438 U.S. 265, 317 (1978).

3. The Seattle plan required parents .to identify their child as a member of a particular racial group, but if a parent identified more than one race on the form, the application was not accepted and, if necessary, enrollment personnel would check one box.

4. Up to 75 percent of the places in the freshman class were filled through the state legislature–approved Top Ten Percent Plan.

5. 2020 Democratic Party platform from Peters, G., & Woolley, J. T. (n.d.). The American Presidency Project. University of California at Santa Barbara. https://www.presidency.ucsb.edu/documents/app-categories/elections-and-transitions/party-platforms.

6. 2012 Democratic Party platform.

7. 1984 Democratic Party platform.

8. 1948 Democratic Party platform.

9. 1944 Republican Party platform from Peters, G., & Woolley, J. T. (n.d.). The American Presidency Project. University of California at Santa Barbara. https://www.presidency.ucsb.edu/documents/app-categories/elections-and-transitions/party-platforms.

10. 1948 Republican Party platform.

11. 1960 and 1964 Democratic Party platforms.

12. 1956 Republican Party platform.

13. 1956 Republican Party platform.

14. 1960 Republican Party platform.

15. 1960 Republican Party platform.

16. 1960 Republican Party platform.

17. 1968 Democratic Party platform.

18. 1968 Democratic Party platform.

19. 1972 Democratic Party platform.

20. Republican 1972 platform.

21. 1980 Republican Party platform.

22. 2004 Republican Party platform, 1980 Republican Party platform.

23. 1996 Republican Party platform. Gay rights is one area where conservative statements on diversity, equity, and inclusion (DEI) are distinctive from Democrats', as they consistently opposed same-sex marriage from 1980 through 2016.

24. Lyndon B. Johnson, Executive Order 11375—Amending Executive Order No. 11246, Relating to Equal Employment Opportunity from Peters, G., & Woolley, J. T. (n.d.). The American Presidency Project. https://www.presidency.ucsb.edu/node/239383.

25. Parren J. M. (1983). Federal affirmative action for MBE's: An historical analysis. *National Bar Association Magazine*; Congressional Research Service. (2022, March 9). *SBA's "8(a) Program": Overview, history, and current issues.* https://sgp.fas.org/crs/misc/R44844.pdf; LaNoue, G. R., & Sullivan, J. C. (1994). Presumptions for preferences: The Small Business Administration's decisions on groups entitled to affirmative action. *Journal of Policy History*, 6(4).

26. Congress provided a legislative framework for these regulations by enacting them via 1978 amendments to the Small Business Act. Congressional Research Service. (2022, March 9). *SBA's "8(a) Program": Overview, history, and current issues.* https://sgp.fas.org/crs/misc/R44844.pdf.

27. Urofsky reports that still in 1981 the US Commission on Civil Rights defined affirmative action as "efforts that take race, sex, and national origin into

account for the purpose of remedying past and present discrimination and its effects." It was "because of the duration, intensity, scope and intransigence of the discrimination women and minority groups experience, affirmative action plans are needed to assure equal employment opportunity." See: Urofsky, M. I. (2020). *The affirmative action puzzle: A living history from Reconstruction to today*. Pantheon Books, xi–xii.

28. Parren, J. M. (1983). Federal affirmative action for MBE's: An historical analysis. *National Bar Association Magazine*; Congressional Research Service. (2022, March 9). *SBA's "8(a) Program": Overview, history, and current issues*. https://sgp.fas.org/crs/misc/R44844.pdf; LaNoue, G. R., and Sullivan, J. C. (1994). Presumptions for preferences: The Small Business Administration's decisions on groups entitled to affirmative action. *Journal of Policy History*, 6(4).

29. George Bush, Remarks at a White House Ceremony Commemorating the 25th Anniversary of the Civil Rights Act from Peters, G., & Woolley, J. T. (n.d.). The American Presidency Project. https://www.presidency.ucsb.edu/node/263611.

30. George Bush, Remarks at a White House Ceremony Commemorating the 25th Anniversary of the Civil Rights Act from Peters, G., & Woolley, J. T. (n.d.). The American Presidency Project. https://www.presidency.ucsb.edu/node/263611.

31. Executive Order 13279—Equal Protection of the Laws for Faith-Based and Community Organizations, December 12, 2002, and George W. Bush, Fact Sheet: Compassion in Action: Producing Real Results for Americans Most in Need from Peters, G., & Woolley, J. T. (n.d.). The American Presidency Project. https://www.presidency.ucsb.edu/node/283124.

32. William J. Clinton, Executive Order 13160—Nondiscrimination on the Basis of Race, Sex, Color, National Origin, Disability, Religion, Age, Sexual Orientation, and Status as a Parent in Federally Conducted Education and Training Programs from Peters, G., & Woolley, J. T. (n.d.). The American Presidency Project. https://www.presidency.ucsb.edu/node/227869; Department of Justice. (2001, January 18). Executive Order 13160 guidance document: Ensuring opportunity in federally conducted education and training programs. *Federal Register*. https://www.federalregister.gov/documents/2001/01/18/01-1494/executive-order-13160-guidance-document-ensuring-equal-opportunity-in-federally-conducted-education.

33. Stephanopoulos, G., & Edley, C., Jr. (1995, July 19). Affirmative action review. The White House. Last accessed 5/5/2022 from https://clintonWhitehouse4.archives.gov/WH/EOP/OP/html/aa/aa-lett.html.

34. Barack Obama, Interview with Ta-Nehisi Coates from Peters, G., & Woolley, J. T. (n.d.). The American Presidency Project. https://www.presidency.ucsb.edu/node/331727.

35. Joseph R. Biden, Executive Order 14035—Diversity, Equity, Inclusion, and Accessibility in the Federal Workforce from Peters, G., & Woolley, J. T. (n.d.). The American Presidency Project. https://www.presidency.ucsb.edu/node/350596.

36. Butler, J. (1998). An affirmative view. In R. Post & M. Rogin (Eds.), *Race and representation: Affirmative action*. Zone Books, 179.

37. Butler, J. (1998). An affirmative view. In R. Post & M. Rogin (Eds.), *Race and representation: Affirmative action.* Zone Books, 179.

38. Butler, J. (1998). An affirmative view. In R. Post & M. Rogin (Eds.), *Race and representation: Affirmative action.* Zone Books, 181.

39. Halpern, S. C. (1995). *On the limits of the law: The ironic legacy of Title VI of the 1864 Civil Rights Act.* Johns Hopkins University Press, 291.

40. Halpern, S. C. (1995). *On the limits of the law: The ironic legacy of Title VI of the 1864 Civil Rights Act.* Johns Hopkins University Press, 290.

41. For more on the evolution that began during Reconstruction, see Urofsky, M. I. (2020). *The affirmative action puzzle: A living history from Reconstruction to today.* Pantheon Books.

42. National Advisory Commission on Civil Disorders. (1967). *Report on the causes, events, and aftermaths of the civil disorders of 1967.* United States, Kerner Commission, US G.P.O.

43. Brown, A. (2020, February 25). The changing categories the U.S. Census has used to measure race. Pew Research Center. Last accessed 5/8/2022 from https://www.pewresearch.org/fact-tank/2020/02/25/the-changing-categories-the-u-s-has-used-to-measure-race/; Cohn, D. (2016, October 4). Federal officials may revamp how Americans identify race, ethnicity on census and other forms. Pew Research Center. Last accessed 5/8/2022 from https://www.pewresearch.org/fact-tank/2016/10/04/federal-officials-may-revamp-how-americans-identify-race-ethnicity-on-census-and-other-forms/; Cohn, D. (2014, May 5). Millions of Americans changed their racial or ethnic identity from one census to the next. Pew Research Center. Last accessed 5/8/2022 from https://www.pewresearch.org/fact-tank/2014/05/05/millions-of-americans-changed-their-racial-or-ethnic-identity-from-one-census-to-the-next/.

44. Pollock, E. E. (2012). *Race and the Supreme Court: Defining equality.* Peppertree Press, 15–18.

45. Pollock, E. E. (2012). *Race and the Supreme Court: Defining equality.* Peppertree Press, 18.

46. Tamir, C., Budman, A., Noe-Bustamante, L., & Mora, L. (2021, March 25). Facts about the U.S. Black population. Pew Research Center. Last accessed 5/8/2022 from https://www.pewresearch.org/social-trends/fact-sheet/facts-about-the-us-Black-population/#:~:text=The%20Black%20population%20of%20the,roughly%2036.2%20million%20Black%20Americans.

47. Massey, D. S., Mooney, M., & Torres, K. C. (2007). Black immigrants and Black natives attending selective colleges and universities in the United States. *American Journal of Education, 113*: 243–271.

48. McClain, P. D., Carter, N. M., DeFrancesco Soto, V. M., Lyle, M. L., Grynaviski, J. D., Nunnally, S. C., Scotto, T. J., Kendrick, J. A., Lackey, G. F., & Cotton, K. D. (2006). Racial distancing in a southern city: Latino immigrants' views of Black Americans. *Journal of Politics, 68*: 571–584. https://doi.org/10.1111/j.1468-2508.2006.00446.x. See also: Wilkinson, B. C. (2014). Perceptions of commonality

and Latino–Black, Latino–White relations in a multiethnic United States. *Political Research Quarterly, 67*: 905–916.

49. Corral, Á. J. (2020). Allies, antagonists, or ambivalent? Exploring Latino attitudes about the Black Lives Matter Movement. *Hispanic Journal of Behavioral Sciences, 42*: 431–454.

50. Shihadeh, E. S., & Barranco, R. E. (2010). Latino employment and Black violence: The unintended consequence of U.S. immigration policy. *Social Forces, 88*: 1393–1420.

51. Kennedy, R. (2013). *For discrimination: Race, affirmative action, and the law*. Vintage Books, 143.

52. Schmidt, P. (2007). *Color and money: How rich White kids are winning the war over college affirmative action*. Palgrave Macmillan, 195. Schmidt reports that in the 2003 University of Michigan cases, 60 briefs were submitted in support of the admissions program. Among the more than 300 organizations backing Michigan were 88 colleges, 50 higher education associations, and dozens of minority-advocacy and student groups (18).

53. Kennedy, R. (2013). *For discrimination: Race, affirmative action, and the law*. Vintage Books, 143.

54. Quoted in Jaschik, S. (2007, February 1). The immigrant factor: Study documents that disproportionate number of Black students at top colleges are new arrivals in the U.S.—and offers only clues about why. *Inside Higher Ed*. https://www.insidehighered.com/news/2007/02/01/immigrant-factor.

55. *Regents v. Bakke* (1978), 438 U.S. 265, 316.

56. Testimony from University of Michigan Law School admissions director Erica Munzel.

57. Testimony from Law School Dean Jeffrey Lehman.

58. Previous Law School Admissions Director Dennis Shields.

59. Justice Kagan did not participate in this decision. Also missing from this vote is the late Justice Antonin Scalia.

60. Schmidt, P. (2007). *Color and money: How rich White kids are winning the war over college affirmative action*. Palgrave Macmillan, 198–199.

61. Sander, R. H., & Taylor, S., Jr. (2012). *Mismatch: How affirmative action hurts students it's intended to help, and why universities won't admit it*. Basic Books.

62. 2000 Republican Party platform from Peters, G., & Woolley, J. T. (n.d.). The American Presidency Project. University of California at Santa Barbara. https://www.presidency.ucsb.edu/documents/app-categories/elections-and-transitions/party-platforms.

63. 2004 Republican Party platform.

64. 1984 Republican Party platform.

65. 1992 Democratic Party platform from Peters, G., & Woolley, J. T. (n.d.). The American Presidency Project. University of California at Santa Barbara. https://www.presidency.ucsb.edu/documents/app-categories/elections-and-transitions/party-platforms.

66. 2012 Democratic Party platform.

67. 2020 Democratic Party platform.

68. Democratic Party platform.

69. 1972 and 1976 Republican Party platforms.

70. 1984 Republican Party platform.

71. 2000 Republican Party platform.

72. 1980 Republican Party platform.

73. 1960 Republican Party platform.

74. 1984 Democratic Party platform.

75. 1980 Democratic Party platform.

76. 1972 Democratic Party platform.

77. William J. Clinton, Remarks on Affirmative Action at the National Archives and Records Administration from Peters, G., & Woolley, J. T. (n.d.). The American Presidency Project. https://www.presidency.ucsb.edu/node/221889.

78. Barack Obama, Remarks at a Naturalization Ceremony at the National Archives and Records Administration from Peters, G., & Woolley, J. T. (n.d.). The American Presidency Project. https://www.presidency.ucsb.edu/node/311427.

79. Barack Obama, Remarks at a Naturalization Ceremony at the National Archives and Records Administration from Peters, G., & Woolley, J. T. (n.d.). The American Presidency Project. https://www.presidency.ucsb.edu/node/311427.

80. Richard Nixon, Statement About Federal Policies Relative to Equal Housing Opportunity from Peters, G., & Woolley, J. T. (n.d.). The American Presidency Project. https://www.presidency.ucsb.edu/node/240233.

81. Jimmy Carter, Address at the National Italian-American Bicentennial Tribute Dinner in Washington, DC, from Peters, G., & Woolley, J. T. (n.d.). The American Presidency Project. https://www.presidency.ucsb.edu/node/347544.

82. Ronald Reagan, Remarks in New York City on Receiving the Charles Evans Hughes Gold Medal of the National Conference of Christians and Jews from Peters, G., & Woolley, J. T. (n.d.). The American Presidency Project. https://www.presidency.ucsb.edu/node/245920.

83. Donald J. Trump, Press Release—President Trump's Bold Immigration Plan for the 21st Century, from Peters, G., & Woolley, J. T. (n.d.). The American Presidency Project. https://www.presidency.ucsb.edu/node/334409.

84. Sakpal, M. (2019). Diversity and inclusion build high-performance teams. Gartner, Inc. https://www.gartner.com/smarterwithgartner/diversity-and-inclusion-build-high-performance-teams.

85. Hunt, V., Layton, D., & Prince, S. (2015, January 1). New research makes it increasingly clear that companies with more diverse workforces perform better financially. McKinsey & Company. https://www.mckinsey.com/business-functions/people-and-organizational-performance/our-insights/why-diversity-matters?zd_source=hrt&zd_campaign=2448&zd_term=scottballina.

86. Georgeac, O., & Rattan, A. (2002, June 15). Stop making the business case for diversity. *Harvard Business Review*. Accessed 3/10/2025 from https://hbr.org/2022/06/stop-making-the-business-case-for-diversity.

Epilogue

1. Kennedy, R. (2013). *For discrimination: Race, affirmative action, and the law*. Vintage Books, 34–35.

2. Jimmy Carter, Address at the National Italian-American Bicentennial Tribute Dinner in Washington, DC, from Peters, G., & Woolley, J. T. (n.d.). The American Presidency Project. https://www.presidency.ucsb.edu/node/347544.

3. 2008 Democratic Party platform.

References

303 Creative LLC v. Elenis, 600 U.S. ___ (2023).

Abraham, H. S. (1992). *Justices and presidents: A political history of appointments to the Supreme Court.* Oxford University Press.

Adarand Constructors v. Mineta, 534 U.S. 103 (2001).

Adarand Constructors v. Pena, 515 U.S. 200 (1995).

Adarand Constructors v. Slater, 528 U.S. 216 (2000).

Administrative Office of the United States Courts. (n.d.). *United States Courts.* Last accessed 5/1/2022 from https://www.uscourts.gov/statistics-reports/funding-and-budget-annual-report-2021.

Alba, R., & Abdel-Hady, D. (2005). Galileo's children: Italian Americans' difficult entry into the intellectual elite. *Sociological Quarterly, 46*(1): 3–18.

Alexander, M. (2020). *The new Jim Crow: Mass incarceration in the age of colorblindness.* 10th anniversary edition. Free Press.

Anderson, T. H. (2004). *The pursuit of fairness: A history of affirmative action.* Oxford University Press.

Arlington Heights v. Metropolitan Housing Development Corp., 429 U.S. 252 (1977).

Associated Press. (2016, August 19). "What do you have to lose?" Donald Trump appeals for Black vote. *Guardian.* https://www.theguardian.com/us-news/2016/aug/20/what-do-you-have-to-lose-donald-trump-appeals-for-Black-vote.

Associated Press–NORC Center for Public Affairs Research. (2018, March). *50 years after Martin Luther King's assassination: Assessing progress of the civil rights movement.* https://apnorc.org/wp-content/uploads/2020/02/50-years-after-Martin-Luther-King%E2%80%99s-Assassination.pdf.

Ballotpedia. (n.d.). State affirmative action information. Last accessed 5/7/2022 from https://ballotpedia.org/State_affirmative_action_information.

Baum, L. (1988). Measuring policy change in the U.S. Supreme Court. *American Political Science Review, 82*: 905–912.

Baum, L. (2001). *American courts: Process and policy.* Houghton Mifflin.

Baum, L. (2001). *The Supreme Court.* 7th edition. CQ Press.

Baum, L. (2003). The Supreme Court in American politics. *Annual Review of Political Science, 6*: 161–180.

Baum, L., & Devins, N. (2010). Why the Supreme Court cares about elites, not the American people. *Georgetown Law Journal, 98*: 1515–1581.

Bearak, B. (1997, July 27). Questions of race run deep for foe of preferences. *New York Times*.

Bickel, A. M. (1986). *The least dangerous branch: The Supreme Court at the bar of politics*. 2nd edition. Yale University Press.

Black, R. C., & Owens, R. J. (2016). Courting the president: How circuit court judges alter their behavior for promotion to the Supreme Court. *American Journal of Political Science, 60*: 30–43.

Black, R. C., Wedeking, J., Owens, R. J., & Wohlfarth, P. C. (2016). The influence of public sentiment on Supreme Court opinion clarity. *Law & Society Review, 50*: 703–732.

Bobo, L. (1997). Race, public opinion, and the social sphere. *Public Opinion Quarterly, 61*: 1–15.

Bobo, L. D., & Fox, C. (2003). Race, racism, and discrimination: Bridging problems, methods, and theory in social psychological research. *Social Psychology Quarterly, 66*: 319–332.

Bobo, L., & Hutchings, V. L. (1996). Perceptions of racial group competition: Extending Blumer's theory of group position to a multiracial social context. *American Sociological Review, 61*: 951–972. https://doi.org/10.2307/2096302.

Borter, G. (2023, February 15). Most Americans think college admissions should not consider race. Reuters/Ipsos poll. Accessed 1/17/2024 from https://www.reuters.com/world/us/most-americans-think-college-admissions-should-not-consider-race-reutersipsos-2023-02-15/.

Boston Firefighters Union Local 718 v. Boston Chapter, 461 U.S. 477 (1983).

Boyd, C. L., Ringhand, L. A., & Collins, P. M. (2018). The role of nominee gender and race at U.S. Supreme Court confirmation hearings. *Law & Society Review, 52*: 871–901.

Brigham, C. C. (1923). *A study of American intelligence*. Princeton University Press.

Brown v. Board of Education, 347 U.S. 483 (1954).

Brown, A. (2020, February 25). The changing categories the U.S. Census has used to measure race. Pew Research Center. Last accessed 5/8/2022 from https://www.pewresearch.org/fact-tank/2020/02/25/the-changing-categories-the-u-s-has-used-to-measure-race/.

Bump, P. (2020, July 6). It's not that Trump doesn't want to tackle racism. It's just that he's focused on perceived racism against Whites. *Washington Post*.

Butcher, J., & Gonzalea, M. (2020, December 7). *Critical race theory, the new intolerance and its grip on America*. The Heritage Foundation. https://www.heritage.org/civil-rights/report/critical-race-theory-the-new-intolerance-and-its-grip-america.

Butler, J. (1998). An affirmative view. in R. Post & M. Rogin (Eds.), *Race and representation: Affirmative action*. Zone Books.

Caldeira, G. A., & Gibson, J. L. (1992). The etiology of public support for the Supreme Court. *American Journal of Political Science, 36*: 635–664.

Caldeira, G. A., & Wright, J. R. (1988). Organized interests and agenda setting in the U.S. Supreme Court. *American Political Science Review, 82*: 1109–1127.

Cameron, C. M., Cover, A.D., & Segal, J. A. (1990). Senate voting on Supreme Court nominations: A neo-institutional model. *American Political Science Review, 84*: 525–534.

Caplan, L. (1987). *The tenth justice: The solicitor general and the rule of law*. Vintage Books.

Cardozo, B. (1921). *The nature of the judicial process*. Yale University Press.

Carmines, E. G., & Stimson, J. A. (1989). *Issue evolution: Race and the transformation of American politics*. Princeton University Press.

Carr, M. K. (2018). Prudential supreme court opinion writing. In *The rhetorical invention of diversity: Supreme Court opinions, public arguments, and affirmative action*. Michigan State University Press.

Casillas, C. J., Enns, P. K., & Wohlfarth, P. C. (2011). How public opinion constrains the U.S. Supreme Court. *American Journal of Political Science, 55*: 74–88.

Chemerinsky, E. (2014). *The case against the Supreme Court*. Penguin Books.

Chow, K. (2017, April 19). "Model minority" myth again used as a racial wedge between Asians and Blacks. NPR. https://www.npr.org/sections/codeswitch/2017/04/19/524571669/model-minority-myth-again-used-as-a-racial-wedge-between-asians-and-Blacks.

Cillizza, C. (2015, August 17). Donald Trump on "Meet the Press," annotated. *Washington Post*.

Cirillo, F. J. (2020, August 7). Colorblindness has become a conservative shield for racial inequality. *Washington Post*.

CNN. (2023, May 17). 'Star Trek's' Zoe Saldana on racism: 'I'm not going to talk about it.' https://www.cnn.com/2013/05/17/us/star-treks-zoe-saldana-on-racism-im-not-going-to-talk-about-it.

Cobb, J. (2017, March 8). Ben Carson, Donald Trump, and the misuse of American history. *New Yorker*.

Cohn, D. (2014, May 5). Millions of Americans changed their racial or ethnic identity from one census to the next. Pew Research Center. Last accessed 5/8/2022 from https://www.pewresearch.org/fact-tank/2014/05/05/millions-of-americans-changed-their-racial-or-ethnic-identity-from-one-census-to-the-next/.

Cohn, D. (2016, October 4). Federal officials may revamp how Americans identify race, ethnicity on census and other forms. Pew Research Center. Last accessed 5/8/2022 from https://www.pewresearch.org/fact-tank/2016/10/04/federal-officials-may-revamp-how-americans-identify-race-ethnicity-on-census-and-other-forms/.

Congressional Research Service. (2022, March 9). *SBA's "8(a) Program": Overview, history, and current issues*. https://sgp.fas.org/crs/misc/R44844.pdf.

Corral, Á. J. (2020). Allies, antagonists, or ambivalent? Exploring Latino attitudes about the Black Lives Matter movement. *Hispanic Journal of Behavioral Sciences, 42*: 431–454.

CQ Press. (1964). First federal pay bill rejected; compromise enacted. *Congressional Quarterly Almanac 1964*. CQ Press, a division of Sage.

Crosby, F. J. (2004). *Affirmative action is dead; Long live affirmative action*. Yale University Press.

Cross, F. B., & Nelson, B. J. (2001). Strategic institutional effects on Supreme Court decision making. *Northwestern University Law Review, 95*: 1437–1493.

Crugnale, J. (2014, June 5). Morgan Freeman says not to make race a "bigger issue than it needs to be." The Wrap. https://www.thewrap.com/morgan-freeman-disputes-race-plays-factor-in-income-inequality-video/.

Curtis, L. P. (1971). *Apes and angels: The Irish in Victorian caricature*. Smithsonian Institution Press.

Dahl, R. A. (1957). Decision-making in a democracy: The Supreme Court as a national policy-maker. *Journal of Public Law, 6*: 279–295.

Daniller, A. (2021, March 18). Majorities of Americans see at least some discrimination against Black, Hispanic and Asian people in the U.S. Pew Research Center. https://www.pewresearch.org/fact-tank/2021/03/18/majorities-of-americans-see-at-least-some-discrimination-against-Black-hispanic-and-asian-people-in-the-u-s/.

Davern, M., Bautista, R., Freese, J., Morgan, S. L., & Smith, T. W. (n.d.). *General social surveys, 1972–2021*. NORC, 2021: NORC at the University of Chicago [producer and distributor]. Last accessed 2/16/2021 from the GSS Data Explorer website at gssdataexplorer.norc.org and "racopen" variable.

Davis, A. L., & Graham, B. L. (1995). *The Supreme Court, race, and civil rights*. Sage.

De Velasco, A. (2010). *Centrist rhetoric: The production of political transcendence in the Clinton presidency*. Lexington Books.

DeFunis v. Odegaard, 416 U.S. 312 (1974).

Dobbs v. Jackson Women's Health Organization, 597 U.S. ___ (2022).

Duster, T. (1998). Individual fairness, group preferences, and the California strategy. In R. Post & M. Rogin (Eds.), *Race and representation: Affirmative action*. Zone Books.

Edsall, T. B. (1992, June 14). Clinton stuns Rainbow Coalition. *Washington Post*.

Epstein, L., Knight, J. L., & Martin, A. D. (2001). The Supreme Court as a strategic national policymaker. *Emory Law Review, 55*: 583–611.

Epstein, L., Martin, A. D., Quinn, I. M., & Segal, J. A. (2007). Ideological drift among Supreme Court Justices: Who, when, and how important? *Northwestern University Law Review, 101*: 1483–1542.

Epstein, L., & Posner, E. A. (2016). Supreme Court justices' loyalty to the president. *Journal of Legal Studies, 45*: 401–436.

Epstein, L., & Posner, E. A. (2018). The decline of Supreme Court deference to the president. *University of Pennsylvania Law Review, 166*: 829–860.

Epstein, L., Segal, J. A., Spaeth, H. J., & Walker, T. G. (2007). *The Supreme Court compendium: Data, decisions & developments*. CQ Press.

Equal Employment Opportunity Commission (EEOC). Affirmative action appropriate under Title VI of the Civil Rights Act of 1964, as amended, 44 F.R. § 4422 (1979).

Factbase. (n.d.). Remarks: *Donald Trump delivers remarks on the Fourth of July in Washington—July 4, 2020*. Last accessed 5/7/2022 from https://factba.se/transcript/donald-trump-remarks-fourth-of-july-independence-day-july-4-2020.

Fagan, E. J. (2018). Marching orders? U.S. party platforms and legislative agenda setting 1948–2014. *Political Research Quarterly, 71*: 949–959.

Felton, E. (2022, February 25). Supporters say they have the votes in the House to pass a reparations bill after years of lobbying. *Washington Post*.

Firefighters Local 1784 v. Stotts, 467 U.S. 561 (1984).

Firefighters v. City of Cleveland, 478 U.S. 501 (1986).

Fiscus, R. J. (1992). *The constitutional logic of affirmative action* (ed. S. L. Wasby). Duke University Press.

Fisher v. University of Texas, 570 U.S. 297 (2013).

Fisher v. University of Texas II, Docket 14-981 (2016).

Flemming, R. B., Bohte, J., & Wood, B. D. (1997). One voice among many: The Supreme Court's influence on attentiveness to issues in the United States, 1947–92. *American Journal of Political Science, 41*: 1224–1250.

Fletcher, M. A. (1998, September 19). President accepts report on race. *Washington Post*.

Ford, H. J. (1915). *The Scotch-Irish in America*. Princeton University Press.

Fullilove v. Klutznick, 448 U.S. 448 (1980).

Garrow, D. J. (1978). *Protest at Selma: Martin Luther King, Jr., and the Voting Rights Act of 1965*. Yale University Press.

Gibson, J. L. (1990). Review of *Public Opinion and the Court*, Thomas R. Marshall. *Public Opinion Quarterly, 54*: 289–290.

Gibson, J. L., & Caldeira, G. A. (2011). Has legal realism damaged the legitimacy of the U.S. Supreme Court? *Law & Society Review, 45*: 195–219.

Gibson, J. L., Caldeira, G.A., & Spence, L. K. (2003). The Supreme Court and the U.S. presidential election of 2000: Wounds, self-inflicted or otherwise? *British Journal of Political Science, 33*: 535–556.

Giles, M. W., Blackstone, B., & Vining, R. L. (2008). The Supreme Court in American democracy: Unraveling the linkages between public opinion and judicial decision making. *Journal of Politics, 70*: 293–306.

Ginsberg, B. (1976). Elections and public policy. *American Political Science Review, 70*: 41–49.

Goldstone, L. (2020). *On account of race*. Counterpoint Press.

Golub, M. (2018). *Is racial equality unconstitutional?* Oxford University Press.

Gramlich, J. (2023, June 16). Americans and affirmative action: How the public sees the consideration of race in college admissions, hiring. Pew Research Center. Accessed 1/17/2024 from https://www.pewresearch.org/shortreads/ 2023/06/16/ americans-and-affirmative-action-how-the-public-sees-the-consideration-of-race-in-college-admissions-hiring/.

Gratz v. Bollinger, 539 U.S. 244 (2003).

Gray, W. R. (2001). *The four faces of affirmative action: Fundamental answers and actions*. Greenwood Press.

Greve, J. E. (2023, July 9). "Democracy is at risk": Inside the fight for Supreme Court reform. *Guardian*. Accessed 1/18/2024 from https://www.theguardian. com/law/2023/jul/09/supreme-court-reform-conservative-justices.

Grutter v. Bollinger, 539 U.S. 306 (2003).

Guinier, L. (1994). *Tyranny of the majority: Fundamental fairness in representative democracy*. Free Press.

Hall, M. E. K. (2011). *The nature of Supreme Court power*. Cambridge University Press.

Halpern, S. C. (1995). *On the limits of the law: The ironic legacy of Title VI of the 1864 Civil Rights Act*. Johns Hopkins University Press.

Handlin, O. (1991). *Boston's immigrants, 1780–1880: A study in acculturation*. 50th anniversary edition. Harvard University Press.

Hannah-Jones, N. (2015, June 25). Living apart: How the government betrayed a landmark civil rights law. ProPublica. https://www.propublica.org/article/ living-apart-how-the-government-betrayed-a-landmark-civil-rights-law.

Hannah-Jones, N. (2021). *A new origin story: The 1619 Project*. One World.

Hansford, T. G., & Spriggs, J. F., II. (2006). *The politics of precedent on the U.S. Supreme Court*. Oxford University Press.

Harris, F. R., & Wilkins, R.W., eds. (1988). *Quiet riots: Race and poverty in the United States—The Kerner Report twenty years later*. Pantheon Books.

Henschen, B. M., Walsh, M. H., & Strauss, J. (1992). Courting constituents? An analysis of the Senate confirmation vote on Justice Clarence Thomas. *American Political Science Review, 86*: 997–1006.

Herndon, A. W., & Glueck, K. (2020, May 22). Biden apologizes for saying Black voters "ain't Black" if they're considering Trump. *New York Times*.

Higham, J. (1975). *Strangers in the land: Patterns of American nativism, 1860–1925*. Revised edition. Atheneum.

Holmes, S. A. (1998, September 18). Clinton panel on race urges variety of modest measures. *New York Times*.

Hood, J. L. (1993). The Nixon administration and the revised Philadelphia Plan for Affirmative Action: A study in expanding presidential power and divided government. *Presidential Studies Quarterly, 23*: 145–167.

Hopwood v. Texas, 78 F. 2d 932 (1996).

Hunt, V., Layton, D., & Prince, S. (2015, January 1). *New research makes it increasingly clear that companies with more diverse workforces perform better financially*. McKinsey & Company. https://www.mckinsey.com/business-functions/people-and-organizational-performance/our-insights/why-diversity-matters?zd_source=hrt&zd_campaign=2448&zd_term=scottballina.

Jackson Lee, S. (2020, May 22). *H.R. 40 is not a symbolic act. It's a path to restorative justice*. ACLU. https://www.aclu.org/news/racial-justice/h-r-40-is-not-a-symbolic-act-its-a-path-to-restorative-justice.

Jaschik, S. (2007, February 1). The immigrant factor: Study documents that disproportionate number of Black students at top colleges are new arrivals in the U.S.—and offers only clues about why. *Inside Higher Ed*. https://www.insidehighered.com/news/2007/02/01/immigrant-factor.

Johnson v. Transportation Agency, 480 U.S. 616 (1987).

Kahlenberg, R. D. (1997). *The remedy: Class, race, and affirmative action*. Basic Books.

Kahn, M. A. (1992). Shattering the myth about President Eisenhower's Supreme Court appointments. *Presidential Studies Quarterly*, 22(1): 47–56.

Kastellec, J. P., Lax, J. R., & Phillips, J. H. (2010). Public opinion and Senate confirmation of Supreme Court nominees. *Journal of Politics*, 72: 767–784.

Keck, T. M. (2004). *The most activist Supreme Court in history: The road to modern judicial conservatism*. University of Chicago Press.

Kennedy, R. (2015). *For discrimination: Race, affirmative action, and the law*. Reprint. Vintage Books.

Kidd, Q. (2008). The real (lack of) difference between Republicans and Democrats: A computer word score analysis of party platforms, 1996–2004. *PS: Political Science and Politics*, 41: 519–525.

Klarman, M. J. (2006). *From Jim Crow to civil rights: The Supreme Court and the struggle for racial equality*. Oxford University Press.

Knobel, D. T. (1986). *Paddy and the republic*. Wesleyan University Press.

Knopp, C. (2005, December 14). "Morgan Freeman defies labels." *60 Minutes*. Retrieved on 2/23/2024 from https://www.cbsnews.com/news/morgan-freeman-defies-labels-14-12-2005/.

LaNoue, G. R., & Sullivan, J. C. (1994). Presumptions for preferences: The Small Business Administration's decisions on groups entitled to affirmative action. *Journal of Policy History*, 6: 439–467.

Leiter, W. M., & Leiter, S. (2010). *Affirmative action in antidiscrimination law and policy*. 2nd edition. State University of New York Press.

Lemon, J. (2020, July 21). Majority of Americans now support removing confederate statutes, up 16 points from 2018: Poll. *Newsweek*.

LGBTQ+ Rights. (n.d.). Gallup.com. Accessed 1/17/2024 from https://news.gallup.com/poll/1651/gay-lesbian-rights.aspx.

Link, M. W. (1995). Tracking public mood in the Supreme Court: Cross-time analyses of criminal procedure and civil rights cases. *Political Research Quarterly*, 48: 61–78.

Local 28 of Sheet Metal Workers' International Association v. Equal Employment Opportunity Commission, 478 U.S. 421 (1986).

López, I. H. (2006). *White by law: The legal construction of race.* New York University Press.

Lord, E., Trenor, J. J. D., & Barrows, S. J. (1970). *The Italian in America.* Reprint edition. R & E Associates.

Luskin, R. C., McIver, J. P., & Carmines, E. G. (1989). Issues and the transmission of partisanship. *American Journal of Political Science, 33*: 440–458.

Marshall, T. R. (2008). *Public opinion and the Rehnquist Court.* State University of New York Press.

Martin v. Wilks, 490 U.S. 755 (1989).

Masterpiece Cakeshop v. Colorado Civil Rights Commission, 584 U.S. ___ (2018).

McAdam, D. (1999). *Political process and the development of Black insurgency, 1930–1970.* University of Chicago Press.

McClain, P. D., Carter, N. M., DeFrancesco Soto, V. M., Lyle, M. L., Grynaviski, J. D., Nunnally, S. C., Scotto, T. J., Kendrick, J. A., Lackey, G. F., & Cotton, K. D. (2006). Racial distancing in a southern city: Latino immigrants' views of Black Americans. *Journal of Politics, 68*: 571–584.

McCloskey, R. G. (2016). *The American Supreme Court.* 6th edition. Revised by S. Levinson. University of Chicago Press.

McGuire, K. T., Vanberg, G., Smith, C. E., & Caldeira, G. A. (2009). Measuring policy content on the U.S. Supreme Court. *Journal of Politics, 71*: 1305–1321.

McGuire, K. T., & Stimson, J. A. (2004). The least dangerous branch revisited: New evidence on Supreme Court responsiveness to public preferences. *Journal of Politics, 66*: 1018–1035.

Meinhold, S. S., & Shull, S. A. (1998). Policy congruence between the president and the solicitor general. *Political Research Quarterly, 51*: 527–537.

Meredith v. Jefferson County Board of Education, 551 U.S. 701 (2007).

Metro Broadcasting v. FCC, 497 U.S. 547 (1990).

Miller, B. (2020, September 28). *It's time to worry about college enrollment declines among Black students.* Center for American Progress. https://www.americanprogress.org/article/time-worry-college-enrollment-declines-among-Black-students.

Mills, D. (1992, May 13). Sister Souljah's call to arms. *Washington Post.*

Min Kim, S., & Barnes, R. (2021, December 28). Supreme Court term limits are popular—and appear to be going nowhere. *Washington Post.* https://www.washingtonpost.com/nation/2021/12/28/supreme-court-term-limits/.

Minnick v. California Dept. of Corrections, 452 U.S. 105 (1981).

Minority Business Development Agency, U.S. Department of Commerce. *The history of the MDBA.* Last accessed 5/5/2022 from https://www.mbda.gov/about/history.

Mishler, W., & Sheehan, R. S. (1993). The Supreme Court as a countermajoritarian institution? The impact of public opinion on Supreme Court decisions. *American Political Science Review, 87*: 87–101.

Mishler, W., & Sheehan, R. S. (1994). Popular influence on Supreme Court decisions. *American Political Science Review*, 88(3): 716–724.

Mishler, W., & Sheehan, R. S. (1996). Public opinion, the attitudinal model, and Supreme Court decision making: A micro-analytic perspective. *Journal of Politics*, 58: 169–200.

Monroe, A. D. (1983). American party platforms and public opinion. *American Journal of Political Science*, 27: 27–42.

Monroe, S. J., Assistant Secretary for Civil Rights, U.S. Department of Education. (2008, August 28). *Dear colleague*. https://www2.ed.gov/about/offices/list/ocr/letters/raceassignmentese.html.

Moore, N. (2000). *Governing race: Policy process and the politics of race*. Praeger.

Moore, N. (2015). *The political roots of racial tracking in American criminal justice*. Cambridge University Press.

Moraski, B. J., & Shipan, C. R. (1999). The politics of Supreme Court nominations: A theory of institutional constraints and choices. *American Journal of Political Science*, 43(4): 1069–1095.

Morton v. Mancari, 417 U.S. 353 (1974).

Murray, C. (1984). *Losing ground: American social policy, 1950–1980*. Basic Books.

National Advisory Commission on Civil Disorders. (1967). *Report on the causes, events, and aftermaths of the civil disorders of 1967*. United States, Kerner Commission: U.S. G.P.O.

New York Times. (2015, July 8). Excerpts from the Confederate Flag debate in the South Carolina House. *New York Times*. https://www.nytimes.com/interactive/2015/07/08/us/09carolinaexcerpts.html.

Nixon, R. M. (1978). *RN: The memoirs of Richard Nixon*. Grosset & Dunlap.

Northeastern v. Florida, 508 U.S. 656 (1993).

Norton, M. I., & Sommers, S. R. (2011). Whites see racism as a zero-sum game that they are now losing. *Perspectives on Psychological Science*, 6: 215–218.

O'Brien, D. M. (2014). *Storm center: The Supreme Court in American politics*. 10th edition. W. W. Norton.

Office of Fair Housing and Equal Opportunity, Housing and Urban Development. (2021, June 10). *Restoring Affirmatively Furthering Fair Housing definitions and certifications*. Last accessed 5/5/2022 from https://www.federalregister.gov/documents/2021/06/10/2021-12114/restoring-affirmatively-furthering-fair-housing-definitions-and-certifications.

Office of Federal Contract Compliance Programs, U.S. Department of Labor. (n.d.). *History of Executive Order 11246*. Last accessed 5/7/2022 from https://www.dol.gov/agencies/ofccp/about/executive-order-11246-history. (Note: As of 2025, this URL is no longer viable.)

Office of Policy Planning and Research, U.S. Department of Labor. (1965, March). *The Negro family: The case for national action*. https://www.dol.gov/general/aboutdol/history/webid-moynihan.

Office of Public Affairs, Department of Justice. (2018, July 3). *Attorney General Jeff Sessions rescinds 24 guidance documents*. Last accessed 5/7/2022 from https://www.justice.gov/opa/pr/attorney-general-jeff-sessions-rescinds-24-guidance-documents.

Overby, L. M., Henschen, B. M., Walsh, M. H., & Strauss, J. (1992). Courting constituents? An analysis of the Senate confirmation vote on Justice Clarence Thomas. *American Political Science Review*, *86*: 997–1006.

Owens, Ryan J. (2010). The separation of powers and Supreme Court agenda setting. *American Journal of Political Science*, *54*: 412–427.

Parents Involved in Community Schools v. Seattle School District No. 1, 551 U.S. 701 (2007).

Parren J. M. (1983). Federal affirmative action for MBE's: An historical analysis. *National Bar Association Magazine*.

Patterson v. McLean Credit Union, 491 U.S. 164 (1989).

Perry, B. (2007). *The Michigan affirmative action cases*. University Press of Kansas.

Peters, G., & Woolley, J. T. (n.d.). The American Presidency Project. University of California at Santa Barbara. https://www.presidency.ucsb.edu/documents/app-categories/elections-and-transitions/party-platforms.

Peters, J. W., & Chira, S. (2018, September 29). Kavanaugh borrows from Trump's playbook on White male anger. *New York Times*.

Piven, F. F. (1998). Affirmative action. In R. Post & M. Rogin (Eds.), *Race and representation: Affirmative action*. Zone Books.

Plessy v. Ferguson, 163 U.S. 537 (1896).

Pollock, E. E. (2012). *Race and the Supreme Court: Defining equality*. Peppertree Press.

Potter, H. (2014, June 26). *What can we learn from states that ban affirmative action*. The Century Foundation. https://tcf.org/content/commentary/what-can-we-learn-from-states-that-ban-affirmative-action/.

Price Waterhouse v. Hopkins, 490 U.S. 228 (1989).

Quinnipiac University Poll. (2009, June 3). U.S. Voters Disagree 3–1 with Sotomayor on key case, Quinnipiac University National Poll finds; most say abolish affirmative action. https://poll.qu.edu/Poll-Release-Legacy?releaseid=1307.

Racial Advisory Board. (1998, September 18). *One America in the 21st century: Forging a new future. The President's Initiative on Race*. Last accessed 5/5/2022 from https://clinton.presidentiallibraries.us/items/show/88862.

Regents of the University of California v. Bakke, 438 U.S. 265 (1978).

Rehnquist, W. H. (1986). Constitutional law and public opinion. *Suffolk University Law Review*, *20*: 751–769.

Ricci v. DeStefano, 557 U.S. 557 (2009).

Richmond v. Croson, 488 U.S. 469 (1989).

Rizzo, K. (1997, June 13). Lawmaker calls for apology to Blacks for slavery. AP News.

Root, D., & Berger, S. (2019, May 8). *Structural reforms to the federal judiciary: Restoring independence and fairness to the courts*. Center for American Progress. https://www.americanprogress.org/article/structural-reforms-federal-judiciary/.

Rosenberg, G. N. (2008). *The hollow hope: Can courts bring about change?* 2nd edition. University of Chicago Press.

Ruckman, P. S., Jr. (1993). The Supreme Court, critical nominations, and the Senate confirmation process. *Journal of Politics, 55*: 793–805.

Saad, L. (2022, June 2). *"Pro-choice" identification rises to near record high in U.S.* Gallup.com. Accessed 1/17/2024 from https://news.gallup.com/poll/393104/pro-choice-identification-rises-near-record-high.aspx.

Sakpal, M. (2019). *Diversity and inclusion build high-performance teams.* Gartner, Inc. https://www.gartner.com/smarterwithgartner/diversity-and-inclusion-build-high-performance-teams.

Samson, F. L. (2013). Altering public university admission standards to preserve White group position in the United States: Results from a laboratory experiment. *Comparative Education Review, 57*: 369–396.

Sander, R. H., & Taylor, S., Jr. (2012). *Mismatch: How affirmative action hurts students it's intended to help, and why universities won't admit it.* Basic Books.

Savage, C. (2017, August 1). Justice Dept. to take on affirmative action in college admissions. *New York Times.*

Schmidt, P. (2007). *Color and money: How rich White kids are winning the war over college affirmative action.* Palgrave Macmillan.

Schuette v. Coalition to Defend Affirmative Action, 572 U.S. 291 (2014).

Schuwerk, R. P. (1972). The Philadelphia Plan: A study in the dynamics of executive power. *University of Chicago Law Review, 39*(4): 723–760.

Segal, J. A., & Spaeth, H. J. (1993). *The Supreme Court and the attitudinal model.* Cambridge University Press.

Segal, J. A., & Spaeth, H. J. (2002). *The Supreme Court and the attitudinal model revisited.* Cambridge University Press.

Segal, J. A., Timpone, R. J., & Howard, R. M. (2000). Buyer beware? Presidential success through Supreme Court appointments. *Political Research Quarterly, 53*: 557–573. https://doi.org/10.2307/449198.

Segal, J. A., Westerland, C., & Lindquist, S. A. (2011). Congress, the Supreme Court, and judicial review: Testing a constitutional separation of powers model. *American Journal of Political Science, 55*: 89–104.

Sheer, M. D. (2023, June 29). "This is not a normal court": Biden denounces affirmative-action ruling. *New York Times.* Accessed 1/18/2024 from https://www.nytimes.com/2023/06/29/us/politics/biden-supreme-courtaffirmative-action.html.

Sheeran, T. J. (1976). Title VII and layoffs under the "Last Hired, First Fired" seniority rule: The preservation of equal employment. *Case Western Reserve Law Review, 26*: 409–482.

Shihadeh, E. S., & Barranco, R. E. (2010). Latino employment and Black violence: The Unintended Consequence of U.S. Immigration Policy. *Social Forces, 88*: 1393–1420.

Shull, S. A. (1989). *The president and civil rights policy: Leadership and change.* Greenwood Press.

Shurberg Broadcasting v. Federal Communications Commission, Appellee, Astroline Communications Co., Intervenor, 876 F.2d 902 (D.C. Cir. 1989).

Simas, E. N., & Evans, K. A. (2011). Linking party platforms to perceptions of presidential candidates' policy positions, 1972–2000. *Political Research Quarterly, 64*: 831–839.

Simmons, A. D., & Bobo, L. D. (2015). Can non-full-probability internet surveys yield useful data? A comparison with full-probability face-to-face surveys in the domain of race and social inequality attitudes. *Sociological Methodology, 45*: 357–387.

Simon, R. J., & Alexander, S. H. (1993). *The ambivalent welcome: Print media, public opinion, and immigration.* Praeger.

Spann, G. A. (1993). *Race against the Court: The Supreme Court and minorities in contemporary America.* New York University Press.

Spann, G. A. (2000). *The law of affirmative action: Twenty-five years of Supreme Court decisions on race and remedies.* New York University Press.

Staff, Committee on Energy & Commerce, U.S. House of Representatives. (2020, January 9). Memorandum on "Lifting voices: legislation to promote media marketplace diversity." https://www.congress.gov/116/meeting/house/110373/documents/HHRG-116-IF16-20200115-SD002.pdf.

Stanley, H. W., & Niemi, R. G. (2015). *Vital statistics on American politics 2015–2016.* CQ Press.

Stephanopoulos, G., & Edley, C., Jr. (1995, July 19). Affirmative action review. The White House. Last accessed 5/5/2022 from https://clintonWhitehouse4.archives.gov/WH/EOP/OP/html/aa/aa-lett.html.

Stimson, J. A., MacKuen, M. B., & Erikson, R. S. (1995). Dynamic representation. *American Political Science Review, 89*: 543–565.

Students for Fair Admissions v. Harvard, 600 U.S. ___ (2023).

Sunstein, C. R. (1998). Casuistry. In R. Post & M. Rogin (Eds.), *Race and representation: Affirmative action.* Zone Books.

Swann v. Charlotte-Mecklenburg Board of Education, 402 U.S. 1 (1970).

Tamir, C., Budman, A., Noe-Bustamante, L., & Mora, L. (2021, March 25). Facts about the U.S. Black population. Pew Research Center. Last accessed 5/8/2022 from https://www.pewresearch.org/social-trends/fact-sheet/facts-about-the-us-Black-population/#:~:text=The%20Black%20population%20of%20the,roughly%2036.2%20million%20Black%20Americans.

Teamsters v. U.S., 431 U.S. 324 (1977).

Texas v. Lesage and U.S., 528 U.S. 18 (1999).

Treisman, R. (2021, February 23). Nearly 100 Confederate monuments removed in 2020, report says; More than 700 remain. NPR. https://www.npr.org/2021/02/23/970610428/nearly-100-confederate-monuments-removed-in-2020-report-says-more-than-700-remain.

Ulmer, S. S. (1970). Dissent behavior and the social background of Supreme Court justices. *Journal of Politics, 32*: 580–598.

United Automobile Workers v. Johnson Controls, Inc., 199 U.S. 187 (1991).

United States Courts. (2001, March 14). *Judicial Conference adopts strategy to improve pay for top government officials.* https://www.uscourts.gov/news/2001/03/14/judicial-conference-adopts-strategy-improve-pay-top-government-officials.

Urofsky, M. I. (2020). *The affirmative action puzzle: A living history from Reconstruction to today.* Pantheon Books.

U.S. Department of Justice, U.S. Department of Education. (2011, December 2). *Guidance on the voluntary use of race to achieve diversity and avoid racial isolation in elementary and secondary schools.* Last accessed 5/5/2022 from https://www2.ed.gov/about/offices/list/ocr/docs/guidance-ese-201111.pdf.

U.S. Department of Justice, U.S. Department of Education. (2013, September 27). *Joint "Dear Colleague" letter.* Last accessed 5/7/2022 from https://www2.ed.gov/about/offices/list/ocr/letters/colleague-201309.html.

U.S. Department of Justice, U.S. Department of Education. (2018, July 3). *Dear colleague.* Last accessed 5/7/2022 from https://www2.ed.gov/about/offices/list/ocr/letters/colleague-title-vi-201807.pdf.

U.S. Department of Justice. (2001, January 18). Executive Order 13160 guidance document: Ensuring opportunity in federally conducted education and training programs. *Federal Register.* https://www.federalregister.gov/documents/2001/01/18/01-1494/executive-order-13160-guidance-document-ensuring-equal-opportunity-in-federally-conducted-education.

U.S. Department of Justice. (n.d.). *The compelling interest to remedy the effects of discrimination in federal contracting: A survey of recent evidence.* https://www.justice.gov/crt/page/file/1463921/download.

U.S. Equal Employment Opportunity Commission (EEOC). Affirmative action appropriate under Title VI of the Civil Rights Act of 1964, as amended, 44 F.R. § 4422 (1979).

U.S. House of Representatives, 117th Congress, George Floyd Justice in Policing Act of 2021 H.R. 1280.

U.S. House of Representatives, 117th Congress, H.R. 40—Commission to Study and Develop Reparation Proposals for African Americans Act.

U.S. Steel Workers v. Weber, 443 U.S. 193 (1979).

U.S. v. Paradise, 480 U.S. 149 (1987).

Vance, J. D. (2016). *Hillbilly elegy: A memoir of a family and culture in crisis.* Harper.

Vu Tran, H. (2020). *Race, law, and higher education in the colorblind era: Critical investigations into race-related Supreme Court disputes.* Routledge.

Wards Cove Packing Co. v. Atonio, 490 U.S. 642 (1989).

Washington v. Davis, 426 U.S. 229, 1976 (1976).

Waters, M. C. (1990). *Ethnic options: Choosing identities in America.* University of California Press.

Wedeking, J., & Zilis, M. A. (2018). Disagreeable rhetoric and the prospect of public opposition: Opinion moderation on the U.S. Supreme Court. *Political Research Quarterly, 71*: 380–394.

Weinberger v. Rossi, 456 U.S. 25 (1982).

Whittington, K. E. (2006). Presidents, senates, and failed Supreme Court nominations. *Supreme Court Review, 2006*(1): 401–438.

Wilkinson, B. C. (2014). Perceptions of commonality and Latino–Black, Latino–White relations in a multiethnic United States. *Political Research Quarterly, 67*: 905–916.

Wilson, W. J. (1978, 2012). *The declining significance of race: Blacks and changing American institutions*. University of Chicago Press.

Wilson, W. J. (2001). *The bridge over the racial divide: Rising inequality and coalition politics*. University of California Press.

Wittke, C. (1956). *The Irish in America*. Louisiana State University Press.

Wygant v. Jackson, 476 U.S. 267 (1986).

Index

www.ingramcontent.com/pod-product-compliance
Lightning Source LLC
Chambersburg PA
CBHW020334270326
41926CB00007B/180